PEAKS
and LAMAS

PEAKS
and LAMAS
by Marco Pallis

Shoemaker & Hoard
Washington, D.C.

Library of Congress Cataloging-in-Publication Data is available
ISBN 1–59376–058–2

Printed in the United States of America

Shoemaker & Hoard
A Division of Avalon Publishing Group, Inc.
Distributed by Publishers Group West

10   9   8   7   6   5   4   3   2   1

༄༅། ཨོཾ་ན་མོ་གུ་རུ།

TO THE FOUR LAMAS

THE HERMIT ABBOT OF LACHHEN

THE LAMA DAWA, BURSAR OF SPITUK

THE LAMA PAINTER, KONCHHOG GYALTSAN OF P'HIYANG

THE LAMA WANGYAL, OF DREPUNG, LHASA

Who for my benefit

and for the good of all creatures

set in motion the WHEEL OF THE DOCTRINE

this book is reverently dedicated

Contents

PART FOUR   AFTERTHOUGHTS

Illustrations

EREMURUS IN THE ALP OF NIMARG

TISTA FOREST

Following page 202

KANGCHHENDZÖNGA AND SIMVU FROM SINGHIK

PAVILION IN THE SHALIMAR GARDENS

MUGHAL LATTICES AND INLAYS

BETWEEN DRAS AND TASGAM

SHEPHERD ON THE ZOJI LA

OASIS NEAR KARGIL

KARGIL

MULBEK

Following page 234

LADAK PEASANT HOUSE

LADAKI PEASANT

THRESHING BARLEY

STORM CLOUDS OVER YURU

PAINTINGS AT YURU

LIKHIR

THE PRECENTOR OF LIKHIR

LIKHIR, CORNER OF A LAMA'S ROOM

DESERT TRACK BEHIND SPITUK

THE LAMA DAWA, BURSAR OF SPITUK

A NOVICE OF THE GELUGPA ORDER

Following page 266

LEH AND CASTLE OF THE KINGS OF LADAK

YAKS FROM A TURKI CARAVAN

THE LATE HADJI MUHAMMAD SIDDIQ

"THE YELLOW MAN"

THE ART OF POURING TEA

HIMI GOMPA

BEYOND THE CHANG LA

Maps

Introductory Notes

A FORMAL PREFACE would serve no useful purpose in this book. All that had to be said has found a better place in the actual narrative: there is no object in preparing the reader's mind for things that he will discover soon enough for himself. I shall therefore confine myself to giving a few explanations of a purely practical nature, concerning the spelling of place-names and the use of special terms. At the same time I shall discharge the pleasant duty of thanking the many friends without whose help the book could not have been written nor the work done that furnished the excuse for writing it.

Spelling of Indian and Tibetan Names. I have all along tried to reproduce the correct sounds, as spoken, and have disregarded the original spellings. Therefore the name of a celebrated monastery in Ladak, though spelt Himis on maps, is here written Himi, since in conversation I have always found the *s* to be muted. Similarly in referring to a Tibetan valley that lies near the north frontier of Bhutan, I write Hlobrak instead of the orthographically correct Lho-brag. The name of a certain divinity called Chenrezig is so written here, though by its spelling it would be Spyan-ras-gzigs. The book is intended in the first place for the general reader, not for scholars; the latter will in any case know what the spelling should have been. The only exceptions to this rule of writing phonetically are names such as Lhasa and Darjeeling, which are now practically English words. To have turned Lhasa into Hlasa, because it is so sounded in Tibetan, would have been pedantic and confusing.

In the Tibetan language, generic terms derived from places are made by the addition of the suffixes *-pa,* *-wa,* or *-ba.* Thus a man of Ladak is Ladakpa, a Londoner is Londonwa. By this method many circumlocutions like "a man of Kham" can be avoided. I have therefore permitted myself its free use; in the example given I should simply say Khamba.

Phonetics. Vowel sounds may be taken as being roughly like the Continental ones, say in Italian. The diphthong *au* in Indian words and the modified vowels *ö* and *ü* in Tibetan should be pronounced as in German.

In a few Indian words stress accents have been added, wherever the tendencies of English were likely to predispose people towards wrong accentuation. Nine Englishmen out of ten who have not had some connexion with India will call the capital of Kashmir Srinagár, instead of the correct Srinágar, unless the stress is marked as I have shown it.

Aspirated consonants need special attention. In both the Indian and the Tibetan languages the *h* sound must be distinctly pronounced, even after *p* or *t*. To make sure that no one falls into the error of reading *ph* with an *f* sound, or *th* as in "then," I have marked an apostrophe, thus: *p'h, t'h*. In the word *t'hanka,* meaning a painted scroll, the *t'h* should therefore be spoken as in "tha*t h*ouse."

For the sake of accuracy I have followed scholars in indicating a particular sort of *t* and *d* sound that is found in Tibetan thus: *ṭ* and *ḍ*. They occur in words where the main consonant is followed by a muted *r*, which lends to the preceding letter a slightly explosive character. To produce it, the tongue must be pressed hard against the palate. The words *Ṭulku,* an Incarnation, and *Ṭashilhunpo,* the great monastery near Shigatze where the Panchhen Lama resides, are a case in point: so also is *Ḍikhung,* the name of another monastery.

Use of the Terms "Tradition" and "Lama." In treating of doctrines, both Hindu and Tibetan Buddhist, I have been faced with a difficulty over the choice of terms to express certain fundamental ideas. The chief trouble has been over the use of the word "religion," which seems unsatisfactory when applied to the two examples mentioned, for they differ markedly in their modes of thought from those of Christianity, Islam, and Judaism, the three typical religions of the world. In the religions the doctrine, though necessarily metaphysical in its essence, has been expressed in a special manner suitable to the mentality of peoples in whom sentimental tendencies were powerful. It is this special adaptation that characterizes the "religious" point of view properly speaking, affecting the doctrinal forms. The personal aspect of divinity is emphasized, knowledge appears chiefly as faith, moral and social interests are greatly stressed, as well as oppositions such as "believers and heathen." I do not say that these limits are not transcended in principle; but religion is too constantly associated in men's minds with a certain type of organization and a certain outlook, to allow of its being applied, without grave danger of misinterpretation, to doctrines where the point of view is very different. Of all possible choices, the word "Tradition" seems the best. Another alternative, "philosophy," is even less satisfactory than "religion"; for it is too often associated with closed systems and with the persons of their founders. I therefore reject such phases as "Hindu religion" or "Tibetan philosophy" as being misleading; I will refer to them as the "Hindu and Tibetan Traditions." To bring out the distinction still better, I would say that "the Christian religion is a special mode of Tradition peculiar to the West."

Tradition, because of its universal character, defies definition; but a few indications may make it clearer. It embraces the whole of a civilization, in all its modes and departments, so that it cannot be said of any element that it exists independently of the traditional influence; there is no place for a "profane" point of view. A traditional civilization has its roots set in a doctrine of the purely metaphysical order, from which all the other constituents of the tradition, whether ethical, social, or artistic, down to the most petty activities of daily life, derive their sanction. Metaphysical ideas are the cement that binds every part together. The whole body of thought and action must be viewed as a hierarchy, with pure metaphysic at the head.

The process by which the truth is made to circulate is the tradition from Master to pupil, which stretches back into the past and reaches forward to the future. By the doctrine so handed down, all parts are related to one another; they derive from it both stability and elasticity. No set boundaries can be recognized by Tradition as a whole; it can only be taken as the equivalent of Knowledge itself.

Something must also be said concerning the use of the word "lama." Spelt with a capital, it is used in its technical sense of either a saint, a personal spiritual director, or else one of those abbots in Tibet who are venerated as embodying the spiritual influence of their predecessors — they are often, but quite improperly, spoken of as "living Buddhas." However, when I have only wished to refer to clerics or monks, which is the usual meaning when speaking of lamas in English, I have used the small *l.* Thus we have "the Lama who founded the Yellow Order of monks," but "a group of lamas in the village."

Photography. Most of my illustrations have been taken from photographs by my companions on the two expeditions. For 1933 they are mostly by C. F. Kirkus and Dr. Charles Warren; for 1936 some of the Sikkim ones are by J. K. Cooke, some by R. C. Nicholson, and one by F. S. Chapman, while all the Ladak ones are by R. C. Nicholson. None of these illustrations is signed; I have only added the names underneath if the photographs have been taken by friends not belonging to my own parties. I have much pleasure in acknowledging the privilege of reproducing these extra photographs, which have filled important gaps.

My thanks are also due to a large number of people who have assisted me in a variety of ways. I have indeed been surprised at the trouble taken on behalf of both expeditions by all sorts of busy people, from maharajas and officials downwards. Not the least of the rewards that have fallen to me and my companions have been the many friendships that have arisen in this manner, both at home and in the East, both among our own people and with Indians and Tibetans. I can assure all who have contributed information, advice, gifts, or any other form of help to us that their kindness is neither forgotten nor forgettable.

To Pamela Freston my debt is beyond all thanks. The whole book passed through her hands three times and received from her a most rigorous, though sympathetic, criticism, which got rid of countless clumsy passages and other faults of style. I have reckoned that she pointed out over two thousand major and minor blemishes. Her contribution has been such that I look on her now not so much as an adviser, but rather as a collaborator.

MARCO PALLIS

Additional note on the
revised edition

The original version of this book was published in 1939. Since that time a great deal has been learned (or so one hopes), with the result that a number of minor mistakes of fact and still more cases of false emphasis have had to be put right. Furthermore a good deal of "padding" has been cut out, while several important additions have gone in, especially on the doctrinal side; these include one whole fresh chapter. In consequence of the above changes the present version of the book is the only one to be regarded as fully authoritative and any prospective translators into foreign tongues must be sure and base themselves on the American text, no other.

M. P.

Kalimpong, February 1948

PART ONE

Ganges and Satlej -- 1933

Chapter I

The Birth of an Expedition

THE STORY OF two Himalayan journeys which fills this book presented a peculiar difficulty in the telling, because of the many and sometimes bewildering sudden alternations of mood required of the reader. At one moment, in our company, he would be living on the purely physical plane while pitting every ounce of strength against a giant of the mountains; or else in the midst of flower-filled meadows or in a secluded glade of the primeval forest he would be recovering from the fatigues of defeat or success. Yet directly afterwards, having moved on but a few short miles, he would be found sipping tea from silver-mounted bowls and exchanging formal courtesies with representatives of one of the earth's most civilized peoples; or again, with intellect whetted to its keenest edge, he would be trying to keep pace with the descant of some contemplative recluse upon a theme of pure metaphysic.

To have suppressed some of the contrasting elements, leaving the others in a position of unchallenged preponderance, would have been simple; advisers were not wanting who urged this course. But somehow, when it came to be tried, the journey so described seemed to be no longer the same that I remembered: a stranger had gone on it, a man more single-eyed than the author. I resolved, therefore, to risk a long story and to relate the adventures of our party in all their diversity, allowing the pendulum to swing where and when it willed, leaving out nothing that really mattered, and only praying that my would-be companions might have the patience to adapt themselves. Whoever is willing to bear with these apparent caprices will find, I hope, as I have done, that the bodily exertion of climbing, by forcing the mind to lie fallow for a time and concentrate on purely animal needs, will have prepared it in just the right way for subsequent excursions into more subtle realms. There is some advantage in first reducing mental, no less than physi-

cal weight before calling on the spirit, thus lightened of its
ballast, to take flight towards the stars.

Indeed, there is everything to be said for letting unaccustomed impressions soak in slowly, without system, to find their
own level in their own time. A vague idea, born of some chance
event, presently ripens into sharper definition as fresh incidents
bearing on it occur at intervals and are pieced together with
other impressions already stored in the consciousness. The first
allusion may have been superficial and soon forgotten, while
one turned from the path to attempt some peak that caught
one's passing fancy. Later the same question comes up again.
Possibly an increasing fluency in the language, fruit of daily
practice, has enabled one to debate it seriously with some person qualified to throw light on it. So one is led on by small, dis-
continuous steps, till at length one is swept into very deep
waters.

At the end of the narrative portion of the book, two or three
chapters have been added in which general subjects such as
Tibetan art, which previously had been touched on piecemeal,
are dealt with in more orderly fashion and some wider conclusions drawn. Since much of the material on which these depend will by then have become familiar, it should not be difficult, on meeting it again assembled on a logical plan, in just
relation, to judge whether the facts cited do indeed warrant
the interpretation that has been put upon them. I have all
along attempted to leave out nothing relevant, and conscience
does not accuse me of wilful inaccuracy either by suggestion or
suppression. Whenever a fact has not come under my personal
notice, but has been accepted on hearsay, I have been at pains
to show who was the author of the statement, so that his com-
petence to make it might be the more easily criticizable. As to
books of reference, whenever there has been the least feeling
of doubt, information obtained from them has, if possible, been
corroborated by someone trustworthy.

In particular, a number of passages concerning Tibetan doctrines have been checked with the help of a learned Mongolian lama from Lhasa, the Rev. Dr. Wangyal, who passed
several weeks of the summer of 1937 at my home. I have seen
so many other writers duped by having taken on trust the word
of experts holding apparently good credentials, whose work
later proved to be tainted, that I am resolved to lean to the
side of scepticism lest I too make myself into an unwitting
agent for passing on inexact or prejudiced information. When

once a man begins to delve in the Oriental field, he finds out only too quickly how many so-called authorities owe their standing rather to the bulk than to the accuracy of their researches. The grotesque travesties of doctrines that they try to fasten upon the thinkers of India and Tibet would be laughable were they not apt to be employed as weapons by persons having an obvious axe to grind, for carrying on subversive propaganda in those countries. The only safe way of separating the grain from the chaff is by submitting even the most innocent-looking assertions for verification by duly accredited exponents of the doctrines in question.

So much, then, for principles: the hour has come to pack up our baggage and set out on this our first visit to the mountain ranges of the East. It is All Fools' Day, 1933, and the group of five well-seasoned climbing friends is waving farewells to parents and relatives, and drawing the fire of cameras on the dockside at Liverpool, where the good ship *Custodian,* which is to be their home for the next four weeks, is taking on its last belated bits of cargo.

The members of the party must now be introduced by name: RICHARD NICHOLSON, a son of the famous builder of yachts, and a fellow musician of mine, for many years my companion on almost every climb, both in the Alps and at home; F. E. HICKS, a schoolmaster and notable rock-climber and ski-runner, one of the strongest and gentlest of men, owner of physical and mental gifts blended in such a nice proportion as to make him, to my mind, the very ideal of an all-round mountaineer; C. F. KIRKUS, who works in insurance, one of the two or three best rock-climbers in this country, pioneer of many new routes, especially in Wales; * DR. CHARLES WARREN, a man of considerable Alpine experience, who afterwards acted as medical officer on several Everest expeditions; lastly myself, rather older than the others, with a number of Alpine seasons behind me and an affinity for Oriental, especially Indian, history and art dating back to early childhood: a reasonably strong party, and even-tempered, a thing that counts for much in the wilds.

When the last cable that joined us to England had been cast loose and the ship began to move out into the river, there was a brief moment of excitement; then a pleasant feeling of relaxation began to steal over us, to which we had long been stran-

---

* He eventually lost his life in a raid over Germany while serving with the R.A.F.

gers; for the preliminaries of such an expedition, new to every one of us, which had occupied our leisure for twelve months or more, had been strenuous: drawing up lists of equipment and estimating rations, unpacking parcels, sorting, checking, repacking, weighing, working out a foolproof method of cataloguing simple enough not to break down under field conditions, consulting every accessible authority living or printed and sifting their often contradictory information, cadging contributions in kind from sympathetic firms, poring over maps, or, ensconced in armchairs before the fire, calling up those alluring phantoms that by and by materialized into feasible plans — these were but a few of our occupations.

In addition, certain items of equipment had to be put to practical trial so as to preclude the danger of unpleasant surprises on the mountain. The most plausible design often hides lurking weaknesses that are only detected through actual use. Clumsiness in handling tackle too, due to ignorance of the appropriate drill, may entail exhausting struggles in the rarefied air of high altitudes. We held sleeping-bag parades, tentless, on the windy summits of Ben Nevis and Snowdon in mid-winter, following them up with a grand dress-rehearsal, tents and all, played under mock-Himalayan rules, as realistic as we could devise them, in the Valais Alps. Nothing was taken on trust; there were no serious mishaps when the hour came for real testing.

Fair weather attended us from the outset of the voyage, but some days elapsed before we began to feel inclined for anything except sleep. After we had rounded Gibraltar, however, and entered warmer seas, and turtles with orange shells had swum past, and we had looked on the ineffable transparency of the Algerian ranges, still clothed in winter snow, our torpid energies began to reassert themselves. As we were the only passengers on board, the jovial Irish captain gave us the run of his ship and a number of "rock-climbs" were soon discovered. The most important activity, however, was connected with the study of languages. The *Custodian* was promptly converted into a floating university; in every corner you could have found grammars and dictionaries left by students who had been diligently compiling useful vocabularies under headings such as "On the March," "Pitching Camp," "Buying Food in a Village, "Visiting a Shrine," when they were summoned to the saloon by the clang of the dinner-gong.

In the tropics, while lying on the deck sunbathing and watching the shoals of flying fish skimming the crests of waves like volleys of silver arrows, we concocted strange dialogues, now Hindustani, now Tibetan. The classic "Have you taken the pen of my uncle? No, you will find it in your grandmother's garden" was replaced with "Is there a camping-ground in the woods behind the village? No, it is on the glacier to the east of the mountain pass." Presently, as the combining of phrases began to come more easily, they were tried on the dog — that is to say, on members of the Lascar crew, who at first affected not to know the language at all for Hindustani, till one day it dawned on them, when they broke out into such volubility that they left us all guessing.

Many people intending to travel in the Himalaya are, in the matter of languages, ready to accept a rather low standard, ignoring the rules of grammar and contenting themselves with a hundred words or so. No doubt this can be made to do for elementary needs, and even for forging the links of a genuine, if inarticulate, comradeship with the native porters. But it seems a pity to put up with such a narrowing of possibilities; for many people are not nearly so incompetent at languages as they imagine, and good teachers are to be found to help them over the more awkward stiles. The reward for trying lies in the possibility of a real exchange of thoughts with the inhabitants of a foreign country, which is surely one of the greatest joys of travel.

For us so occupied, four weeks slipped by all too quickly, and it was with mixed feelings that we saw the mangrove-fringed coast near the mouth of the Hoogli slowly loom into sight and knew that it was the last time we should hear the cheery voice of Captain O'Connor summoning us to his cabin, at the end of the day's work, to join him in a "sundowner." But there was a thrill in the thought that this turbid waterway, with its jute factories and barges, its feathery palms and slimy mud-flats, suited to the siestas of crocodiles, was a mouth of the selfsame Ganges that we were about to follow all the way to its source, goal of many pilgrims, where it issued from the parent glacier.

Calcutta saw us for the inside of a day; at night we made our way to Howra terminus and entrained for Dehra Dun, the railhead for the hill station of Mussoori. As we walked down the thronged platform we noticed a white cotton thread, apparently endless, extending away from us into the distance; it might have been taken for the clue bestowed on Theseus by Ariadne to guide him through the labyrinth. Moved by curiosity we traced it out; but our Minotaur proved to be an obese, elderly Bengali, white-robed and clutching the inevitable, untidily furled umbrella, who was waddling along through the tittering crowd, all unconscious of the mirth he was causing by reason of the reel of cotton in his pocket ever unwinding, the free end having caught itself somewhere on the way. As no one seemed to be making a move, one of us picked up the strand and, nudging the old *babu* on the elbow, handed back his straggling property. The old fellow gathered it up with a startled movement and then broke out into such effusive thanks that our simple action might have been an unprecedented act of chivalry. Could it really have appeared out of the ordinary? Or did his pompous gratitude mask some age-long reproach?

We spent the railway journey, or at least its waking hours, gazing out of the window. Charming rural scenes, familiar through the miniatures of the Rajput school in our museums, passed before us, villages of reddish mud and thatch surrounded by mango trees, hump-backed cattle watched by half-naked urchins, grazing upon what seemed bare earth (for it was near the end of the hot weather), women in gay saris — it must have been a festival day — waiting their turn at the well or walking home with the gait of princesses, their polished brass pots balanced on their heads. By a queer reversal, it felt as if all this was meant to illustrate the miniatures, instead of the contrary. With what deep understanding those old artists had caught hold of the spirit of village life, where beats the real heart of India!

A number of sites of historical interest flashed by. Here was Benares, sacred city of the Hindus; over its many-stepped bathing-places and conical-roofed temples towered the twin minarets of the Mughal Aurangzib, who, unlike his ancestors, was no builder and erected them there principally in order to impress his non-Moslem subjects. We also caught sight of Jaunpur, glorious in the stately Saracenic gateways of its numerous mosques, the former capital of a dynasty bearing the proud title of Kings of the East, now reduced to a quiet country town.

Later came temple-girt Ayodhya, scene of the childhood of India's epic hero, Rama, mighty bender of the bow. In the station a family of brown monkeys was waiting, father, mother, and frolicking babies, apparently hoping to catch the next stopping train.

But what astonished us most of all on the journey across India was the abundance of animal life: we saw foxes, jackals, and monkeys, and a great variety of birds. Remembering the songless countryside of so much of Europe, one was tempted to ask how it was that this Indian plain, densely inhabited and cultivated since remote times, was still able to support so large an animal population. Surely the interests of some, at least, of the creatures that we saw must be competing to a certain extent with those of man. Does the explanation lie in the fact that Hindus, in their abhorrence of killing, for which people sometimes presume to ridicule them, are ready to overlook a moderate toll levied by animals on their crops, and do not make this into an excuse for wholesale extermination, though these Indian peasants have little enough to spare, as compared with many of their fellows in other countries?

One of the minor peculiarities of an Indian tour is the sheer hopelessness that attends any search for a drinkable cup of tea, although this is the land that contains Darjeeling and Ceylon. Neither prayers nor threats will make the Indian servant on the railways or in hotels believe that every Englishman does not like his tea *ystrang* — that is to say, of such a consistency that I could easily have written this book by filling my fountain-pen from the teapot. As to serving a jug of hot water with the tea-tray, that is simply not done, not even in good hotels. If pressed, the waiter, after a prolonged show of incomprehension, will first take away the pot and dilute the ink, or if one goes on insisting, he will go and fetch a second teapot full of boiling water; but the convention as we know it at home is simply not recognized. It is strange that the British, who in their time succeeded in imposing so many of their institutions on their Imperial possessions, should have failed over this. It is as if the Indians said: "You have conquered us in other ways; in this one thing, a thing moreover very close to your hearts, we defy you!"

Early on the second morning we woke up in a climate markedly cooler: we were passing through a belt of jungle; when we emerged, we saw hills at last. Then the train draw up alongside Dehra Dun platform, and we stepped out to shake hands with Dr. R. Maclagan Gorrie, a distinguished member of that admirable service the Department of Forests, who bade us welcome to the Himalaya. His help and advice at this stage were invaluable, for we suddenly felt tongue-tied by shyness and in no mood for making decisions. He piloted us through our first awkwardness, interviewed candidates for the post of head porter and selected one who had been overseer to a gang

of road-menders, a Hindu of the name of Jai Datt. Dr. Gorrie
also took two of us for a whole day in his car across the lovely
forested Dun to call on H.H. the Maharaja of Tehri-Garhwal,
in whose principality our mountains lay. To the prince also and
to his prime minister our thanks are due, for the kindness of
their reception and for their readiness in arranging all facilities.

Clouds hung low on the ridge, and we walked up the short
distance into Mussoori, from where the motor road ends,
through a fine drizzle. A regimental band was giving selec-
tions from light opera on the parade, and the doubtful cheerful-
ness of the tunes seemed to add a touch of melancholy to the
rawness of the evening. Knots of Garhwalis huddled in shop
doorways, their brown blankets drawn over their heads. We
passed a lighted shop-window that displayed a fashionable
frock draped superciliously on its lay figure. A young man in
evening dress rolled by in a rickshaw. As we turned down off
the parade towards our hotel, there was a sudden crash overhead as a band of monkeys hurtled out from among some
scarlet rhododendrons, chasing one another across the road,
and disappeared down the hillside.

That first evening we assembled for dinner only four out
of five: one member of our party was confined to his room
indisposed, truly a matter for agitation. We were on the threshold of our adventure, and a man gone sick already! What
precaution could possibly have been neglected? Had we not
let our insides be turned into a bacteriological laboratory and
our skins into sieves with I know not how many inoculations?
It was in vain that other visitors in the hotel explained that
it was the commonest thing to be slightly upset by the sudden
rise from the plains to seven thousand feet. He who has come
with ambitions to climb to a height of twenty thousand or more
is loath to believe himself of the same clay as ordinary hotel
guests. His mind is prone to wildest alarms about nameless
exotic diseases. Little was said, but a jumpy uneasiness lurked
behind the desultory conversation as we drifted in and out of
one another's rooms or up and down the veranda, listening to
the whirring of cicadas or stopping to examine the unfamiliar
moths round the electric lamps. In the light of later experience
how easy and how unfair it is to laugh at those exaggerated
fears!

The sun rose in a clear sky next morning and for a brief
hour or two the matchless panorama of the Gangotri peaks was
uncovered. Our goal stood outspread before us; catching that

"If I Forget Thee, O Jerusalem"   *See page 229*
Monastery at Likhir, Ladak

THRESHING-FLOOR, BARAHAT VILLAGE

GORGE SCENERY ON THE PILGRIM ROUTE   *See page 26*

SATOPANT'H PEAKS   *See Chapter IV*
From camp below Gaumukh

High Bivouac *See page* 39

CENTRAL SATOPANT'H   *See Chapter* IV

SATLEJ ABOVE POO   *See page* 59

SATLEJ GORGE SCENERY   *See Chapter* VI

first glimpse of the land of our dreams, what a passionate eagerness welled up in us to set out, leaving all tedious last-minute organization to run itself! We longed to start, not the day after the day after tomorrow, but in that very instant, along the winding tracks that cross the seventy miles of forested foothills to the base of the snowy ranges. Whoever has had experience of a get-away into the Himalaya must be familiar with this impatience. One remembers several evenings standing knee-deep in the debris of packing, to watch the twilight in the valleys snuffed out by the over-hasty fingers of subtropical nightfall, and sighing because yet another day's work stands between oneself and departure. The vow is fiercely registered each time to travel lighter and yet more light; and in fact, if it is to be purely a question of travelling, that is easy enough, as we have since found out; but when the program includes mountaineering, with its siege tactics, a certain minimum of climbing-gear and provisions for spending several weeks on glaciers is unavoidable, and that minimum when stacked together in one place can look disconcertingly elaborate.

Before 1933 few expeditions had gone up from Mussoori. There was no precedent behind the formation of a *bandobast* such as exists, for instance, in Kashmir. This was not without its compensations, for we escaped the regiment of touts that falls upon the greenhorn in those other places, with its nicely graded tariffs based on the degree of "roughing it" required or apprehended: so much for tents, chairs, tables, camp-beds, commodes, and tin baths, with slight reductions on omitting any one or other of these almost indispensable articles. How we laughed on a certain morning three years later in Kashmir when we rode up behind a young servant trotting along with the meat-safe strapped to his shoulders and Sunday's joint visible through the wire on its white china dish! But if we enjoyed the advantage of being early in the field in Mussoori, there was correspondingly more for a stranger to find out and more work to be done.

The hotel manager kindly made over to us one of his sheds in which to complete the packing and interview porters and candidates for the all-important office of cook. Several mornings were spent down there weighing up loads on a spring balance, squeezing out any object regarded at the last minute as superfluous, and all the while fending off the inquisitive, the hasty, the officious would-be helpers, who buzzed like a cloud of bluebottles round the door, threatening at any moment to reduce everything to a state of chaos. The bazaar knew, of course, all about the expedition, and besides those whose names had been entered officially on the head porter's list, countless hopefuls hung round from morning till night. It was during these operations that a little Puck-like fellow called Urbi Datt first caught my eye. We used to pick up two or three assistants from the crowd and one day the lot fell to him, a happy chance, since he was to turn out the most able of any of our servants during this early part of our travels. We soon saw that here was a first-class man, from his unhurried manner, his quickness to catch on to an idea, and his ability not to meddle in matters that did not concern him. Also he had a way with the crowd that was an invaluable protection when one's back was turned.

At home we had read a good deal about the sufferings of mountaineers at the hands of their cooks, though the grumblers rather betrayed themselves by having made no serious effort to change cooks. It seems so unnecessary to put up with unwholesome food. The Englishman's readiness to allow a low standard to be imposed on him and his almost criminal timidity about experimenting with outlandish cookery partly accounts for these tales. A man may be an expert in cooking the food he is used to and at the same time may make a hopeless failure when invited to reproduce the foreign recipes that his sahib demands. How else can one account for the fact that though skilful cooks abound in India, so much of the food served up to Europeans there is uneatable? In the long run it is better for the digestion, as well as pleasanter, to experiment a little in the native dishes that one's cook already knows how to prepare than to expect him to try his hand at the English style at short notice. If he is a professional he will at first assume that English dishes are expected of him; but he will probably be overjoyed and begin to turn out food of a very different quality when firmly told that one prefers to feed like an Indian.

A friend had advised us, when choosing a cook, to avoid the professionals and to teach our few special requirements to an intelligent porter, who would be bound to know the common Hindu dishes and would not have great pretensions. We followed his advice both then and ever since, and in consequence have never had to complain of bad catering. On this first occasion in Mussoori, however, the cook question was complicated by our inexperience, so that of the many warnings we did not quite know which to believe. People who prided themselves on their mastery of the mysterious lore known as "understanding how to manage the natives" alleged that the number of religious customs which had been invented solely as traps for ignorant travellers was legion. To fall into one of them would infallibly cause the porters to rise in insurrection and the expedition to end in a humiliating fiasco. "You should do this, you mustn't do that. Believe me, I have lived twenty years in this country; I understand the native mind. You can't go without a regular cook; it's simply not done!"

We inquired of Urbi Datt if he would take on the job, but he very properly replied that, being a strict vegetarian, he was afraid of being asked to handle what was ritually impure. Though disappointed, we still hesitated, because a few interviews with professional applicants for the post did not tend to predispose us in their favour. We had heard that the subdivision of functions had gone far in India, but the question was how far? Did custom entitle the cook to demand one menial to fetch water for him, a second to scour his dirty pans, a third to blow up his fire, and a fourth to carry the food to the sahib's table? Or was this simple jobbery? We saw our caravan growing into an army. When it came to a request for a cookhouse tent to shade the meats from the sinister influence of hooded crows or even of a passing cloud, suspicion turned to conviction. Here was nothing more or less than a ramp to provide a couple of months' employment for brothers and cousins and in-laws.

Eventually a porter named Maidar Singh was chosen. For a few extra annas he was prepared to do his share of carrying, as well as our own domestic work. He was a big, rough fellow whose shirt protruded from beneath a tight-fitting blue waistcoat even on the hottest of days and who professed, with what turned out to be false modesty, to know very little about cooking. Actually, I think, he was nearly first-class, and we soon learned our place and abandoned any amateurish attempts at interference with his art. He managed to gather three helpmates for the kitchen, including one of suitable caste to do the washing up, which he himself was not allowed to touch. But as they all carried ordinary loads and were counted the same as other porters, he was welcome to them.

Maidar Singh was a child in his habit of fishing for praises: "That was a very nice curried chicken you gave us this evening; I hope we shall have it often." "Ah! Ah!" he purred, drinking in our words. A few minutes later there would be a scratching at my tent-flap. "What is it, Maidar Singh?" "Did the sahib like the curried chicken? Was it good?" "But certainly, Maidar Singh, I told you so. You must do some again tomorrow." "Ah! Ah!" A quarter of an hour would pass and the identical ceremony had to be gone through again. "Ah! Ah!"

One other controversy led to prolonged heart-searchings. It is a convenience when trekking to carry personal belongings in one's own rucksack and to be independent of servants. It had been hinted, however, by some of "the initiated" that this practice would at once lower our prestige. We were by no means above taking hints; quite the reverse, for in our hearts we did feel some diffidence in setting out to control sixty or seventy men in this unfamiliar land. The climax came when it was discovered that if we carried packs the head porter must do likewise; naturally he could not be seen walking unburdened behind his loaded masters. Jai Datt was much dashed when his nice new rucksack was handed to him, for he was a man of rather feeble character, morbidly sensitive about losing face. His redeeming feature was that he never tried to abuse or bully his subordinates. There had been some difficulty in securing anyone better for the job, as the man engaged for us before we left England had gone off to Everest at short notice. Dr. Gorrie had done the very best possible in the time.

I forget if Jai Datt resorted to the persuasion of tears on the first or second day. "Please don't make me carry it," he whimpered. "Everyone on that route knows me for the friend of important people, of forest rangers and even deputy collectors. What will they think when they see me with a load like a coolie? They will make a mock of me." "But, Jai Datt, they will see us carrying packs too: we will walk beside you whenever you have to go through a village." In the end he was forced to yield and his forebodings proved unjustified; but he never felt easy about it and took every opportunity of handing over his rucksack on the quiet to one of the other porters.

It is to be hoped that we did not socially degrade the rather pitiable Jai Datt. As to ourselves, what with one thing and another, our loads became of quite respectable weight; but this, far from losing us the respect of our porters, enhanced it noticeably. In fact, it produced a crop of topical jokes. A man would come up and feel my pack. "That's quite heavy. Why not get a fresh porter?" (That, doubtless, with an eye to providing an extra job for some cousin.) "I'm doing it for practice. If I lose my money and all else fails, I shall take up the profession of coolie." This sally never failed to bring the house down.

At last the morning of May 10 came: all was in readiness, "venesta" plywood boxes and kitbags were stacked according to their several marks; ice-axes and an awkward parcel of skis — which, when carried upright, turned its owner into the likeness of a monster praying-mantis — were standing in a corner, ropes and line were neatly coiled, and the pile was completed by a couple of empty kerosene tins grandiloquently called "canister" and used for fetching water, washing the sahibs' socks or shirts, or for the sahibs themselves to wash in. The march appointed for the first day was a short one, only seven miles, to a camping-ground called Magra, near which was a shop where the men could buy food to last several stages out of their first day's pay. No one could understand why I insisted on everyone reporting at the store-shed as early as six thirty, with a view to an eight o'clock start. If truth must be told, I did not wish to air my still halting Hindustani or to make a display of incompetence in controlling men under the critical eyes of those of the hotel residents who might have been tempted to look on. It was better to know that they were all safely ensconced in their beds.

It is extraordinary how, till one has tried, one fails to think of quite simple expedients such as ordering the porters to stand in a line so that they should pick up their loads one by one. The management of these matters was left to Jai Datt, for we had yet to plumb the depths of his incapacity. Almost all the men pressed forward simultaneously and settled on the pile of waiting loads like swarming bees, each man determined to weigh every one of the sixty-five packages with his own hands in search of the lightest. In vain we shouted above the uproar that they were all equal, fifty pounds, neither more nor less. For a few moments confusion threatened, while poor Jai Datt stood turning the leaves of his notebook and sucking a pencil, his usual signal of distress. Then somehow, probably with the help of Urbi Datt, the hubbub was stilled and in small groups the men started off down the road.

There is a special excitement belonging to any first occasion. For pure delight what can equal a first day's trek out into a fresh landscape? On such an occasion the commonest object fascinates — every viewpoint, every plant, bird, or beetle. The business of the day, reaching a destination, becomes quite secondary. I, for one, am given to peering inside thistles and turning over dock leaves for fear of missing something. It does not worry me if the local inhabitants stop and stare at the mad foreigner.

It was misty that morning and the air was softly caressing. Before turning north off the ridge towards Magra, we stopped to take a last look at the plains. The clouds had lifted, revealing the white stony bed of Lady Ganges, where she issued from the mountains, winding away endlessly. The sound of many cuckoos calling in the woods below came as an almost annoying surprise. In that exotic landscape the cuckoo, which, like the nightingale, suggests a copse with primrose, dog-violet, and anemone — the heralds of an English spring — had no place. Rounding a corner, we came upon a clump of tall rhododendron, trees rather than bushes, carrying their dark leathery foliage and clusters of blossoms upon smooth, russet-coloured branches. A pair of Himalayan pie floated off into the woods, trailing their graceful powder-blue tail-feathers behind them. No homely associations could outlive that sudden vision of crimson blooms and brilliant plumage, and we walked on engrossed again in the examination of the new and the strange.

The path had veered sharp left over the crest now, and we found ourselves beginning to drop down the farther slope, following a small ravine. "I, no other, supervised the making of this bit of road," exclaimed Jai Datt proudly. At last, in a grove of fir, we caught a glint of fires. Our men had already made themselves at home; some were engaged in carrying water from the stream, others were squatting over stew-pots or merely enjoying that sweet art of doing nothing which we are, to our loss, on the way to forgetting in this hard-driven society of ours. This was Magra, our first camp in the wilds.

Chapter II

The Pilgrim Way to Gangotri

CERTAIN ANXIETIES attend the setting of a first camp. The whole carefully planned system of packing becomes open to suspicion if on this occasion a tent is discovered without its attendant pegs; nor is the suspicion allayed if out of another tent-bag there clatter enough pegs to anchor a marquee. The porters have not been drilled in the handling of your particular brand of tent; confusion and damage may result if you cannot keep their zealous hands off the gear while you yourself carry out a demonstration pitch. Indian porters seem constitutionally slow at learning the principles of guy-ropes. Even after repeated and patient coaching they keep reverting to their own idea of tightening, which is to stick a peg through the ring at the end of the line, pull hard, and then force the peg into the ground, using a stone to hammer it home if it resists. If the adjustment of some other guy-rope causes their line to slacken, they uproot the peg and haul on it again.

Light fabrics or aluminum pegs will not stand such treatment for long; that is why tent-pitching and striking should never be left entirely to underlings. If only hasty and thoughtless handling can be restrained, it is remarkable how small are the effects of wear and tear even after a strenuous season. It will have been gathered from this that I am somewhat of a fanatic on the subject of camp technique. I have developed so fine a nose in this matter that I can usually smell out, better than any African witch-doctor, the intention of pulling on a guy-line even before the potential culprit has lifted a finger, merely by the way he walks and looks. I believe that I should rise from my deathbed at the sight of a tent being treated cruelly.

At Magra a fortnight's walking lay between us and Gaumukh, source of the Bhagirat'hi, one of the several head waters of the Ganges, itself the continuation of the great Gangotri Glacier. Gaumukh means Cow's Mouth. It is the Hindu custom

to attach symbolical names to the salient features in a landscape, the intention being to conjure up ideas rather than to
refer to historical events or to evoke the memory of famous
men. The Ganges, which plays so prominent a part in Hindu
symbolism, is pictured as having its source in the mouth of that
gentle, patient creature, the chosen type of the animal kingdom, whose protection is enjoined on all Hindus. To a stranger
in his ignorance "Cow's Mouth" might seem an unromantic
name for one of Nature's grandest display-places; yet when the
meaning is made known, one revises one's opinion. Looking
with the eye of a pilgrim at the flood of waters gushing forth
from amethystine caverns concealed beneath the ice, a sculptor
could have found inspiration in the name and felt moved to
carve some great animal head, a sphinxlike Colossus, through
whose jaws the waters of the infant Ganges might flow.

The second morning's march continued the descent into the
valley of the Aglar. The unforgettable memory of that day
was a magnolia bush at a curve of the road; its few flowers
were of shell-like purity, their frilled petals shaded to a deep
rose. The trunk and branches were gnarled and twisted into
shapes so fantastic that one would have said it had been consciously trained to serve as a model for some divine old Chinese
artist. Each man stopped as he caught sight of it in breathless amazement. At a later stage we found more magnolias,
larger and covered with flowers; but that first one contained
the quintessence of them all, an unfading picture imprinted on
our minds.

Between us and the Bhagirat'hi Valley there still lay two
passes, each about eight thousand feet high. Twice we saw the
Gangotri peaks from these points of vantage overlooking the
wooded foothills. For the second pass it was desirable to make
an early start since the descent on the farther side was said to
be long and hot. With the dawn we broke up our camp on the
hillside at Chapra, below the first pass, and plunged down into
the cool shadow. At the bottom we paddled through a shallow
torrent in which a Hindu devotee was performing his morning
ablutions; we had noticed him the night before, sitting in deep
meditation in a villager's garden among opium poppies and to-
bacco plants. He had greeted us with a motion of the hand and
a dreamy, far-off look; our passing scarcely distracted him for
a second from the vision that held him.

For a couple of hours we climbed up the opposite hillside.
Peasants here and there were tilling narrow strips of field,

walking behind the small wooden harrows drawn by slow, plodding oxen; little boys, the colour of the soil, were sitting on the ploughs, using their scanty weight to drive the plough-shares deeper. About eight o'clock we arrived on the col. I remember how we all stood in silence before the glorious line of peaks glistening in the early morning sunlight. Close at hand on either side a soft breeze was brushing across the barley, while overhead eagles wheeled against the blue. The porters came up close behind us, some of them bringing handfuls of yellow raspberries. As each man topped the pass he sang out boisterously in praise of the Holy Ones. "Hail to Jamnotri!" (source of the Jamna). "Hail to Gangotri!" "To the white lord of Kedar, homage!" (Its Weisshorn-like pyramid occupied the centre of the picture.) "To Badrinath" (sacred to Vishnu), "all hail!" We would willingly have gazed all day, but the thought of the heat awaiting us in the valley below made us cut short this joyous moment and we set off on the descent to Dharasu.

Our way followed the Bhagirat'hi Valley, now making height steadily, now rising suddenly when rocky narrows forced the path to take a higher level. We had got into our stride now, arrangements were working smoothly, and we felt in a carefree frame of mind, able to let our attention wander among the countless new things that met us at every turn. To allude to them all separately would need a volume; so I will first describe a typical day, and afterwards mention one or two happenings that stood out with special prominence.

We usually woke about five and while breakfast was cooking we strapped up our holdalls and struck the tents; for the porters would be already hovering round impatient to get off in the cool. Then, after indicating a place some fifteen miles away for the next camp, we let them straggle off, each at his own pace; the faster ones, to whom things first needed on arrival had been entrusted, forged on ahead, while the older ones trudged behind slowly. We were then free to employ our own time on the march as we pleased, pausing to take photographs or to bathe in an inviting pool or to pass the time of day with some friendly pilgrims bound like ourselves for Gangotri.

This valley is sacred to Shiva, the Aspect of the Hindu Trinity who stands for the transformative and also, but only by extension, for the destructive function in the Godhead. We passed many small temples, like elongated beehives; almost all were dedicated to Shiva under one or other of His aspects, such as the Conqueror of Demons. Within, in lieu of an image, there

is often placed a black conical stone, the phallic emblem of the
God. The corresponding valley on the east of the Gangotri
Mountains in Eastern Garhwal, that of the Alaknanda, is con-
secrated to the cult of Vishnu, the divine Aspect that is the complement of Shiva's, that of conservation and redemption; His
temple at Badrinath draws a still larger yearly pilgrimage.

The pilgrims themselves belonged to every province of India
and came from all ranks of society. First we met a sturdy
peasant, half hidden under a huge bundle of bedding overflowing from his long wicker basket, like the ones used in
Switzerland, which was slung over his back. On the top of
it his wife was perched, her legs dangling; yet the Orient is
called ungallant! Then we came across a wealthy dame,
borne aloft in her palanquin on the shoulders of four stout
attendants, looking, but for her clothes, like one of her eighteenth-century predecessors, the pious Austrian or French great
ladies, Romeward bound.

I remember also a mysterious person whom we passed and
repassed frequently, a very tall man in a flowing toga, with eyes
that pierced like stilettos, his coal-black hair gathered up in a
knot, in his hand an iron-shod staff like a spear. He strode
along haughtily, and whenever he came upon a big stone that
had rolled on to the path, he picked it up as if it were a feather
and tossed it over the precipice with a gesture of disdain that
was rather terrifying in its suggestion of power. We thought
of him as the god Wotan, disguised as the Wanderer — for he
really might have stepped straight out of *Siegfried*. When he
brought his staff sharply down on the rock, I momentarily
expected sparks to fly out.

Many swamis, or devotees wearing saffron robes and turbans,
each of them carrying a drinking-pot of burnished metal,
passed us by. Most of them eyed us coldly, as if suspicious of
our presence; their demeanour came as somewhat of a shock
after the unfailing smiles and salaams of the common pilgrims.
There was also another class of devotees to be found in large
numbers, so-called sadhus, men naked save for a loincloth, be-
smeared with grey ash from head to foot, their faces often
made to look repulsive by blotches of ochre. The conception
of the true sadhu is an exalted one: he is the type of the
spiritually independent man, who asks guidance of no power
but his inner light and has passed beyond all that social life
can give, whether rights or duties. For him, renunciation implies no idea of sacrifice of the "good things of the world" —

that conception, peculiar to European monasticism, is unknown to India, Tibet, and other Oriental traditions; this is an important point to grasp, lest one be drawn into a false analogy. On the contrary, the genuine sadhu rejects the world "with pleasure, just as a man would find satisfaction in taking off a filthy and ragged garment." He makes himself like an outlaw, abandoning the privileges of family and caste in the present, of past fame, and of aspiration for the future life, and tramps the highways, begging for his meagre livelihood, driven on by the wind of the spirit, which bloweth where it listeth.

This way, however, is not for the many: by no means all the ascetics who frequent sacred places can approach it. There is also a host of hangers-on, charlatans usurping the title, who, to do them justice, adopt an uncomfortable existence, but whose spiritual status would, in other respects, take some proving.

In the afternoon we used to go ahead of the porters to choose the best site for a camp in beautiful surroundings. Having read of the uncleanness that spoils many usual camping-grounds in Garhwal, we made a point of avoiding them and choosing ground of our own, not too close to villages. It is a better plan not to leave this important matter, affecting both comfort and pleasure, to head porters, who will of course invariably do as everyone else does and pick for preference some fly-infested area in the middle of the village, near a stream that receives the sewage of all the houses. Indians are extremely clean as far as their persons, clothes, and eating-vessels are concerned, but utterly insanitary in their use of ground in the vicinity of habitations. Within a radius of two miles round Gangotri temple, for instance, the soil is badly polluted. Near villages or cultivation one cannot be too careful about the water; in fact, we never risked drinking it unboiled till we were past human settlements. Lest anyone should be tempted in the midday heat, we made it a rule that each European must carry in his rucksack a flask of boiled water. Should any man desire to undertake a worthy work of piety, he might try to install a system of simple latrines along the pilgrim route. I should like to see it established not as an innovation in the name of foreign hygiene, but rather as an offering to Shiva, for a purification of His holy ground.

It is lucky that carcasses of cows and goats are dealt with by the vultures, which circle continuously overhead at a great height and scan the country for dying animals. Outside the village of Uttarkashi we came upon a dozen of them which had just finished picking a skeleton clean. How magnificent they looked as they flapped their mighty wings, and how different from the listless captives of our zoos, which are made into a gazing-stock for the supposed education of children! It is surely base ingratitude towards a fellow creature, which, even from the narrow point of view of our own self-interest, should be saluted as the unpaid ally of the sanitary squad and the health inspector.

Even after tents had been pitched and tea made, the work of the day was by no means over, for some of us at least. News that we had a doctor in our midst spread quickly, and soon a long string of people demanding medicine appeared at the edge of the camp. First they had to be sorted out, and then the doctor examined each in turn. One of us acted as his interpreter and helped to dispense in small envelopes the pills or powders that he prescribed. We saw some sad and many amusing cases.

One man reported various symptoms affecting almost every limb and organ in his body, which seemed hard to square with an appearance of robust health. Pain in the shoulder, in the hips, headache, shivering — what next? Fever? — the thermometer belied him. "There is nothing wrong with you. Why do you come and waste our time?" cried the doctor. "Oh, no, Sahib!" he answered. "It's not I who am ill, it's my wife. She lives at the village back yonder, two days' journey away. You can give me the medicine."

Another man demanded something for his horse, also not present. All this had to be carried on in full publicity, with the whole village enjoying the show. Some of the bystanders, bitten with a desire to share in the excitement, were seized with sudden ailments and looked quite crestfallen when the doctor refused to prescribe for them like the others.

The outpatients' clinic not infrequently lasted till dark, with an overflow meeting before we started in the morning. No one could say that Dr. Warren idled his time away. Some consider that it is justifiable to distribute fizzy salts to all and sundry and send the people away happy, but that was not the view of either Dr. Warren or Dr. Roaf, who acted in his place in 1936. Of course it is little enough that one can do to relieve sufferers when one is moving from place to place: many cases are beyond such temporary treatment. But there are others who can be helped, those who require, above all, advice — to them it is usually best to give a little medicine too on some pretext;

otherwise the advice will be disregarded. To those who are able and willing to travel to a hospital a letter can sometimes be given; minor surgical cases — gathered fingers or teeth needing extraction — these are among the ones who benefit positively. To malingerers one need not be afraid to tell the truth. In quite unmanageable cases like cancer it is best to avoid raising false hopes, and of course single doses of anodynes, such as injections of morphia, seeing that they cannot be followed up, will only add to the suffering and are out of the question.

At long last came the big meal of the day, supper, usually a curry of sorts; and then half an hour's yarning round the camp-fire, in which some of the porters joined, reduced everyone to somnolence. By eight thirty or nine we were all asleep.

The commissariat proved an unqualified success, thanks to the fresh food we bought daily and to Maidar Singh's skill in cooking it. During the course of travel in the hills one learns to know the essential requirements, what must be brought from home, and what can be purchased locally. Experience has shown that in most districts the village shop can be relied on for flour, rice, lentils, *ghi* (clarified butter), sugar, onions, and pepper. Eggs, milk, and often a few vegetables such as potatoes, a kind of spinach, and large sweet radishes can be bought direct from the peasants. We accustomed ourselves to a diet of these foods; our imports amounted to only a few luxuries.

The quality of the native foodstuffs is on the whole excellent; the fatal cult of whiteness and regularity of shape has not caused half their goodness to be "purified" away, nor has their flavour been dissipated in the crazy worship of size and number. To give one instance, the native sugar, slightly greyish of hue, sweetened twice as well as our imported refined sugar. The native potatoes, about the same size as our new potatoes, are the tastiest known to me. After getting used to the small, hard rice of India, unpolished of course, the white, big-grained, "high-grade" rice usually sold in stores at home is insipid to the point of being unusable, and its nutritive properties are no less deficient.

In retrospect, the preparations made at Mussoori in 1933 with such care appear needlessly elaborate. It has become, in fact, difficult to believe that those quantities of big and little tins, with their garish labels, which exhaust superlatives in proclaiming the unique virtues of their contents, could ever have been thought indispensable. Those ugly, aggressive little objects have unfortunately got their uses on the mountain; but

elsewhere they are never missed. They are the spurious sub-
stitutes for things that can be better bought at the local shop,
where one can see honest, rough flour being shoveled from big
sacks and hear the patter of rice grains in the scales.

The highest-lying villages in Garhwal, along the Tibetan
border, are inhabited in the summer months by a semi-nomadic
tribe called Jadhs or, farther to the east, Bhotias. These people
are a typical frontier product, mixed racially and in tradition,
who make the best of two worlds in any border dispute. The
Tibetan half predominates in the Jadhs, however; six days
out of seven they are Buddhists and, when they are not wearing European cast-offs purchased while wintering on the edge
of the Indian plain, they clothe themselves in Tibetan style.
In summer they pasture their flocks and ponies in the uplands,
or cross into Tibet to barter Indian produce for a consignment
of salt or borax.

A party of Jadhs happened to be encamped near a place
called Kot'h Bangla the afternoon we arrived there. Their gaily
coloured tents, unusual clothes, and flat faces at once attracted
our attention. We stopped to stare and they, for their part, returned the compliment with interest. Then I took my courage
in both hands and spoke a short sentence in Tibetan, my first
remark in that tongue to a native of the land. There was stony
silence till I spoke again; then everyone burst into roars of
laughter, shouting: "Why, he's talking Tibetan, he's really talking Tibetan!" It was rather disconcerting to have one's linguistic efforts laughed at with such unconcealed frankness; but it
was not long before I discovered that what tickled their sense
of humour was not so much my halting speech as the extraordinary fact that a white man should speak in Tibetan at all! There
was among them one man in particular who caught my eye;
we asked him to visit us so that we might continue the new
talking-game. Sure enough, he turned up in an hour's time,
bringing a young companion with him, and they spent the rest
of the afternoon in our company. Mutual sympathy developed
from the start. We found that he spoke, and even could write,
Hindustani as well as Tibetan, and what was still more exciting,
that he was no Jadh but came from Poo on the Satlej, a place
that stood on our itinerary for Part Two of the expedition's
program: for it was our intention to climb at Gangotri till the
rains broke and then to cross the Ganges-Satlej watershed to
a district beyond the monsoon's influence and, passing through
Poo, to attempt, as a grand finale, the ascent of the great peak

of Riwo Pargyul. Our new-found friends seemed to have turned up providentially; before they left our camp that day we had invited them both to join us. The man of Poo asked for a brief delay in order to go back and consult his wife, but promised to bring an answer before the day was out.

In the evening he returned with the glad news that everything was settled and that he and Djun Singh, his friend, who looked as strong as a young bull, would most certainly come with us as far and as long as we liked. As if to seal the compact, he made me a present of a little wooden bowl with a silver base and received a knife in exchange. His name was Odsung in his own country; but he kept the alternative one of Ishwar Singh for use when associating with Indians. In time he was to become the head of our porters, and three years later both he and Djun Singh joined us again in Sikkim: far-reaching results from a chance meeting by the roadside. Ishwar Singh's rapid decision to throw in his lot with total strangers, for a journey of six hundred miles, was characteristic of Tibetan independence and love of roving.

Chapter III

Porters and Sahibs

FOR THE MAN who loves trees and plants, even if he be no more than an amateur, the walk along the Bhagirat'hi is one long succession of delights; for each day's gain in height is faithfully reflected in corresponding changes of vegetation. Dharasu, the point where one enters the valley at the low level of 2,500 feet, lies in a warm zone in which even small palms are found — outposts of the flora of the plains. The blue-grey of the long-needled pine colours much of the landscape. White roses are massed along the path for miles on end; *Erythrina,* the coral tree, lends here and there a touch of fire; this part of the valley is the favoured home of the pink magnolia.

At about 7,000 feet that king of forest trees, the Himalayan cedar or deodar, makes its appearance, its roots clinging to ledges on the cliff face, its trunk leaning precariously out over the swirling rapids. A few miles short of a place called Gangnani the road crosses temporarily to the left bank and penetrates a belt of mixed forest, maple, oak, and chestnut, of almost tropical density. The shed petals of tree rhododendrons turn the path into a crimson carpet, as if in expectation of a royal progress. Jasmine and wild hops wreathe the boughs with festive garlands. The slender shoots of bamboo, so delicate yet so impenetrable, bar the way to the interior forest, guarding the glades where the wild peonies gleam like folds of white satin.

One more day and the scene changes to typical Alpine country, a flat-bottomed valley through which the Bhagirat'hi winds along its shingly bed, hardly recognizable for the same stream as the raging torrent lower down. Mixed woods have disappeared and the hillsides are uniformly forested with stately deodars; violets look up from the grass; the light airs bring with them the fragrance of thyme. One is glad to pull on a sweater, for in mid-May the snow is still lying quite low and evenings soon turn chilly.

At the farther extremity of this valley there is a small hamlet called Harsil where, according to our program, we had planned to make a three days' halt in order to pay off our Mussoori coolies and replace them by local men, better inured to the rigorous climate of the glaciers. We had been counting on the Jadhs to furnish the whole of our new personnel, but found that at that date only a few advanced bands had yet come up from the winter grazing-grounds; the remainder were still scattered down the valley. The only alternative was to make up the number from near-by villages, though we knew that the nomads, whose life is one long trek, would have answered our purpose far better than the peasants, whose hearts were in their fields and who elected to come for the pay, but came reluctantly. There was no choice, however, so word was sent to the villages stating our requirements. Presently three headmen arrived at the camp to parley over terms. They were striking figures, thickset and powerful, bearded and beaked, natural orators and possessed of an inborn dignity with a dash of cunning. As soon as we saw them we christened them the Canaanite "Kings," rulers over "cities" that might have resisted Joshua. At every turn in the debate the three chieftains consulted one another from the corners of their eyes and then one of them, say the King of Eglon, would take the leading part, while the others stood by to lend moral support.

"I require twenty porters by tomorrow," said I.

The trio exchanged hasty glances.

"Tomorrow twenty men cannot possibly be found," answered the King of Eglon.

"No indeed," chimed in the King of Jarmuth.

"Can't be done," echoed the King of Ai.

"Suppose we collected them in three days' time?" said Eglon.

"Yes, in three days it shall be," agreed Jarmuth.

"By the fourth day from now they can be here," corroborated Ai.

"Oh, but I can't wait so long as that; besides," I added, "you will find it worth your while if you do get them sooner. Now, what about splitting the difference? Say two days from today?"

Another hasty ocular confabulation. Ai picked up the ball.

"In two days from now it could be done."

"Indeed it could," assented Eglon. "You just leave it to us; in two days!"

Jarmuth ratified the treaty; at which all three marched off to set the wheels in motion.

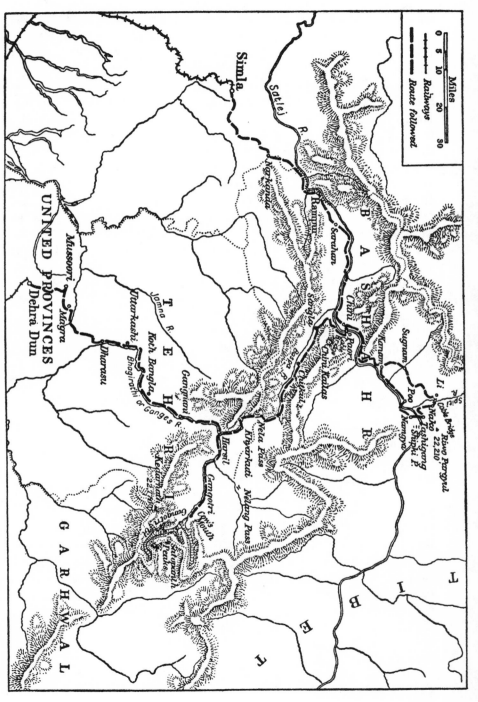

It should be noted that only the principal mountain chains have been indicated; most of the area shown, however, is mountainous.

Meanwhile at our end there were also jobs to be done. First we had to decide who were the four best men to keep with us at our glacier camp for work on the mountains. As recently as 1933 it was still generally believed that Europeans were only just capable of becoming sufficiently acclimatized to climb their peaks, and that in the absence of native porters to do their fetching and carrying for them they had hardly a hope of success. For one European climber to go high, several natives had to accompany him. It is not difficult to calculate what a multiplication of personnel and baggage resulted from this hypothesis: for the attendant natives themselves needed food and shelter, which entailed again more porters and so on for ever. In fact, it could be proved mathematically that by this process one European party would eventually involve the whole human race, and still the problem would be no nearer solution. We were, I believe, one of the earliest parties to break decisively with this custom, both from our own wish for privacy, which was incompatible with the presence of a regiment requiring a sergeant-major to manœuvre it, and because our pioneer theories received firm encouragement from Dr. Longstaff, who always maintained that Himalayan climbing could be treated very much like Alpine, save in the case of certain exceptional peaks. The chief argument of all in favour of reduced numbers lay in the knowledge that whatever climbs were accomplished would be due to the climbers' own efforts, and that the satisfaction derived from success would not have to be scaled down proportionately to the number of their helpers. It would be a sad story if porters in the Himalaya were to be turned insidiously into something like guides in the Alps, namely middlemen, admittedly competent ones, interposed between the amateur and his mountains. Since 1933 we have seen most of the younger climbers reach the same conclusions, and the soundness of the method has been incontestably proved on very high peaks indeed. One has only to think of the brilliant explorations of Shipton and Tilman in Eastern Garhwal, which for magnitude of accomplishment, coupled with exiguousness of expenditure, perhaps constitute the finest piece of mountaineering recorded in history, or the tackling in 1937 of the extremely difficult Mana Peak by Smythe and Oliver, which of all ascents appeals to me most for its "artistic" qualities, or again the success of Tilman's party in 1936 on Nanda Devi, when, owing to sickness among the coolies, all carrying on the upper reaches of that formidable mountain was done by Europeans. A significant point in that expedition was the inclusion of Professor Graham Brown, who, though not young in years, did his full share of the work and, by so doing, helped to lay the old acclimatization bogy.

Our complement of only four porters was probably rather short commons, since it meant less than one coolie per European: we found in practice that we wasted more of our own energy than we could afford in long-distance carries over the glaciers. I have said four; but in reality they were but three and a half, for one of the men selected, our new-found friend from Poo, Ishwar Singh, was not very strong and did not undertake serious carrying. He more than made up for it, however, by being the perfect caretaker of a camp, ready to turn his hand to anything, and a suitable man for sending down to the villages to order fresh supplies or to engage porters to clear our stuff when the climbing was all over. His friend, Djun Singh, the Jadh, was a powerful fellow. The other vacancies were filled by two young men from Eastern Garhwal, one of whom was an old soldier, in more senses than one, who had served with the Garhwal Rifles. He was perpetually saluting and clicking heels; but he was active as a cat on rocks. He also performed prodigies of weight-lifting and speed on steep slopes. Had we asked for his life he would have given it; but that did not preclude his trying to score off us in petty ways from time to time. Apart from that, as a mountain porter he could not have been bettered.

A further job at Harsil was the dumping of half our baggage, which, not being immediately required, was intended for use during the second or Satlej part of the journey. Everything was handed into the charge of the district forest ranger, a very obliging Hindu who stored it in a safe place against our return from the glacier.

The third job was a melancholy one for all concerned; namely, the paying off of the old set of porters who had served us so faithfully. Nine days of acquaintance may not seem long, but the Indians, when treated considerately, attach themselves easily; the men seemed genuinely sad to be leaving us as they walked up in turn to the box that served as a table, to receive their wages. We were particularly sorry to say good-bye to Maidar Singh and Urbi Datt. We would have liked to stretch a point and keep on the latter; but he was rather a delicate man, inclined to suffer from a chronic cough, so it would hardly have been fair to take him high. Some weeks later, by good luck, he came back to us for a time; the pleasure of that reunion was all the greater for the previous parting.

This opportunity must be taken of testifying to the uniform level of honesty that we have found among the mountain peoples. In 1933 we changed porters five times and employed Indians, Jadhs, Tibetans, and Kunáwaris from the Satlej. During the whole time we did not miss so much as a lump of sugar; not that we took precautions; we soon learned that it was a waste of trouble. Everything was strewn about the camp. In how many countries of Europe or America would it be possible to pick up fifty chance comers and yet enjoy perfect immunity from anxiety on the score of pilfering? Sometimes in the case of Indians, though not of the other races, those who were entrusted with the job of buying provisions were inclined to add an anna or two to the bill; but even here a distinction must be made between regular perquisites sanctioned by convention, amounting to a tiny percentage levied on all shopping transactions, and attempts to exceed just limits by taking advantage of the ignorance of an employer new to the game.

Honesty and deceit are governed by fashions which vary greatly in different countries: it is the unfashionable dishonesty that evokes public censure. Many people in England, for example, seem to consider semi-deliberate slackness in repaying a loan or failure to settle a tailor's bill or a doctor's fee distinctly less heinous than other forms of cheating. Among Indians it is probably in connexion with the seeking and accepting of commissions that there is more room for criticism. Making all due allowance for local variation in the standards of serious and petty crime, my experience of the Himalayan peoples is that the general level of honesty is pretty high. All the races we had to do with in 1933 seemed entitled to full marks on the score of not stealing. When it came to truthfulness the difference was greater. The Tibetans and allied peoples tend to be extremely accurate, while the Indians are sometimes inclined to romance, more from a desire to please than from any wish to deceive. There is much truth in the tale of the tired English traveller who asked the distance to the next village. "Not far," was the answer. "What do you mean by that? Is it about three miles?" "Yes, your honour." But the Englishman still entertained some doubts. "Are you sure it's only three miles? Or is it six?" "Yes, six, your honour." Losing his temper, the Englishman cried: "What the devil do you mean by saying it's three miles and then six? Don't tell me any more lies; which is it,

three or six?" "It's as your honour pleases." In a small way this
sort of thing often happens, and it is good to be prepared for it.

The three headmen were as good as their word; at the appointed hour the new coolies duly paraded for their loads.
Physically they looked equal to any call; but their faces struck
us as rather empty, with a dash of slyness combined with obsti-
nacy. They were much better clad than the Mussoori men, for
their hand-woven garments contrasted favourably with the
heterogeneous collections of European misfits that have been
adopted by a great number of the hill Indians. This regrettable
practice cannot justify itself on the mere plea of cheapness, for
the local cloth, often still worn by women even when their hus-
bands have discarded it, is spun and woven at home from the
wool of their own sheep and costs them next to nothing. Furthermore, it is hard-wearing and warm as well as beautiful;
made from it, even the rags of a beggar look dignified. That is
really the test of good cloth; machine-made materials are tolerable when new and smart, but their old age is ugly. The more
sophisticated the garment, the worse it looks when once it is
worn out; nothing looks more forlorn than a well-cut dinner-
jacket that is soiled and shabby. It is partly the desire to raise
their social status by emulating the sahibs, and partly the easy
temptation of getting things ready-made that causes many Indians to despise their own goods. I have occasionally put leading questions to some of these people concerning their motives,
and their replies bear out these conclusions. It is worth noting
that women are less prone to lose their heads in this way than
men — the male is the unstable sex. A marked strain of Tibetan
blood is usually a safeguard; but not always, for that fine race
of men, the Nepali Sherpas, justly famous as mountain porters,
are great offenders. If only the climbers who employ them
would make a point of encouraging them to revert to their national costume, it would be doing them and the world a service.

It did not take us long to discover how much we had been
spoiled by our Mussoori coolies. As usual, having indicated the
stage for the day, we left the men to their own devices, knowing that they were not yet in training and expecting them to
follow slowly. After going some miles, I sat down for rather
longer than usual and began to wonder why nobody had yet
put in an appearance. Having waited some time, I walked back
to a commanding point, but not a soul was in sight. Slightly
concerned, I retraced my steps; but I had to go a long way
downhill before I encountered Jai Datt, who had been retained

in his office of leading porter, and who announced that most of
the men were dawdling miles back. Some time later we came
upon them all sitting down, their loads off, taking turns at
puffing their charcoal pipes, and to all appearances settled there
for ever. When we started to protest, some of them stood up
sulkily and raced a few steps uphill at an absurd pace, only to
collapse once more. Out came the pipes again quite blatantly.
This performance was repeated at intervals all the afternoon,
and we reached Bhaironghati, the resting-place for the night,
with frayed tempers. It was dark before the rear guard
slouched in at last; not a good outlook, for we were still following a path, whereas the next day we were to enter trackless
country. Working out that day's rate of progress, I made it not
much more than one mile an hour, as compared with the normal two and a half miles.

In the morning things at first looked a little more cheerful:
there was a perfumed freshness in the air that left little room
for worries. In this part of its course the river had hewn its
way through a succession of deep chasms, racing through their
depths in a thin line of foam. The fantastic rock walls of the
cutting were unlike anything I had seen elsewhere; and yet
there was something reminiscent about them, but I could not
just lay my finger on it. Eventually it dawned on me: it was
the rocks in Giotto's frescoes. The whole scene would have
served to illustrate the Inferno of Dante; thus I picture murky
Acheron, or Styx, on which if an oath be sworn, even a god
is bound by it.

Towards ten o'clock the temple of Gangotri, the end of the
pilgrim road, came into view, a pleasantly porportioned domed
building of grey stone that did not look very old; I should have
guessed no earlier than eighteenth-century, though this may not
be quite accurate. It stands on the river bank, against a background of noble deodars. We were received by a priest who
offered to show us round. We gave him a small present, and
besides, following the ancient custom of feeding a specified
number of poor Brahmins, we distributed alms to some of the
neediest-looking of the pilgrims. In front of the temple steps
we removed our shoes and were then permitted to approach
near enough to peer vaguely into the dark interior. A tray with
sweetmeats that had stood in front of the image was brought
out and we were each invited to taste a piece, and then our
foreheads were marked with powdered sandalwood, to the
accompaniment of triumphant shouts from the bystanders led

by Jai Datt. Sightseeing, lunch, and a long rest filled a couple
of hours before the signal was given to continue the march.

At once a chorus of moans rose from the porters, who had
evidently been counting on our readiness to accept the few
miles between Bhaironghati and Gangotri as the equivalent of a
day's work. Wringing their hands, they whined: "Please, please
don't make us go farther today. There is no path, it is a terrible
wilderness full of leopards and bears. We shall be killed by
falling stones, and there are no camping-grounds!" At length,
having exhausted themselves in vain lamentation, and seeing
that we were not to be moved from our purpose, they lifted
their loads with an ill grace and started off. Several truants
hid among the temple outhouses, hoping to be overlooked, and
had to be rounded up by Jai Datt and the forest ranger, who,
uninvited, accompanied our column.

The wild Gangotri Gorge, the passage from the temple to
the Cow's Mouth, is crossed at that season by huge drifts of
compacted winter snow which bridge the river and allow free
crossing to and fro. In summer these get washed away and the
approved route follows the left bank and crosses to Gangotri
by a bridge. The other side is blocked by formidable cliffs
lashed by the torrent that boils against their base. When we
came down in the monsoon, though the main body took the
left bank, two of us, ignorant of the obstacle, followed the right
bank and only just got through, after a strenuous day's rock-
climbing along ledges and up cracks, all the time haunted by
the fear that in the end we might find ourselves cut off.

The porters soon began to repeat the previous day's tactics,
but with even more frequent halts, a policy that was favoured
by the abundance of cover. Every inch was contested. Sometimes a man would move not more than twenty paces and then
subside under a bush and slip his arms out of the loops of his
carrying-rope. Poor Jai Datt lost his head completely and
showed abject irresolution before his men, while the ranger,
being made of sterner stuff, preferred futile threats to entreaties.
At last, when we had crawled a couple of miles, things came
to a head. A ringleader, ordered to get up from behind a boulder where he was crouching, refused. Abandoning his load, he
declared that he could not go a step farther. Thereupon Ted
Hicks snatched up the package and slung it over his own shoulders, saying: "If you are too weak to carry this light box, I can
do it myself." The man was utterly taken aback by the unprecedented sight of a sahib actually doing a job of work; he sprang

up and rushed after Ted, begging to be allowed to take back his load. A general stampede followed, and before we knew where we were, we had gone quite a distance. For the moment we were in control of the situation; but it was doubtful how long the emotion that had befriended us would last, so as soon as I saw a possible site for a camp I called a halt. It was elementary generalship to be the first to offer — indeed, to order — the very thing that the other party was still screwing up its courage to demand.

At tea-time we held a council of war. It was evident that we were facing a crisis; for had the discontent resulted in a strike and the dumping of our baggage, it would have taken us days to extricate ourselves from the mess. Gangotri is not a village; we could only have sent back for fresh porters to Harsil, the very place from which the present lot were drawn, and we should have been more than ever in their power. Nor would the monsoon have stayed its hand for our convenience. A loss of time at that moment could not have been made up later. As things turned out, it would have meant utter disaster, for the rains came on a full three weeks before the expected date, so that we had only a bare month on the glacier. In addition, we had visions of the sarcastic comments of those prophets who had shaken their heads over the imprudence of five amateurs venturing to run an expedition without an experienced transport officer. Heroic remedies were obviously called for.

The first move was to get rid of Jai Datt and the officious ranger; their presence as intermediaries was only adding to our difficulties. After that, remembering my army training, I worked out a new order of march, by which a slow but unflagging pace was to be imposed on all, on the fast few as well as on the many loiterers; they were to keep in one body, with official halts at stated intervals. We went the round of the camp-fires that night and explained the morrow's plans; we found everyone in better humour and more ready to listen to us in person than to Jai Datt's hysterical appeals.

We pointed out to them that at the present rate we were never going to reach Cow's Mouth; and that this rushing on a few steps and then stopping was actually the most tiring method imaginable. We pointed out that they were mistaken in thinking that we did not intend them to have time to rest; we promised, on the contrary, to arrange regular halts and they would see for themselves how much earlier they would make camp and how fresh they would feel. We said that the next

day no one would be allowed to go fast, but all must go at
a set pace; every half-hour there would be five minutes' halt,
after an hour ten, after two hours a long rest. They were not
to sit down except at a given signal, nor to start without another. Between the halts they must keep moving at an even
pace. We assured them that they would thank us in the end,
when they realized how much less tired they were. The men
seemed disposed to respond to this appeal to their reason; we
retired to bed still feeling anxious though somewhat more optimistic, and blessing the extra time we had spent on linguistic
studies, without which such complex explanations would have
been impossible.

After breakfast we lined up the men facing the loads and
called the roll, so that the day might start in an atmosphere
of calm. When all were ready, we formed them in single file,
placing two of our party at the head, two at the tail, and one
to act as liaison in the middle. Then we set off; but, at first,
success hung in the balance. Several men attempted to sit
down and had to be hooked up with ice-axes by their girdles.
As soon as the hands of my watch pointed to the half-hour I
called a halt and sat down. This seemed to affect certain notorious sluggards with an irresistible enthusiasm for going on;
they had to be forcibly restrained and made to rest.

The next period went better: by the end of the second
hour, when a lengthy pause was due according to schedule, we
knew we had won the day. The coolies had caught on to the
idea; their step had become springy and their whole manner
changed. We had no further trouble with them, and during
the next two days in the gorge everything went smoothly. At
the finish the tables were turned; for when we had nearly arrived in sight of the glacier snout the porters could no longer
be restrained, and one and all raced off at breakneck pace
across the slopes, so that we hardly knew them for the feeble
creatures who three days earlier seemed hardly capable of
putting one foot in front of the other. The whole episode was a
valuable lesson to us, our first real experience of porter management. The story may make the hard-bitten traveller smile,
but to five novices it seemed no small adventure.

Some little distance short of the Cow's Mouth and separated
from it by an expanse of clean sand we camped in a leafless
birch wood, surrounded by long drifts of snow. Ahead loomed
the vast glacier, measuring a mile across, its rubbish-covered
surface broken up into mounds, which turned out to be hillocks

quite a hundred feet high. Peaks rose on every side in wildest confusion; not even in Sikkim have I seen anything like the mountain scenery round Gangotri. Dominating all was the glorious group of the Satopant'h peaks, a magnet for our ambitions during our stay there — one of them was eventually scaled by two of the party — but it is useless to try to describe the grandeur of the scene: there are perfections about which the only eloquence is silence.

During the following three days the baggage was transferred on to the glacier, to a spot close under the left moraine, which had been chosen for the base camp. Across the opposite side, in a branch valley, a slope covered with low bushes of juniper provided plentiful firewood. After we had settled in, the majority of the porters returned home, leaving only the chosen four to keep us company. We now split up into pairs and began to make exploratory forays and to look for climbable peaks; we rejected at sight a nightmare version of the Matterhorn that overhung the camp. I do not propose to enter into minute details of our mountaineering round this region, for it is now old history, as an Austrian expedition has since explored the Gangotri district. But briefly, one small, one larger, and three medium peaks — not to mention two abortive attempts — were climbed before the warm rains descended upon us prematurely, to the accompaniment of a barrage of falling stones and avalanches, and put an end to operations.

The highest as well as the most formidable of these excursions was the ascent, previously mentioned, of Central Satopant'h * by Kirkus and Warren. Of this a full description will be given in the next chapter, written by C. F. Kirkus himself. At the time when the account first appeared it did not, to my mind, receive the general attention that it deserved. Not only was the ascent a fine piece of mountaineering, but it afforded a triumphant vindication of the theory that Europeans were capable of carrying out such enterprises without the help of porters. In this case the two climbers did the whole of their portering on a difficult mountain, involving several bivouacs, unaided from start to finish, and at the height of 21,000 feet negotiated a rock pitch that would have counted as severe at sea level: it is this difficult rock-climbing at a high altitude that makes their achievement so outstanding.

* As a result of the Austrian party's explorations there is now reason to believe that the peaks known to us as *Satopant'h* should be named the *B'hagirat'hi* group.

Chapter IV

Central Satopant'h

(by C. F. Kirkus)

ON THE AFTERNOON of June 14 Warren and I arrived at our advanced base, a pleasant camp at a height of about 15,000 feet, pitched on turf. It would have made an ideal base camp if only our transport arrangements had enabled us to get all our equipment up the extra seven miles of glacier.

We were still undecided about our next move. It was a warm and sunny day, the kind of day that inspires one to make bold plans for the morrow, and until the morrow comes, to relax in delightful idleness. Across the glacier to the east was the great rock mass of the Central Satopant'h Peak, 22,060 feet. Its face was a fearsome yellow cliff, crowned by a snow-capped ridge of red rock. This looked possible on the right, where it sloped down to a col and, providentially, a long, curving, easy-looking ridge led up to this col. We wanted to climb a big peak, but we wished for no more slopes of endless, heart-breaking snow. The gleaming snow and silvery rock of Central Satopant'h, standing up so boldly against a sky of deepest blue, proved quite irresistible and we decided to start the attempt on it next day.

There seemed to be two doubtful stretches on the route we had planned — a rock tower on the col and a vertical step in the ridge immediately above. This step was several hundred feet in height and looked formidable enough to stop us unless we could manage to turn it. The whole peak, in fact, looked definitely difficult and we were none too optimistic about our chances.

We set off at eight o'clock next morning, stumbling and cursing across the mile-wide glacier. Never is scree so villainous as when it is resting on ice; never are the limpid depths of glacier lakes less appreciated than when one is faced with the prospect of falling into them. We each carried a sack weighing about twenty-five pounds, containing sleeping-bags, bivouac tent, a week's supply of food (chiefly pemmican and boiled sweets), solidified spirit cookers, and a Primus. Everything had been cut down to a bare minimum. A very pleasant slope of grass and grey boulders, with scarcely any snow on it, led us to a ridge, clustered with grotesque pinnacles of red rock.

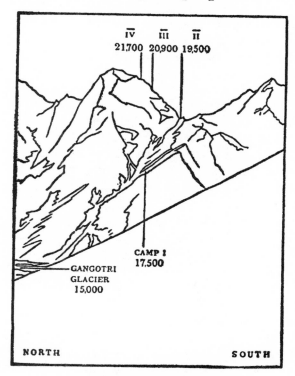

Central Satopant'h

Soon afterwards we had to rope for a fascinating arête of grey rock, which reminded us of Snowdonia, wonderfully firm and rough and technically quite difficult. It made us feel almost homesick and was altogether an exhilarating interlude in this rather grim business of Himalayan mountaineering.

We had to traverse off finally, to avoid a wall that would have given good sport in gym shoes, but we had no trouble in getting back to the ridge again. We pitched Camp I at about 17,500 feet, right on its jumbled crest. The only flat place was a miserable patch of snow, four or five feet square; this we had to build up with stones until it was big enough to take our four-foot by six-foot tent.

As usual, it came on to snow in the afternoon and a bitter wind harried us. I kept myself comparatively warm by building a cairn and a wall worthy of the old Romans. By the time we went to bed, there was half a gale blowing and we were afraid that our tent might be swept off its precarious platform.

It was still horribly cold in the morning and the tent was frozen stiff as a board; we had to wait for about an hour before it was soft enough to pack. We had to rope very soon for a small pinnacle and then were forced off the ridge on the left, across a slope that looked from a distance like snow, but proved to be composed of small prickles of ice, about three feet high, frozen on to rock. Then we got on to slabs, smooth and hold-less and covered with snow wherever snow would lie. The route-finding was very tricky and the climbing difficult and in-secure, with a great scarcity of belays. All the time we were getting farther and farther away from the crest of the ridge, with less and less hope of regaining it. And this was the part that we thought would be an easy scramble up to the true peak above the col.

I came round a slabby corner and to my joy saw that an easy snow gully led right up to the ridge. Here we made some tea and basked in the sunshine. We were now 3,000 or 4,000 feet above the glacier, which looked like a great sweeping river of speckled grey and white. An astonishing array of peaks surrounded us. There was the huge pinnacle that we called the Matterhorn, half spire, half tower, red rock at the bottom, snow-powdered yellow at the top; beautifully alluring, hide-ously inaccessible. We unroped with profound relief and made our way across a slope of mixed snow and stones on the right. This was made necessary by a curious kink in the ridge, where it almost ceased to be a ridge at all. We climbed easily up-wards by interesting rock pitches and little knife-edges of snow. I felt well and happy and was able to enjoy the noble scale of the scenery. Especially impressive was a weird and shadowy ice-valley, dizzily far below on the right, into which a hanging glacier, perched on top of 2,000 feet of cliff, rained showers of ice-splinters.

Then followed two towers, the second rotten and snow-sprinkled, after which a descent of a hundred feet or so brought us, still unroped, to our longed-for col. It was an ideal spot — flat, slaty ground with convenient stones all ready for laying on the tent-flaps and there was even a water-supply where a stone had melted a hole in some snow and left a small pool. One could not hope to find a better spot at 19,500 feet; it was amazing luxury not having to camp on snow. A full vertical mile below was our base camp and the whole dreary ribbon of the glacier. In front was the face of our mountain — 3,000 feet of the smoothest, sheerest yellow-silver rock, almost luminous against the clear blue of the sky. Behind, over the Ganges, the clouds were gathering — monsoon clouds had we but known; but who would have expected the monsoon to come three weeks early?

We had now a chance to examine the ridge above us, the final peak. It rose in a great step of rotten red rock, streaked with yellow. Even foreshortened as it was, it looked very formidable, but not quite out of the question, should all else fail. However, it seemed possible to turn it on the right, across a slope that rose at an angle of 40° to 50° for 2,000 feet, snow where snow would lie, and the rest loose stones. In some parts of the Himalaya, from tales we had heard, such a slope would have been suicidal. However, the Gangotri mountains seemed to be no more prone to avalanches than the Alps, so we decided we were quite justified in venturing on this eastern face of the ridge. We discovered one interesting fact: our col was not a main col of the Satopant'h range as it had appeared to be from below, but only a subsidiary neck on our particular ridge. The main col was behind and the two ridges joined about 1,000 feet higher up.

It snowed as usual in the evening, but soon cleared up. There were only 23 degrees of frost in the night and we had a comfortable sleep. We set off at eight o'clock, leaving the Primus stove and some pemmican behind. The first tower, which had looked so imposing from the glacier, gave no trouble at all; it was easily turned on the right. Then came the traverse, horribly unpleasant. We got on to some rotten rocks, covered with wet snow and loose slate. It was very trying and disheartening; after going for two hours we had hardly risen a foot, and it was a miracle that not a stone fell; in such a place in the Alps there would have been a bombardment.

At last we entered a gully of steep snow-covered slabs, where we had to run out the whole hundred feet of rope to find a stance, let alone a belay. The return traverse to the ridge, however, went quite smoothly, though it was unpleasant going. The ridge was very rotten — mud and snow and loose shale. There was one pitch in particular, a vertical tower about fifty feet high composed of great red blocks like paving-stones rest-

ing on top of one another. It looked as though the whole structure would fall to pieces, and, added to that, the final overhang
was decidedly difficult.

We pitched Camp III on a miserable spot at about 20,900
feet. Before we actually put the tent up I wandered on alone
and had a look at the next section. It was only 1.15 p.m. and
I thought we might have gone on a little farther, but, as Warren
pointed out, there was quite a possibility that we might not find
another suitable site in time. It is Dr. Longstaff's golden rule
of Himalayan mountaineering always to bivouac by three
o'clock. If you are later it gets cold before everything is done,
and the result is confusion and discomfort. Just above was a
wall of rock. I climbed up the first forty feet, but stopped
at the final portion, which looked terrifying, overhanging ominously at the top. I descended and rejoined Warren. The only
place on which to put the tent was a little snow ledge at the
top of a very steep snow-slope that descended several thousand
feet to the glacier on the east. This ledge was just too small,
so we had to build it up on the right and dig it out on the left.
One of the ice-axe extensions (we used ice-axes as tent poles
with bits of bamboo added) was dropped and slid rapidly out
of sight. We hoped that the tent would not follow in the middle
of the night.

It was a desolate spot, almost overhung by cliffs, so that the
sun set on the tent at three o'clock. We went fifty feet down
the ridge and found the sun again. At five p.m. it got too cold
and we struggled and gasped and panted our way back to the
camp and crawled into our sleeping-bags. Then there was the
miserable business of cooking and eating pemmican; that night
it seemed nauseating fare. We were using solid spirit cookers
now, and their choking fumes filled the tent and made our eyes
smart. Fourteen hours in a cramped tent is a weary business.
Sleep does not come easily at this height and the first few hours
are usually spent in regretting the food one has eaten.

It snowed all night and when we got up at 6.30 a.m. we felt
rather pessimistic. There had been only 16°F. of frost — an
ominous sign at this height. However, at 7.30 there was a clearing in the cloud and we had a magical view of a summit across
the glacier, an island of gleaming ice floating in a sea of cloud
with a vivid sky above. It must have been very marvellous, for
I crawled out of the tent specially to photograph it. Soon all
the peaks appeared, and the snow evaporated from the ground
in a few minutes. When we set out just before nine o'clock the

valleys were still shrouded in mist, while streamers of cloud lapped the peaks like angry waves against sea cliffs.

We soon got into the shade where the rocks were icy cold and the snow still lay on every ledge. I had to take off my woollen gloves for the difficult pitches and my fingers were soon stiff and numb. At high altitudes I always feel sick and weak in the morning for the first two hours. This, coupled with the bad conditions, made even the first pitch seem much more forbidding than it had done the night before. And now we were standing under the final wall which was to decide the fate of our venture. We were in a vertical corner of red rock. The holds were flat but not incut, and very rotten, and at the top there was an overhang of at least two feet.

With Warren belayed some forty feet below, I climbed up to this overhang, having first divested myself of my rucksack. The overhang seemed hopeless, but on the nose on the right was a projection like a wafer, about two inches thick and jutting out horizontally a yard or so. I pushed off the top layer, which was obviously loose, and then looked at it. If I could trust my weight on it I could cheat the overhang. Three days of grim and anxious effort could not wait on one doubtful hold. I stood on it — it had to be near the edge for me to keep my balance — and it held. That was the only time on the whole climb that I was really frightened. The pounding of my heart was not due entirely to the altitude. Another anxious step — only just in balance — and I lay panting on the scree above.

An easy slope of slates and snow led to a little tower and we were able to see what lay ahead. The ridge was narrow and very serrated — not at all the solid smooth slope it had looked from below. Quite close was a great snowy rise; behind, dimly seen through the mist, a shadowy pinnacle; steep snow on the left; almost vertical rock falling for thousands of feet on the right. This we took to be the summit. We climbed the pinnacle. At the top the snow turned to ice, and, after a good deal of step-cutting, we had to take to the awkward slabby rocks on the left. We reached the top of the pinnacle at 11.25 a.m., rather tired. We dumped our loads and decided to make an attempt on the summit that day. It looked very close, but I was dubious; things are always three times as far away as they seem in the Himalaya. I thought it would take us at least two hours.

Before starting out we made some tea. Water boils at about 175°F. at this altitude (about 21,750 feet) and all the tea-leaves floated, so that we had to drink them. It was about the most unpleasant tea I have ever tasted, but it had a marvellously refreshing effect. We started off again at 12.25, without our rucksacks, feeling fit and excited. We had to ascend a narrow ridge of snow, corniced on the right above the great rock cliffs and dropping very steeply on the left. The cloud shut off everything except the immediate foreground; we seemed to be very much alone on the crest of the world. We moved one at a time; it is safer that way and also the rests are welcome.

At 1.05 p.m. — surprisingly soon — on Sunday, June 18, we stood on top of the Central Satopant'h Peak, 22,060 feet above sea level. It seemed an eternity since we had left the advanced base camp three and a half days before. I felt very little elation — altitude deadens all emotion — only a great relief; for I had been very much afraid that we should not succeed. We had no view — there was thick, depressing cloud all around.

We could just make out the other summit, marked 21,991 feet on the map. We decided we ought to include this, so after ten minutes' halt we set off again. There was an ice-cornice on the right and a steep ice-slope on the left leading down, as we knew, to 3,000 feet of cliff. Between the two, the cornice and the slope, was a little snow-filled crack. We walked on this to save step-cutting, which does not appeal at 22,000 feet. Even so we had to cut some steps. The other summit was about 500 feet away. We still moved singly, but led through. The actual top was such a narrow point of ice that there was room for only one at a time. We solemnly stood there in turn, then retreated without a word. We regained the higher summit after an absence of one hour.

It had grown colder now and the weather was threatening. As usual I felt weak and empty when descending and progressed in a curious bent-up attitude. We regained our rucksacks at 2.15 p.m. and descended the big pinnacle to an ideal shelf of flat snow, just the right width for a tent, at its foot. Here we pitched Camp IV (about 21,700 feet) under a large sheltering rock, at 3 p.m. It began to snow just as we got in. I had a very poor night with a violent headache and thirst. We had not enough fuel left to melt snow for drinking at odd moments. Also my pillow was most uncomfortable. This pillow consisted of my rucksack, containing boots and an air cushion. When the boots came uppermost I rarely had a good night.

We set off at 8.15 a.m. on a perfect morning. It was a long and tiring day; we were rather short of food and again I felt weak and empty. On the ascent I had been keyed up with the urge to get to the summit; now a reaction of listlessness had set in.

When we reached the crux of the climb, the great rock wall, we roped down it, cutting a loop off our line. I went down first and then Warren let down my rucksack with the ice-axe insecurely attached, with the result that it fell out, but luckily it stuck in the rock. As I was going to get it, a large piece of rock that I had grasped began to slide. I held it up as long as I could and then jumped to the right, luckily landing on a ledge. The rock crashed down the other way and did not hit me. As if that had not been enough, the buckle got torn off my rucksack and I was just in time to save the tent. Our position would have been very unpleasant with only one axe and no tent. I was shaken by the incident and found relief in several minutes of continuous cursing.

We reached the site of our old Camp III (20,900 feet) at 9.50 a.m., made some tea, and left at 10.15. Against Warren's counsel I decided to try the snow-and-rock slope on the left. We soon found it quite hopeless — loose snow on ice and sliding stones — and we had to make an awkward upward traverse back to the ridge. A lot of snow had melted and the ledges were covered with slippery mud. One just had to hope that all the handholds would not give way at the same time as all the footholds. Climbing down the red rock tower without a rucksack proved to be much easier than I expected. Then we were faced with the problem of finding our way off the ridge. We found vague signs of our old footmarks and followed them. The snow was in a wickedly dangerous condition. We managed with a fair degree of safety by leading through in short run-outs and, after a good deal of difficulty, found the top of our gully. We also found avalanches sliding into it. Most of them were small and stopped at the top of the gully, but the stones were more serious. They came down in bounds of 400 feet at an incredible speed and hit anywhere in the gully with terrifying cracks. We did not stay here longer than was necessary. Now that the monsoon had arrived, the Himalayan snow-slopes were certainly justifying their reputation.

We found an easier traverse back to the col than the way we had taken on the ascent. We kept a little lower and avoided the steeper rocks. We were so tired that we continued to move singly, leading through. I still remember what a blessed relief it was, when all the rope had run out, to sit down and wait for Warren to pass me, and what an effort it was when I in turn

had to move. I have two recollections of this traverse — one
of Warren, far ahead on the skyline, signalling to me to come
on; the other of rounding, interminably, corner after corner
and always seeing an endless distance between me and the col.

We finally reached the col (19,500 feet) — our Camp II of
the ascent — at 3.15 p.m., very tired. Although clouds hid the
sun, even at five o'clock it was warm enough to sit outside. I
had quite a good night in spite of a headache. At five in the
morning it started to snow; at dawn it looked quite hopeless.
There had been only 10°F. of frost in the night and we felt sure
that this must be the monsoon, in which case it might go on
for days. The outlook was distinctly unpleasant; it certainly
seemed at though we should not get down that day. We had
only one tin of pemmican and a few biscuits left, two days'
provisions at the most. Added to this, Warren was partially
snow-blind, from having left off his goggles the previous day,
and was in some pain. I put my head out of the tent and dug
the Primus stove out of the snow. It was nearly empty and
would not work at this altitude. After nearly setting the tent
on fire several times, we barely managed to melt some snow
and had to content ourselves with a cold drink.

About eight o'clock the other side of the glacier became
visible, although it was still snowing, so we decided to descend.
It was quite warm and, once we were outside the tent, it was
not nearly so unpleasant as we had expected. Several inches
of snow had fallen and we had some trouble in unburying the
odds and ends that we had put outside the tent before going
to sleep. However, we managed to start off by nine a.m. It
stopped snowing at ten o'clock, but the cloud remained, making route-finding rather a problem. We cut out a lot of the difficult traversing by an awkward descent on a doubled rope and
managed to miss the lower rocks altogether. We finished down
the turfy slope that we had left nearly a week before. Now
streams of crystal-clear water were flowing across it and little
alpine flowers were springing up all around in soul-satisfying
contrast to the grimness above. There could hardly have been
a more idyllic ending to our climb.

We reached the advanced base at three o'clock. Warren had
to remain there for an extra day because of his eyes, but there
was not enough food for me to stay as well, so I put some
drops of cocaine in his eyes and left him with the remaining
food and fuel and thirteen matches. I got lost in the mist and

finally reached the base camp and a long dreamed-of meal at 6.30, just before dark.

The Central Satopant'h Peak is definitely a rather difficult mountain. Above Camp II — for four days, that is — we were moving one at a time almost the whole way. We had some severe rock-climbing at 21,000 feet; we had bad weather most of the time and ended by being caught in the monsoon. Yet I think we managed the whole climb with a very fair degree of safety.

Chapter V

The Ganges-Satlej Watershed

THE LAST DAYS of June found the party on its way down the Gangotri Gorge, between mountains that hid their snowy heads under a pall of impenetrable mist. Nature, which still slumbered when we had passed upward five weeks earlier, was fully awakened now. The woods were gay in their mantle of young leaves. We had to push our way through thickets of pink ramblers that barred the gaps between the huge birches. Many unfamiliar shrubs were in flower and mingled their honeyed perfume with the incense of cedars. In open spaces banks of white lilies proclaimed the return of spring.

An interlude of several days at Harsil, where the surplus baggage had been deposited, passed in pleasant uneventfulness. Unstinted fresh food and sleep was all that glacier-weary men asked for. Two of the party, Hicks and Kirkus, who were now due to return to England, packed up, leaving the other three of us to make the crossing of the divide between the basins of the Ganges and the Satlej, into the country of Kunáwar, known to readers from the pages of *Kim*. Its own people call it Khunu, a name that I like better than its Indianized variant. A fresh troop of porters, drastically reduced in number, was engaged. This time there were plenty to select from, as all the Jadhs had come up to the summer pastures; also a number of Tibetans had crossed the frontier seeking work. We were therefore able to confine our choice to these two races and to exclude doubtful or troublesome elements.

From the moment that we began to have dealings with the Tibetans we felt ourselves in sympathetic company. Though no one could then have foreseen the far-reaching effects fated to spring from this fresh contact, we felt from the outset that here was something entirely new and that we had stepped right out of the circle of influences that had enclosed our lives hitherto. Naturally, our impressions were concerned with outward things: but from under the surface the power of an unfamiliar tradition let itself be half inferred, half sensed intuitively. As regards appearances, we had evidently said good-bye to everything machine-moulded. Men's souls showed as little trace of it as did their clothing. The Occidental world might not have existed, for all the notice that these people had taken of it; whereas the same could not be said of the Garh-walis, or even of the Jadhs, all of whom, in one point or an-other, showed evidences of having at some time impinged on the sphere of modernity.

Most of these Tibetans were drawn from the district of Sarang, just across the border. Their clothes, even those of the poorest, were invariably made of materials that filled us with envy. Their dark woollen gowns were worn over white shirts fastened on one shoulder in the Chinese way. Their legs were thrust into high cloth boots with flexible yak-hide soles, held up by coloured garters. Most of them went bare-headed. Some allowed their hair to hang wild and matted; others had it plaited into pigtails, which they wound round their heads. A few wore black felt caps with fur-lined earflaps. Nearly every-one owned some jewellery — the poor, an irregular string of uncut pebbles, the better-off a silver chain with a chased box containing an amulet. One ear was always pierced to take a gilt and turquoise ear-ring.

They were mostly big-boned men with hairless faces dark-ened many shades deeper than sallow through the effects of exposure and of not washing: the severe climate of Tibet does not favour frequent removal of the natural oil of the skin. A few had broad features that might have been called repellent but for the friendly smiles that sometimes illumined them. Others had a curiously feminine look, which was matched by their high-pitched voices, so that it took us a little time before we learned to tell the sexes apart with any certainty. While remaining serious for the most part, they could also be up-roariously gay, breaking out into noisy and unrestrained laugh-ter. They were open in expression, in manner respectful yet dignified. When accepting money they never troubled to count it. Their womenfolk were equally cheerful and robust-looking. No one could have thought of applying to them the epithet of weaker partners.

Tibetans of lower rank have a curious manner of showing respect by sticking out their tongues. Anyone unfamiliar with this custom might easily misinterpret it. I remember an amus-ing story told me by a general who, while yet a young sub-

altern, accompanied the military forces that occupied Lhasa in
1904. As he was going along the road a man passed him on
horseback and of course politely thrust out his tongue at him.
Enraged at the fellow's apparent insolence, the officer seized
hold of him and pulled him out of his saddle. The more he
shook him, the more the wretched man tried to propitiate the
angry Englishman by stretching out his tongue still farther, to
the great mirth of a Gurkha orderly who had seen the joke, but
had no intention of enlightening his superior officer!

During the final preparations at Harsil we were cheered by
daily visits from a little lama who had also come over from
Sarang to minister to the horse-dealers and shepherds encamped in the valley. He was the first Tibetan priest whom
we had met and he created a favourable impression of his
Order, which time has not caused us to modify to any material
extent. With him, even more than with his lay companions, we
felt ourselves in the presence of an unseen power, which, if I
must give it a name, might be called compassion. It is a virtue
of peculiar flavour, not identical with, though not unrelated to,
that charity which is radiated by the best Christian people.
Our lama's love possessed a note of serenity that seemed to
distinguish it from the similarly named but usually more passionately expressed virtue found among Europeans. I do not
believe that this compassion, said by some to be special to Buddhism, really differs in essence from its Christian counterpart;
but it is, as I shall try to explain later, more consciously linked
with a certain intellectual concept, of which it is the corollary
— a recognition of the relations that exist between all creatures,
including men, based on an insight into the true nature of the
universe, and not dependent on a vague emotional appeal. This
intellectual basis is, or ought to be, just as indispensable in the
Christian doctrine; but in practice Christians often allow the
sentimental side to predominate.

When the day of departure came, the lama was invited to
bless the caravan in the presence of the entire village. He
turned up in full canonicals, an under-garment of orange damask, and over it his rust-red gown. The company was made to
sit in a semicircle on the turf; he then passed three times along
the line, reciting sacred formulas. The first time he poured
water from a teapot-shaped sprinkler into each man's hands.
The recipient made a gesture of ceremonial washing and also
sniffed some of the liquid up his nose. At the second round a
bunch of peacock feathers was waved in our faces, while at

the third passage he blessed each of us again on the head with his rosary. The Tibetans do not confer benedictions collectively on a crowd of people as in Europe; for the blessing to be effective either there must be direct contact or else the celebrant must bestow power by an intentionally aimed concentration of thought upon the postulant.

A faint path that rises sharply round a spur just behind the village gives access to the first great torrent valley joining the Bhagirat'hi from the north-west. This is the beginning of the route by the Nela Pass into the valley of the Baspa. Our way led into this side valley, through cedar forests with an undergrowth of the mock-orange blossom, or syringa, which was in full flower and gave out an overpowering sweetness. I once showed a photograph of this wood on the screen at a lecture in one of our industrial cities. After it was over, a lady, prominent for her municipal activities, came up quite indignantly and offered the following comment: "How shocking to see all that valuable timber tumbled about. It is high time something was done to tidy the place up and stop such appalling waste." Heaven protect the Himalaya if she and her kind ever get busy there!

The track continued rather steeply for some hours through denser woods, chiefly of ancient birches dividing into many trunks. Strawberry plants made a pleasant carpet for our bare feet, until we discovered that this wood was haunted by large adders. The next two short marches lay across open meadows crossed by bands of birch, new country for us. Near Gangotri the sides of the valley had been too uniformly steep and rugged to form alps. Here the grassy hillsides were scored by streambeds, edged with birch scrub. It might have been Scotland but for the flowers, purple iris and potentillas — yellow, deepest crimson, and magenta.

There was also a dwarf species of lily, cream-yellow in colour, some bulbs of which we dug up and eventually sent to England, where they proved new to our gardens and quite hardy. They were identified as *Nemocharis oxypetala,* which had been described by a botanist close on one hundred years ago. It was in this place that we first made the acquaintance of the poppies of the genus *Meconopsis,* now becoming such favourites in English gardens; in this instance the colour was mauve, not blue, with an orange centre. A species of rhododendron formed the undergrowth of the higher birch woods. The huge flower-heads were dazzling white, like snowballs. The kitchen garden was

also represented, for we gathered bundles of wild rhubarb, a
welcome addition to the bill of fare. In the wild variety only
the young stalks are worth stewing, as the older ones are
stringy and acrid.

At the alp of Khyárkuti, a wide flat at the junction of several
glens, the flora was so rich that we decided to stay there an
extra day. This pleased Djun Singh greatly because it gave him
an opportunity of displaying before us the wealth of his family
as represented by the flocks and herds that, with a few ponies,
were grazing on the luscious pasture. "These are our sheep,
those goats are ours, over yonder it is our own men you see!"
We were able to get plenty of fresh milk and a sheep for the
whole company to feast upon. The humane killer, a gift of the
Royal Society for Prevention of Cruelty to Animals, was much
admired; we carefully explained its purpose, which was to
spare the animal the anticipation of death, and then demon-
strated its use on the sheep, which continued to crop the grass
unconcernedly up to the last minute. Though two of us have
since altered our views on the question of slaughtering at all,
members of most other expeditions will doubtless continue to
demand meat, so to them we strongly recommend the use of the
captive bolt pistol. It anyway eliminates such risk of cruelty
as might result from entrusting the killing to incompetent or
callous hands; also the public pointing out of the moral is worth
something in itself. It is interesting to note that on all occasions
when this implement was used it was welcomed; there was no
hostile reaction such as has often followed its first introduction
into parts of Europe. Slaughtering is a serious job, which, in
general, is best not left to underlings. The suitable person to
act as butcher is really the most sensitive member of a party,
not the toughest: for then one can be sure that no effort to
minimize pain will be neglected. Perhaps executioners ought
to be chosen from the ranks of the most humane and tender-
hearted citizens too!

At Khyárkuti we passed beyond the birches, but stunted willows still formed diminutive woods. Higher up nothing that
could be called a tree was found, though dwarf willows crept
in and out of the stones. The large-blossomed rhododendrons
too had been left behind and replaced by a small lemon-yellow
variety, which covered the slopes just like the familiar "Alpine
rose" of Switzerland. Immense auriculas of the deepest purple,
ten inches high, grew under the bushes and three kinds of
fritillaria, one with a speckled green bell shaped like the hood

of a cobra, another white, and a third delicate mauve. There were, besides, asters similar to the Alpine ones, and wherever snow had just melted, tufts of golden kingcup. We were surprised not to find any members of the carnation tribe — but there may have been a campion — nor did we see any gentians or saxifrages, though various unknown rock plants abounded. The most conspicuous plant of the district, covering some slopes like a white sheet and overtopping the yellow rhododendrons, was an anemone with a circlet of flowers on a fleshy stalk. Judging from photographs and published lists, the flora of our valley must be very similar to that of the Bhyundar Glen, in Eastern Garhwal, made famous by Smythe under the name of *The Valley of Flowers*. From the extreme localization of such rich assemblages of flowers it seems evident that even in this latitude sheltered places alone favour dense concentrations and multiplicity of species. The perpetual cold draught of the greater glacier valleys is probably rather discouraging to plant life and partly neutralizes the advantages of subtropical sun and generous rainfall.

The next day's march was a very short one, only three hours; but we had to halt near the limit of firewood on this side of the watershed because there was not time to cross from Khyárkuti to the corresponding point on the farther side of the pass in one day. We camped near a small green lake with tiny icebergs floating on it, not far from the end of a long moraine that leads conveniently to the foot of the actual pass. Two of our porters were Baspa men and knew the route, which is used to some extent by the local people. The mountains were more Alpine than anything we had yet seen, long jagged rock ridges enclosing combes filled by icefalls.

The Nela Pass itself is long and monotonous: it is advisable to make an early start, as the snowfields lie steep enough to let their angle be felt, but not sufficiently steep to help one gain height quickly. In the heat of the day, after snow has begun to soften, the walk up the airless trough is tiring, nor is the scenery interesting enough to make one forget fatigue. Unfortunately, being inexperienced in the psychology of porters, we let them dawdle at the start; the weather was dull and inclined to rain, and porters hate to move before the sun is up. We also found out later that they had not bothered to cook a proper meal although they knew that it would be an unusually long carry over the 18,000-foot pass. They are happy-go-lucky and rarely carry food to provide a snack at halts. It is a mistake to leave such questions to the porters' own initiative, and the person in charge must himself supervise every detail. Lack of food made them slow, and when we stopped at the rocky rib that marks the real pass we became convinced that the next firewood in the upper part of the Baspa Valley would never be reached before dark. Snow began to fall, turning to rain lower down, so we decided to pitch camp in an unpleasant spot on loose stones and wait for the stragglers. Night had fallen when at last they drifted wearily into camp. Though it was not part of our agreement to provide shelter for the porters, we thought it only fair to pitch all our tents and squeeze into a single one ourselves, so that, with some shelter, the night might be less miserable for them.

One lad called Gonu caused anxiety by narrowly escaping frost-bite. Men who lack boots usually wrap cloths round their feet when going through snow, and that is quite effective; but this youth, who was wearing flimsy shoes, took them off and struggled up the slope in bare feet. Two of us who were waiting to see everyone safely across the pass noticed that his feet had turned a queer colour; on closer examination they proved to be quite numb. There was no time to linger, as snow was falling and a biting wind rising, so we could only rub his feet with our gloved hands for a few minutes. Then we made him put on two pairs of dry socks, and let him walk in them, without shoes, down to the camp, where he was handed over to the care of the doctor for first aid. His feet were carefully dried with wads of cotton, and he was placed in a tent, and instructions were given that he must wear a larger size of boots with several pairs of socks and be carried across streams and wet places bodily, to make sure that his feet remained dry. His load was handed over to another man. Though his feet looked alarmingly bad for a day, a naturally good circulation did its work in time and Gonu suffered no ill effects. In crossing snow with porters, the care of feet and eyes should not be left to the men's own initiative. On that same day three men were affected by snow-blindness from neglecting to shield their eyes against the glare. It is a painful ailment while it lasts, though it rarely has permanent consequences.

While descending the Baspa Valley, some little trouble was experienced in crossing torrents in spate; in fact we had to camp on the bank of one of them, waiting for the flood to abate in the early hours of the morning, when the melting process on the parent glacier had slowed down. The porters excelled at this game of torrents, fearlessly threading a way through the swirling eddies and jumping from foothold to foothold; but in the worst places a rope had to be used. There was one porter, a native of Nesang in upper Khunu, called Ts'hering Tendzin, an elderly man of dignified appearance, who had a special flair for detecting a practicable passage. He had slanting Tartar eyes and a pointed beard and wore a short double-breasted tunic of white wool with a cap to match. He looked like one of the Mongol archers of the twelfth century just stepped out of a Persian miniature. Djun Singh, his nephew by marriage, also used to treat torrents with complete disdain, plunging in headlong with no apparent precaution. In fact he became somewhat conceited about his skill. At last we reached the edge of a broad stream, across which some of the more timid of us, myself for one, after taking soundings with axes, worked out an intricate zigzag route; but Djun Singh, with his habitual recklessness, leapt straight into the middle and, having chanced this time on a deep hole, suddenly disappeared under the flood, while his load, which contained tents, was seen floating away towards the Baspa. Fortunately, his uncle was on the watch and hauled him out by the hair, while another excellent porter, called Naranhu, whom we later kept on as a permanent climbing coolie, retrieved the precious bundle. Poor Djun Singh emerged from his chilly bath suffering even more from chagrin than from the cold; we gave him dry clothes from our rucksacks and rubbed him back to warmth; but his pride received a damping from which it took days to recover.

It was in the upper Baspa that we first saw the blue *Meconopsis* poppy; it grew in the most unlikely-looking places among big scree. Strangely enough, we never came across large collections of these plants such as one would expect from the number of seeds that cram their seed-pods; but we kept finding single specimens every quarter of a mile or so, growing among the stones in solitary aloofness.

Chitkul, the first village after the Nela Pass, is built amid glacier boulders in a magnificent situation backed by a great curtain of fiercely sharp peaks. We had reached the birch line only just before; but below the village, forests of deodar cedar occurred again, carpeted with pale turquoise Aquilegia. We elected to pitch camp on the other side of the river just across a bridge, where a good spring of fresh water issued from the bank only a few feet above the level of the river. The usual camping-ground lies in the middle of the village close to a torrent, which receives all the refuse, so that its water cannot be drunk unboiled. A peculiar race inhabits Chitkul and its sister villages of Raksam and Sangla, whose affinities I have not been able to ascertain. There is no trace of the Mongoloid in their faces; neither do they look like Indians. They are tall, powerful, and strikingly beautiful. I have seen no other race to compare with them for looks, except the Khambas of eastern Tibet.

One of them picked up the load of one of our porters on two fingers, exclaiming scornfully: "That's not a man's load, anyway!" We met men and even children carrying enormous logs on their backs, yet the people seemed to preserve their physique to an advanced age, for all their heavy work. The men had long flowing locks and short beards like those of the ancient Persian kings; their dress was a grey homespun tunic girded with a violet sash. The women were like Greek goddesses; even quite elderly women had an unwrinkled complexion and a full contralto timbre of voice that would have been the envy of many of their younger sisters elsewhere. The young girls, merry and rosy-cheeked, invited us to fall head over heels in love at first sight. By their dress they recalled Tanagra statuettes, with a flat round cap and a shawl fastened with a brass pin, its design also reminiscent of ancient Hellas. The children were little angels of beauty, but they had impish smiles; their bearing had the dignity found everywhere among those accustomed to spend much of their time alone in the wilderness. No artifice of the schoolmaster can provide a substitute for that sort of independence. It was a great disappointment that the photographs we took here were failures.

I remember particularly two people whom we met at Chitkul. The first was a young man who would surely have put Adonis out of countenance. He knew it too; but this cannot be called conceit, for who could be the possessor of such supreme comeliness and pretend not to know it? In his dress there could be detected an extra care in the choice of material (white wool instead of the usual grey) and a distinctive jauntiness in the way he wore it. On his finger we noticed a ring of unusually fine craftsmanship. It was the work, so he told us, of the best smith in all Khunu, whose fame had spread throughout the province. He dwelt at Sugnam beyond the Satlej, more than a hundred miles away, and his products were everywhere in demand. Later we met the artist himself.

The other person who lives in my memory was a woman,

wife of one of the elders. She was middle-aged, but still possessed a rare beauty, shadowed by obvious signs of suffering; for she had a cancer of the breast, not uncommon in that district. It was tragic that nothing could be done for so sweet a creature.

When the first of our party came in sight of the houses, a tall figure detached itself from a group that was holding a discussion on the veranda of the temple and came running towards us; it proved to be the headman, who, with marks of profound respect, made us welcome and explained that he had been expecting us. We wondered how he came to have heard of our approach, and it transpired that the Superintendent of Hill States, Simla, had, unsolicited by us, very kindly written to inform the Raja of Bashahr that we were coming over the Nela and he, in turn, had sent word to all his people to receive us hospitably. This order was faithfully observed in all the villages under his jurisdiction.

Chitkul is almost entirely built of wood, and every house, as well as the principal temple, is adorned with notable carvings, in which, unlike the woodwork observed in the Ganges Valley, Mughal influence is hardly evident. The style of design is based on square forms and seemed to us to have a connexion with that of the older Hindu and Jain temples of the north of India. The temple was a masterpiece of the woodworker's craft, with rich floral devices, elegant verandas, and pierced panels. A small detached pavilion, standing in the open space close by, was, if anything, still more perfect. Round it hung a fringe of wooden drops, which produced a curious soft jangling in the wind, like the ghost of a xylophone.

Chitkul divided its allegiance between two Traditions. The temple already described, which was dedicated to the *Devta* or local divinity, was nominally Hindu; but there was another, newer temple, looked after by a ragged and unprepossessing lama — a regular tramp — which was Buddhist and built in Tibetan style. To the first shrine we were not admitted for fear of pollution; but the second, like all Buddhist places of worship, is open to strangers. This contained some crude mural paintings, which nevertheless had a certain liveliness. In particular I remember the figure of a huge slate-coloured Warden brandishing a sword, a St. Michael barring the way to heaven against the wicked. The Tibetan influence appears to have been brought to Chitkul from the adjoining valley to the north, over the Charang Pass.

The central part of the Baspa Valley is friendly and parklike, with stretches of fertile farming, alternating with belts of conifer and groves of walnut. In places we found wild apricots bearing small but quite palatable fruit. Sangla, the richest of the villages, is a station of the Forestry Service. The Forestry officer, Mr. Deans, was in residence accompanied by his wife and two friends, and they kindly invited us to spend the night. They were the first English people whom we had met since leaving Mussoori many weeks before and we had almost forgotten how one behaves when faced with china, knives, forks, napkins, and a tablecloth. Pulling ourselves together, we managed to acquit ourselves fairly creditably, though I admit I did fall asleep at the dinner-table once.

Below Sangla the scenery becomes rather uninteresting; we hurried past it impatient to see the Satlej. That great river, which at this confluence has already run over three hundred miles of its course, is so impressive that it seems immediately to reduce the Baspa to the inferior status of a minor tributary. There is something awe-inspiring about the Satlej that many other rivers do not share. Man is not alone in feeling its secret power, for, according to certain authorities, Nature herself recognizes it by making the river into an easterly boundary of the kingdom of the goats. The horned species that are to be found farther east of that line, despite their goatlike appearance, are all sheep or antelopes, with the one exception of the *t'har*. The ibex, whose range extends even as far west as Spain, when he comes to the Satlej hears a mysterious voice whispering in his ear: "Thus far, but no farther!"

Chapter VI

The Hindustan-Tibet Road

WE CROSSED to the right bank of the Satlej by the *jhula* or cable bridge of Paori. Such bridges are frequent in the Tibetan countries and are rather amusing to negotiate. The passenger or baggage is fastened on a wooden platform suspended from the main cable, which is then drawn across by means of a second rope. Ferrymen are deputed to work the *jhula* from each end; at Paori there were ferrywomen too, real Amazons, who pulled as vigorously as the men. While doing this job they wore their jewels, and their appearance would not have disgraced a wedding. Pack-animals were slung by a girth passed under their bellies and then hauled across, dangling over space. Ponies seemed rather nervous of this passage and began to kick when they got near the landing-place; but donkeys faced the ordeal with stolid unconcern, never moving until all four feet were safely over the land.

Opposite Paori the path zigzags up a long rise to Chini, winding through dry and open fir woods, with occasional cornfields in the clearings. We had now said good-bye to the monsoon, and rain troubled us no longer, though clouds still clung to the mountaintops. At Chini there is a post office and a delightful forest bungalow with a terraced garden planted with apples, plums, and every sort of English vegetable, commanding a surpassing view across the Satlej towards a splendid group of mountains, the Chini Kailas.

Chini is also an important post on the Hindustan-Tibet road, which connects Simla with the trade-mart of Gartok. All along it bungalows have been erected at convenient intervals by the Public Works Department; we were glad to use them, for they are comfortable and invariably placed with an excellent eye for a commanding view. Staying in these houses we gained additional enjoyment from being able to have regular chamber music every evening, playing on two viols, treble and alto, which had accompanied us so far without our having found an opportunity for using them.

String music that sounds complete in two parts, needing no accompaniment, is not easy to find. Our great stand-by was the book of two-part *Inventions* by Bach, which, though composed for the keyboard, transcribe excellently for viols. We also had a set of fantasies in two parts by Thomas Morley, which are authentic viol music. Finally we arranged a number of sixteenth-century English and Spanish tunes in such a way that, by the generous use of double stops, they sounded like a full quartet. It often happened that, unperceived by us, a little group of porters would gather quietly round us and listen intently. They formed a perfect audience, unobtrusive yet seeming to possess the true faculty for listening. Playing our national music to these foreign but sympathetic listeners, we could not help recalling the words of Thomas Mace, a Fellow of Trinity College, Cambridge, who wrote a book in the middle of the seventeenth century entitled *Musick's Monument*. In the last chapter he speculates on the method of communication that will be used in heaven by members of the diverse nationalities there assembled. There must, so he argues, be a common language intelligible to all mankind, and the only known language that fulfils that condition is music.

On quitting Chini the woods begin to thin out rapidly and the country takes on the character of semi-desert, with patches of cultivation only at points where the waters of snow-born torrents can be tapped for irrigation. Here the beauties of the landscape are quite different from those of the wooded regions, with open views and especially vivid colours. We felt sudden stirrings of emotion each time we came to greenness after hours of walking through parched country. The combined effect of dry air and an average altitude of about 8,000 feet is extremely exhilarating. The flora changes to the arid type: thyme and other aromatic herbs and various thorny plants are scattered sparsely over the hillsides; only high up, close to the melting snows, is there any grass for summer pasture.

Such a climate suits the apricot: orchards surround each village, and the trees appear from a distance like little dark-green islands in a golden sea of barley. The houses are well built and the general aspect of the villages is more prosperous than in Garhwal. As one approaches the frontier of Tibet, timber becomes scarce, and the chalets and carved wooden temples with their high-pitched roofs give way to an exclusively stone style of architecture with flat roofs. The roofs are used for drying piles of apricots, which do not rot, but are turned by the sun's rays to every shade between orange and deepest crimson. When dry, they form a staple winter food.

On entering a village, the road passes through a gateway something like a lych-gate; under its pointed roof is placed a *chhorten,* or *stupa,* to give it its better-known Indian name, the Buddhists' emblematic monument, which replaces the crucifix of Catholic lands. *Chhorten* means literally "receptacle of offerings" or "reliquary": some of them do shelter relics of saints as a protection against the entry of evil influences; others again are cenotaphs. The interior of the gateway consists of a shallow dome from which rows of saints of the Tibetan calendar peer down gravely upon the traveller. These paintings are excellent and probably of considerable age, though, judging by the freshness of the colours, some of them have been renovated in modern times.

Besides *chhortens,* each entrance to a village is marked by a *mendong* or *Mani* wall, a low cemented breastwork upon which innumerable flat stones carved with sacred texts in low relief have been laid, the accumulated offerings of local piety. The commonest text is *Om mani padme hum,* from which the name is derived. Its significance will be explained later. Where such a wall occurs the road divides, leaving a free passage on either side of the *Mani,* so that passers-by, whether men or beasts, are enabled to walk on its left side — that is, turning their own right sides towards it. It is an invariable rule in Tibet that any sacred object must be passed on the left; neglect to do so will be considered both disrespectful and unlucky. There is a popular saying: "Beware of the devils on the left-hand side." To turn the right flank is a sign of assent to the doctrine inscribed on the stones or enshrined in the *chhorten;* the left side is turned towards the devils, personifying sins and errors, in token of defiant rejection of their blandishments.

The basic food of the people in this land of Khunu is barley, first parched and then ground into flour, in which form it is consumed. This is called *tsamba,* and takes the place of bread in all countries of the Tibetan group. Frequently it is eaten mixed with buttered tea to form a kind of stiff porridge; when dry it is not unlike sweetened sawdust — an acquired taste! Along the Satlej excellent potatoes are also grown and a sort of white radish, the size of a turnip. Rice is imported and a little sugar. In summer little meat seems to be eaten; the chief, and almost the only regular source of fat is the butter melted into the tea. To this list must be added apricots fresh or dried. On this diet both men and women maintain a magnificent physique. Their teeth are invariably excellent and likewise their eyesight, though it is said that certain illnesses of the eyes are not uncommon in the Tibetan countries. One does not come across many decrepit-looking old people; I do not know what is an average expectation of life among them.

On July 28 we reached the important village of Kanam, notable as the place where a systematic study of the Tibetan language by a European first began. A Hungarian, named Csoma de Kőrös, arrived in western Tibet about 1825 and settled at Kanam, where he resided several years. The ostensible object of his researches was the origin of the Hungarian race and language, over which there was controversy. Like ourselves, he immediately fell in love with the character of the Tibetans and in consequence found no difficulty in adopting the hypothesis that a people so endowed with charm and intelligence could not but be cousins of his own Hungarians. He pursued his studies most conscientiously, living exactly like the people and assimilating their ideas by the one method that, to my mind, is likely to yield reliable results — namely, by steeping oneself in the life of the country and by seeking information only from those who, by their own traditional standards, are qualified to impart it. Second-hand learning, based on observations made from the outside, notebook in hand, hardly seems worth the trouble of amassing.

At the time of our visit Csoma's lamasery was being drastically reconditioned, having become rather dilapidated. We were fortunate in seeing the work in its early stages. The temple had been partly pulled down and the walls had only risen again to half the intended height. Round the courtyard, which was encumbered with timber and stones, the residential buildings were arranged; cells occupied the upper story and access was gained to it by a "ladder" — that is, by a tree trunk with nicks cut in it, more alarming than many a rock-climb.

The work was being directed by a tall and dignified-looking person in a long robe, with a silver chain round his neck, from which hung a cylindrical charm-box. His beard was sparse and his hair gathered into a pigtail. Across his forehead were scored three parallel wrinkles as straight as if they had been drawn with a ruler. He was introduced to us as a painter from Ladak who had been engaged to be the *capo maestro;* under him

senior monks acted as foremen, while for labourers he had
juniors and peasants of both sexes who were giving their spare
time as an act of devotion. Thus it could be claimed that the
entire labour employed was amateur, except for the director.
But it must not be forgotten that the practice of building is
common in this country: most people would have done such
work at some time or other on their own houses, so that it would
be false to describe them as unskilled. The masonry and woodwork were excellent. It was probably the artist's intention eventually to line the walls with paintings. It was indeed exciting
to witness the same process by which our own cathedrals and
parish churches were built in the Middle Ages, when ecclesi-
astics had a practical understanding of construction and could
collaborate intelligently with their technicians without being
helplessly at their mercy; while the laity contributed that vol-
untary labour which best adorns a sacred purpose and edifies
the donors much more than money offerings. The most surprising architectural feats of antiquity were not accomplished by
architects trained during a protracted university course to draw
elaborate plans, with every single detail prejudged, in an office;
nor was the planning of a church handed over to Messrs. X—
the atheist and Z— the cynical capitalist. The processes of building, except in the case of structures that verge on engineering,
are evidently not beyond the comprehension of the average person. I wish we had thought of offering ourselves and our men
to take part in the building. It would have been a rare experience; but, as so often happens, the idea occurred to us too late
and can only be added to the list of missed opportunities.

The painter invited us to follow him up the ladder into an
upper chamber supported on pillars and furnished with some
elegance. He was using it for a workshop, and a number of
unfinished figures of painted wood were drying in a corner. We
were also shown a scroll painting of the type found universally
in Tibet, called a *t'hanka,* in brilliant colours on cotton impreg-
nated with lime, and mounted on Chinese brocade, with a
baton at either end so that it could be rolled up like a map.

One fact puzzled us at first: whereas on the *t'hanka* the colours, though vivid, produced a harmonious effect, the wooden
images stared at us from under a coating of shiny and rather
offensive pigment. How could the same eye and hand have
produced these two incompatible results? Suddenly the explanation dawned on me and I said to our host, "Surely those
are not Tibetan paints you have used for the images?" "That

is true," he replied. "I bought some foreign paints for doing wood, but I always employ Tibetan paint for pictures."

There is little doubt that he had at some time been tempted into buying factory-made chemicals of cheap grade to save the trouble of grinding up his own paints. Once he had accepted this compromise with his artistic standards, his senses, in their turn, had duly registered the result and become correspondingly coarsened. His taste was now partly vitiated, remaining sound when doing pictures, but over-tolerant when painting statues, probably for no stronger reason than because the amounts of paint necessary for the latter are large and tedious to prepare. These were the first symptoms of a disordered critical faculty. Later, perhaps, under the specious whisperings of intellectual laziness, the bad paints would invade the pictures, and so things would go gradually from bad to worse.

The painter of Kanam had probably been infected with the disease all unconsciously, and it may well have stopped there without developing aggravated symptoms. One can only hope so: but having come across many other cases of loss of judgment from similar causes, I feel in a position to trace out the stages by which this disorder runs its normal course.

Beginning with:

1. Acceptance of inferior materials;
   it proceeds via:
2. Damage to the sense of colour;
3. Seduction by the idea of saving trouble;
4. Disturbance of colour-sense, which in its turn disturbs the sense of form;
5. Bewilderment — general atrophy of taste;
6. Collapse of the sense of tradition in the artist, who becomes a prey to the idea of novelty and begins to imitate misunderstood foreign models, usually the worst.
   And so to the last stage:
7. Extinction of the art.

That, alas, is the history of a great part of Asia; whether in our time we shall be permitted to descry the first faint signs of a turn in the tide cannot be told; but it is not easy to be optimistic.

There was a separate temple in the village known as "The House of the Kangyur" (the collection of canonical scriptures corresponding roughly to the Bible), where, in semi-darkness, an enormous number of scrolls hung, all rather dusty, but including among them some extremely fine examples. We offered the community an adequate sum towards the building fund if they would sell us two *t'hankas;* we did not feel that this was a wrongful offer, for the pictures were being neglected and a fair equivalent was paid for them and applied to a necessary sacred purpose. It is always a nice question, however, how far it is lawful to buy objects dedicated to religious use. If a competent authority is willing to sell, it is, of course, admissible legally; and should the work of art be perishing from neglect, it seems morally so; but on the other hand, in cases where the object is still fulfilling its proper purpose and being duly cared for, every means should be taken to encourage the custodians to continue to treasure it: indeed, they should be warned against parting lightly with their precious possessions. Collectors and archæologists, in their insatiable thirst for rare antiques, sometimes develop a lack of scruple that would hardly stick at murder or burglary; certainly bribery and undue pressure of every sort are resorted to in order to wrest sacred treasures from the hands of their owners. One has read of people publicly glorying in the tricks by which they have overcome the qualms of their victims. It should not be difficult to determine the ethics of each case; but, if there is any doubt, a conservative policy is to be preferred.

It was at Kanam that we had our first taste of tea made in the Tibetan way. A broad-leaved kind is used, compressed into bricks, and brought mostly by yak caravan from western China. The Tibetans have such a preference for this sort of tea that even when living on the south side of the Himalaya, where Indian tea would be cheaper to obtain, they go to no end of trouble to import their favourite brand. In preparing the infusion the leaves are put into cold water and then brought to the boil. When the proper strength has been reached, salt, with a pinch of soda, is added, then butter, whereupon the whole is thoroughly mixed in a churn. It is afterwards warmed up again and served from the teapot.

Not far from Kanam a certain Tibetan Lama from the Chumbi Valley, adjoining Sikkim, was then living; he was called "The Chumbi Precious Doctor" and was famous in every corner of Tibet for his sanctity. He had spent years in caves communing with higher Powers and, like the old anchorites of Europe, enjoyed an extraordinary influence over animals. Our head porter related to us with emotion how bears and leopards waited on him in the wilderness, even as the ravens served

Elias. He had come to Kanam in order to "set the wheel of the Doctrine a-turning" — that is, on a mission to reawaken the faith of the people and to illumine their ignorance. There is no doubt about his immense reputation, which extended even outside the limits of his own communion. Everyone spoke of him with reverence. A Hindu official told us that one look at the Lama's face was enough to make one realize how great a saint he was. We naturally felt a longing to call on him on the return journey; but when the moment came we let trivial obstacles turn us from our purpose. The same occurred in 1936 when he was residing at Ghum, near Darjeeling. Again we put off the meeting till too late; we have since had news of his death, so that chance is gone for ever and we are left with vain regrets.

The two best silversmiths of Khunu belong to this neighbourhood. One is the man mentioned in the previous chapter as the maker of the ring that we had so admired at Chitkul. His village was Sugnam, a few miles up a side valley, where Richard Nicholson went to visit him. Assisted by his son, he was working to supply a very wide market, chiefly with silver clasps and trinkets for the country women, who delight in jewellery. His colleague, who came to call on us, lived quite close to Kanam, in an outlying hamlet called Labrang, conspicuous for its old watch-tower. They both were men of fine presence, typical of master craftsmen the world over. That profession, with its happy blend of head and hand, the intellectual and the practical, seems to include some of the best types of humanity, and its members might well style themselves the "salt of the earth." Their extinction, under the pressure of the modern industrialism that is overrunning the Orient, must be regarded as a social no less than an artistic disaster.

Metalwork is the craft at which the Khunuwas excel. Teapots in brass, decorated with silver and copper bands *appliqués*, are in common use; the combining of several metals is typical of Tibetan work. Handles are usually made in the shape of dragons, which exhibit almost endless diversity of detail but fall roughly into two generic types, the fishlike and the pure dragon type with horns, related to Chinese models. The spout issues out of the jaws of a monster rather like an elephant, but said to inhabit the sea; it is called the *Makara*.

Ornamental woodwork is also to be found in the better houses and temples, happily combining both boldness and grace; but this craft is seen at its best in the villages of lower Kunáwar, in the well-timbered tract between Chini and Simla.

The next halt after Kanam is called Poo. We had been listening to tales about the wonders of this place for weeks before we reached it, because Ishwar Singh, or, to give him his proper Tibetan name, Odsung, lived there. We had recently appointed him head porter, as he had proved exceptionally reliable and intelligent. "The sweetest potatoes come from Poo." "Apricots! You don't call these apricots; you wait till you get to Poo and then you will learn what's what." "Woodworkers? The ones here all overcharge; besides not one of them can hold a candle to the carver at Poo!" This became a standing joke; but to do our friend justice, his home village did not fall far short of his claims: it was a charming place, with quite the most succulent apricots, the tastiest potatoes, and the most intelligent inhabitants in the whole district.

The first sight of the village is dramatic. As the crow flies, the distance from Kanam is not great, but a deep re-entrant has to be contoured, which prolongs the road to some twenty miles. Trees, already sparse and small, resembling Mediterranean pines, cease altogether beyond Kanam, and the vast stony tract of western Tibet begins. The road descends to the edge of the Satlej and follows it for some miles through an extremely hot gorge; then suddenly quitting the bank, by a sharp rise to the left, it takes a sweeping curve round a combe to a small pass between the main hillside and an isolated knoll above the river. On this pass stands a conspicuous *mendong* that, even from a distance, makes one feel as if something exciting is about to appear. From this gap one looks straight across a ravine to Poo, with its terraces of well-built stone houses relieved by elegant wooden balconies, and surrounded by barley fields and apricot orchards. At the edge of the village stands the pleasant little rest-bungalow in a garden full of hollyhocks, probably introduced by the British. When we arrived, the loaded apricot trees were being stripped by boys who had climbed up into the branches and were beating down the fruit with poles. It was then gathered into baskets by their mothers and sisters. The caretaker of the rest-house, one Namgyal, seemed like an old friend before we had been an hour under his roof. As soon as we entered the bungalow, tired and thirsty, Namgyal offered us tea together with a wooden platter piled with a pyramid of unusually tasty *tsamba*, bidding us welcome with a courtesy of language noticeable even in one of his polite race.

The people of Poo are well-to-do peasants, and the cultivated

land is shared out among the various families. Besides tilling
the fields and taking their flocks up the mountains to graze,
they also do a certain amount of trading, especially in the
autumn, when a series of great fairs is held, at which merchants
from Ladak, Garhwal, and other distant places gather together
to exchange their wares, first at Gartok in Tibet itself, then at
Kanam, and lastly at Rampur, capital of the state of Bashahr,
of which this district forms a part. The Poopas lead a well-
balanced life, free from strain, which has its times of leisure as
well as hard work. Ready money is scarce, but they are fully
provided with food, clothes, and good housing. The artistic
influences emanating from independent Tibet are apparent in
the high quality of most of their possessions.

We were invited to supper in Odsung's home. The family
consisted of his mother, a widow, and numerous brothers and
cousins, whom we never quite managed to identify since the
term "brother" is indiscriminately applied to both. Their house,
which was two-storied and built round a court, was planned
on generous lines. The chief living-room was left half open on
one side, commanding a magnificent view down the Satlej to
the snowy summits of the Kailas. Our hostess at first refused to
come and sit with us at table, till I got up and pleaded with
her, saying: "If the mountain will not come to me, then I shall
have to go to the mountain myself."

The old quotation, thus adapted, gains additional piquancy
on being turned into Tibetan, because the words referring to
the other party — the mountain in this instance — can be placed
in what is called the honorific language, while to oneself only
common terms are applied. To give a rough paraphrase of the
sentence, it reads something like this: "If the honourable mountain will not deign to proceed to me, the insignificant fellow
(myself) will have to go to the mountain."

It should be explained that the Tibetan language reflects in
its vocabulary the nicely judged grades of feudal society. For
every noun, pronoun, or verb and for many of the adjectives,
not one but two words must be learned, a common one, which
applies to ordinary folk, and an honorific, which must be used
when speaking to or about persons of quality. Turning the
idea into an English equivalent, my gardener simply "walks,"
but my readers "proceed." Similarly, a thing is "shown" to a
servant, but in the case of an aristocrat one "petitions the coming of the honourable eye." Sometimes even three words exist
for the same notion, the third being a "high honorific," which

can be applied only to representatives of the most exalted political or ecclesiastical authority. A subtle play of compliments
can be introduced by timely selection of this or that word,
especially as at the other end of the scale a further weapon
lies to hand in the form of self-depreciatory words, denoting
one's own worthlessness or humility. Normally, one simply uses
the ordinary non-honorific words in referring to oneself; but in
extreme cases, especially in letters, it is possible to use in place
of "I," "the trifle" or "the naughty boy." Even words like "liar"
or "murderer" have their honorifics; they are an essential part
of the language, employed by all classes, and not a precious
affectation of the educated, though the latter naturally have a
fuller command of them. A few especially high expressions
can be used only about the Dalai Lama and Panchhen Lama,
the two senior Pontiffs. There is, for instance, a word meaning
"to come" which is normally applied to any dignitary over a
certain rank; but it can, by special extension, be used of the arrival of a cup of tea for the Dalai Lama. "The goblet of honourable tea," as it were, "ambulates into the Dalai Lama's chamber,"
or rather ("the insignificant trifle petitions for His Holiness's absolution") what I intended to say was not "chamber" but "loca-
tion of the cushion of repose."

In the evening the Poopas invited us to watch an entertainment of folk-dances performed by torchlight and accompanied
only by drums. The dancers provided their own music by singing songs at the same time. These dances are rustic in character,
simple ring groupings, which reminded me of the old Scotch
brawl. One of them was broadly comic. A huge circle was
formed, half of men and half of girls, turning clockwise. Suddenly one group of men, without warning, would violently reverse the direction, causing a general collapse, which was
greeted with shouts of laughter.

On another occasion some wandering lamas performed a
more formal dance for our benefit. Every man played two instruments. In the right hand he wielded a small drum, called
damaru, held by means of a wooden handle, to which a string
was attached tipped with a small weight. By manipulating the
drum to the right and left the weight was made to swing
and thus beat the instrument. In the left hand the performer
grasped a bell with a fascinating silvery tone; for the Tibetans
excel in the casting of bell metal. Since he also sang at the
same time, it might be said that each man constituted a self-
contained trio.

We were sorry to leave Poo, but time was slipping away and we wished to tackle the last item on our program by attempting the highest peak of Khunu, Riwo Pargyul. Crossing the Satlej by a bridge, we made for the last village on this side of the frontier, Namgya. The country now became barren and stony, even the river's margin showing no trace of green. We passed the junction of the Spiti and Satlej, where the rock had been eroded to form a chasm of such depth that the water was not visible from the path. Namgya is a beautiful village with many fine houses and carvings. We camped on a terrace of stubble in an orchard; all night long we could hear a soft patter on the tent roof, as the trees, gently shaken by the wind, rained down ripe apricots.

Fifty yards along the terrace some other tents were standing, guarded by a terrifying Tibetan mastiff, a regular Cerberus, all snarl and fang, who strained furiously at his chain when we approached. We found that this camp belonged to a notable scholar, the Italian professor Giuseppe Tucci. He had just come down the Spiti Valley on his way into Tibet, accompanied by one companion, Captain Ghersi, who filled the twofold function of doctor and photographer. Professor Tucci kindly invited us to share his dinner, so we sat down with him to an appetizing menu of five courses. During the meal the professor kept up a running lecture in excellent English, on archæology, history, and art, out of his inexhaustible fund of scholarship and enthusiasm; at the same time he carried on whispered negotiations in Tibetan, spoken *prestissimo e sempre accelerando*, over the purchase of an antique ceremonial apron made from carved plates of human bone joined by strings of beads of the same material, such as are used in certain rites. It was being offered for sale by a mysterious person hovering in the background.

Food, archæology, and bargaining became hopelessly entangled. "Have some hors d'hœuvres." (Aside, to a servant who was playing the go-between: "Yes, you can offer him two hundred." In a whisper: "No, I won't give more.") "Do let me pass you some spaghetti." ("Say yes, if he offers it for two hundred and fifty, I'll take it.") "As I was saying, about the year 1250 — yes, I have read Schnitzelfresser's paper. No, he's not a scientist; he actually confused Vajrapani with —" ("Yes. What? He can go and think it over — no, I won't offer any more.") "Do please help yourself to cheese, Dr. Warren. In the sixteenth century the King of Tsaparang was attacked by . . ."

Over the coffee, we were shown photographs taken in the ancient temples of Spiti, which contain some of the most precious relics of Tibetan art. The professor explained that the unusually perfect examples that existed at Tabo were in considerable danger of disappearing. The prosperity of the country, and consequently its culture, had been declining steadily in the last century, and the upkeep of ancient monuments was lapsing. The school of painting to which the Tabo examples belong is unique, so perhaps some authority may devise measures to protect them. It is often only a question of blocking up a few cracks, which, if neglected, will eventually let in the weather. In other respects this dry climate is the most perfect conceivable for the preservation of antiques.

From Namgya the path once more descends to the Satlej and crosses a bridge to the right bank, whence it rises again to a small grove of willows, below Tashigang, the see of the presiding Lama of all Khunu. From there a track rounds the spur that fills in the angle of the two rivers, and the Spiti Valley is entered at a height of about 12,000 feet. The rest of the way to Nako, our base of operations for the mountain, is about level, rising to 13,000 feet at times.

At first the hillside was devoid of vegetation. From far above us some big stone-falls, which looked as if they could not miss the path, came crashing down with a thunderous din. Round the corner we came to plants again. First there were enormous rose bushes, covered with pink flowers, which grew out of crannies or climbed up the face of the cliff. Then a patch of vivid violet revealed the presence of a magnificent bushy delphinium among the stones. Later, in the Spiti Valley, the path was bordered with Alpine flowers — speedwells, harebells, rockroses, and saxifrages — that reminded us of Switzerland.

Nako is built among the boulders brought down by old glaciers, and a walk through its "streets" involves constant scrambling. Behind the village extend the endless scree-covered slopes of Riwo Pargyul, which, when we arrived, hid its head under a cap of cloud. On the outskirts numerous *chhortens* and *mendongs* look as if they have sprouted like mushrooms among the stones. At every street corner there are prayer-wheels containing cylindrical paper rolls inscribed with prayers, which are set in motion by passers-by. The best place to camp is on the edge of a small lake fringed with willows, which are among the few trees that survive this altitude. It is too high for apricots, but not for barley, which is supposed to be of special

quality when grown at this height. There are three big tracts
of cultivation, to which water is conducted through a leat from
the Riwo Pargyul main glacier stream.

Our baggage had been brought from Poo on ponies, the first
pack transport we had used. It was pleasant to notice how
well the animals were cared for. The local people, like most
Tibetans, were devoted to their animals and did all that was
possible for their comfort; they never thought of settling down
to cook their own meal until saddles had been removed and
fodder distributed. They carried rounded sickles in their
girdles, and in this barren country they often had to go some
distance before they found any grass to cut. I have rarely heard
impatient abuse addressed by a Tibetan to a horse or mule, nor
seen one flogged or goaded. The races of the Mediterranean
littoral, where somewhat similar climatic conditions prevail,
might well take a few lessons in animal management from the
Tibetans, as much for their own interest as on moral grounds.
But when people regard animals as having no real rights and
as merely existing for the service of man, it is difficult to persuade them to control their tempers or to exert themselves on
their beasts' behalf, even on utilitarian grounds. The clear emphasis laid on the position of animals in Buddhist teaching undoubtedly influences the people in the right direction.

Though we were intending to set out for the mountain next
day, we found time to visit the ancient temple, ascribed to a
famous saint of the tenth century called Rinchhenzangpo. He
is surnamed *Lotsawa*, which means Translator or Interpreter;
it is a title accorded to a few scholars, in honour of their having
made the Indian sacred books accessible to their own countrymen. The same sage was the founder of most of the Spiti
temples.

A Translator, in the sense recognized by the Tibetans, is
not to be taken for a mere scholar who, aided by dictionaries,
turns a certain text from one language into another and leaves
it at that. A text interpreted according to the whim of every
reader, however uninstructed, is a public danger, since the seed
of a whole crop of errors may be sown, which in their turn en-
gender new errors, which again, in course of time, may themselves become invested with the prestige of acknowledged
authority. One has only to recall some of the ill-founded theories of Orientalists, due to the distortion of texts by persons
who had, half-unconsciously, read into them their own personal
habits of thought, assimilating any words of doubtful meaning

to specious equivalents in their own tongue and thus conjuring up an entirely inappropriate set of associations.

An elementary example will serve to show how easy it is to slip into this pitfall. There is a popular proverb in Tibetan which says that "without the Lama no man can be delivered." Europeans have quoted it with indignation. "See how the lamas try to keep the people in subjection!" was their comment. "Here's priestcraft for you, here's jesuitry!" Actually they have been betrayed by a slight yet crucial inaccuracy over the word *Lama*. The word, which means "exalted," should, strictly speaking, be applied either to a Teacher, "one's own Lama" or personal spiritual director, or else to eminent members of the clergy. On all formal occasions, or in writing, this is the meaning the name *Lama* bears. In ordinary conversation the body of clergy is occasionally called *the lamas* indiscriminately, but it is comparatively rare to find the word so used; among the clergy themselves this colloquialism practically never occurs. The proper word for a cleric is *trapa*, and that is the one commonly in use. Thus the foreign critics, accustomed in their own language to giving the word a different shade of meaning, and also being predisposed by their own anticlerical upbringing to place an unfavourable construction on the whole phrase, have committed the sin of those who possess a little learning. This is a simple case, typical of countless similar ones. The real interpretation of the proverb quoted is "without a Teacher, no man can be delivered." It refers to the fact that, in common with all Orientals, the Buddhists regard study at the feet of a Teacher or Lama as the normal and virtually indispensable prelude to "entering the current" — that is, imparting to one's spiritual aims a definite direction towards Enlightenment. I had a talk on this very matter with the hermit of Lachhen in Sikkim, which will be related in Part Two.

To return to the real Translator: his task was indeed a formidable one. His first duty, before putting pen to paper, was to seek out some adept of the doctrine expressed in the treatise which he wished to translate and be properly instructed over a period probably lasting years. Then, having experienced the meaning of that doctrine in his own person, he was prepared to turn the Sanskrit text into Tibetan with more than mere verbal accuracy. That task completed, he carried back the manuscript to Tibet and proceeded to reverse the process he had himself followed, by expounding the doctrine in all its aspects to his own disciples, at the same time placing the text in their hands. Thus the tradition was truly imparted. Several divines besides the Nako founder have been accorded the title of Translator; one of the most renowned was Marpa, tutor of Tibet's ascetic poet Mila Repa, about whom much more will be said later. Even nowadays, as the Lachhen Lama emphatically declared, it is useless to try to read sacred books except under the guidance of a competent teacher. According to this conception the word "read" begins to mean something more than skimming through so many pages. If this line of thought were to be pursued, it would also radically alter the meaning of the word "education."

In former times Nako and the whole Spiti Valley belonged to the kingdom of Gugge, which attained an extraordinary degree of civilization. Since the extinction of that kingdom there has been steady decline. Cultivated areas have shrunk, populations have dwindled, and the sands of the desert are invading the surviving settlements. Gugge was the province of Tibet first visited by European missionaries, in 1624. Portuguese Franciscans established a mission in the capital, Tsaparang, the modern Chabrang Dzong. They were received by the king with all the honour that Tibetans are ready to accord to the bringers of unknown doctrines. The friars, at one moment, had some reason for hoping that they were about to effect a royal conversion; but it is also possible that their optimism may have been somewhat exaggerated. The Tibetans are always ready to offer worship to any sacred object, and do not necessarily confine their homage to the more familiar forms. They do not feel that by so doing they are tacitly admitting the superiority of the foreign tradition or showing infidelity towards their own. They will bow as naturally before the Crucifix as they would at the feet of a Buddha, whereas our own people, accustomed to the sectarian exclusiveness of Europe, usually feel that by offering reverence in a church with the tenets of which they disagree they are condoning its errors. The Hindus have a label for that section of mankind, regarded by them as spiritually immature, who are unwilling to honour anyone's gods but their own. They are called *Pashu* (from the root *pash* =bound) and are supposed to be blind to the larger Unity of the Godhead, though within the parochial limits they lay down for themselves they may be worthy of all respect and praise. They are described as men in whom a tendency towards obscurantism is strong, who exaggerate the distinctions of mere form or name; this makes them all too prone to speak con-

ABOVE NAKO   *See page 78*

PAINTED CEILING OF A VILLAGE GATEWAY

WANDERING LAMAS SERENADE US

"INCOMPARABLE MONUMENTS OF MUGHAL ART"   *See page* 93
The Pearl Mosque in Agra Fort

TIBETAN T'HANKA   *See page* 63
In the possession of H. H. the Maharaja of Sikkim

LACHHEN *See page* 111

EARLY SPRING IN ZEMU VALLEY *See page* 118

ZEMU FOREST *See page* 118

FIRST BREAKFAST ON THE ZEMU GLACIER *See page* 121
Siniolchu in the background

temptuously of the beliefs and practices of others. Far superior to the *Pashus* are the men who fall into the class known as *Viras,* or heroes. They are those who recognize that though modes of thought are many, yet metaphysical realization, wheresoever obtained by direct intuitive identification of the knower with the known, is one and only. It is that which counts; it is that truth which underlies all symbolism and is the object of every traditional ritual. The Buddha Himself counselled His followers against abruptly curtailing the gifts that they had been accustomed to offer to the Brahmans; that spirit still prevails today. One young lama told me that they were taught from childhood not to speak ill of other religions, but on the contrary to treat them with every respect. Similarly, along the Chinese-Tibetan border, it is said to be conventional at any chance meeting of strangers for one to ask the other, after the first greeting: "Sir, and to which sublime tradition do you belong?"

Chapter VII

Riwo Pargyul

THE PEAK that was to be the last objective of our journey possessed a topical interest in that it had been ascended to a point well over 19,000 feet quite early in the nineteenth century by two enterprising Scotsmen, the brothers Gerard, who travelled all over the country of Khunu and published a diary, which shows them to have been honest observers, unblinded by racial prejudice. In those days, when travel was more of an adventure than it is now, doubtless only those attempted it who were impelled by a keen curiosity to see and learn. It would be sad if the development of rapid communications were to end in doing away with all possibility of genuine travel, as seems likely. Considering the early date of their expedition, when only thirty years had elapsed since the first ascent of Mont Blanc, and when the Pillar Rock in our own Ennerdale was still virgin ground, the height that the two Gerards attained is a highly creditable preformance, though that does not imply that they went in for any serious climbing. The snow-line is very high and a number of subsidiary points could be reached in a couple of days' laborious plodding over scree, without setting foot on snow. But for all that, to have braved such an altitude involved real enterprise at that time.

Many legends connected with Riwo Pargyul exist, for in common with all permanent snow its twin peaks are regarded as sacred by the Tibetans. One of the chapels in the temple at Nako is dedicated to the genius of the mountain; but it is now derelict, devoid of an altar and all furniture. On a rock near by, the imprint of the god's huge foot is pointed out.

There are even tales of early ascents; a pious lama, so it is rumoured, had actually climbed to the summit long ago. In more recent times a party of four villagers ascended the mountain in quest of sapphires. When they reached the highest pinnacle they found it to be formed out of a huge sapphire about a foot across and worth millions of rupees. They managed **to** dislodge it and were already well on the way down with their booty when a terrible storm arose and overwhelmed them all. The story sounds most credible to judge from our own experience on what we must, therefore, reluctantly claim to be no more than the third ascent. Exactly how the accident to the second party came to be reported with all its details is unexplained! There are other legends too; at Poo we witnessed a folk-dance performed to the strains of a ballad in which Riwo Pargyul figured prominently; but we were unable to secure a copy of these verses.

On the evening of our arrival at Nako we started to sort out the miscellaneous things required for the assault on the mountain, and made them up into forty-pound loads. There was food for the body, and food for the soul in the shape of Chaucer's *Canterbury Tales*, and paraffin for the Primus, which, by some silly miscalculation, was measured out short, and all the usual climbing-apparatus.

Two Jadh porters, Djun Singh and Naranhu, were chosen to come high with us, while three men from Poo were told off for the initial carry to a camp just below the snow. After following the main road northwards a mile or two, we veered sharp right up the valley of a torrent that we believed, correctly as it proved, to issue from the central glacier basin between the two main peaks. The lower slopes are a chaos of old glacier debris, waterless save for the leat, fringed with gentian-spangled turf, that brings the main water-supply down to the village. Higher up, from about 14,000 feet, patches of grazing occur, and low thorny bushes, the inhabitants' only source of fuel. Between 15,000 and 17,000 feet, some way below the zone of melting snows, lie the summer pastures, which support quite a number of cows and sheep. There is a fairly rich Alpine flora, which was only just coming into flower when we passed on the upward way, but had reached full bloom by August 11. We saw two or three kinds of blue gentian and a light mauve delphinium with large rounded blooms, growing in clumps among the stones.

For the last couple of hours before approaching the terminal ice of the glacier, at a height of some 17,500 feet, we passed along a succession of boulder-covered moraines. A drearier landscape could not well have been imagined, for lateral ridges confined the view to a crumbling world. These containing walls of the valley were no more than great rubbish-heaps, an aimless accumulation of rocks piled crazily one upon another; only at the lower extremities of the ridges, where they faced outward towards the Spiti, their tips were still sheathed in a carapace of slabby rock, like the rams of some monster ironclads still standing in mock defiance long after the rest of the hull had rotted away.

A Tibetan hermit in search of a place in which to rest in meditation, as so many do, on the great principle of Death and Impermanence, would have found these surroundings peculiarly appropriate. "The Universe is running down . . . down . . . *tout passe, tout casse, tout lasse*," seemed to be whispered by a thousand expressionless voices. "Where's the glacier now, that viscous flood which once upon a time overran all these slopes? It was active then, look where it reached to; but now it's getting old, and one day it will die; there will be no ice to melt and the water will dry up; then the gentians will be dried up too and the crops of the people of Nako, and the men also will die out. The stones that remain, they too are gradually dying; death is not an appanage only of the apparently living, nor are they alone in being subject to death; in this is to be seen the pattern of all things." Thus would muse the hermit — a faint whisper of this message reached even our own ears — and a great love and pity would be kindled in his heart for all the deluded creatures blindly chasing the will-o'-the-wisp of happiness, trying to fix it firmly, now in this life, now in the next. Not to realize this, say the Tibetan sages, is to remain the plaything of ignorance and of the suffering born therefrom, but to know it, is reality and freedom, which is called Buddhahood.

We pitched our second camp — for we had taken two days to approach the glacier — in a hollow, and then walked up to a point whence we hoped to obtain the first view of our mountain; but its face was veiled in mist. Though Riwo Pargyul has a very low rainfall and is considered to stand outside the monsoon's influence, the proximity of rain-clouds at that season is enough to produce constant mist, hanging round the mountaintops though not falling in actual showers. Beyond that point the moist vapours are cut off sharply by the dry Tibetan winds. One of our principal hindrances in climbing the peak was our inability to obtain any save the most fleeting glimpses of the upper parts of proposed routes. In the end we had to hazard a partial guess in making our choice. There is evidence that this mountain does not enjoy very good weather as a rule, for other travellers have remarked on it. Possibly the fact that it stands considerably higher than anything for many miles around may account for this, for it seems to collect all the weather.

In the evening the miscalculation over the paraffin was brought home to us, for when we set about cooking a meal for the porters on the Primus we were not long in finding out that a single boiling of rice used our meagre supply of fuel at such a rate that it threatened to jeopardize the commissariat arrangements. Something had to be done without a moment's delay, for time was precious. An anxious debate ensued, after which it was resolved that one of the men should be sent down next day to Nako to collect more paraffin from the big carboy left in charge of Odsung, while the rest of us, to make doubly sure, were to postpone the pressing reconnaissance and to go down to brushwood level and lay in enough fuel to stock the camp for two or three days. A man named Djambal, a strong and willing young fellow with flowing locks, volunteered to run down with the message. That night we retired to bed feeling rather depressed over the bad management that had caused the waste of a day.

Next morning we all trekked off downhill again, bearing empty rucksacks and ground-sheets, not at all relishing the idea of having to retrace our steps across the unending screes. But luck favoured us in an unexpected way; we had gone but half the distance and arrived at the upper pastures when Djun Singh, with an exclamation of joy, pointed to some droppings of cattle scattered about the slope and dried hard by the sun. "Here is good fuel," he cried, "and lots of it. It's what we always burn in Tibet." So we set about with a will stacking the dung and filling our sacks, taking care to reject any that was still at all damp. By afternoon we were loaded up and on our way back to camp, cheered by the knowledge that we need not raid the precious store of paraffin for at least three days. The dung was found to yield quite a fair heat, smouldering like peat and surprisingly free from unsavoury smell; but it is rather difficult to coax it into a good fire and, in default of bellows, Djun Singh kept up a steady blast from his lungs.

We had prayed that the sun would shine on our efforts to reconnoitre the approaches to the peak, but mist continued to harass us all day long, hanging disobligingly round the 20,000-foot level, now tantalizingly lifting a little, now threatening to ring down the curtain over the whole scene. The party had agreed to split up, two men going into the main basin, while I explored a snowy col on a ridge uniting the west flank of the

north peak to a small spur. Nearer portions of the mountain
had already been ruled out. The south peak, which consists of
a long rocky ridge bristling with pinnacles, looked as if it would
offer good sport; but as it was slightly the lower of the two we
felt more drawn to the north peak, which was of an entirely
different character, consisting of a huge rounded white mass,
portions of which looked ominously grey, suggestive of ice and
hours of step-cutting. A great shoulder not easily attainable in
a day indicated a pitch for an upper camp, but the sides
seemed badly exposed to stone-fall; even if we had got up that
way it would hardly have been justifiable to have let porters
return down it alone. So we decided to look farther afield.

In the afternoon we forgathered again to compare notes.
Those who had been to the glacier had drawn a blank. They
found no practicable col on the ridge connecting the peaks, as
the basin was walled in by forbidding cliffs of mixed rocks and
ice. I was able to give a better report, however, of the snowy
col on the west side: the approaches were gentle and the
ground was safe till quite close under the col, where there was
a lake of the purest azure and one or two crevasses that had
caused me, being alone, to restrain my curiosity to look over the
other side. As to the route up the west flank, it seemed promising, since it consisted entirely of snow without a trace of rock.
The only snag was an icy bulge on the skyline just below the
mist, which looked as if it either might be easily contourable
or else might indicate a row of formidable ice defences; but it
was well worth chancing. All voted in favour of adopting this
route, and we sat down to await the return of Djambal and
the paraffin; nor were we kept waiting long, for he soon turned
up with a bulging pack, looking as if he had been out for a
stroll instead of having raced all the way from Nako over bad
ground with a heavy load.

Eagerly we undid the package — "Ah! I see Odsung has sent
some extra biscuits; thoughtful of him. Butter? Well, I should
have thought we had enough, but no matter — all is grist
for the mill. Chocolate — matches — that can't be all? Look
here, where's the paraffin?" Djambal turned on us an uncom-
prehending eye. "The paraffin, the paraffin! Why on earth — ?"
But it was useless to go on lamenting — the awful fact was
there: a misunderstanding had occurred and the wrong stores
had been sent. We were as far as ever from getting on to the
mountain.

There was no help for it; we must face another delay. Who

would go down next day to Nako while we carried on with
pitching a camp on the western col? The stout Djambal was the
first to jump up and offer his services a second time for the
tedious errand; this time, however, to make doubly certain,
Richard Nicholson, who was not intending to come beyond the
next stage thus leaving two for the final dash, offered to descend at once and see that no further blunder occurred. As
there were still some hours of daylight, they started immediately. The two of us who were left retired to our tents chafing
at this new delay, for time was getting short and the weather
did not promise many extra chances in case of initial defeat.

The job of carrying stores and a good-sized tent as far as the
col occupied the next day. The camping-site proved to be excellent, a few minutes from the west flank of the north peak.
Northwards, a great glacier (the Chango Glacier) lay outspread, possibly for the first time, to human gaze, surrounded
by serried rows of peaks of every kind, easy ones and hard
ones, snowy ridges and forbidding needles, first cousins of the
Aiguilles of Chamonix. How we wished that half the season were
still before us! We could even discern, on a flat piece of moraine
across the other side, the exact spot for a base camp; and there
were some enticing passes that beckoned us over into Tibet.
We slept on the col that night, sending back the porters to the
lower camp, where our two Jadhs were ordered to collect the
paraffin and bring it up with all speed. The Poo men were dismissed, as there was not enough work to keep them busy.

The following morning passed in enforced idleness; but in
the afternoon the porters returned with the eagerly expected
supplies of paraffin. At last all was ready for the start and
even the weather began to show signs of clearing up. This
promise was fulfilled, for the morning of August 8 was sunny.
We started off in good spirits, but had not climbed more than
a couple of hundred feet before we found that the snow was
turning into pure ice, though luckily not of the toughest black
variety, which occurs so frequently in the Himalaya. A long
spell of cutting lay ahead and it was evident that we should be
unable to reach the upper shoulder, where we hoped to bivouac, in a single day, unless the ice gave way to soft snow
higher up, which at the time seemed unlikely. This day had
therefore to be devoted to the job of cutting a well-graded staircase to a point as far up as possible that would serve as a jump-
ing-off spot for completing the ascent afterwards. So we started
in an unhurried manner and worked our way upward, chipping

careful steps in the ice-slope, equally safe for descent and ascent. We were unexpectedly lucky, however, for just below the ice-bulge, past which we could not yet see, we discovered a tiny platform, barely wide enough to take our bivouac, but not a bad pitch, if rather airy, with clear ice-slopes leading the eye down in all directions and with the bulging cliff of ice blocking the upward view. It was a blessing to have found any flat ground at all at such a convenient level, so we called it the site for Camp IV and retreated to the col in an optimistic frame of mind.

Unfortunately, we were reckoning without our host, Riwo Pargyul himself, and his reputation for storms. At about nine o'clock that night a tremendous blizzard suddenly arose, driving hard from the north across the ridge. It was so furious that we were afraid lest the fragile-looking bivouac-tent, which we were to use at Camp IV and in which the porters were now sleeping, might have been torn away from them. So we got up at midnight and shouted to inquire if all was safe. Contented, sleepy voices answered that they were quite snug. The little tent had never stood such a testing before; it was a high tribute to the toughness of the thin material and reflects great credit on the specialists in light-weight fabrics, Camptors of London, who constructed it to our specifications. Though weighing only three and a half pounds, it accommodates two people in comfort, if not quite in luxury.

The sight of our lovely staircase so laboriously cut, or rather the sight of the place where it had been — for it had disappeared under a coating of fresh snow — was not the best of morning greetings. The hurricane had blown itself out, but the weather still looked ominous and another day of impatient waiting confronted us. If things went on at this rate it was important for supplies to be made to spin out to the latest possible moment, so we resolved to dispense with porters' help even at the cost of making our loads to Camp IV heavier than was pleasant. Our men were therefore told to join the others at Nako and to await us there.

Towards evening the sky began to clear and pessimism gave way once again to rising hopes. Packs, weighing about thirty pounds each, were hastily shouldered and off we went towards the old steps, which the wind, once it had ceased to bring snow with it, had cleared as if to atone for its earlier misdeeds. The bivouac was successfully pitched on the platform, and we were soon inside consuming an energizing brew of pemmican. We did not sleep very much during the night, partly from excitement and partly because we were listening anxiously for signs of a return of the storm. The earlier performance of the tiny tent should have made us confident, but the fact that we were pitched on hard ice, not dug into snow, and anchored with the spikes of our crampons in the absence of stones, in a very exposed situation, left little margin for accidents.

August 10 dawned radiantly; zero hour at last. Bolting our breakfast, we set about dismounting the tent by withdrawing the two ice-axes, which with their bamboo extensions served as poles, one of our several dodges to save weight. Prospects of reaching the top that day seemed so bright that we felt it was worth while to go light and take only one rucksack with spare clothes and the utensils for brewing fresh tea. Some people prefer vacuum-flasks, but these always give the tea an unpleasant taste, a mixture of tin and stale cork; they are fragile, moreover, and the liquid has to be doled out in miserly doses. Some spirit and an aluminum lamp weigh no more than the flask and provide really good tea in fairly generous draughts, the best of stimulants on a climb.

We were of course expecting to have to continue hewing out steps, and we also had the bulge to negotiate, but our luck held; the bulge proved innocent enough, being only part of a small isolated projection on the mountainside. To the left of it the passage was clear and, still better, free from ice. A splendid slope of hard snow, in which the points of our crampons gripped safely, extended before us into the distance. We happened to notice that down on the left there was a labyrinth of crevasses which showed that our line of ascent had been the best possible one. This observation was to prove useful later in an unexpected way.

Some hours of walking in wide zigzags eventually led us on to a huge plateau, "the shoulder," from which we could see the sharp crest of a ridge, continuing steeply upwards, perhaps the final lap. It was now just after noon and we were thirsty, so we chose that moment for rest and the making of tea. It was so hot that we debated whether to climb the last bit in shirt-sleeves; but Charles Warren, being a prudent mountaineer, said that on these high places one never knows what abrupt changes are in store and that it would be wiser to take spare clothes, leaving the rucksack behind. We were full of excitement trying to imagine the view that awaited us on top; it must surely be one of overwhelming grandeur, since Riwo Pargyul is not only

the highest point of vantage for a wide tract of country, but
stands midway between groups of still higher peaks. Without
being quite sure of the lie of the land, we thought of the Karakoram to the north-west and our own Gangotri Range to the
south. But most of all we were looking forward to our first sight
of Tibet; our recent contact with its people, their fine sturdy
character, and their ideas had forged a bond between us and
Tibet that was destined to influence us in the future more profoundly than we dreamed of. A longing to pass within its closed
gates had taken possession of our hearts; already it would be a
milestone in our pilgrimage to look into the promised land.
With such thoughts to urge us on, we advanced towards the
foot of the ridge.

The giant was taking his noonday siesta when he was awakened by a slight tickling on the shoulder. Looking to see what
was the matter, he perceived two minute dwarfs just starting
to climb up his neck, making for his head. "What, at it again?"
he exclaimed. "Wasn't the drubbing I gave you the night before
last good enough to teach you manners? You just wait and see
this time!" So speaking, he shuffled off to his cave as fast as his
legs would carry him. The four winds who were imprisoned
inside were holding a rehearsal of the chorus *"Zerreisset, zer-
sprenget, zertrümmert die Gruft,"* by Bach.

"*Zerreisset!*" they yelled as they battered on the door. "Just
hold on a minute, my hearties," growled the ogre, "till I un-
fasten the padlock." Then out they charged, driving black
thunder-clouds before them, till the whole mountain became
enveloped so that the world was blotted from view. Back and
forth they lashed, snarling round corners and whistling athwart
the ridges, while the thunder-spirit added his counterpoint,
now decrescendoing to a low growl, now administering a succession of *sforzandi* that would have roused the envy of a Beethoven, now coalescing into a roar like a continuous barrage,
now taken up in canon by a choir of echoes.

We looked at one another. To advance or not to advance,
that was the question. "Let's go on a few more steps up the
ridge." Sss . . . sss . . . sss! "What's that?" One of us had

waved an axe and it emitted a prolonged hiss. From the direction of Tibet came up an icy draught. We drew on our windproof suits and caps, and as we did so our hair crackled uncannily. The axes by now were sizzling: it sounded as if the storm were drawing nearer. It seemed unsafe to keep hold of steel, so the axes were planted in the snow on the crest while we cowered some way off to leeward. Again we debated whether to persevere or not: "We must not leave the descent until too late, for it may be extremely hard to find our way off the slopes in the mist. Snow is certain to come soon and all tracks will be covered."

"Yes, but the top can't be far off now. Let's give it a few moments more" (listening) — "I think the storm seems to be moving away a bit."

Every mountaineer knows the difficulty of such decisions. The confronting of an insurmountable obstacle, as happened to us on Simvu three years later, leaves no choice and therefore no sting; but to turn back for bad weather always involves doubt whether one might not have pushed on with a little more firmness of purpose. No worse dilemma could be imagined than that of a climber who had reached a point, say, two hundred feet below the summit of Everest and saw the weather changing or realized the danger of becoming benighted. If he turned back he would, probably rightly, be praised for moral courage; but most climbers would suffer cruel searchings of heart or they would not be climbers at all.

The storm, with occasional threats of returning, did indeed seem to draw away from the ridge, though the blackness was as dense as ever, save for brief moments when glimpses of ghostly glaciers appeared away in the depths. The axes, though still sizzling occasionally, were growing more silent and we judged that we might try our luck by pushing on a few steps. We agreed, however, on a time limit of three o'clock, after which, if the top was not in sight, we must retrace our steps at all costs. To ease the strain we took it in turns to lead on short stretches. Fortunately the snow on the ridge kept good and firm. Suddenly two black specks appeared ahead. What could they be — rocks? But when we caught sight of the upper part of the ridge earlier in the day, we had noticed that there were no rocks save on the very top. We must be there! A moment later and Charles Warren stepped on to the summit and saw the other two main ridges disappearing into the mist below. Nearly three p.m., but the mountain had surrendered; the whole of Riwo Pargyul's 22,210 feet lay under our feet. "Thou shalt tread on the lion and the basilisk."

"Whose feet did I hear you mention?" whispered an unseen Lama. "How can you talk of 'your' feet, when there is no real person of the name of 'you'? There exists indeed a certain bundle of mental and physical properties temporarily associated, ever changing: soon they will be dissolved again; which of them then will keep the right to say that he was Marco? 'You' have not conquered Riwo Pargyul, for there is no Riwo Pargyul either, though there exists an aggregation of stones and grains and bits of ice called, purely for convenience, by that name. If there be no vanquished, there can be no victor. If you still believe those old legends, you are far from the road to freedom. There can be no true achievement so long as there persists the slightest hankering after an individual enjoyment of its fruits. If you don't realize that, why do you climb?" So commented the unseen Lama, but his meaning was at that time hidden from me.

No view was vouchsafed us, and Tibet might have been the Atlantic Ocean for all we could see. It was no time to linger, not even to hunt for sapphires, for already the first stray snow-flakes, harbingers of the blizzard, were drifting over. We turned and hurried down the ridge; but by the time we had got to the rucksack, snow was falling heavily and all trace of our foot-steps had vanished, so that the problem of keeping direction on the featureless slopes was not easy. As we made our way down, trusting to a sixth sense more than anything else, we were pursued by periodic bursts of hail, like volleys of pins. It was strange that with so much wind the mist could remain so unmovingly opaque.

We had come a good way down, but were beginning to doubt our bearings, when we saw close under us the margin of a huge crevasse, then another, and then a third; we were certainly off the route, and in that weather there was but a poor prospect of setting ourselves right. We wondered, if we were benighted, whether one of the crevasses might offer us shelter, only temporarily, we hoped. But surely we had noticed a crevassed area on our left when we started out in the morning? If this was it, we ought to contour, with a faint downward trend, and then might strike the proper route. We altered direction accordingly, crevasses were swallowed up in the mist, and we found ourselves again on open snow. Then something loomed ahead: ice pinnacles; were we approaching another crevassed system — in which case had we miscalculated in the first instance? But surely there was something familiar in the shape of that bulge! Could it be *the* bulge, the one above Camp IV? Yes, it must be, and beyond it was a black speck marking the dismounted tent. Snow had not fallen densely here; the mist, too, was thinning.

Thankfully we came to the tent, all anxiety now dispelled. We had finished with the mountain and the last item on the expedition's program could be ticked off. In a flash our thoughts were homeward bound, speeding across the seas. The tent and the second rucksack were hastily packed and all unnecessaries were sent spinning down to the glacier; then, leaving the last traces of the snow-storm, we walked down the ice staircase and by six p.m. found ourselves back on the col by our big tent. Fatigue began to steal upon us, and made us feel too lazy to cook, so we contented ourselves with a cup of malted milk and then curled into our sleeping-bags.

Indescribable was the fury of Riwo Pargyul at having allowed his prey to checkmate him. All night long he raged impotently, like a blinded Cyclops, lashing the upper parts of his mountain with storm after storm; but we, peacefully sleeping, knew nothing of this till, on waking up rather late in the morning, we found that masses of snow had piled up against the sides of the tent. Looking out, we saw a wintry landscape extending some thousand feet below us. The weather, too, seemed to have broken again decisively: it was evident that the only possible day for the climb had been the one chosen by or rather for us. Thinking back now, one can see that the north peak, under reliable conditions of weather and if free from ice, would not be a difficult mountain; but for all that, it was a grand adventure.

Having struck the tent and gathered whatever of value was left, we started down the 7,500 feet that separated us from Nako. By the time we and our excessive burdens had struggled across the wilderness of boulders and at last reached the road, we felt thoroughly tired and longed to be relieved of our loads for the last mile. As if in answer to a prayer, as we rounded a bend within view of the houses, two figures sprang up and came running towards us. We felt a sudden lightening as the loads were whisked from off our backs, and our strength seemed to rush back to us in that moment. Our two faithful coolies, who had been watching for our return, were overjoyed to hear of the success of the climb and spread the news among the villagers standing near. Someone made a joke, evidently at our expense, the tenor of which eluded us, and the whole company burst out into uproarious guffaws: it was better than fulsome congratulations and so typical of the jovial ways of the Tibetan country-folk.

Chapter VIII

"Back to Civilization"

"MEMBERS OF THE PARTY that has been exploring the X glacier and lately climbed Mount Y have just got back to civilization after spending four months in the wilds. All are in good health."

There is not an expedition about which something like this has not been said, our own case being no exception. The wretched cliché crops up with unfailing monotony in newspaper articles and reviews of books, in the remarks of chairmen before lectures, and from the lips of proposers of after-dinner toasts. Anyone who chooses to spend some of his time off the beaten track, be he surveyor or mountaineer, geologist, or bug-hunter, student of archæology, or merely a traveller for his own pleasure, is equally victimized; and that quite irrespective of the nature of the country in which he has been staying or of the kind of people with whom he has been associating.

How different, nevertheless, was our own experience as we walked the last few miles of the Hindustan-Tibet road towards the corrugated-iron-roofed summer capital of the Indian Empire. The trek back from our mountain on the frontier ridge of Tibet had been sheer joy. Nothing to worry about, the entire program accomplished without serious hitch, everyone feeling fit after four months of an ideally healthy life, lovely country to traverse, a perfect climate at the enlivening height of 8,000 feet.

Our favourite coolies, who had been with us from start to finish, were still in attendance. There was little for them to do, so we treated ourselves to the hitherto forbidden luxury of walking unloaded and handed our personal rucksacks over to them with instructions that they should keep close at heel in case of a sudden call for camera or notebook. The first time I stopped, my heel landed on someone's toe; as I turned abruptly, I collided violently with one of the faithful coolies, who had interpreted his orders with literal exactitude.

The first few days we passed through familiar country. From Nako, at the foot of the mountain, we plunged down the steep side of the valley to the stony banks of the Spiti River, which we crossed by a rope bridge to the prosperous fields and orchards of Li. Then over a pass covered with Alpines, to the Satlej again and our beloved Poo. After this came Kanam with its monastery and the joy of the first woods, and the taste of ripe apples as good as Ribston pippins in the garden of the delightful Forest bungalow of Chini. There we beguiled the evening playing over the old English and Spanish airs on our viols, which, judging by their tone, shared our pleasure.

From there we began to tread new ground. The Tibetan language and Buddhism were now things of the past, and the village *devtas* belonged to the Hindu Pantheon. But the Kunáwari peasants, with their long hair and beards and homespun gowns with purple sashes, were still with us, and their artistic talents were in evidence, now that timber was plentiful, in the decoration not only of temples, but of ordinary houses, on which the carvings were of great boldness and originality. There was not a veranda or window-frame, beam or rail or string-course that was not appropriately beautified.

Gone, however, were the laughing, self-confident faces of the women of upper Khunu; their sisters here looked shy and rapidly aging, and the golden rings they wore in their noses made their wizened features look all the more dejected.

After Urni we entered the zone of rains again; the monsoon was sending down the last few drops from its bucket. All kinds of butterflies were flitting to and fro in the river gorges; some looked like huge orange-tips or brimstones, yellow, white, and red; we also saw fritillaries and swallow-tails, some of them velvety black and others, the commonest species, dusted with golden-green powder and with an electric blue mirror on the hind wings. They settled on moist patches of the road, and rose in clouds when disturbed. Numbers of large grey-green lizards lurked on the rocks, lying in wait for the yellowish grasshoppers that swarmed everywhere. Having seized their prey, they carried it off struggling in their jaws to a hole before gulping it down.

In the more humid parts the forest rioted in tangled luxuriance. Balsams, pink, yellow, or white, bordered the track, and in one place a rock that oozed moisture was half hidden behind a curtain of pink begonias. The ground was covered with a thick carpet of ferns and selaginella.

At Sarahan we were received in audience by H.H. the Raja of Bashahr; we welcomed this opportunity of thanking him for his kindness and all his subjects for their willing help. Our head porter, the man of Poo, on this occasion suddenly shed the character of Odsung the half-Tibetan Buddhist and appeared again in the guise of Ishwar Singh, the complete Hindu, with a sash and a turban like a monstrous onion, in which his flat features were most comically framed. Thus attired, he paraded before his ruler to the accompaniment of many bows and claspings of hands; we always thought he would have made a perfect Vicar of Bray.

Then down from the woods we went to another dry valley, along stubbly hillsides dotted with euphorbias looking like weird candelabra, and so on into hot and stuffy Rampur, the capital of the state. After a night spent in the Raja's guest bungalow, we continued our way to Nirt'h, with its graceful temple spire, which seemed to tell us that we were really back in India, and then, after bidding good-bye to our old friend the Satlej, we climbed again to 8,000 feet and the frontiers of British India at last. We were now all impatience to get to Simla and its luxuries. The expedition was over, and long unheeded cares and desires, like an elbowing throng of ghosts come to life, began to jostle us.

We arrived at Narkanda in a heavy shower and stood rooted in horror gazing on its hutments covered with old kerosene tins hammered out flat. For nearly three months we had not looked on an ugly thing and had begun to take the beauty of the world for granted, even including the works of man. Now the unclean hand of encroaching slumdom had reached out to welcome us home even here in this glorious situation.

The dak bungalow's charges, though perfectly normal, struck us as terrific. For a single man's meal we were expected to pay what had hitherto sufficed for the expenses of the party for a whole day. When the caretaker quoted the price, our porters turned on us such a look of reproach that we simply could not face it. We managed to find cheaper lodgings in a house that, so we were told, had belonged to some missionaries but had now been abandoned and converted into a private hostel. The house was of wood, shockingly put together; not a decent joint in it, every window-frame warped, cracks in the plaster, furniture both uncomfortable and unsightly, and a few irrelevant ornamental details on the mantelpieces that could be traced back to some obscure Roman source. Tea, black as pitch and bitter as gall, was served. We hated to sit down or to touch anything. That night, for the first time for weeks, under the influence of these distressing emotions, it took me more than a few moments to drop off to sleep.

So missionaries were responsible for this jerry-built place! I think they must have been the same ones whom Kipling wrote about in the story of "Lispeth" in *Plain Tales from the Hills*. They lived at Kotgargh then; but that lies only a few miles from Narkanda. What we saw was doubtless part of their efforts to "educate the natives." Could they not have found models a few miles away in the charming and solidly constructed peasant chalets? What could anyone wish for better? Probably in Narkanda they built like that too, formerly; but when they saw that the sahibs did things differently, they followed suit and the old local craftsmen, finding themselves out of a job, were driven to other occupations and their skill died with them. Everything was mean and ugly, and yet a couple of days' march back, the people seemed to possess unerring taste and a love of sound workmanship, as well as that poetic fancy which, from the old forms, is ever turning out something fresh and alive — I will not call it new, but ageless.

As I lay restless on my bed, I heard a curious scurrying and snapping going on as if a pair of huge rats was at work gnawing behind the wainscoting. I prayed that they might be successful in rearing a numerous progeny to collaborate with them in their useful and civilizing efforts.

After Narkanda, continuing along the ridge, we entered the devastated belt, though the valleys on either side looked fair enough still. Rickshaws turned up and the coolies offered to draw us to Simla. The inhabitants were now all dressed in the cast-off reach-me-downs of Europe mixed with loin-cloths and turbans in all sorts of unlikely combinations. Once, however, when we halted for lunch, we came across a young shepherd with an extraordinarily spiritual face and the body of an athlete, comely in his peasant dress of grey wool. He was amusing some children who played around him with shouts of merriment. How did he manage to keep himself untainted in such surroundings? Or had we been speaking unwittingly to Lord Krishna himself?

Lastly came Simla, with its inevitable thoughts of luxuries long untasted. The spell was broken: "civilization" had claimed us back, for the time being at least, filling our minds with conflicting desires and impressions.

We still had a few days left before catching the steamer at Bombay, so we decided to spend most of them at Agra, visiting its incomparable monuments of Mughal art. At Kalka junction, where the narrow-gauge railway from Simla joins the main line, we said good-bye to the two Jadhs, Djun Singh and Naranhu, who had continued to attend upon us in the hotel. In fact, there had been some difficulty in persuading them that Simla was not a nest of robbers and that it was really needless for them to lie across our threshold at night like watchdogs. We had suggested to them that they should walk back to Mussoori by a high-level route, instead of descending to the plains and going round via Dehra Dun; but Djun Singh, who, if so commanded, would have gone alone across five hundred miles of Tibetan desert without turning a hair, absolutely declined to risk himself in this tame bit of Indian territory, declaring it to be swarming with crooks and brigands! Ishwar Singh, alias Odsung, refused to be parted from us till the last possible moment and accompanied us as far as Bombay, whence we saw him off on a return train the day before we sailed. When the coast of India began to fade from sight, though we were full of excitement at the prospect of home, we could not help feeling some twinges of regret, which made us aware of how hopelessly we had lost our hearts. The Himalayan germ, once caught, works inside one like a relapsing fever; it is ever biding its time before breaking out again with renewed virulence. Dr. Longstaff had warned us when we set out, "once a man has found the road, he can never keep away for long." "It is certain you will return," had declared Professor Tucci over supper that evening at Namgya; to which I could only answer "Amen" in all sincerity.

PART TWO

Sikkim ~ 1936

Chapter IX

The Antechamber of Tibet

MARCH 1936 found us back again in the Himalaya, as the prophets had foretold; or rather two of us, Richard Nicholson and I, for of the other members of the old party, Ted Hicks and Colin Kirkus were not free to join us, while Charles Warren had been yielded up, grudgingly, to the Everest expedition.

In the interval between the two journeys not only had our study of the Tibetan language continued with unflagging diligence, but also there had been a good deal of general reading and thinking round the subject of Tibet and its institutions. A path was beginning to be cleared through the maze of new and exciting impressions that we had collected, so that they could be sorted into some degree of order and related to our ordinary life.

Our return into Occidental society, after having spent some months separated from it, made it possible to examine in a new and critical light many things that had hitherto been taken for granted. Indeed, reversion to the old conditions came in many ways as a shock, for the restless, noisy daily round seemed strangely futile after the manageable pace to which we had accustomed ourselves. We missed the quietness and the physical well-being of the mountain life, and we looked round in vain for any adequate substitute for that sense of poise which, more than anything, distinguished the people among whom we had lately stayed.

As soon as we began to make definite plans for another visit to the East we invited two more climbers to join us, J. K. COOKE,* a very able mountaineer with whom I had been associated both in the Alps and in Wales, and F. S. CHAPMAN, of Greenland fame, a keen field ornithologist, who, after leaving us, accompanied the Political Officer of Sikkim to Lhasa as private secretary and finally capped his varied adventures with a first ascent of the lofty peak of Chomolhari. The medical offi-

* He was killed at Dunkerque in 1940, while serving with the Navy.

cer's place was filled by Dr. R. ROAF of Liverpool, who, though he had done but little mountaineering, shared many of our other interests, especially the artistic ones.

The projected expedition was to be divided roughly into two parts. First, we wished to attempt one or more of the peaks situated near the margin of the Zemu Glacier in Sikkim, before the arrival of the monsoon about June. In the second half Cooke and Chapman were to be free to continue climbing in the north of Sikkim if they so wished, while the other three of us devoted ourselves to Tibetan studies. Permission to enter Tibet proper was solicited from the Government of India, which promised to take an early opportunity of forwarding our application to the Lhasa authorities. The district for which we required a passport was called Hlobrak, which means Southern Crag. It is a valley adjoining the north frontier of Bhutan and is reputed both to be of extraordinary natural beauty and to contain a number of ancient monasteries of great interest, in one of which we hoped to be allowed to stay and receive instruction.

Hlobrak is famous as the birthplace of one of Tibet's great divines, Marpa, who, like the founder of the Spiti temples, earned the rare title of Translator, from having brought back doctrinal books to his country from India. He is still more renowned as the spiritual guide of Tibet's most popular saint and national poet, Mila Repa. The latter had started life as a notorious sinner. When his father died, his uncle and aunt seized on the inheritance and drove Mila and his mother out into penury. The widow vowed vengeance and called on her son to show himself a man by exacting a cruel punishment from the usurpers of his patrimony. But his uncle only mocked them both, saying: "If you are many, declare war on us; if few, cast spells on us!" The young man took them at their word and went in search of a sorcerer able and willing to teach him the art of black magic. Eventually he found his man and became initiated into the mysteries of witchcraft. When he felt his powers sufficiently matured, he made his preparations and launched spells against his uncle's house, condemning all who dwelt there to perish except two, his uncle and aunt, who were to be spared so that they might experience the anguish of their loss to the full. At that moment a feast was in progress and the horses belonging to the guests were stabled on the ground floor of the house, as is still customary in Tibet today, while the family entertained their friends on the first floor. A maidservant, sent down on an errand and deluded by the spell, imagined she saw a scorpion as big as a yak tugging at the central pier that formed the main support of the building. Unhinged by terror, she rushed shrieking from the stable, and her alarm communicated itself to the horses; upon which all the stallions hurled themselves madly upon the mares and a terrible fight ensued. The whole house was shaken so violently that it toppled down, burying all the company under the ruins except the wretched aunt and uncle.

The news did not take long to reach the ears of the old widow, who hastened to the scene of the disaster and added her triumphant gibes to the sorrows of the hapless pair. To escape the consequences of his crime Mila Repa had to flee the country; but in exile he began to be tormented by remorse. His highly sensitive and spiritual nature craved to understand the true meaning of life. A chance acquaintance happened to mention to him the name of Marpa the Translator, and Mila instantly experienced, as many young Tibetans still do, a conviction that he, and he alone, was the Master to lead him into the Path of Truth. He set out at once for Hlobrak, where Marpa, who is represented in pictures as a rather stout, choleric-looking man, already expected him, having sensed his approach through second sight. Mila offered himself body and soul to his Lama, and prayed that he would impart to him his special doctrine. "What!" cried Marpa, feigning anger. "Do you think I am going to hand over secrets which I brought all the way from India at great trouble and risk to the first comer, to one moreover who is a wicked sorcerer, the slayer of I know not how many human beings? It is only after a long probation that I may, if I see that you are really in earnest, instruct you in the doctrine." Mila, having agreed to Marpa's terms, awaited his commands.

The Lama, who discerned in Mila's enthusiastic personality a wealth of possibilities that were only waiting to be released as soon as his past misdeeds had been expiated, deliberately put him through a testing that would have broken the spirit of any ordinary man, treating him with the utmost harshness, snubbing him on every possible occasion, and displaying a shortness of temper and despotic capriciousness which belied the deep respect that he really felt for his disciple. Marpa is still held up to admiration as the type of an uncompromising trainer of character, who shrinks from no discipline that he thinks likely to aid the spiritual development of his pupil. If

few men have quite equalled Marpa in his ruthless interpretation of a preceptor's duties, many of the modern lama teachers
today would be found to act on his principles to a surprising
extent.

One of the measures taken by Marpa will perhaps astonish
my readers, though to a Tibetan it would appear more natural.
He ordered Mila Repa to use his magic arts to coerce the people
of a village who, so he said, had offended him in some way.
Mila, who was by this time consumed with shame for the
murders that he had perpetrated by his sorcery, crimes that
he now appreciated at their true worth, suffered the pain of
realization a hundredfold, now that he had to repeat them in
cold blood; but, like a true pupil, he never for a moment
dreamed of disobeying his master. The strange-sounding command was really a means of bringing home to Mila, in a way
that no mere precepts could have done, the real enormity of the
sin of violence, revealing it to him in its true colours. The sole
object of a genuine Lama's training is realization; whatever
does not conduce to that end is a waste of time. Innocence, if
due to nothing more than unconsciousness of evil, is considered
of little worth. Not the new-born baby, but the experienced
sage is the Tibetan ideal. It must be admitted that in the history of these events Marpa got out of a difficulty by restoring
to health the men, rats, and birds that had suffered from his
so drastic experiment. He also invented another series of tests.
He ordered the building of a house on a certain site and specified the exact design. Mila was to erect it unaided, bringing
every stone with his own hands. When after unspeakable toil
it was completed, Marpa came along and said casually: "Who
ordered that absurd building to be put up there?" "It was Your
Reverence," answered Mila. "I must have been crazy when I
said it. Pull it down and re-erect it here." This episode, with
variations, was enacted again and again. Mila was even made
to replace the stones where they had come from, miles away,
carrying them on his back.

At last when the young man had proved that, though pushed
to the limit of endurance, his steadfastness was utterly unshakable, his formidable tutor relented. Mila could hardly believe
his ears when he heard the news that the coveted initiation was
to be his at last. Then, in the centre of a *Khyinkhor*, or Sacred
Circle, Marpa admitted his favourite pupil into his spiritual
family, while foretelling for him a most glorious achievement.

Then follows one of the most moving episodes of the whole

story, the description of the parting of the old Lama from his beloved disciple. After the stern lesson of Mila's cruel labours, the poignant tenderness of this farewell is strangely affecting.

Mila Repa's autobiography, which he dictated later to one of his own pupils, is the great masterpiece of Tibetan prose and has fortunately been competently translated into English, and into French still better. It gives a clearer impression of how the Tibetan mind works than any other book that I know, and as a picture of daily life it holds good today, though these events happened about the time of William the Norman.

Mila Repa became one of the greatest saints and by his extreme power of concentration succeeded in telescoping into the space of a single earthly life all the stages that must precede the Supreme Illumination of a Buddha. He spent most of his remaining years in reclusion in caves, some of them not far from Mount Everest, where one can still meet a few of his spiritual children. There he meditated upon the Truth for the good of all creatures. The Order of Lamas which Marpa and he founded on Earth is called *Kargyudpa* or White Tradition Order. It hands down, in golden succession, doctrines which perhaps represent the richest manifestations of the Tibetan spirit. The saint has revealed his most intimate musings in a collection of poems, characterized by an extreme succinctness of expression. The autobiography is also a model of brevity; the style is vigorous and free from padding and the dialogue is vivid in the extreme.

It was to the scene of St. Mila's apprenticeship, to the mountain valley hallowed by his footsteps, that we hoped to go, perhaps to receive there some faint reflected glimpses of the teachings that he had dared to face in their dazzling effulgence. After an uneventful voyage we landed at Calcutta, buoyed up by hopes, little dreaming that we were fated to be thwarted in every single item of our program: that we should fail on our peak, and be unable to set foot in Tibet; that our arrangements would work less smoothly than when we came out, quite inexperienced, three years before; and that luck would only turn at long last, when we had left our chosen ground and migrated to the opposite end of the Himalaya, where, at P'hiyang in Ladak, a spiritual descendant of Marpa of Hlobrak would instruct us!

At Siliguri on the edge of the plain, where passengers for Kalimpong detrain, the sight of the flat-nosed, high-cheek-boned faces of the hill-men filled us with excitement. We packed into

a car driven by a Nepali chauffeur and sped off along a road
bordered by dense jungle, said to harbour tigers and elephants.
A sharp turn into the hills, and the river Tista, flowing between
banks overgrown with luxuriant tropical foliage, came into
view. There we saw the polished leathery leaves of wild banana
and of the indiarubber plant, palmlike cycads that called to
mind remote geological ages, the light fronds of bamboo,
screwpines or pandanus and creepers in amazing variety. The
trees, covered with ferns and orchids, exhibited the characteristic phenomena of damp tropical vegetation; fine air cables
like telegraph wires, buttressed roots and subsidiary trunks
growing out of the ends of branches so that a whole grove
might really consist of but a single tree. Monkeys played overhead, and here and there huge butterflies, known hitherto only
from collections, flitted past.

Having once spent some weeks in the forests of equatorial
South America, I was expecting to find the jungles of the Tista
Valley equally prolific, since the rainfall of Sikkim is enormous,
some 120 inches in the outer ranges. They were on a markedly
smaller scale, however. The trees themselves were perhaps
half the size and did not produce the stately cathedral-like impression of the more highly developed tropical rain-forest.
Creepers also, though numerous, were mostly of the fine jasmine type. Thick-stemmed lianas were relatively few: I noticed
the rattan or climbing palm and the pothos, a scansorial member of the arum family, and another creeper with broad heart-
shaped leaves. On the whole, these forests admit a good deal
of light, so that the plants have a less severe struggle to reach
it and are not forced to resort so generally to complex expedients like air roots, such as commonly occur in forests where
every gleam of light is precious. By the Tista there were open
paths, which on the Essequibo of Guiana would have been
roofed over by creepers in less than a couple of seasons. Insects
too, though common and splendid, did not hover round in anything like the same numbers. It must be supposed that the
slightly higher latitude (27° North, actually outside the tropics), the sharper division into seasons (the dry season tends to
act somewhat like a winter), and perhaps also the proximity of
the plains of India, which are comparatively poor in species,
have jointly conspired to water down the intensity of Nature's
energy; but even so, the forest is of great magnificence, such
as temperate vegetation, even at its best, does not quite equal.
The beauty of the latter may not be less perfect in itself, but

its possibilities are more limited. If temperate woods resemble the Pastoral Symphony of Beethoven, tropical forests are a fugal concerto of Bach or a six-part motet by Palestrina.

After crossing the Tista, the road winds upwards in numerous bends to a ridge 4,000 feet high, with the bazaar of Kalimpong straggling along its crest. This place, which once belonged to Bhutan, forms part of a district annexed to British territory in 1865; it owes its commercial importance to its position as a terminal of the Lhasa-India trade-route. Thousands of mules and ponies come and go, bringing the wool of Tibet to India and carrying in exchange cotton, manufactured goods and also silk and other Chinese products. In Kalimpong's rambling street of shops many races rub shoulders, Bengalis and merchants from Marwar celebrated for business acumen, neat little Nepalis and high-cheeked Tibetans, lanky bullet-skulled Bhutanese in short striped tunics, heroic-looking Khambas with their broadswords stuck through their belts, lamas trading on behalf of their monasteries or intent on a visit to Bodh Gaya in Bihar, where the Victorious One obtained His final revelation. The best shops, neatest, cleanest, and most tastefully arranged, are those kept by Chinese; the smiling faces of their owners strike a friendly note as one walks through the bazaar.

The presiding genius of Kalimpong at that time was the Very Reverend Dr. J. A. Graham, sometime Moderator of the General Assembly of the Church of Scotland. Having come out as a missionary, his attention was drawn to the crying evil of unwanted children of Anglo-Indian parentage, who, like Kim of old, hung about the streets of India, deserted and neglected. Dr. Graham came to their rescue, and starting from small beginnings, built up a wonderful organization to deal with the problem, including a school where the boys and girls were fostered, educated, and eventually placed in suitable trades or professions. Many firms, as well as private persons, have recognized the great public benefit of this work by becoming regular subscribers to its upkeep. It was a moving experience to visit the homes in company with the saintly man who acted as father to this huge family. The unfeigned joy that lit up the rows of faces as he pushed open the doors of successive class-rooms, the general atmosphere of health and confidence, the pleasant cottages among which the children had been subdivided into small groups instead of being allowed to grow up under barrack conditions, all these things made the St. Andrew's Homes deserve the much-abused name of Charity.

During my stay at Kalimpong I spent every available moment in trying to improve my Tibetan. Having picked it up in the western provinces and gone on building upon that foundation, my ear was not attuned to the dialect and accent of Lhasa, which is the lingua franca of educated Tibetans everywhere. I had several teachers at Kalimpong, one of whom, an elderly layman, used to come and coach me on the hotel veranda. One day, as we were sitting at our lesson, I happened to see an ant crawling up the hem of his gown and picked it off and put it on the grass. "You have done well," said the teacher. "I rejoice to see that you did not unthinkingly squash the ant. You must be familiar with the doctrines that enjoin respect for life however lowly." "Yes," I answered, "I have heard the popular saying that any insect one sees has probably been at some time one or both of one's parents." This is a way of expressing the idea that all beings are continuously passing from one state to another, according to the actions that consciously or unconsciously affect them, so that all living things are brothers, and all things whatsoever, one. This doctrine will be explained in detail in the chapter on the Round of Existence.

While at Kalimpong I had many opportunities of investigating the attitude of the Tibetans towards animals, as not a day passes but long trains of mules or ponies come and go along the caravan route. I had already noticed in 1933 that Tibetans acted kindly and thoughtfully towards their animals, and that ill temper, cursing, and beating seemed unknown among them. This first opinion was reinforced by what I heard and saw at Kalimpong, in Sikkim, and later in Ladak. I think one is safe in declaring that genuine cruelty is uncommon and that in their relations with the animal world the Tibetans might serve as an example for most other races. Their theoretical position is sound from the start. Animals are sensitive beings, differing in degree, not in kind, from ourselves, and must be treated accordingly — so runs their teaching. Hunting and fishing are discountenanced by the law, and foreigners admitted into Tibet are obliged to give a pledge that they will respect this prohibition. Wild animals are in consequence often very tame. Feeding of birds and fishes is considered a pious act. Meat-eating, though general because of the scarcity of other kinds of food on the plateau, is indulged in as a regrettable necessity, but never defended, and the stricter lamas and any others who abstain from it altogether are much respected.

Pack-animals travelling along the trade-routes suffer from frequent sores caused by the rubbing of the wooden pack-saddles. I have seen many bad open wounds, while there is hardly one mule or pony that does not show some patches of white hair where an old sore has healed over. In Europe a bad sore on a horse is taken as clear proof of cruelty. Should not the same be said here? I think that a different construction should be put on the evidence, and that the evil is almost entirely due to the nature of the ground over which the caravans have to go. The paths are often strewn with boulders; successions of high mountain passes must be crossed where blizzards overtake the travellers; early or late in the season deep snowdrifts add to the difficulties. I was told that a driver is usually put in charge of from twenty to thirty mules; the men battle hard to help their animals, but the task is beyond one man's strength. If the ponies themselves were like the nervous creatures that we know in England, the number of casualties would bring all traffic to a standstill; but the Tibetan pony or mule is as tough as his master. When he falls over, if there is no one at hand to help, he just scrambles up and goes on his way. One Kalimpong resident also told me that the animals eventually become hardened to the pack-saddles and that the second-growth skin is less liable to sores than before. An improved saddle was once designed, but it was impossible to get it tried seriously, as the existing pattern is time-honored and slightly cheaper too. One knows at home how difficult it is to overcome the conservatism of simple people.

In southern Europe, where sores on animals are common, they are to be found invariably associated with emaciation from underfeeding, beating, goading, and especially with the habit of leaving the pack-saddles on day and night out of sheer laziness. In Tibet I regard the sores, though greatly to be regretted, as a comparatively minor ill among the many evils by which man, as Schopenhauer said, has "turned the earth into a hell for the animals," both because the sores seem to recover under good treatment on reaching home, and because they are chiefly the outcome of extremely hard conditions of life, which the men also endure in equal degree; they are not caused by malevolence, indifference, denial of the animals' just rights, or, as so often happens, simply by indolence. All this mitigates the evil considerably, and though one would not exactly choose to be born a mule on an Asiatic caravan route

if one could avoid it, I continue to rate the Tibetans high in
their treatment of animals. Above all, they admit the right principle, so that, in case of abuse, there is something to appeal to.

At the same time it would be easy to misread the motives
that govern the Tibetans in their attitude towards cruelty.
Their treatment of animals, in which their standard is above
average, must not lead one to ascribe to them an extreme
tender-heartedness or an inability to witness pain without re-
pugnance. By no stretch of imagination could they be called
humanitarians, even when their acts conform to the humane
code. With us the chief objection to cruelty is the actual pain
inflicted; not so with the Tibetan, whose powers of enduring
pain without flinching are great and who can also look unmoved upon suffering that would horrify us. For him, the feeling of hostility which leads to the doing of an injury is far
more serious than the pain involved in the cruel act. The two
points of view differ profoundly, even if they sometimes approach in their results.

The Buddhist takes for his starting-point the rights of all his
living fellow creatures, rights that he recognizes in theory,
whatever may be his own practice. The sinfulness of ill treatment lies in the ignorant denial of those rights and in the
indulgence of anger or self-interest. For our part, we make a
marked distinction of principle between the rights claimed for
man and those accorded to animals. The latter can vary between moderately full rights — sometimes marred by a patron-
izing attitude — slight recognition, and non-existence. On the
other hand, our objection to pain is extreme. We fear it greatly
for ourselves and, by a projection of our own highly developed
sensibility, we recoil from the idea of inflicting it on others.

The Tibetans, on the other hand, take little stock of pain
as such. A man who would not commit a cruel act himself
could be unmoved by the severest torture suffered by either
man or beast provided he was convinced that it was inevitable
or deserved. If it were purely the result of chance, he would
probably feel no strong impulse to seek a way to remedy it. A
man who would put himself to no end of trouble in order to
spare his animals might experience little horror on witnessing
an accident to one of those same animals; even a deliberate act,
such as a painful penalty decreed by the criminal law, would
not stir his feelings.

For us pain is a comparatively rare occurrence; where it
exists we try to hide it from public gaze. Our fear of it for our-

selves, as well as the humane teachings, have sharpened our imagination, so that we no longer feel able to apply it even towards the worst criminals. We only tolerate it openly in war, and to some extent in scientific research; in the latter case our besetting fear of the pain of disease works the other way and overcomes our normal inhibitions. There are of course other horrible cruelties, like trapping for furs; but they are allowed to continue because the pain is out of sight and the appeal to cupidity is great; and the same applies to some of the measures taken against those wild animals that are counted as "vermin."

The virtues of the Tibetans in their relations with animals they owe chiefly to their Buddhist principles, which remain unquestioned even if they are not always applied consistently. Were such to be the case, indeed, it could not but bring about the abolition of all cruelties. But of objection to pain for its own sake there is little, and inhuman practices hallowed by custom, such as the slaughter of animals in certain districts by suffocation, do not stir the public conscience.

One of my pressing duties after my arrival was to go over by car to Gangtok, the capital of Sikkim, and introduce myself to the Political Officer, Mr. B. J. (now Sir Basil) Gould, who controlled the issue of passports into Tibet. He had very bad news for us. A report had arrived concerning an untoward incident on a different part of the frontier which, it was feared, had annoyed the Lhasa authorities. In consequence the promise of forwarding our application for a permit to go to Hlobrak could not be fulfilled. It was a great blow: all our plans were in the melting-pot. There was nothing to be done now, however, but to carry on with our immediate program of climbing in Sikkim. We spent several days at Gangtok organizing transport. Mr. Gould most kindly offered us the hospitality of the Residency and its lovely garden, while H.H. the Maharaja of Sikkim received us several times and treated us with every possible consideration; I should like to express to him the grateful thanks of all our party.

By far the most interesting of the sights at Gangtok is the new temple attached to the palace, which has only recently been completed by the reigning prince. Both the structure and the interior decorations and fittings are new. It is significant that a work has been carried through in this little Himalayan principality that would nowadays be wellnigh impossible in the capitals of the richest countries in the world. Externally the building is plain, built in two stories like all Sikkim temples. The nave, well proportioned and resting on pillars with the usual Tibetan bracketed capitals, is lined with mural paintings by the best contemporary artists from Tibet. Symbolical figures, illustrating metaphysical doctrines, scenes from the life of the Buddha and from local sacred history, together with bands and panels of conventional foliage, have all been executed with precision and in animated style. The colours are clean and well blended; the only fault that can be alleged against them is their rather aggressively new appearance, intensified by the fact that they had to be overlaid with a coat of glossy varnish, to protect them from the humid climate. It is to be hoped that time will tone them down.

Besides the royal shrine there is a conspicuous monastery on the top of Gangtok hill, to which we paid a call, at the hour of afternoon service. When I knocked on the door to ask admittance, the lama doorkeeper must have been puzzled by my appearance and accent: I suppose I pronounced Tibetan rather differently from an Englishman. I overheard him whispering: "He must be from Ladak" — prophetic words, as it happened. I thought of Madame David-Neel when she stayed at Lhasa disguised as a beggar, for she also had been taken for a Ladaki.

The service was not edifying. The lamas who forgathered in the choir seemed bent on getting through their orisons in the briefest possible time. They gabbled mechanically and turned to stare and gossip quite unashamedly. It was the "vain repetition" mentioned in the Gospel, vain by reason of its inattention, for repetition is not in itself harmful and has its uses. In Tibet the delinquents would soon have heard from the monastic censor, and maybe felt the weight of his whip too! There is plenty of room for reform in the Sikkim lamaseries — real reform, not revolutionary innovation, but a return to earlier practice and a stricter enforcement of rules that already exist. There is a great difference between these two policies.

Unlike so many Hindu and Moslem rulers, the Maharaja and his court invariably wear their traditional dress. This wise and salutary practice, in keeping with the dignity of a prince, is unfortunately not copied as it ought to be by the officials of petty rank. Postal servants, overseers on roads, and, most serious of all, schoolmasters are frequent offenders. This last case is especially regrettable because of the teachers' influence upon the character of their youthful and uncritical charges. I used to meet the schoolboys returning home in the evenings with their satchels: some of them looked in the picture, but far too many were got up as grotesque travesties of European children. There is no law I should welcome more than one making it a duty of every employee of the state to wear his national costume. The same rule should be applied to schoolchildren. Designers of school buildings and Government offices might follow this principle, so far as is practicable, in regard to the style of the architecture and furnishing. It is only long after people have relinquished their heritage that they begin to feel regrets; but then the attempt to reconstruct the past is only too liable to result in a mere romantic affectation, like the Gothic revival in Europe. The time for devising counter-measures against the evil tendency is now, before it has had time to gather its full force.

I believe that this question of costume, external though it may appear at first sight, is a crucial one for India, China, Japan, and other nations too. It has become a symbol of something far more deep-seated, a touchstone by which the traditional and anti-traditional souls can be distinguished. That I am not alone in thinking so is proved by the actions of those to whom, in this matter, I feel most opposed. I call to witness the inveterate Occidentalizers, Kemal Atatürk and his Persian and Afghan imitators, for they, though from diametrically contrary motives, came to the same conclusion as myself. They wished to uproot tradition, for they too felt the power of symbols; that is why they persecuted all the outward signs of native culture and forcibly imposed trousers and bowler hats, Romanized architecture, and jazz orchestras. They accepted, for a criterion of civilization, conformity to the Western model, and that alone. In their eyes such an object as a typewriter was more than a useful tool to do a certain job; it became invested with mystical qualities, like an emblem of progressiveness in the new era. Their ideals matched their outward trappings. Militaristic nationalism, identification of propaganda with education, hatred of religion and denial of the private authority of conscience — above all, the exaltation of feverish action over thought in every sphere — these were their ideas of culture.

In encouraging contrast, I must tell the story of how in 1937 I was visited in my home in Liverpool by the Mongol lama Wangyal, whom I have mentioned before and to whom this book owes so much. He came over in his national dress and always wore it while in England. On the voyage some Indians tried to frighten him by prophesying that he would be laughed at; they even told him that the police would interfere with him if he did not change into European clothes! Not only did no such thing happen, but people who met him went out of their way to comment favourably on his appearance. That is how the question struck English people. I wish some of my Oriental friends would lay this to heart.

A general reversion to the traditional costume on the part of male Indians, and Chinese and Japanese of the educated classes, especially students and officials — women seem usually to have more courage and sounder instincts in these things — would, in my opinion, earn general respect from Europeans. Self-respect is the first step towards friendship with others. Slavish imitation is the way to get oneself despised, when all talk of equality or reconciliation becomes merely futile.

Chapter X

Defeat on Simvu

THE VALLEY OF the Tista, approached by a short descent from the Penlong Pass, is the ordinary route from Gangtok to northern Sikkim. It is a sylvan fairyland, which should have inspired poets; but its name has been more often associated with the unpleasant topics of malaria and leeches. True, the disease is common in the lower parts of the valley, especially during the rains; but the upper reaches, along which the path of expeditions lies, are, except for one stretch, free from it. It is only in the rainy season that certain sections are overrun with leeches; at other times of the year they are only found in large numbers in some unusually moist side valleys.

When our caravan marched up the four stages between Gangtok and Lachhen, at the gate of the Zemu Glacier valley, the drought had not yet broken and vegetation was not showing at its best. There were few insects or flowers; only here and there a vivid purple splash indicated a plant of dendrobium orchid perched up in a fork of the branches. I will leave more detailed description till our return in the monsoon, when everything had come to life again. In the space of a few days on our outward journey we went through the gamut of the year's seasons in reverse, starting from the perpetual high summer of the subtropical zone, passing within a few hours into an evergreen subtemperate summer, then gradually rising to temperate spring, till finally, after climbing abruptly on to a much higher shelf, where stand the pretty chalets of Lachhen, we were back again in a landscape of leafless trees, except for the conifers; the first touch of spring was just showing in the red of tree rhododendrons, the waxy white blooms of magnolias, and the mauve of primulas dotted over the brown turf. When we reached the glacier, after a brief stay in the village, we had taken the final step back into a wintry snowbound world.

Lachhen stands on a minor caravan route leading into Sikkim from Tibet, which has been followed by several Everest

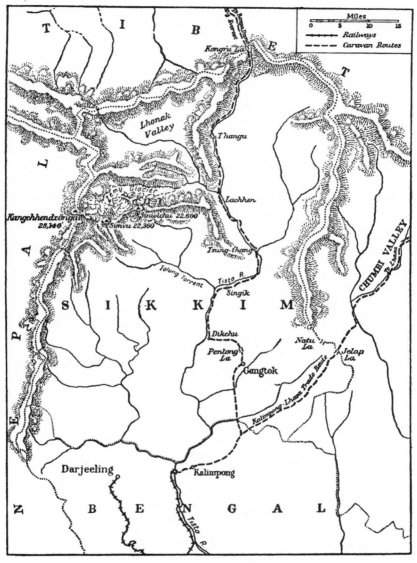

It should be noted that only the principal mountain chains have been indicated; most of the area shown, however, is mountainous.

expeditions. The Zemu torrent, which feeds the Tista with the drainage of a huge group of snow mountains, culminating in the gigantic massif of Kangchhendzŏnga, comes out some two miles beyond the village, which thus occupies a strategic position on the path of parties intent on climbing in these parts. The villagers, who provide a good deal of the porterage, are well aware of their power to hold the climbers up to ransom; they do it with some show of rustic cunning, though quite good-humouredly. Their idea is to try to spin out the stages between Lachhen and the proposed base camp so that they, being paid not by distance but by the day, may reap the maximum profit. It is necessary to be wary when making an agreement with them and to drive a keen bargain oneself, if possible laying down beforehand what stages will be officially recognized irrespective of the time taken. Lachhenpas can be astonishingly quick when there is nothing extra to be gained by being dilatory; when about their own business they cover great distances at a remarkable speed, carrying superhuman loads, and never resting till they have reached the other end, when they let themselves relax. These people are all born pleaders. They will talk interminably before they accept your terms, but once an agreement has been made, they will not try to violate it; for they are not educated to the ways of the great outer world and have yet to learn that one can always find a loophole for wriggling out of one's pledges.

The village runs its affairs on a largely co-operative basis. Property is privately owned, but all take their share of work that affects the community as a whole. Rules have been made that aim at preventing one family from getting an unfair advantage over the others by such means as an early sowing, or a reaping of the crops before the date laid down by the commune, which meets to debate in an open space on the edge of the village. Regulations having this end in view are often enforced with unimaginative rigidity, not taking into account whether a field faces the sun or has a different kind of soil. Madame David-Neel, who spent several years near Lachhen, tells some amusing stories of how the principle is apt to be interpreted. She was herself nearly forced to accept a whole pack of hounds because a family that sold her one dog was considered, by so doing, to have tried to steal a march on its neighbours.

The headman, recognized by Government, is the person who acts as go-between for strangers. At the time of our visit, he was an obliging and intelligent man in the early thirties, who had been to school in Gangtok and could speak, and even write, a little English. As spokesman for his people, he always tried to obtain for them the most advantageous terms; but he also saw to it that his part of the bargain was faithfully carried out.

One morning he presented himself at the rest-house and asked to see the doctor. He wished to be overhauled, for he was suffering from an annoying complaint, and another medical man whom he had consulted had shown himself incapable of prescribing a remedy. Whenever he drank a lot of brandy, so he said, his eyes began to water; but the other doctor had suggested nothing more helpful than that he should in future abstain from taking brandy, an obviously impossible solution. He hoped that Dr. Roaf would give him a medicine to stop the flow of tears without interfering with other paramount interests!

Above the village there stood a small monastery, of not more than twenty lamas, which nevertheless had acquired considerable fame through its abbot, a most remarkable man, who styled himself the Lachhen hermit. He occupied a thatched cottage adjoining the temple and had gained his title by spending several years in meditation in mountain retreats. He was considered to have advanced very far on the road to Buddhahood.

We naturally felt a wish to make his acquaintance, so we sent word to ask leave to come and pay our respects. When we arrived at the monastery, we were told to wait a few minutes as the abbot was not quite ready to see us. While we stood outside, several lamas rushed hither and thither in a feverish search for five chairs, considered indispensable to the proper reception of the party. After four stools had been carried into the abbot's room, a fifth one, a wicker armchair, was produced; but the door was too narrow to admit it. As the lamas struggled to force it through the entrance, I tried in vain to explain that so much trouble on our behalf was unnecessary. When once a Tibetan has made up his mind that politeness demands a certain course of action, no power on earth will turn him from his purpose. The guest may be made to wait all night out in the cold, but that is preferable to insulting him.

When their frantic efforts to coax the armchair into the doorway proved fruitless, they turned their attention to the window. One young monk heaved vigorously from the outside while another pulled with all his strength from within. We feared that the whole cottage would collapse, but suddenly, with a crash, the armchair lurched through the window. In a second, agitation gave way to their normal bland demeanour, as we were smilingly ushered into the august presence.

We stepped into a dimly lit room, furnished with altar, lamps, scrolls, and books. On a rug by the window, turned so that the disturbing rays of the sun should not fall directly on his face, a rather fat man in orange robes was seated, cross-legged. His face was broad, with twinkling, humorous eyes, his hair long and wispy; from his ears hung a pair of large gold rings. The great thickness of his neck was increased by a prominent goitre; the whole effect might have been comic but for the aura of power that seemed to radiate from his person, making one feel at once that here was no ordinary mortal. Actually, I have never looked on a more impressive face, despite its grotesqueness.

We presented a ceremonial scarf and were then invited to take our seats in strict hierarchical order, with myself in the armchair. After this there followed a brief and formal conversation, during which I asked him to be so kind as to bless the porters before we started up the Zemu.

On the following day the stage was set for the blessing ceremony on the open space before the temple, where a high seat was installed for the abbot and, facing it, five lower ones covered with small Tibetan rugs for us. The porters, both Lachhen men and our nucleus of Darjeeling Sherpas, gathered round, and then the hermit, attended by his lamas, mounted the dais. He was wearing on his head a queer hat of papier-mâché, shaped rather like a top hat and secured under the chin with a string, which made him look even more peculiar.

Before the service began, offerings were presented on behalf of ourselves and our party. The porters gave him a white scarf, which is as indispensable in Tibetan social intercourse as a visiting-card in nineteenth-century England, and a silver coin, while I handed him a large *t'hanka* of the green Dolma, a divinity who plays a part analogous to that of the Blessed Virgin in the Christian religion. It had been sent to me from North China and we had brought it out to Sikkim in accordance with our policy of giving as presents only those things that would fit in with their surroundings in every sense of the word. For gifts to temples I had brought three such scroll-pictures and two silver lamps made in Greece over a century ago; for highly placed personages there were rings and a pendant made by my goldsmith brother. We had, besides, a number of semi-precious stones, unset, such as garnets and amethysts, cornelians and lapis lazuli; these were suitable for persons of medium status, while for people of higher rank we had reserved a few aquamarines and tourmalines.

Stones, being endowed with an intrinsic beauty that cannot be affected by time or fashion, provide a simple solution to the whole problem of presents. For instance, an ambassador, if he also took unset stones, could grade them so as to suit every rank from the highest downwards. To the sovereign a diamond, to a minister an emerald, to a local governor an opal, and so on. It is easy to be thoughtless and play the part of a tempter, offering things that will help to corrupt people's taste by playing on their mere love of novelty. In ancient times, when the products of every country were more or less artistic, such precautions were needless; indeed, quite the contrary, for the exchange of artistic products between nations was a means of mutually stimulating their creative instincts. But now it is different, and most of our present-day "art products" are a disgrace to human taste. Their introduction into a society whose artistic sense is uncorrupted is dangerous. The precious stones are always unexceptionable as presents, and their influence cannot but work in the right direction.

The abbot's benediction differed entirely from that of the lama who officiated for us at Harsil in 1933. The Lachhen prelate remained seated throughout and let us file up one by one to receive from him a few drops of a strange decoction. We sprinkled our hands with it and sniffed a little up our noses, after which he gave us an equally mysterious pill to swallow. Then, to the accompaniment of an invocation, rice grains were thrown up into the air and the service concluded with a distribution to everyone of small muslin scarves, knotted in a peculiar manner by the abbot himself. As he handed out each scarf, he said: "May your stay in the mountains be fortunate."

Rather late on our last evening I wandered out alone by the path that led to the entrance of the Zemu Valley; the others were still busy packing. As I was returning homewards I saw a pathetic sight. Two men were approaching from the side of the village, weighed down by bulky burdens, at least eighty pounds apiece. One of them walked ahead at a brisk pace and the second, who was blind and tied to him by two bits of string, arm to arm, followed without hesitation over the irregular ground. "Where are you bound for?" I stopped to ask. "We are

going over the Kongra Pass to Kampa Dzong" — that is, over
a pass 17,000 feet high across the mountains at a season when
snow was still lying quite deep! "Alas," cried the blind man,
"woe is me; for twelve years I have not seen the light. Who is
there to take pity on me?" I felt much affected, but could think
of nothing to say. I saluted them and had moved off a few
paces when I suddenly recalled a story in Madame David-
Neel's book about her famous journey to Lhasa. She tells how
she met a dying man by the roadside and found a way of comforting him. I turned and ran after the pair, who were walking
away rapidly. I nudged the leading man's arm and he turned
round in surprise. "Listen, friend," I said, "to the possessor of
the eye of the doctrine there is no darkness. In the Western
Paradise of the Buddha who is named Boundless Light the sun
shall rise for you once again." A flash of joy chased the blank
despair for a moment from the blind man's face, while his com-
rade thanked me with a touching look of gratitude.

Next day the whole party set out by the same path on which
I had met the blind man. Before we had gone a mile I noticed
that the Lachhenpas were walking badly, advancing a hundred
yards at excessive speed and then putting down their loads and
starting to gossip. The symptoms were unmistakable: I saw
the ghosts of the troublesome porters at Gangotri rising again.
But this time I was no longer a raw hand. If they were working for a prolongation of marching time in order to earn more
days' pay, we could manœuvre for position too. One thing to
do was to pick out the willing elements and play them against
the malcontents, and another to anticipate intended halts and
rush the men quickly past attractive camping-sites on to ground
where a stop was not so alluring. At each inviting spot I
was ready for them and managed to hustle a few beyond it,
without betraying my feelings. The men were argumentative but friendly, and often a jest was enough to keep them on
the move.

Our three days' trek to the Zemu passed off quite satisfactorily in the end, though it required constant vigilance to control
the recalcitrant elements among the porters. In the evenings
the leading trouble-makers used to harangue us eloquently
on the scarcity of camping-grounds and fuel for the next day;
we countered this by proposing an exceptionally distant place
as the end of the following march, in language no less rhetorical. This little game was played without ill feeling, and the
compromises that we reached worked out about right.

In the end we became fast friends. The Lachhenpas liked us to sit at their camp-fires while they played dice. Each man had his "system": one would shake the dice-bowl in a special way, another would shout out some luck-bringing ejaculation, and a third would bang down the dice on the cloth with a whoop. Most Tibetans love games of chance. On rest-days, whether it stayed fine or whether it rained, the porters spent their entire time, from early morning till far into the night, with little piles of coins by their side or chips of wood for counters, passing the dice-bowl round, shouting and laughing, but never quarrelsome. I found that if any petty dispute among porters did arise, it could usually be settled by an appeal to their sporting instinct. An award based on drawing lots or tossing up was invariably found satisfactory by all parties.

The Zemu Valley is richly wooded with conifers and mixed rhododendron scrub. In April the tall red variety is flowering; in order to see the vast number of smaller kinds one must wait till the end of May. On our upward journey we found great snowdrifts lying on the path under the trees; the ground underfoot was often quite hidden by masses of primroses, like the English ones except that they were mauve instead of yellow.

Trees ceased near the snout of the glacier. Beyond that point the whole country lay under snow and at night it was very cold. We followed a trough between the left moraine and the mountainside, making for the "Green Lake" where former parties had camped, opposite the side glacier coming down from Simvu, the mountain that we wished to attempt. In the end, however, we chose another spot about three miles lower down, a sheltered bay that caught all the sun, where a patch of grass had already been thawed clear of snow. The Lachhen men then left us, promising to return when the camp had finally to be struck. We kept on five Sherpas and our old friends Odsung and Djun Singh, who had been with us in Garhwal days. We had only intended to retain four of the Sherpas, but one man called Ang Babu had so set his mind on going up the mountain with us that we had not the heart to send him away. He turned out to be the keenest of them all. He had a monkey-house face, an asset in his chosen part of professional humorist; he kept everyone continually amused with his sallies. At the second camp on Simvu, when we were all feeling fagged after a carry up bad snow, he set to work immediately on arrival and modelled a large snow elephant and then rolled on it, squashing it flat, and pulling a face that set us all laughing helplessly.

At the end of the expedition he was rewarded with the gift of a fine ice-axe.

Weather favoured us for the first few days on the Zemu, which were spent in finding out the lie of the land and in surveying routes up Simvu from neighbouring heights. Two lesser points on the left bank of the glacier were climbed, one evidently a Bavarian peak, judging by the neat masonry of the cairn found on the top, suggestive of German thoroughness. The other peak was new (Point 19,420 feet) and consisted of a pleasant rock ridge, giving out on to a rounded cap of pure ice, with a diminutive crevasse right on the very top. We felt in a hopeful frame of mind, for acclimatization seemed to be proceeding satisfactorily for everyone; this was proved by the absence of signs of distress when walking up to 18,000–19,000 feet and confirmed by certain tests carried out by the doctor.

Optimism about the weather turned out to have been premature, however. After a week, when we were just thinking of making a move towards our mountain, the wind changed its quarter and blue skies disappeared behind blankets of grey mist; this was followed by snow soon after midday, which drove us under cover. Late at night the sky cleared again and hopes revived; but next day brought the same order of changes, and the next day after that; and so it continued till we began to lose count of the days, and passed from a mood of chafing to one of blank resignation. The only useful work that could be done was carrying stores across the glacier and making a dump on the moraine that led up towards Simvu. After that there was nothing to do but to be patient and reflect that if this was purgatory, the Everest party on the other side of the mountains must be having hell – a doubtful consolation.

A protracted period of waiting is trying for the nerves, especially in the case of people of athletic temperament, with much energy to spare. As day after day passed with the same tedious routine of early morning sun, followed by mist and then snow all the afternoon, ending in a tantalizingly clear spell after eight o'clock at night, everyone began to feel the strain of inactivity, which translated itself into a curious sense of guilt, as if we ourselves somehow were to blame for the delay. Our company was an extremely good-tempered one; but a similar experience in a large, ill-assorted party must be most unpleasant.

One morning we had just finished breakfast and were settling down to yet another wasted day when suddenly we noticed that something unusual was happening to the mist across the glacier. A rift opened in the clouds and the graceful Gothic pinnacles and flutings of cathedral-like Siniolchu appeared, glistening against an azure background, a sight which, at that hour of the day, had long been denied us. Then in ten minutes, as if under the stroke of an enchanter's wand, the mists dissolved into nothingness and on every side the peaks stood out clear and sharp against the sunlight. We leaped up, galvanized into instant action. Orders were shouted, lists hastily consulted, kit was packed, and in less than a couple of hours we were ready to start. The porters, in their green windproofs, gathered round a big boulder outside the camp before shouldering their packs and kindled their ritual fire, on which they piled branches of juniper and sweet-smelling azalea, with shouts of *"Hla gyaló!"* ("The Gods conquer!")

I do not propose to give a lengthy description of our attempt on Simvu, nor to tell how we worked our way up the great snow-slopes towards our ridge. Successions of camps, numbered or lettered, are familiar to readers of climbing-books. Their unavoidable repetition can only be compensated by the conquest of the peak. When that is not achieved, it is wiser to cut short that part of the story.

We spent ten days on the mountain, and established three camps, the highest being placed at about 20,000 feet, close to the foot of the north-east ridge. The promise of good conditions on the day we started was not fulfilled, and we reverted to a slightly improved version of the previous weather. The mornings were usually sunny till about eleven; then mists began to swirl over from the south, followed by a cold wind that brought snow in the early afternoon. Thus every day counted but half its normal length in climbing-hours, and this made upward progress extremely slow.

Except on the crest of the ridge itself we never touched good snow. It was always quite soft, even early in the day, so that the carrying of loads and the kicking of steps was a laborious business. We often used to sink up to our thighs in the snow and a good deal of care was required to keep clear of hidden crevasses, for when sounding with an axe one could rarely touch bottom even on safe ground.

From the Upper Simvu Saddle, where we established our principal depot, we saw, through gaps in the mist, an overwhelming panorama of peaks, culminating in the monstrous mass of Kangchhendzönga. To the south, on the other hand,

across the steamy Talung Valley, source of the bad weather, a
sea of trees extended as far as the eye could reach; we knew
that it only ended at Siliguri, on the edge of the Bengal plain,
where passengers for Darjeeling were even then sitting in the
station restaurant consuming their coffee and bacon and eggs.
Looking back, we had before us the terrifying Talung face of
Siniolchu. It looked a most inaccessible mountain and it was a
great surprise to hear, in the autumn of 1936, that it had actually been climbed, by a dangerous route from the Zemu side,
by that most dashing of parties, Paul Bauer and his Bavarians.
The men who climbed Siniolchu certainly earned their glory.

But there was something else that, in the clear hour after
daybreak, drew our gaze even more than that icy spire. To the
left of it, through a distant gap in the mountains, we could just
make out lines of rolling purple hills that seemed to belong to
another world, a world of austere calm, of deserted plateaux
and colourful downs, which made the snowy Himalaya seem
strangely young and assertive. It was a corner of Tibet. My
eyes rested on it with an intensity of longing. I sometimes
wondered whether I should ever be privileged to approach the
vision any closer. Tibet is well guarded, as it should be; nor is
it always easy to distinguish between the genuine seeker after
knowledge and the charlatan or the sensation-monger intent on
"getting into Tibet" merely because of its reputation as a closed
and mysterious land.

The final assault on our peak occupied two days. First we
tried a side of the ridge from a point about 400 feet above our
highest camp, where a steeply inclined snow-slope led through
a breach in the formidable ice defences that ring the mountain. Had the surface of this slope been hard, it would certainly have led us out on to the higher part of the ridge; but
it was found to consist of shallow rotten snow, adhering precariously to a substructure of pure ice, and ready to avalanche
at the slightest provocation. We pushed on as far as we could;
but eventually even the most daring among us voted emphatically for retreat.

Early next morning we explored another line of weakness, a
similar slope starting level with the camp, but it was no safer.
One can deal with pure ice if one has time enough, but that
disintegrating film of snow, ready to part company with its
glassy base at any moment, was more than nerves could stand.
We proceeded to work along the bottom of a quite vertical
curtain of ice cliffs, of the purest white and conspicuously

layered, till we came to the very steep nose of the ridge, which fell away into hazy depths that looked bottomless. I happened to be walking behind when I heard a shout: "Come on quickly! We've found the passage!" I rounded the corner of the cliff and saw that we were close to a comparatively short ice-slope, free from snow, which joined the crest. Everyone put on spiked crampons and I led out on the ice.

We had often, in Switzerland, spent off days practising the making of steps up and down the steep pinnacles of glaciers; but we had never yet been called upon to tackle ice at such a steep angle on an actual mountain. I still remember that slope as one of the most exhilarating bits of climbing of my life. I worked my way in a wide zigzag, out over the abyss, into which the ice-chips went sliding down with a silvery tinkle. I graded my steps with the same unhurried precision that I would have shown on a purely experimental pitch. Not having especially strong arms, I did not try to cut fast, but I was glad to note that accurate aim, with its consequent economy of strokes, was resulting in sufficiently speedy progress. Our long enforced spell of idleness at the base camp had brought about a very complete acclimatization, and we felt a mastery over our movements, without any greater strain than we would have experienced on a Swiss peak. Having cut a long course to the right, I returned on the left tack and suddenly felt the dancing resiliency of the ice give place to a dull "plop," as the head of my axe buried itself in snow. A few steps higher and I stood on the ridge and had plunged the stem of the axe into firm, deep snow. Attached to it by a loop of the rope, I was in a position to hold a whole party. Everyone followed up quickly and then unroped, for before us the ridge extended upwards broad and easy. We felt that the first trying obstacle was behind us and that we could relax a little before tackling the summit ridge some 1,000 feet ahead, which, though it looked jagged, did not suggest insurmountable resistance.

We sat down to lunch in a hollow. Then, without roping, we advanced once more over the next bump. To our amazement we found that we were gazing down into a huge gulf. A crevasse, as broad and deep as a castle moat, cut off all communciation between our part of the ridge and its continuation. Up and down its lip we walked, looking for a bridge, but the harsh truth was not to be charmed away: the upper part of the mountain was cut off from us. It was the very ease of that middle portion of the ridge that had been our undoing. On a narrow ridge such a split would not have appeared. Simvu is a mountain where it is difficult to discover even a speck of bare rock, and its huge massif lies buried under a thick ice-cap which has overrun every rock, like icing squeezed out by the hand of a giant maker of cakes. On the gentler portions of its ridges splits in the ice occur, though not deep enough to expose the rock foundation.

We had no alternative but to retreat. The situation was rather comic: there was no arguing with stark impossibility. We descended to the head of the ice staircase and only took a few minutes to reach the lower slopes again. As we drew near the camp, the first flakes, harbingers of the usual blizzard, began to eddy round us. The rest of the day had to be spent in our sleeping-bags.

A day sufficed for us to clear the upper camp and descend to the Zemu. Tufts of a tiny mauve azalea, the first moraine plant to open to the sun, caught our eye from afar, by sheer brilliance and purity of colour. The spring — and the monsoon — were at hand. That same night we crossed to the base camp and celebrated our defeat by lighting the plum pudding, a festivity to which the Sherpas were also invited. We hid a rupee in it and there was great excitement when one of the porters unearthed it from his slice. The honest fellow, doubting his luck, came round after supper to ask if he was expected to return it.

Had more time been available we should have continued climbing on other peaks; but the weather was showing by unmistakable signs that the season of rains was beginning. Word was therefore sent down to Lachhen to arrange for the collecting of our baggage, while we and the Sherpas enjoyed a brief rest at Tset'hang, a beautiful clearing in the Zemu forest.

Sikkim at the end of May is famous for its rhododendrons. They are of every conceivable size and colour, from tiny white or purple varieties found above the tree line, to showy bushes covered with huge tufts of blossoms, which make up the tangled undergrowth of the woods, and colour the slopes mauve and white or, most wonderful of all, yellow. On the way down from the snout of the glacier we kept discovering fresh species. For variety, the primulas almost equalled them; there were mauve ones, and deep purple, and yellow ones on all the grassy banks. Blue *Meconopsis* poppies were also at their best, but the great yellow poppy that we had been hoping to see was not yet out and only showed as a rosette of leaves. In the forest, festoons of white clematis bound tree to tree.

At Tset'hang we parted company with two of our friends, Cooke and Chapman, who were intending to go up north into the Lhonak Valley and continue climbing. They were joined there by a third friend and, in spite of poor weather, managed, among other things, to make the first ascent of the difficult Fluted Peak.

The last few miles before Lachhen brought more changes in the plants. Among the new kinds of rhododendrons there was one of a fiery scarlet with flowers hanging down like bells. Another species, in its efforts to evade the competition of its neighbours, had ingeniously made its home forty feet above ground, as an epiphyte on old and mossy pine trees, which it adorned with bunches of snow-white flowers. There was an orchid also, on the same pines, called *Pleione*, tinged with a delicate mauve. Bushes of orange azalea flamed round the entrance to the torrent valley.

Sikkim hills in rhododendron-time deserve the epigram that the Mughal Emperor Shah Jahan wrote over the gate of his palace:

"If there be a heaven on earth, it is here, it is here!"

Chapter XI

The Round of Existence

PERHAPS OUR DEFEAT on Simvu was symbolical. We climbed no more peaks of ice and snow on our travels, for we were led into a different world. We became pilgrims of the Tibetan Buddhist Tradition; but before I tell of these adventures of the spirit, it is necessary to explain a few fundamental teachings of the Doctrine, so that those who read of our journeyings may, by understanding the nature of the quest, share in the treasures that are to be found along the Path.*

When any man sets out to expound the principles of one of the great Traditions, the first thing to beware of is any tendency to systematize. Such an explanation should never be oversimplified in the vain hope of bringing it within the effortless comprehension of all men; facile diffusion of an idea can be achieved only to the detriment of its purity. It is not for the Doctrine to abase itself to the common level, but for those who can to exalt themselves to its height. That is why a doctrine spread by organized propaganda is liable to be reduced to a hollow shell, empty of the essentials. The Truth may be likened to a difficult mountain peak, which, though free of access to all mankind, is yet actually scaled by a chosen few, by those who are willing to pay the price in self-discipline, steadfastness, and risk. Though it is no one's private preserve and all have an equal right to possess it, yet all do not attain it simultaneously, for there are those who feel no urge to seek, and those who suffer from vacillation, doubting whether the quest is worth the trouble. Others again must measure painfully every step on the Path, inch by inch, over an indefinitely protracted period of effort. A few rare souls find it possible, like Mila Repa, by

---

* For a more general account of the Buddhist doctrine the reader is advised to consult A. K. Coomaraswamy: *Hinduism and Buddhism* (New York: Philosophical Library; 1943). This exposition is masterly in its conciseness and can be accepted as perfectly accurate both factually and traditionally (which cannot be said of most books in European languages); the same applies to the section dealing with the parent tradition of Hinduism.

supreme concentration, to compress into one the several stages that ordinary flesh and blood must needs take successively. That road is known to the Tibetans as the "Direct Path"; but it is not for faint hearts to think of braving its perils.

It is therefore not without misgiving that I have decided to include the present chapter; for I may, in spite of these warnings, be luring someone into rash generalizations, not warranted by these gleanings from my own elementary knowledge. Nevertheless, it seems imperative for me to try to clear up certain basic ideas; otherwise many of the illuminating talks that I had with the lamas may not be fully understood, since terms will have to be used and references made that are unfamiliar to the reader though common knowledge among Tibetans. More than that, there is no phase of Tibetan life which is not pervaded by the subtle influence of the Doctrine, as by an ether; the whole Tibetan picture must be viewed in that light for it to become intelligible. What I wish to do for my reader is to help him to place himself, as far as possible, at the same viewpoint as a Tibetan, so that allusions to the traditional doctrines, whether explicitly made or only implied, may not fall on his ears as on those of a merely curious onlooker.

One minor point must be stressed. It should be understood that I have had no first-hand contact with Buddhism except in its Tibetan form. When I speak of the Doctrine, I mean the tradition that has come down through the Lamas. Of other schools, such as the Southern School of Ceylon, I know little, and that little is taken from books.

It is not unusual for European writers to reproach the Northern School, which includes Japan and China as well as Tibet, with being "impure," because it has incorporated elements from other traditions. The Tibetans have been greatly beholden to Shivaite Hinduism; it is from there that the Tantrik doctrines, a favourite target for abuse, derive. Students who approach every question mainly from a historical angle are given to overstressing the importance of "primitiveness" in estimating the validity of a doctrine. If doubt is cast on the antiquity or on the exact authorship of a certain saying, its claim to embody authentic teachings is thereby held to have been exploded. Historical research can assuredly throw useful light on the background against which the teachings were unfolded; but it can never furnish the test by which their authority stands or falls. The origin of a doctrine or the historical personality of its author is a trifling matter compared with its truth.

If some of the profound metaphysical teachings of the Tibetan Tradition are historically traceable to a Hindu origin, that in no wise invalidates them. The power of drawing on any and every source for the illustration of the Doctrine, and of pressing the most unlikely tools into its service, constitutes the "Note" of Catholicity, which unites all the authentic Traditions. However widely separated may be their viewpoints, there resides, under what at a superficial glance may seem like irreconcilable differences, one and the same metaphysical knowledge, which is allowed to clothe itself at will in whatever guise best suits its immediate purposes, without yielding up one jot of its reality or one tittle of authority.

On page 128 is a picture of the conventional representation of the doctrine of the Round or Wheel of Existence, as displayed in the porch of every Tibetan temple. It is said to have been first drawn by the Buddha Himself in rice grains on the ground, and it was one of the very earliest lessons that He communicated to His disciples. Readers will find it helpful to refer to the picture frequently, for it is essential to familiarize oneself with this fundamental theme.

The Wheel consists of a circle subdivided into six sectors, with a small concentric circle in the centre and another of wider diameter outside, so that a continuous border runs round the main circle. The whole is a diagrammatic scheme of the principle of Existence, whereby it is not conceived as a single episode in Time, affecting a basically fixed individuality and finally determining the future status of the being concerned, but is viewed as a connected series of changes, a continual passage from one state into the next, without a single one of the participating elements remaining exempt from modification. Man is but one of an indefinite number of states of the being. His earthly life is but one episode among many others. No special importance distinguishes the human state from the others, though it is legitimate to treat it as a mean from man's own point of view, seeing that he is situated therein by definition and cannot escape viewing all other beings in relation to it. Therefore it is just for us, and for us only, to call any other being which, compared to Man, is less limited in its possibilities "superior," just as the converse holds good for "inferior" beings which, in comparison with Man, are hedged in by narrower limitations. Thus a passing into one of the former or higher states may also be called an ascendant movement, while the exchanging of the human state for one of the lower degrees can be described as a degeneration or fall.

The agent which keeps the Round moving, ringing the changes between various states of Existence, is the force of Action. Its well-known Indian name of *Karman* means nothing else; it is wrong to translate it as law of Cause and Effect, or

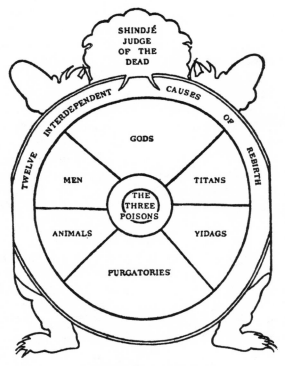

The Round of Existence

Fate, though the two notions are closely connected. It is the play of complex activities that introduces the incessant modifications into every being, and it is legitimate to say that no existence preserves its identity for two successive moments: change in one part entails corresponding variations in all the others. There is nothing but ebb and flow, continual reshuffling of the cards, continual Becoming.

A circle is well chosen as the symbol of this unending process. The Wheel is in a way a misnomer, for when a wheel turns, it is as one solid whole, whereas in the Round it is the contents that remain in motion, a tangle of orbits entering at every moment into new permutations, as the Existences, planet-like, collide, split, cohere, grow, or dissolve. A whirlpool is perhaps the best simile of any.

The Round is described as of indefinite extension, reaching backward into the impenetrable dimness of the past and, in default of Deliverance — that is, of an interruption in the Action that provides the motive power — extending equally relentlessly into the future. The question of Deliverance will be discussed later, however. As the Round includes the state of existence in which we are situated ourselves here and now, it calls for detailed consideration before we turn our attention elsewhere.

The flux of endless change involves each being in accessions of strength and onsettings of weakness, entries into stages marked enough to receive a new name, and exits from previous states; these are what we call youth and age, birth and death. They are signposts, imaginary but convenient points of division in a process that, nevertheless, remains fluid and uninterrupted. So we live out our lives, as corks, playthings of the waves on the ocean of Possibility, or as pebbles ground against one another under the poundings and buffetings of Action's unceasing tide.

We must now consider Action under some of its aspects. It comprises a great deal more than the manifestations that we normally call acts, attributable to beings in virtue of their individual existence. First there is Cosmic Activity, the sum total of effects (themselves already on the way to becoming new Causes) of all the Causes that have occurred throughout the Universe. These include effects of Will, recognizable as such, and the interplay of so-called inanimate forces. Then there is Localized Action, bound up with the conditions that prevail in any subdivision of the Universe considered separately. There is also Racial Action, the united causes and effects definable as Heredity. Finally, there is Personal Action, individual acts and thoughts, with their chains of results. Any one of the many series of causes and effects can be discussed in isolation; but in reality they are all contributors to the General or Cosmic Activity and have no proper existence outside it.

The effects of Action on a given being may be direct, or indirect and produced by unsuspected causes at the other extremity of the world. No series develops in a continuous line like a bundle of endlessly extensile threads: it forms part of a network, throwing out filaments and gathering them in from all directions, beyond hope of unravelling.

Every activity is the result of previous activity, or activities, and bears in it the seeds of future ones. This is one of the fundamental postulates of the Buddhists, summed up in the sentence: "Every effect springs from a cause." Creation, if taken in the sense of something expressly fashioned out of nothing on a certain occasion, is foreign to their ideas. They will admit indefinite combinations and dissociations, changes advantageous or harmful, simplifications or increases of complexity, but never out of relation with the general idea of causality. All that is, whatever its nature, can be referred back to causes in the indefinite past and points forward to effects in the indefinite future. It follows from this that nothing can fail to produce some effect or other, since the merest thought, devoid of observable results, does introduce instant and inescapable modifications in the general Activity of the whole world. This doctrine will be found to have important ethical implications, since it does away with the possibility of a totally ineffective action. No right action, however quixotic it may seem, can be called useless; no foolish action can be excused as harmless. Every activity, be it the most trivial or apparently purposeless, sets in motion, as cause, a new series of effects, which even if they are incalculable to us, are none the less strictly determined.

If the Round depends on Action, Action viewed as a whole is the product of Desire. Every being, even the most inert, must be credited with some form of Will. Attachment or repulsion, which are the same thing viewed under two aspects, are inherent to all existence. Volition may be conscious or reflex or so faintly energetic as hardly to be recognizable for Will; but some response to the impacts of other Existences is there all the same. In a conscious being, attachment is the aspiration after pleasant experience and its repetition, repulsion the avoidance of the unpleasant and of its recurrence. Each attempt to catch and hold and repeat the former produces a new chain of Action; so does every endeavour to change painful or disadvantageous experience; and so the Round goes on turning.

But the argument can be carried back another stage. What is it that prompts Desire or Attachment? This is declared to be none other than Ignorance, the want of realization of what things really are and how they really work. If the search for the pleasant and the shunning of the disagreeable only results in going round in a circle, if the action planned to that end as a result of those desires is not, in fact, calculated to yield the results aimed at, then that action of seeking and shunning is unreasonable, based upon false information, on a failure to fathom the mechanism of the Universe. It deserves the epithet "ignorant." Were true Knowledge to be present, assuredly a totally different method would have to be followed and with quite different ends in view. No one, in that case, would go on doing exactly those things which were bound to perpetuate his wandering in the Round; he would devote his energies rather to *Undoing.* Therefore so long as Ignorance, unawareness of the true constitution of the World and of oneself, persists, so long must be postponed any hope of breaking the Vicious Circle. Obstinate attempts to cure disastrous Activity by still more Activity, Desire by fresh Desire, are as futile as the babblings of those who would make War to end War or cast out devils in the name of Beelzebub.

"By Action men enjoy happiness," says the book called *Great Liberation,* "and by Action again they suffer pain. They are born, they live, and they die slaves of Action. . . . As a man is bound, be it by a gold or an iron chain, so he is bound by his Action, be it good or evil." It must never be forgotten that the Action referred to is always associated with some degree of Ignorance. Everything can be changed by real Knowledge.

Activity and War have something in common; both are largely remedial in intention. If there is nothing to be set to rights, no livelihood to be gained, no want to be supplied, no loss to be made up, then there can be no incentive towards action, even the most creative and altruistic action. The fiddle that is guaranteed to play eternally in tune does not require any turning of pegs. Peace or Harmony belongs to Non-Activity. The cessation of action will result in peace; but how is such a pacification to be brought to pass? So long as Ignorance is still there, it must remain a dream; there is no cheating the inexorable law inherent in the very nature of things. Ignorance, teeming womb of Desire and Action, supplies the power that keeps the wheels turning, as in a factory where the machinery must never be allowed to stop by day or night. All else depends on this: were Ignorance to be interrupted for a second, the Round would automatically come to rest.

The world passeth away and the lust thereof.

We must now return to the examination of the diagram of the Round of Existence. We have already noticed that there are six compartments, corresponding to six groupings or classes of beings. The number is arbitrary: it should really be indefinite, for they merge into one another imperceptibly; the classification is a mere matter of convenience, a symbol. Attention must be drawn to one omission. All the six classes that we are about to name can be termed Animate beings. Ought not inanimate existences such as stones or air to occupy a class also? Logically speaking they should, for no sharp boundary is really admissible; but those who devised this symbolism for popular use, like their colleagues of other faiths, gave most of their attention to those beings that showed affinity with the human, and treated all that was inorganic, and even plants, as so much furniture. Nevertheless, they ought to recognize the omission; though I once had difficulty in getting a lama to admit that plants were alive in the same way as animals. This slight crudeness is in the iconography, not in the theory. That the more profound thinkers were in no two minds about the essential Oneness of everything can be proved by a quotation from a Japanese sage who declared that "the very mountains can become Buddha."

The six classes are named respectively:

1. Gods
2. Non-Gods or Titans $\Big\}$ higher than man
3. Man
4. Animals
5. *Yidags* or tantalized ghosts
6. Tormented beings in the purgatories, including devils $\Bigg\}$ lower than man

Popular belief, which, all the world over, tends to a literal interpretation of the external symbol and to an overlooking of the principle symbolized, makes of these six classes so many closed realms, entered by successive individual rebirths. Similarly, it has read into the Universal law of Causality a law of Retributive Justice and turned those effects which flow from Action as its unavoidable continuation — a fruit inherent in the seed — into so many moral sanctions punishing the wicked, and so many rewards earned by the merits of the virtuous, on a basis of a strictly kept profit-and-loss account. This is the commonest attitude everywhere; but it need not imply that the symbolism fails in its purpose. As was said before, it is for those who can to raise themselves to the heights of the Doctrine. Symbolism is the ladder and some may never climb farther than its lowest rungs. But the other rungs are all there, in proper succession, so that the climber may pass, according to capacity, from what is crudely external, through stages where the spiritual is half seen, till he rises to the height where the Doctrine will dawn on him in its universal applicability.

For the ordinary man the abode of gods is a delightful kingdom into which suffering does not penetrate and where all wishes — and whims — will be gratified. Thousands pray for rebirth in that sphere and look no farther. They are content to enjoy its pleasures — while they last. As with us, the heavenly scene may be spiritualized or gross, according to each person's mental development; but in any case it is an *individual* enjoyment that is imagined, as in our own popular conceptions of paradise — that is to say, an enjoyment which is the fruit of Desire and in which Ignorance continues to play its part. Such joys, therefore, contain all the elements that perpetuate the Round, which will, in due course, bring back change and pain.

A word should be said about the use of the name "gods," since it is liable to cause misunderstanding. The gods here referred to are not immortal and self-sufficient deities, but simply beings occupying a degree higher than ours, possessed of wider powers than man's, such as longevity, unfading beauty, and freedom from pain, except at the last when they are about to cease from being gods and turn into something lower; for then their charms begin to wither and their fragrance turns to stench so foul that their goddess-wives flee from their presence. Such gods as set their minds on nothing but pleasure and feel no incentive to listen to the Doctrine will come to a miserable end. When they suddenly become aware of the danger, it is too late. Confused by the Ignorance that they have done nothing to diminish, they flounder helplessly and fall even into hell. "Many long-lived gods are fools," said a lama to me. One cannot help comparing this with *Paradise Lost*, where Milton makes Lucifer, after his fall, deteriorate by imperceptible degrees from a divinity, still endowed with personal beauty, a noble address, and courage of a heroic order, until he turns into Satan, repulsive, crafty, wholly evil. These changes are not punishments imposed on him by a sentence of the Divine Judge, so much as self-imposed consequences, fruits of his own wrong-headedness or, as the Buddhist would say, of his own Ignorance.

It would have saved some confusion if we could have called these gods "supermen" or "angels" or some such name. Technically speaking, they should have their full denomination of "Gods of the Round" (to worship whom is idolatry), in order to distinguish them from true Divinities, those who are free of the Round, Buddhas, and high degrees on the road to Buddhahood; but in common speech Tibetans employ the same word, *Hla*, to denote both kinds, leaving the context to explain itself.

Non-gods are another sort of supermen, more powerful than ourselves, but portrayed as warlike and ambitious, discontented with their many advantages because they envy the superior felicity of the gods. Titans is a good name for them.

Next comes mankind, occupying but a small number of places among the innumerable existences of the Round. Man, though he possesses no privilege over the others, is naturally of special interest to us as men. Likewise a cockroach, in drawing the Round, would doubtless have created a special class for cockroaches, probably including man in one of the other sections. Man is spoken of as an enviable state, and many are those whose aspirations do not go beyond a hope of rebirth into a world of men. It is claimed that man's life is, on the whole, a fairly happy blend of joy and pain: not enough joy to dull the senses, as is apt to happen to the gods, and not so much pain as to induce perpetual self-pity, as occurs in hell; both of them fatal distractions from the problem of looking for a way of escape from the Round.

Animals, the fourth class, are creatures for whom the gaining of their daily food is a dominant care, so that they have little leisure to spare for higher things. Their intelligence, too, operates as a rule within a restricted circle. They are objects of pity, because generally they cannot live without preying on one another, a characteristic that they share to some extent with Man. Animal life is therefore counted as the most tolerable among the states called "sorrowful," because the margin for modifying such existence in a favourable sense is necessarily narrow.

Yidags or tantalized ghosts are beings in whom Desire has taken the upper hand. They are pictured as having huge bellies, but pinpoint mouths, so that though their hunger is insatiable, their power of satisfying it is minute. When they drink, the water turns to liquid fire inside them; when they eat, the food swells like undercooked rice and brings on an acute colic. Under this imagery we see a state of Desire so overweening that every attempt to pander to it only serves to make its pangs more consciously felt. One lama, who was telling me about the *Yidags,* said that sometimes they see a refreshing spring or a table set for a feast and hasten towards it, but just as they are about to seize the food, guardians appear, harpy-like, before them, armed with swords, spears, bows and arrows, and rifles — a delightful modern touch — and drive them back. People often perform a rather touching rite and consecrate some morsel of their own food for the benefit of the poor *Yidags.* A special prayer is said over the offering which is designed to counteract any painful results.

Lastly come the purgatories, both hot and cold; to call them hells is really a misnomer, because that word, to the Westerner, denotes a hopeless state, without a chance of eventual escape; whereas in the Buddhist view, torments, however prolonged, must surely, by a turn of the Wheel, when the effects of their evil causes have played themselves out, give place to some other kind of existence, as surely as the paradise of gods will also be exchanged for a less happy state. Inmates of the purgatories are not deemed incapable of good impulses, and even devils — that is to say, beings who have sunk into a state of utmost malignancy — are able to rise in course of time.

To the eye that troubles to look farther than the symbols, all these states are simply corollaries of various sorts of activity. He in whom Desire has become an overmastering passion sees all things in the light of his desire; for him the World is as *Yidags* see it. To the being who has given way to hatred, all the world is spiteful; what is a pleasure to others becomes his torment, and the whole Universe transforms itself into a hell. Man is a comparatively balanced state, with some surplus energy left, after satisfying physical needs, for paying attention to wiser counsels. But men, in this respect, must again be subdivided; for many are forced to lead lives in which the available surplus of free attention is reduced to a minimum. Their lot must be considered unfortunate beside that of their less enslaved neighbours. Rebirth in the humblest station in Tibet offers fuller possibilities than life in a factory town of Europe or America, or even life in the manager's office of a great firm. In hell, suffering is so intense as to leave little time for serious recollection; only by an exceptional effort can a being rise above the distractions of that dreadful environment. Gods, as we have seen, just because of the evenness of their life, are in danger of being lulled into unawareness, till one day their stock

of merit becomes exhausted and a change for the worse super-
venes, an exact reflection of their general condition at the time,
so that they may sink as low as hell itself.

So turns and turns the Round of Rebirth and Redeath. Suffering is inseparable from its process, for some of its classes
are wedded to suffering by definition, and the others are ever
dogged by it, as their cherished happiness ages and fades, or as
change and death remove from them the objects of their love
— friends, possessions, one after another. Even in one's day
of health one knows, beyond question, that deterioration and
disease, if nothing worse, are lying in wait.

> All that liveth impaireth fast.

Even the hope permitted to the damned is only a palliative,
not a cure. If relief is gained for a time, yet the disease will,
of a surety, recur some day. In the Round, real bliss is impossible; to seek it therein is self-deception. Our hope of heaven,
the reward for well-doing to be enjoyed by individuals, as it is
usually conceived, leads into the paradise of gods, but not to
real freedom. The ruler of the Round is disappointment; each
of its so-called joys bears within itself the seeds of insecurity,
separation, and sorrow.

Everyone has, at some time or other, in a moment of extreme
well-being, in the contemplation of a sunset over an estuary,
or while sitting silently beside a chosen friend, experienced that
peculiar pang which is inseparable from intense joy, a drop of
gall distilled into its honey. It is as if one were striving to hold
up Time, to keep the vision immovable for just one moment;
but even in the hour of rapture, in our innermost heart we feel
its beauty slipping away, leaving us bereft. It is the pain of
"Joy, whose hand is ever at his lips bidding adieu."

This brings us to Suffering, the real starting-point of the
Buddha's teaching. The Tibetan books mention two kinds of
suffering, to both of which I have alluded already. There is
the Pain of the Round, found in the purgatories and the land of
Yidags, and in the disease and death that afflict animals and
men, and there is also the Pain of Happiness, the regrets
brought on by change, the turning of youth into old age, of
health into infirmity, the separation that brings friendships to
their close, the dreariness that succeeds to a joy that is gone
over.

SUFFERING is the FIRST of the FOUR TRUTHS or Pointers in
which is summed up the message of the Buddha, His invitation

to seek something less ineffective than the transient rewards of the Round. Suffering is the beginning of His whole argument, chosen because it is a truth that none could think of denying, that calls for no act of faith, since it is seen and experienced in the world around. The Buddhists make no attempt to explain it away by poetical sophistries, or to neutralize it by offering compensations in another life. They regard it as inseparable from all states of existence, a thing not to be fled from but to be faced, here and everywhere. But the important thing is to discover the proper means, if such exist. The remedial activities of the Round are clearly inadequate. Buddhism is primarily a war on suffering, not on its symptoms but on its causes. When a disease has to be diagnosed, what must the good physician do first of all? He must find a cause for the symptoms. Till this is done he cannot treat the disease. What is the cause of suffering? The cause of suffering and the cause of the Round are identical, Ignorance, which leads to ignorant Desire and ignorant Action. Already the SECOND TRUTH or Pointer is discovered. THE CAUSE OF SUFFERING is IGNORANCE.

Ignorance of what? Ignorance of the real nature of things, a mistaken notion of ourselves and our relation to other beings. It is more than an absence of correct belief; it is something entrenched in our nature that must be eliminated and replaced with Knowledge. Mere study is of no avail; there must be realization, bringing about a radical and *irreversible* change in the being. It is not a question of Faith in certain propositions.

Understanding both the illness and its cause, the doctor reassures his patient: the illness is not incurable. This, incidentally, disposes of the rather silly accusation that Buddhism is "pessimistic," as if such words as "optimism" and "pessimism" have any meaning in an investigation of the Truth. As René Guénon has said: "Truth does not need to be comforting; if some have found it so, so much the better for them." Nevertheless, though there are good grounds for hope, the treatment is not easy and must be carried out by the patient himself, who is apt to be his own worst enemy. The THIRD TRUTH or Pointer is discovered, the SUPPRESSION OF SUFFERING; that is our aim and that aim is possible of achievement.

Now it only remains to find the remedy; that is to say the FOURTH TRUTH, the WAY LEADING TO A SUPPRESSION OF SUFFERING. The Buddha tells us what it is. If Ignorance is the cause of suffering, then the opposite, AWARENESS, is the remedy. Ignorance cannot live in the same heart as real Knowledge. Recognize the latter and Ignorance will have been severed at the root. Without Ignorance ignorant desires no longer can arise, nor the Action loosed by them. When useless activity is stopped, the Wheel is deprived of its motive power and stops turning. Action is no longer needed when once the harmony of Knowledge has been achieved. In real Knowledge there can be no action, because there is nothing to change or to improve. Change and imperfection go hand in hand. Once Enlightenment has been attained, the Wheel of Change comes to rest in Eternity, in which there is no action and no rebirth or death. Action breeds action indefinitely. Enlightenment breeds Enlightenment eternally.

The Four Truths are the quintessence of the Doctrine: all else that may be said or written is only a commentary upon them. It is good to reiterate them in order to fix them in the mind:

1. Suffering
2. Cause of Suffering } Diagnosis
3. Suppression of Suffering
4. Way leading to a Suppression } Cure
   of Suffering

Let us now return to the picture and look at the little circle in the middle of the Round. It contains three animals:

A pig typifying Ignorance
A cock typifying Desire-Attachment (To define this as
   Lust alone, as is often done, is to miss the meaning completely.)
A snake typifying Anger

These three, commonly spoken of as the Three Poisons, are the basic evils to which all others can be reduced. In reality Ignorance is the only fundamental vice, for neither of the other two could occur without it. It always accompanies their every manifestation, and their chief result is a renewal of Ignorance. The immense stress laid on the duty of combating Ignorance distinguishes Hindus and Buddhists from Christians. Not that this theory does not also hold good for Christianity; but in practice there has been a great difference of emphasis. Charity, the central Christian virtue, is regarded by the Indian Traditions as the natural consequence of Knowledge. There are comparatively few overt allusions to Knowledge in the Gospels, though the implications are there all the same.

FIRST CAMP ON SIMVU *See page* 120

THE ROUND OF EXISTENCE *See Chapter XI*

ASSEMBLY OF BUDDHAS   *See Chapter XI*
Every gesture has a symbolical meaning

THE BUDDHA *See pages 136–8*
"I only teach two things, O disciples: suffering and release from suffering."

THE GREAT HERMIT THE ABBOT OF LACHHEN *See pages 114–16*

THE ABBOT MOUNTS HIS HORSE

"Om Mani Padme Hum"   *See page 161*

Eremurus in the Alp of Nimarg   *See page 196*

TISTA FOREST *See page* 111

Ignorance is much more than mere lack of information on this or that subject. It includes every kind of sin against the Light, not only false beliefs, but unawareness, loose thinking, woolly-mindedness, obscurantism, and, above all, indifference to knowledge, neglect of the duty of trying to be truthful and intelligent; a life organized in such a manner as to produce constant distractions, dishonest stifling of doubts, doubt as to the necessity of seeking knowledge at all, neglect of opportunities of listening to those who have a doctrine to teach – all these things fall within the scope of Ignorance. The pursuit of Truth must not be left to chance. No number of charitable actions can be a substitute for that primary need. So-called altruistic actions, if uninformed, are not quite what they purport to be. In so far as they are founded on false premises they remain ignorant actions and bring forth some of the fruits of ignorance. You cannot gather figs from thistles. Nor is mere Innocence, due to lack of opportunity rather than to a clear appreciation of the issues, accepted as a sufficient passport to heaven; indeed, if it were so, the greatest blessing that one could wish for a human being would be death in infancy, before the child could experience a temptation to sin, and Herod should be acclaimed as the special benefactor of innocent children. Similarly, sincerity of motive, which is so often stressed among us here, is counted as no palliative for wrong action. The evil, in that case, is the expression of the innermost nature of the agent. Evil resides not so much in an act as in the state of mind that makes the act possible. If the Ignorance of an evil-doer is invincible and he is thereby relieved from doubt, that is a matter for regret, since it holds out little promise of a change for the better. A hesitating sinner, whose conscience is alive, is far preferable to one who is misnamed a sincere, but mistaken, doer.

The second poison, Desire-Attachment, which includes repulsion, is taken in a much more radical sense than mere egotism. An *impulse to individual experience* is the nearest definition I can offer: it has sometimes been expressed by the one terrible word "Thirst." This trait must be taken as appertaining in some degree to all things, though one commonly treats it as if it were only synonymous with conscious volition as found in sentient beings. That is the form in which Desire interests us most directly; but it would be a great mistake to lose sight of its general applicability to the whole of Creation. If we turn to the special case of Egotism, a sharp cleavage is to be noted between the usual Christian conception and that of the Buddhists. In the former it is taken for an overstressing of one's own importance, an arrogation of rights outside one's just limits, with a consequent invasion of the rights of others. Nowadays it tends to become more narrowly restricted to its social applications. The vice is then regarded as springing from an excess of a supposedly legitimate feeling of individuality. But the Buddhist argues that when we confine our condemnation to the examples cited, we are still treating symptoms only. The roots of Attachment lie deeper still, in the centring of attention in an individual self as such, and in the attribution to it of reality, of permanence, and of the rights consequent upon those qualities. Self-denial, for the Buddhist, is literally a denial of self. The separateness that is ascribed to the "ego" is the error. "He is the rogue who playeth every sort of trick," and his Action, which, to our eyes, seems like an independent development *in* the Universe, not *of* the Universe, keeps up a false relation of dualism between the self and what lies outside it. So are engendered the concepts "myself and others."

A Tibetan work, the *Powerful Good Wish*, says: "Immersed in ignorance and obscured by delusion, the Knower (Mind) was afeared and confused. Then came the idea 'I' and 'Other' and hatred. As these gained force a continuous chain of Action (*Karman*) was produced. The Root Ignorance is the abyssal ground of the knower's unconscious Ignorance. The other Ignorance is that which regards self and others to be different and separate. The thought that regards beings as 'two' begets a hesitating, doubting state. A subtle feeling of Attachment arises, which, if allowed to gain force, gradually resolves itself into strong attachment and a craving for food, clothing, dwellings, wealth, and friends. . . . There is no end to the Action flowing from ideas of dualism."

This duality is denied by both Hindus and Buddhists; but their expression of the doctrine takes somewhat different forms and has given rise to long discussions. The Buddhists, in particular, never tire of inveighing against the belief that the "myself" constitutes a true or permanent entity. For them the so-called individual is a bundle of activities, joining and dissolving, and passing into other activities. They do not, of course, contradict the obvious fact of some sort of quasi-individual existence within the phenomenal world of the Round. That would be absurd. But they deny its reality, saying that once its components are dissociated, the individuality also ceases to be, since no single one of those components has the right to act as its nucleus or to continue to bear its name. Selfishness is therefore more than an abuse of legitimate rights; it is an ignorant arrogation of reality to the "ego." What *we* call selfish is but a secondary product. So long as a craving for individual enjoyment and individual reward persists, so long is the root of selfishness kept alive, nourished by mistaken notions of "self." The Christian heaven, as popularly conceived, in which "I" is rewarded and preserved in perpetuity, is, according to the Buddhist doctrine, only a temporary state: its beatitude cannot be anything else, for in spite of good acts the root error is still present, and it offers no more than a provisional salvation.

Many parables have been used to express the Buddhist doctrine of non-individuality. I have taken upon myself to invent my own simile, after the traditional style, which, I think, expresses the idea satisfactorily. The nature of a man or other being may be likened to a river of which the source is undiscovered. Activity is the water. As the river flows along seeking the sea, several tributaries, from tiny brooks to quite big streams, come in to swell its waters. The farmers along its banks have dug irrigation channels and drain some water off and spread it over the land. The Government, under a big inland waterways scheme, has also opened up canals joining the river to other river systems, flowing towards different seas. Part of its course takes it through hot desert, where evaporation is high. In summer the river becomes shallow and broken up into channels. In the rains it swells with the drainage of a huge area. Along its banks stand several modern manufacturing towns, which allow their sewage and all sorts of polluting chemicals to enter the stream. Close to its mouth it becomes a tidal estuary, and the water is brackish. Some of the water of the sea and of the river itself is evaporated and comes down in rain all over the land and into other rivers and lakes, and falls as snow on the mountains where is born the river's unknown parent glacier. The river exists: no one could deny that. Geographers give it a name and draw it on their maps. But which part of the water has the right to say: "I was and still am the river"? The river's existence is undeniable, but the phenomenon of its individuality cannot be called real.

Thirdly comes Anger. Here again we find a slight difference from the common Western notions of anger. When Christ denounced uncharitableness as the deadliest sin, Anger, driven from its first line of defence, entrenched itself behind the question of motive, and assumed a new name under which it hoped to remain unrecognizable. This was Moral Indignation, anger rightly directed, as it is supposed to be, in which case the violence is held to be respectable. The toleration of anger under this disguise has ended by making the Christian teachings of mercy and non-retaliation almost a dead letter; for self-righteous people never fail to find an excuse to justify their resentment against those who, as they say, have not harmed them personally, but have injured other people, whom it is their duty to protect. It is considered unnecessary that such giving of protection should be a coldly thought-out, passionless act, undertaken with a view to serving in the appropriate way the higher interests of both aggressor and victim. On the contrary, all the sentiments of hatred, pent up as a result of the Christian veto upon them, have been able to find channels where they are allowed unrestricted scope. The Buddhists never recognized such a compromise. Anger, whatever its motives, remained anger in their eyes. When people showed hatred and violence, as men do everywhere, at least they were not to be allowed a loophole for self-deception. Hatred in a righteous cause should, logically, be regarded as more heinous than that prompted by pure selfishness, of which anger is, after all, but a natural expression. To degrade the service of Righteousness with such a weapon verges on sacrilege. If the judge must chastise, he must be a judge who weighs up all the evidence, and pronounces an unimpassioned sentence according to the law, free from Ignorance. If the reformer feels called on to fight an abuse, he must never forget that the cruelty of the tyrant is as worthy of pity as the groans of his victims. Moral Indignation is the subtlest form of Anger, which should not even be directed against Satan himself, for he too can become an object of compassion. Our hatred for him is the seal of his kingdom upon our foreheads. So long as the hatred of Satan is allowed to be an exception to the general law of Charity, so long will hatred continue to flourish in human hearts. Moreover it is but a step from hating Satan to hating evil-doers. If Satan is considered as being incapable of redemption, it follows that we ought not to desire his enlightenment, for it would be contrary to the Divine Order. The Buddhist rejects the idea that any single being is unalterably evil, any more than unalterably good. Good and Evil, belonging as they do to dualistic thinking (though valid at their own level), must alike be transcended before one can begin to speak of Knowledge in the absolute sense.

While I was writing these pages, an acquaintance with whom I had been discussing the alarms of the political situation in Europe made the remark, half approvingly — so I thought — and half doubtedly: "I see you take a very detached view of it all, as if you stood apart. But does that not prevent you from getting anything done? Can we really avoid attaching ourselves to a cause, or a party, and putting our enthusiasm into it, shutting our eyes to everything but the main issue?" There seems no valid reason why the detached person, the philosopher in the primitive sense of "lover of wisdom," should be any less capable of effective action than his more passionate neighbour. On the contrary, in so far as with him opinions are opinions — that is, based on all ascertainable evidence — and judgments are judgments — that is, formed after hearing both sides without prejudice — so also this same philosopher's action ought to be intelligent action, not a mixed bag of elements germane to his purpose, together with many irrelevant factors thrown in. The demands of this impartial approach to life are too exacting for it to make an instantaneous appeal. The plausible security of a label is dear to the slothful, whose passionate loyalties often mask an innate passivity of outlook. In any case, one must remember that visible results count for comparatively little. The fruits of Action cannot escape ripening somewhere, some time. There are no such things as fruitless actions; though they may be temporarily lost from sight, they will be stored in the aggregate of Cosmic Activity and will, beyond all question, become causes in their turn. I have mentioned this example, which is my own and not derived from a lama, to show the sort of way in which the general law of Action applies to a given problem. The partisan way of life exemplifies the action of the Three Poisons better than anything else. The root is Ignorance, evinced in an unwillingness to weigh up a question fairly, and in a readiness to allow the will to conform to a so-called opinion, based on evidence selected by methods that would not be followed by a genuine investigator unswayed by sentiment. Above all, in the anxiety not to weaken one's own devotion to the chosen cause, one becomes *indifferent* to accuracy, even more than a deliberate falsifier of facts. The latter state only follows on the former. Anger is represented by detestation of the opposition; this is true irrespective of the rightness or

wrongness of our cause. But it is Desire-Attachment in this case
that incites us and forms the substance of our loyalties and
readiness for self-sacrifice. From a Buddhist point of view the
whole business is corrupt through and through. The same ought
to hold good no less from a Christian point of view, were it not
for the fact that many of the Christian churches have been only
too willing to make things easy for those who actually treat
Attachment and Indignation-Anger as things worthy of encouragement and who, for the sake of obtaining speedy results, are
willing to resort to the demagogue's appeal to Ignorance.

Every poison has its appropriate antidote. For Ignorance the
antidote is Knowledge, Just Views, Awareness. For Desire-
Attachment the antidote is Non-Attachment, including abandonment of ignorant belief in a permanent individual self. For
Anger the antidote is loving-kindness and a consistent refusal
to inflict suffering.

Love, Charity, or Compassion is the first-fruit of Knowledge.
We have seen how, in spite of moments of pleasurable delusion, life in the Round is lamentable. All find themselves in the
same quandary, from the most carefree of gods to the most tor-
tured of fiends. No one is favoured; to each one comes his turn.
This, logically, makes us all fellows in distress: there is not
one corner of the Universe undeserving of pity. Whoever stops
to contemplate the crowds frantically chasing the will-o'-the-
wisp of happiness, or falling over one another as they turn and
flee from a suffering that they believe to be external to themselves, cannot but be seized with boundless compassion.

"That which makes one weep," said St. Marpa, "is the
thought that all creatures could be Buddha, that they know
it not and die suffering. . . . If that is what you are weeping about, you should go on ever weeping without pause." So,
also, wrote a Chinese sage: "With an understanding of the
impermanent nature of all things, devoid of reality in themselves and subject to pain, rises the sun of true wisdom. . . .
Go on with hearts overflowing with compassion; in this world
that is rent by suffering be instructors and wherever the darkness of Ignorance may happen to reign, kindle there a torch."

There is a close connexion between the idea of Compassion
and the teaching on the subject of "self-naughting." Mila Repa
expounds this truth in three lines of one of this poems:

The notion of emptiness (absence of real self) engenders
    Compassion,

Compassion does away with the distinction between "self and other,"

The indistinction of self and other renders the service of others effective.

His sequence of thought is not immediately evident and requires elaboration. His meaning is that once a being is aware of the impermanence of individuality he is brought to the recognition of his oneness with everything that before had falsely appeared to be external to himself. Their sufferings become his sufferings; their liberation becomes identified with his own; his service to others is no longer one-sided generosity, for the distinction between giver and receiver is no more. The Buddhist Tradition denies to "the Ego" any vestige of permanence and refuses to recognize the real existence of a central thread of individuality on which the various qualities of body and mind are strung like beads. It declares repeatedly that the so-called individual soul is but an aggregate, temporary, changing, and devoid of firm foundation, a play of forces derived from heredity, environment, and a thousand other influences, as well as from the effects of its own actions, good and evil.

The aim of the intelligent life is therefore to reach complete Non-Attachment to self, the state that implies final abandonment of the partisan attitude towards life's happenings. The enlightened being perceives that he cannot monopolize the credit for his own acts of charity, because no act is entirely one person's doing, all beings having a share in the causes and consequences of every act. Everyone must likewise accept some responsibility even for the murderer's knife.

One who has realized his complete oneness with all creation, and who has thereby become an initiate of the supreme Doctrine of Non-Duality, is called a Bodhisat, of whom Jesus might indeed serve as an example, since He claimed no merit for Himself but suffered all sorrow, knowing that whatsoever belongs to one already belongs perforce to all others too.

An equable loving-kindness is the only reasonable outcome of the doctrine of the Round; nor can it accept any limits short of the entire Universe. To preferences and aversions, which are really nothing else than extensions of a false belief about self, it cannot stoop.

Now let us suppose that we have been successful in substituting the antidotes for the poisons and that Just Views have replaced Ignorance in our make-up. Being set free from

our individualistic obsession with its fixed idea of dualism, we
are no longer forced to act as a cog in the Wheel of Existence.
The Round ceases for us: we are Delivered or Enlightened.
That is the state called Nirvana, which, translated literally,
means "Extinction." The word has given rise to a number of
foolish interpretations — outside the countries of its origin — by
which the Buddhist is accused of seeking mere nothingness,
annihilation. The perpetrators of this error let themselves be
deceived by the word "Existence" and its associations *for them.*
What ceases to exist, so they argue — because for them existence and reality are associated — must be reduced to Nothingness. The Buddhist understands it in quite another way; for, in
his eyes, it is the Existence of the Round that is the great illusion, the veil over the face of the Real. Enlightenment is nothing to *us,* for it is the beginning of Reality, something utterly
foreign to our present limitations. It is a waste of time trying to
imagine that state; for whatever we think or say must perforce
be taken out of our own experience of the world of phenomena.
"When you will have understood the dissolution of all com-
pounds," says the *Dhammapada,* "you will understand that
which is uncompounded." At present one can only say of Nirvana what the Hindus say of Brahma, the Infinite: "Not this,
not this."

The word Nirvana means extinction, something like the action of the fingers in snuffing out the flame of a candle. That
which is extinguished is Ignorance and its train of consequences. A double negative — the extinction or annulment of
Knowledgelessness — is our only way of faintly suggesting its
positive reality. What Buddhahood, the state of one who has
Awakened, really is, we simply cannot say. He who attains it
knows it. He who has not attained it can only speculate in
terms of his own relativity, which do not apply to it. To be
Buddha is not just one more degree in the familiar series,
like an ascent to a higher existence within the Round. There
is complete discontinuity between that state and the Circle of
Existence, a great gulf fixed, which can only be crossed at a
single leap.

To return for a moment to the diagram. We have still to
mention the border, containing twelve little scenes, which runs
round the outer rim of the circle. These scenes explain, in more
detailed form, the process of rebirth under the influence of
Ignorance. They are known as the "Twelve Interdependent
Origins" and must be studied by anyone who wishes to enter

deeply into the doctrine; but as they are really an amplification of the basic concept Ignorance — Desire — Action, it is unnecessary to analyse them here. They express, in more precise terms, ideas that we have already considered under those headings.

The remedy for Ignorance is Knowledge or Awareness. It goes without saying that by Knowledge is meant something more than ordinary discursive knowledge. Liberation is not to be compassed by attending courses at the university or by reading up manuals of philosophy. Rational knowledge makes its own useful contribution in helping to clear the ground of minor delusions; but Knowledge, the transcendent virtue by divine right, stands above Reason. It is the fruit of a direct intuitive experience, which is not so much a thing acquired by accretion; rather it is a thing that is already there from the moment that the obstacles to its realization have ceased to be. The effort of the seeker after this Real Knowledge is all along directed to the elimination of hindrances, to *allowing* the Knowledge to arise spontaneously, as it will do, the instant the necessary *undoing* has been effected. The presence of Knowledge is reflected in a radical alteration of the entire nature of a being; to know is to be, there is no other way.

Sound Method is inseparable from Wisdom. The Tibetans speak of these two as husband and wife, making Method into the male and Wisdom into the female aspect. They are symbolized, respectively, by the thunderbolt sceptre or *Dorjé* and the handbell or *Dilbu*. These emblems appear everywhere. In pictures they will be seen wielded by the hands of Divinities and every lama possesses a pair for use in the temple rites and at his own altar. His prescribed movements, as he turns them about, represent the eternal dalliance of Wisdom and Method; even to think of divorcing them is to court disaster. "Just as one desirous of reaching a certain city requires the eyes for seeing and the feet for traversing the way, so doth one desirous of reaching the city of Nirvana require the eyes of Wisdom and the feet of Method." Method itself is sometimes made synonymous with Universal Love or Compassion.

The Buddha in one of His early sermons explained the Method by which Awareness was to be gained and suffering destroyed, under eight headings, known as the PATH WITH EIGHT BRANCHES. This is often compared in its scope with Christ's Sermon on the Mount. It therefore corresponds to the last of the Four Truths, the Way that leads to the extinction of suffering. The Eightfold Path is the Buddhist's program of life, and comprises:

Perfect Vision*
Perfect Consideration } relating to spiritual direction

Perfect Speech
Perfect Ordering of Action
Perfect Means of Livelihood } relating to fitting and intelligent conduct
Perfect Effort

Perfect Recollection
Perfect Contemplation } relating to one-pointed concentration

It may at first appear strange that a method of which the avowed aim is the acquisition of Awareness should place Perfect Vision as the first item on its list, for by so doing it seems to beg the question somewhat. Though Awareness, in a sense, must be regarded as the end, from another point of view it is also the starting-point, since were there not some measure of Awareness at the outset, where would be the incentive to embark on the Eightfold Path at all? An earliest vision tells us that it is both possible and useful to seek the Way. As the various virtues of the Path are perfected, so do inferior Visions give place to higher ones, of more universal applicability, leading at the last to the Changeless Knowledge of the Real and the Infinite.

* The use of the word "perfect" in the present context is really far from perfect: the Tibetan adjective that it was intended to render is actually not precisely translatable into our own language, for which reason a little further comment is called for. In its literal sense the word conveys the idea of *purity;* that is to say, the absence not only of any foreign element but also of any excess or deficiency in respect of those elements which are relevant to the given situation. Whatever work is being undertaken or virtue applied must remain "all that it should be and nothing else besides," to quote an illuminating formula belonging to the Muslim tradition. Taken in that sense, the branches of the Eightfold Path, singly and collectively, correspond to the Buddha's thought when He said: "I teach you a Middle Way," a mean, that is to say, between whatever is excessive or superfluous and whatever is in any respect lacking. In seeking for the best translation of the attribute in question one has the following to choose from: *perfect,* chiefly to be taken in the sense of a full and fitting accomplishment or realization; *normal,* i.e. faithful to the norm or manner of being of a thing (concerning the norm, see also the note at the end of Chapter xvii); *proper,* in its root sense of "that which belongs" to the nature of both ends and means, whatever does not so belong being excluded as *inappropriate; correct,* in the sense of rightly ordered to a given purpose. Two other possible choices would have been "transcendent" and "realistic," but these should rather be looked on as free paraphrases, in that they depart rather too far from the root meaning of the term used. Best of all would be if the reader would try to imagine a word that, starting out from the notion of "perfect purity" (here I give the two roots that combined go to form the original Tibetan word), corresponds to a synthesis of all the above ideas.

Similarly, the four branches of the Path concerned with conduct are both a result and a cause of Awareness. As we learn to define our relation towards ourselves, our neighbours, all creatures, and the entire world more and more accurately, so our conduct becomes more appropriate and enlightened. The fruit of fitting conduct is an increase in Awareness, in Realism.

Some degree of Awareness is therefore indispensable from start to finish. If our actions or thoughts are to have the slightest value, they must be fully responsible actions or thoughts, designed and carried out for ends and by methods that harmonize with the facts of the world and with the relations that unite all beings, as far as it lies in our power to ascertain them. Our actions and thoughts are the products of our whole nature at a given moment, and become the causes of its further development for good or ill. A nature that is still mainly emotional, and not brought under proper control by the Intellect, is a weathercock turned by every impulse. In such a condition of irresponsibility, even if an action happens to be right, this is largely fortuitous; for, not being based upon relevant motives, it is properly little better than a foolish action in masquerade. It must be one's constant aim to withdraw as much of life as possible from the power of outside influences and accidents and to bring it into subjection to one's informed will, so that each act may be exactly what it purports to be, no more and no less, each perception a genuine perception uninfluenced by anything irrelevant, each decision a judgment reached after due consideration of all accessible evidence.

It is as a means towards heightened control that the great Teachers so strongly recommend certain disciplines aiming at bringing movements that are normally reflex under the partial rule of conscious volition. To turn matters of instinct and habit into deliberately controlled operations is considered highly beneficial. Conversely, the cultivation of an automatic response to external stimuli, by expedients such as marching in step or shouting slogans, the stock-in-trade of modern European organization, must, Buddhistically speaking, be reprobated as a disastrous abuse, leading to greater and greater irresponsibility and enslavement.

Recollection and Contemplation, the two last branches of the Path, are concerned with the cultivation of calmness and harmony of soul, the attuning of the whole being to the Word, the promotion of a state of perfect receptivity. Like a rippleless tarn in which the snows are seen so distinctly reflected that one forgets which is solid mountain and which the image, so is Meditation, the solvent of distinctions and the gate of the Real. It is an experience that the average person ignores; yet without it and its resultant mastery over self, Illumination cannot be achieved. A state of agitation always fosters Ignorance; therefore all the sages of the Orient counsel the cultivation of the habit of calm, unruffled meditation. In the highest degree, Meditation is the mark of the saint, the serenity which nothing can disturb, not even in the middle of the Round's eddy.

Concerning the branches of the Eightfold Path that deal with conduct, little need be said. Perfect Speech, Perfect Action, and Perfect Effort are indistinguishable from the same virtues as taught by Christ. Selfless Love and all it implies, Mercy and Non-retaliation for injuries, Gentleness, Reverence, in all these there is nothing to choose between the teaching of the Buddha and the Gospel. So striking is the similarity that one lama gave it as his opinion that Christianity was simply an aberrant branch of Buddhism.

Perfect Means of Livelihood deserves a word of its own, for though it is just as implicit in the Christian revelation as in any other, it is apt to be overlooked, and it has been especially disregarded by those subscribers to puritanical tenets who played so prominent a part in the development of big business. According to the Eightfold Path, it is not enough that one's personal conduct should be apparently blameless; one must look farther, lest one may be deriving sustenance from some practice inconsistent with the law of Mercy or Truth, from some brutality or exploitation of fellow men or animals, or from some form of organization that is tending to hinder Knowledge and favour the growth of Ignorance. A Buddhist may not be a trafficker in lives — that is to say, a slave-dealer or a butcher; worse than the actual killing is the failure to realize that animals are alive and sensitive — the unawareness is as bad as the cruelty. The calf led to the slaughter is not to be shorn of its pitifulness by allowing one's sensibility to seek shelter behind that handy word "veal." Neither may a man live by selling drugs (save for medical use), nor may he be an arms-manufacturer. Living in modern times, he should look to his investments lest he be the unwitting accomplice of commercial exploitation of the weak.

There is one application of the law of Causality that is of special interest to Europeans and has been the subject of much contention. Several writers, both Christian and Buddhist, have taken the view that the doctrine of *Karman* or Action and the Christian doctrine of Forgiveness are fundamentally irreconcilable. I have read somewhere that a Buddhist leader from Ceylon once addressed a protest against some young nobles being allowed to attend a school where they were taught "the abominable doctrine of the forgiveness of sins." Was he justified in this particular criticism or not?

If by "forgiveness" is meant the non-arising of an effect from a previous cause or the simple wiping of that effect off the slate after it has been produced, then the answer must be an unqualified yes. Any irregular or arbitrary interference with the succession of Cause and Effect is rigidly excluded by Buddhism, as constituting a denial of Order. But does Christian forgiveness really amount to this? Does Christ wipe out an offence unconditionally, irrespective of what kind of response is made by the sinner? The muddle-headed talk that often occurs in sermons or pious books might lead one to think so. Popular deformations are common enough, especially among those sects that put all their faith in a "conversion" supposed to take place, once and for all, at a given moment in time. Among such people there is always a tendency to mistrust carefully worded dogmatic formularies and to employ sentimental and rhetorical phrases such as would lend colour to the Singhalese critic's fears: but it is just as unfair to treat as a formal exposition of Christianity an emotional reference to the loving Father, who, for the asking, is ready to disburden the sinner, as to regard one of the travesties that are found in missionary tracts against Buddhism as a just presentation of that Doctrine. In such a sentence as "You have only to lay your sins at the feet of Jesus, imploring His pardon, and He will grant it," though the words are unexceptionable if rightly interpreted, there is a certain danger of misunderstanding from the vagueness which allows one to believe, though it does not affirm it, that there is an easy escape from the consequences of one's offences. The emphasis is laid on the remission of the sin, and a discreet silence is maintained on the part to be played by the sinner himself, while the introduction of the word "only" opens the door to further possibilities of confusion. Similarly, when a Catholic says: "If you go to the priest and humbly confess, you can be sure of receiving Absolution," he certainly does not mean to imply that a mere formal ceremony will be sufficient.

A good confession demands more than the recital of a list of misdemeanours, followed by the administration of a grace conferred by the sacramental words upon an entirely passive recipient. Doubtless in practice many people treat it so; but this is no more than to say that many of mankind water down and denature every doctrine to suit their own feebleness of purpose. Were it otherwise we should already be at the millennium. When Catholics are accused of using the sacrament of Penance as a cheap way of escape from the consequence of sin, there is as little accuracy in the accusation as in the complaint put forward by the Buddhist from Ceylon. In any given case he may have been justified, yet the question of principle is really left untouched.

Again it must be asked: Is there any place for Pardon under the strict application of the doctrine of Causes, or are the two ideas mutually exclusive? Sin, under the law of *Karman,* can be viewed with a twofold aspect: first as an effect, the product of Causes dwelling in the sinner's character or in the circumstances governing his life, and secondly as itself a Cause, productive of various results. Sin first affects the sinner's inner being, producing in it a change which we call guilt and which furthermore implies a reinforcement of the tendency towards repetition of the sin. There are also the extraneous consequences of the historical act, its effects on other people and on the world. Granted that there is a possibility of forgiveness, which of these effects will be cancelled by it? The second group of effects can be ruled out, since they lie extraneous to the guilty person. If I commit a murder, no forgiveness will resurrect the murdered man, or stop the police from arresting me, or interrupt the social consequences flowing from the crime, or assuage the sorrow of the victim's relatives. The sphere in which forgiveness can operate is restricted to that of the effects personal to the delinquent; more especially it concerns itself with the washing away of the stigma of guilt.

It must be repeated that if the Remission of Sins were really a tricking of the Causal law, if Christ simply expunged the guilt *motu proprio* without the introduction of another chain of Causes neutralizing the series loosed by the sin and thus changing the direction of the erring soul's development, that would, to the Buddhist, be tantamount to investing the Will of the Ruler of the Universe with the note of capriciousness, an unthinkable proposition. But surely the true Christian doctrine postulates another factor, on the presence of which forgiveness is conditional — that is, Repentance. The word may often be spoken glibly so as to suggest a mere formality; but no one who takes the trouble to think things out would dismiss it so lightly.

The conditions for a perfect act of Contrition — and nothing less is demanded — are not difficult to define. Firstly there must be a recognition that the act repented of was a sin, and why. Whether this be expressed under the symbol of a personal offence against Divine Majesty, or as a disturbance of harmony arising from non-recognition of the true nature of things, it amounts to much the same thing. In either case one admits that there has been misunderstanding or Ignorance, for which Knowledge must be substituted before the act can be seen to be sinful. The Ignorance has let loose one chain of effects — the sin and its secondary consequences. The succeeding Knowledge looses a new set of consequences, working in a contrary direction. The first set is not so much made null as counterpoised by the effects of Knowledge, resulting in a clean sheet. There is nothing contrary to the law of Causes here; indeed, that law, under its ethical aspect, is nothing else than the opposing of Knowledge with its effects to Ignorance with its effects.

The second postulate for perfect Contrition is sorrow for the sin. Sorrow here is an effect, part of the pain that accompanies the changes wrought by wickedness. The punishment inflicted by the police is a direct external effect of the sinful act itself. The sorrow of self-accusation is an internal effect of the act, arising when that act begins to be viewed in the light of Knowledge. Again we are not faced with any challenge to the principles of *Karman*.

A third condition is a sincere intention of amendment, a taking of effective measures to prevent a repetition of the sinful action. Without understanding why the sin was a sin, or what should have been the alternative to committing it, no effective good intention can possibly arise. Again the whole problem becomes centred in Knowledge and its consequences. Once the nature of the sin has been clearly recognized, the intention of changing one's way arises almost as a natural consequence; this intention, becoming in its turn a Cause, leads to the new consequence of taking practical measures in the future. One can dismiss all reactions such as a superficial wave of emotion, a half-desire to escape from the results of sin without paying the price, a passing regret, a half-hearted profession of good intentions. The Divine Judge is not so easily mocked; when we speak of repentance we mean the real thing, with all the conditions accepted in full.

So much for Contrition: now for Forgiveness. Will a sin be forgiven, even by a Saviour, failing Contrition? Surely such a suggestion would be an absurdity cutting at the roots of Orderly Justice. Repentance must be a first condition; if there be no repentance, the Grace of Christ, though proffered by Him, is in fact rejected by the sinner.

If Contrition be genuine, then the guilt is said to be wiped off the soul. If this seems to be an arbitrary reversal, yet on closer examination it can still be explained in terms of Action and the effects of Action. The combination Ignorance-Sin has brought about one sequence of effects, altering the state of a soul by the addition of guilt. Knowledge-Repentance, a separate *Karman,* also brings its own sequence of effects, which are bound to alter the nature of that soul by the addition of Understanding and New Intentions. The first change has been followed by a second change, and an undeniably radical one; for of all possible changes the displacing of Ignorance by Knowledge is the most fundamental. Once there has been a genuine change of heart, the changed situation, as Cause, is reflected as a matter of course in a whole new series of consequences, and the traditional language of forgiveness is applicable without inconsistency.

That forgiveness is not an idea utterly foreign to Buddhism was confirmed for me by the Mongol lama Wangyal, under whom I read the *Lamrim,* or *Stages in the Path,* the principal doctrinal book of the Yellow-Hat Order of lamas, which is the most influential in modern Tibet. He used a terminology which approximated strikingly to that of the Catholic Church, dividing sins into "mortal" and "venial": only when challenged did he admit that "unforgivable sins" really meant sins that required a protracted penance for their expiation. This might last for æons and æons, but eventually an upward turn of the Round must come, just as a downward one would eventually interrupt even the most lasting of pleasures. It will readily be seen that, as between the two traditional forms, there are considerable differences of expression and emphasis; but in other respects the lama's language about contrition and pardon might well have belonged to one of the divines of the Christian Middle Ages.

We have now covered most of the ground. For the sake of

completeness, mention ought to be made of one more detail in the picture of the Round, the fearsome monster who clutches the entire Circle of Existence in his teeth and talons. He is Shindjé, judge of the dead; in his horrible visage we see the true nature of the Round unmasked, and in his domination over the whole scene we recognize the inexorable character of the law of Causation, with which the Round itself is cognate. Shindjé must not be taken for a minister of retributive Justice. He does not dispense penalties in the name of offended Deity, nor do the consequences that accrue from good or foolish actions depend on his private pleasure. Neither gifts nor charms can buy his indulgence.

> I set no store by gold, silver, nor riches
> Nor by pope, emperor, king, duke, nor princes
> For if I would receive gifts great,
> All the world I might get;
> All my custom is clean contrary.

Shindjé's sole office is to operate the mechanism of cause and effect, in faithful obedience to its rules. "Every effect proceeds from a cause." The whole implication of this law is that each act will bring about an appropriate modification in the Universe, which nothing can hinder. Other actions may change its direction, neutralize it, or transform it; but an effect as such can by no means be wiped out. Joy and pain are simply effects of causes, needing no bestowal of grace or word of condemnation from outside to produce them. They are symptoms of the state of a given being at a given moment. The present condition of the whole Universe, viewed as one, is what it is, because, with the history of causes and effects as they have been until now, it cannot but be otherwise than what it is.

In Buddhist countries, as elsewhere, the majority refuse to give up the simple idea of poetic justice. They measure merit as one might weigh potatoes; so many good acts against so much happiness, so many sins against such and such penalties. All those who, in spite of anything they may profess in theory, still show their belief in their own self-sufficient ego naturally continue to hanker after the delusions of individual enjoyment and advantage, in the form of happy rebirths. I remember one lama who told me that he did not feel equal to an immediate effort in the direction of Buddhahood, but he was at least making sure, by a nice balance of his acts, that he would earn rebirth as a man again, so as not to lose his coign of vantage for further progress later. He confessed that he was an inveterate meat-eater — the Tibetans are not given to making hypocritical excuses — but as a counterblast he was as uncompromising a teetotaller as ever came out of Wales. For my friend, the future life resolved itself simply into a matter of efficient book-keeping. Unfortunately for his naïve schemes, he left out of account the besetting sin of Ignorance, which accompanied his well-planned acts of merit. He was a very kind and pleasant man, well above average, yet he will be lucky, figuratively speaking, if he does not obtain rebirth among the *Yidags*. There are thousands more like him, who are still missing the crucial point. Like all of us, they get what they really desire and expect, not what they profess to ask for — therein lies all the difference! "Knock and it shall be opened unto you: seek and ye shall find." That is a profound truth; but much also depends upon which door one knocks at, and for which gifts one asks.

Some may be surprised that in all this lengthy discussion there has been no direct allusion to God. We have had a whole chapter on doctrine without so much as mentioning His name. Is it correct to say, as some have liked to do, that Buddhism is "atheistical," and that it precludes the belief in a Personal Deity? This is a question that loses its substance once it has been realized that Personality already implies some degree of limitation: every specification must always be clearly distinguished from the unspecifiable Infinite. So long as it is accepted that Personality occupies a lesser degree of universality than the Infinite, the Supreme Principle of All, there is no objection to admitting it as one among possible determinations. The enemy to be shunned at all costs is a permanently dualistic conception, an immutable persistence of pairs of contraries that refuse ultimately to be resolved in the unity of a Principle dwelling beyond their distinction. The Hindus, whose metaphysical language resembles that of the Lamas, have separate names for the Infinite (Brahma — neuter form), the Personified Creative Function (Brahmā — masculine form) and Īshwara, the Supreme Principles of Being. Christian theology applies the name of God now to one, now to another, now to all three together, which is slightly confusing. The Hindu terminology could be valid for a Buddhist too, if need were, though, as far as I am aware, it has not actually been used in this way.

The just word on the Buddhist position with regard to God has been spoken by René Guénon, who, more than any other

European, is qualified for the office of interpreter of the traditional doctrines:

"In reality, Buddhism is no more 'atheistical' than it is 'theistic' or 'pantheistic'; all that need be said is that it does not place itself at the point of view where these various terms have any meaning."

Chapter XII

The Hermit and the Pilgrim

SPRING HAD GIVEN WAY to full summer when we got back to Lachhen, and the better-off of the inhabitants, who, like all Tibetans, dislike damp heat, were talking of moving to cooler levels up the valley, away from the heaviest rains. The abbot had already withdrawn to T'hangu (13,000 feet), to a hermitage dependent on his monastery. As we were anxious to spend some time in his society, we prepared to follow him there, but thought it wiser to let him know beforehand, lest he should be entering into one of his periods of seclusion. Meanwhile we camped, in order to save bungalow charges.

Caravans from Kampa Dzong kept coming through the village, laden with wool and barley flour to be exchanged lower down for rice. We stopped them from time to time and asked if they had any rugs for sale. These Tibetan rugs, coarsely knotted on a woolen warp and dyed in sound vegetable colours, fetched very low prices. The patterns were usually variants of one design, consisting of a central field containing one or three circles more or less decorated, with a key-pattern round the border; the style shows unmistakable Chinese influence. The art of making them is common knowledge in Tibet; happy is the artistic condition of a country where such rugs represent the low-water mark of material and craftsmanship, within reach even of the poorest.*

The headman of Lachhen, who had all along been attentive to our comfort, kindly lent us one of his house servants, a young man from Shigatze, named T'hargya, to accompany us up to T'hangu. He was an unusually intelligent and sensitive youth, and we were anxious to retain his services, so we did our best to persuade his master to release him. But he knew T'hargya's value too well and would not yield him up, though he promised to lend him for a future journey if still in his service.

* Unfortunately this local art has collapsed in the last ten years; chemical dyes have come in and designs have been corrupted to match.

The system of hiring such domestics is a kind of indenture. The servant contracts to stay three years. No regular salary is paid; but he is clothed, fed, housed, and given occasional pocket money. In many respects he is treated like one of the family; we noticed that a respectful address towards his employer did not affect T'hargya's ease of manner, free from all servility. When the term of service expires, the employee is given a present in money, or possibly in kind. We found the same system working in Ladak, in the houses of the Lhasa merchants who lived round Leh.

On the way up towards T'hangu the scenery is not specially striking. After a few miles altitude begins to affect the denseness of the forests; yet here, where trees should be prized, denudation is going on apace, due to the habit of clearing new acres by fire in order to sow corn. We passed wide tracts where all the big trees stood leafless, mere blackened skeletons, surrounded by bare soil or low scrub of recent growth. The destruction seems to go on recklessly, and it would be worth some attempt at regulation by a State Forestry Department.

Close to T'hangu big trees give place to vegetation similar to that found near the snout of the Zemu Glacier. The prevalent flowering plants are dwarf rhododendrons of several kinds, purple or white, and primulas, either small mauve, large dark purple, or, in boggy places, yellow ones like cowslips. Blue poppies are also common. T'hangu is not a village; there is only the pretty hermitage, a big cottage surrounded by a circle of prayer-flags, on a grassy knoll, and under it an eyesore of an ugly, ill-constructed rest-house. In June the surrounding hills were clear of snow; the weather was unceasingly damp, with a raw Scottish mist.

There was local excitement at the time because of the completion of a new *Mani* wall near the road, neatly built of masonry and cement, with the sacred inscriptions incised on flat stones embedded in the wall. The letters were left white on a ground coloured red with a kind of clay. The builders were two pilgrims who spent their time going from place to place erecting these walls; but the carving was done by a local man. The moment for consecrating the *Mani* wall had arrived and the headman of Lachhen and several monks and peasants assembled for the ceremony. A large tent with red flounces was pitched, housing a brazier, a table, and a seat for the abbot. We introduced ourselves to the pilgrims, who were standing by, surveying their handiwork. One of them was a thickset man of powerful build, with a merry, open face over which laughter was continually rippling. He was a childlike soul, delighted with the smallest things and radiating a transparent benevolence towards all. His home lay north-west of Lhasa, so he told us, and he had not seen it for twelve years, having spent all his time in pilgrimages to the most remote parts. With delight he recounted the wonders of the Holy Seat (Bodh Gaya in Bihar), where, at the foot of the Bodhi tree, the Teacher sat to receive His Enlightenment. The pilgrim was planning to visit it again, for the third time — but not before winter, for the plains of India are insufferably hot at other seasons. Five years ago, during his travels, he had met his present companion, a monk from the land of Kham, far away to the east on the China border. The latter was not so prepossessing as his friend. He was rough-looking and ragged; but on closer acquaintance we decided that his gruff voice and unkempt appearance did him an injustice. He was a decent, straightforward fellow.

Among the young lamas who had come up from Lachhen for the service there was one called Samdub to whom we felt attracted from the moment we set eyes on him. His features were fine and regular and his expression suggested the youthful saint, for a look of rapture never quite left his face. He greeted us like old friends; it is curious how many people one met with whom the tedious processes of introduction could be curtailed. Social intercourse is undoubtedly made much easier by the absence of servile manners in any class and by the traditional forms of politeness, which, once they have been complied with, indicate exactly where each man stands.

When the stage had been set for the consecration, we looked up towards the hermitage and seemed to see Chaucer's Canterbury Pilgrims approaching in procession. Our old friend the abbot, in full pontificals and wearing a mitre, was riding, not on a palfrey, but on a sturdy mule better fitted to bear the weight of his portly figure. A leopard-skin was thrown over the saddle and a young monk led the animal, while Samdub and others, armed with drums, sacred vessels, and lighted tapers of incense, acted as acolytes. The dedication was long and complicated. Towards the end the abbot issued from his tent, scattered rice on the wall, and offered small conical cakes, after which the procession circled round the *mendong* several times, clockwise.

Mani walls are a typical feature of the Tibetan landscape.

The one at T'hangu was an insignificant affair compared with the vast erections that mark the approaches to villages or monasteries in Tibet proper and Ladak; but it differed from them only in length, and there is still time for it to grow, as offerings of additional inscribed stones by the faithful gradually extend it. The *Mani* wall or *mendong* consists of a cement base on which flat stones are laid, each with its sacred text, of which by far the commonest is the formula *Om mani padme hum.*

The origin of the *Mani* formula is attributed to the "All-Merciful Good Shepherd" Chenrezig, the personage who manifests himself in the Dalai Lama and who revealed it for the profit of creatures, much as the Blessed Virgin revealed the Rosary to St. Dominic. In India, and in Tibet, where religious thought was moulded under Indian influence, a whole science of *Mantra* or Significant Sound is recognized, which, in the same way as visual works of art, gestures, and other rites of all sorts, helps to create "supports" or "props" for the reverence, attention, and meditation of the worshippers. Of all *Mantras,* the *Mani* phrase is the favourite, and it figures not only on the innumerable *Mani* walls leading into and out of every town, village, or monastery in Tibet, but also on many of the prayer-flags, and inside prayer-wheels great or small, operated by hand or turned by wind or water power. Thus every person travelling in Tibet is continually in touch with the idea, bathed in its influence, whether he responds consciously or not. It is wafted to him by all the breezes, in which also the birds are flying. The same words are repeated to him by the emphatic voice of the hurricane. The water he drinks may have passed over it, and fishes swim within range of its message. His eyes, and also those of passing wolves and wild asses, are constantly lighting upon its beautifully shaped script, now chiselled on the face of some prominent cliff, now on a boulder, now on the flat stones of the wayside *mendong,* to pass which, in a correct direction, the traveller is frequently forced to go up a bank or to squeeze awkwardly through a narrow gap. So the whole country, from end to end, is pervaded with a devotional atmosphere; only the wilfully blind can altogether avoid responding to it, while wandering across the austere landscape of the sacred tableland.

Some travellers have been tempted to hold up these practices to facile ridicule. The *Manis* and other texts, the lotus-throned figures of meditating Buddhas that confront them from rock faces or by the roadside, seem to them nothing but the

futile extravagances of childish minds. Yet one might ask oneself which best becomes a civilized nation — the inscribing in
beautiful lettering round the approaches of a city, say London,
or about the countryside, of a verse or two of the Beatitudes
or some of Shakespeare's most pregnant quotations, or the plas-
tering of those same places with posters, vulgarly worded and
printed in aggressive colours, inviting passers-by to prove the
transcendent virtues of Messrs. So-and-so's pills or pig food or
such-and-such a hair oil?

The precise meaning of the *Mani* words has given rise to
much discussion: I should by rights have said meanings, for it
is a characteristic of traditional ritual sentences to bear several
senses simultaneously, some literal and some figurative; a whole
tissue of ideas is woven into them, which can be teased out, one
after another, till the most far-reaching principles become exposed.

The literal translation of the formula is "*Om,* the jewel in
the lotus, *Hum!*" In a general way it may be described as an
act of assent to the divine aim. *Om* (derived from the Sanskrit
aum) stands for Brahma, "the one without second" or "the in-
expressible Absolute." As one writer has put it, "*Om* is the ultimate word that can be uttered, after which there remains
nothing but silence." In it, therefore, are summed up prayer
and praise and worship. *Om* is also the sound of all sounds,
audible to the initiated ear, which is produced by the act of
Manifestation or, as we would say, of Creation, which produces
and nourishes this and other Universes. It might also be compared with Pythagoras' music of the Spheres.

Mani means "jewel"; therefore a precious thing, the Doctrine. *Padme* means "in the lotus"; it may refer to the world
which enshrines the doctrine of Buddha (the jewel), or to the
spirit in whose depths he who knows how to take soundings
will discover Knowledge, Reality, and Liberation, these three
being really one and the same thing under different names. Or
possibly the lotus, the usual throne of divinities and saints, is
simply attached as a divine attribute to the gem of doctrine.
Hum is an ejaculation denoting defiance. Its utterer hurls a
challenge, as it were, at the enemy, at the passions such as lust,
hatred, and stupidity, the poisons that drug beings into submitting to the tyranny of the Round of Existence. Or, viewed in
yet another way, the adversary is no other than the cherished
belief in an indissoluble "myself," and the desire for individual
recompense.

But these explanations are elementary, a mere prelude to the secrets that await discovery by the initiate in the *Mani Mantra*. Even the shapes of the letters that compose it can be visualized and made to correspond to ideas for the mind's eye to fix on. There is no end to the truths that a competent teacher can extract from this one phrase. One of the less profound interpretations current among the lamas is to establish a correlation between each of the six syllables and one of the six classes of beings in the Round. Thus *Om* is made to stand for the world of gods, *Ma* for non-gods, and so on to *Hum*, which evokes thoughts of the beings in purgatory.

A seventh syllable is sometimes appended to the classical six, the word *Hri*. It is said to signify, in the sacred language, the underlying reality hidden behind phenomena, the Absolute veiled by Form. It is therefore, in a way, a quintessence of the whole preceding six syllables.

It must not be imagined that I am claiming that every Tibetan peasant who passes a *Mani* on the left, or tells the beads of his rosary, or every lama who casually walks along the temple courtyard turning the prayer-wheels, is conscious of all these meanings, any more than every Catholic who says "Hail, Mary," is always conscious of its connexion with the doctrine of the Incarnation. There is every degree possible between a vaguely reverent feeling (as when taking off one's hat on entering a church) and a profound awakening of consciousness by the full and right use of the words as an instrument of association with metaphysical ideas. The man who lays a fresh *Mani* stone on the *mendong* may get no farther than a naïve act of piety, aiming, as so much of prayer does everywhere, at securing material benefits. Not strong enough to contemplate escape from the Round into Buddhahood, he possibly dreams only of a pleasurable rebirth in an individual sense, or if he is of a somewhat more aspiring turn of mind, he prays for rebirth in a position more suitable as a starting-point on the Path of Enlightenment than the one he occupies at present. But the whole doctrine is potentially there all the same, awaiting those who care to avail themselves of it. "Knock and it shall be opened unto you." But if you do not trouble to knock, the door remains shut.

I have gone into this example rather fully, in an endeavour to help readers to grasp the theory of "supports" for meditation, on which both ritual and art depend. Even the involuntary act of breathing can be turned into a contemplative discipline. The sounds of intaking and outgoing breath are then evoked as a *mantra*, and serve to symbolize the alternating rhythm of the manifestation and resorption of Universes. The end and aim of both Tibetan and Hindu teaching is to emancipate the being from the separatist illusions of individuality, in order to raise it eventually to an effective and irreversible realization of the non-dual character of all things, something higher even than Unity. Anything whatsoever, a word, a stone, an image, can be the starting-point of the chain of ideas. From any single point in the Universe the whole remainder can be integrated. Tradition concerns itself with the two indispensables, wisdom and method; if it propounds a doctrine, it must also teach the art by which we can raise ourselves to its comprehension. A certain missionary once said that if everything could be turned to a sacred use, "why not worship my boot?" He spoke truth: a modern Balaam, he was taken to curse, "and, behold, thou hast blest them altogether." Not only his boot, but even his person could, to the seeing eye, be taken for a pattern of the divine scheme; but every man has not reached that pitch of discernment and it is for art to supply more generally practical means than this.

Our time at T'hangu alternated between visits to the abbot in his hermitage and to the pilgrims, who had found a comfortable, dry lodging in a cave under a huge boulder that stood in the midst of the valley. Once our friend came to feed with us in camp. He was a most lovable person, childlike, affectionate, and unworried, and obviously engaged in carrying out literally the Gospel precept: "Take no thought for your life, what ye shall eat; neither for the body, what ye shall put on."

The conversations in his cave made the hours slip by unnoticed. One day, after describing different countries through which he had travelled, the pilgrim said: "Are there many goats in England? And sheep? And if I turn up one day at your home will you take me in?" I assured him that it would be an honour. As to animals, there were plenty of sheep but few goats; cows were used for milking. "Oh, cows, how lovely! You have lots of cows?" The thought made him chuckle with pleasure. "Then you will receive me if I come to your house?" After that he inquired about my family and I explained that my mother was nearly eighty. "Did you say that your mother is one hundred and eight?" cried the pilgrim in great excitement. He turned to his companion. "Our friend says his mother is one hundred and eight years old!" (This is a sacred number in Tibet: the beads of a rosary are so numbered and a hundred and eight Buddhas are sometimes found drawn on a single scroll picture. To reach that age is considered exceptionally lucky, a mark of divine favour.)

He showed us his possessions, which, besides clothes, blankets, food, teapot, and cups, included a small library of books wrapped in silk and a set of drawings of Lamas and Divinities, the size of playing-cards. The whole together must have added up to a weighty load for carrying across mountain passes, but his physique was equal to anything.

His friend related to us stories of border warfare with the Chinese, about 1906 and after. Many of his relations had lost their homes, and even their lives, in the disturbances. The Khambas are the most warlike as well as the handsomest of the Tibetan races and are noted for their raiding propensities, their victims being usually the caravans of wealthy merchants trading between China and Lhasa. Kham seems from all accounts to be a romantic country of seers and brigands, artists and armourers, hermits and Homeric heroes. The Chinese in these campaigns were not provided with artillery, and the walled enclosures of the lamaseries were turned into fortresses, which had to be invested in true mediæval style. There were several epic sieges, in which the defenders performed prodigies of endurance and heroism. No quarter was given to the vanquished and both the Khamba irregulars and the Chinese forces inflicted terrible atrocities upon their unfortunate prisoners. Some of the tales are almost past belief; but there is not the slightest doubt about their accuracy, for they have been recorded by the eminent French scholar and traveller Professor Bacot, who passed through some of the subjugated country not long after.

He relates one history that for superhuman heroism must be hard to parallel, that of a young Khamba of noble blood who fell into Chinese hands and was asked to divulge information about his comrades. When he refused he was threatened with torture. I will not harrow my readers with the hideous details; but the ingenious efforts of ten executioners taking turn and turn about without interruption during thirty successive days proved impotent to extort a single word. At last the Chinese Governor, at the end of his patience, suffered him to be put to death.

It is a relief to turn from these horrors to the reports of Sir Eric Teichman, a British official who mediated between the Chinese and the Tibetans and helped to conclude a peace. The

Tibetan regular forces, which took part in the final phase of the struggle in 1918, were commanded by a churchman, the Kalon Lama, who rode to the wars like the old mace-bearing bishops. Sir Eric pays a tribute to the humane treatment of prisoners by order of the clerical general, and the absence of reprisals. The cruelties had been the work of irregulars, desperately defending their homes. The Lhasa regulars, obedient to the instructions of their commander, seem on that occasion to have shown an exemplary restraint.

In their departure our friends the pilgrims were true to their character. They said no good-byes, but disappeared one morning early from the cave, leaving no trace except some clay models of *tormas* (conical votive cakes) in a niche in the rock, a thank-offering to the dæmon of the place. Our friendship with them was a great experience. From the moment we met, it was as if we had known each other all our lives. Should we ever meet again, it will be as if we had parted but yesterday. We never asked their names nor they ours (no one thought of it); it is, perhaps, more fitting so.

The pilgrims' simplicity cloaked no emptiness. Of such is the Kingdom of Heaven — at last we had actually met and recognized the prototypes of the Gospel description.

Our time at T'hangu, apart from brief walks, was spent in the society of the pilgrim and the abbot. Nothing could have provided a greater contrast than these two men. The pilgrim stood at the pole of childlike and unsolicitous trustfulness, while the abbot occupied the opposite pole of extreme intellectuality and knowledge of the world — acquired, however, largely by withdrawing from the world and watching it from without. He had the urbanity, tempered with a dash of satire, that distinguishes the true man of culture everywhere. In the pilgrim we discerned the free spirit that never would grow up. Power meant nothing to him; he neither aspired to wield it nor stooped to worship it; he just ignored it. In this trait he and the hermit met on common ground; for the latter, though possessed of powers both temporal and psychic which brought with them a right to the service and obedience of others as a matter of course, yet set no store by such power because, by a ruthless stripping of all romance and sentimentality from life, he had learned to know it and the sensations that it brings for hollow things. Thus both the men, otherwise so different, conformed in their own ways to the Buddhist ideal of unattachment, towards which they had travelled by routes that suited

their respective natures. Both of them were founded upon the
rock of the same idea, the illusory character of the phenomenal
world and of their own egos; but the one knew it instinctively
and revealed it by his attitude towards the quite simple problems of daily life, while the prelate had the added power of
being able to define his ideas for the benefit of others. He was
a born teacher, a Lama in the technical sense of the word.

Once, at a later date, I made the half-joking remark that
"the Lachhen Lama is one of those who are said by the Tibetans to have passed to the stage beyond good and evil." I had
inadvertently happened on the truth; for, after we returned
home to England, I read in a travel book by the Marquis of
Zetland, then Lord Ronaldshay, of how he had been told by
the same abbot of Lachhen himself that he had reached a degree of realization where pairs of distinctions lose their meaning, even that of evil and good.

"He who shall have mastered this doctrine will be freed
from sin, and also from virtue."

This condition, recognized by all traditions, amounts to a reintegration in the state of Adam before he had tasted of the
fruit of the dualistic tree. Certainly, I have never met anyone
who so impressed me "as one having authority, and not as the
Scribes." During daily interviews with him I felt my attention
captured beyond any chance of straying. His room at T'hangu
was similar to the one at Lachhen monastery. A softened light
entered by the window. There was an altar on which glowed
a single copper lamp; over it hung a truncated cone of paper,
similar to a lampshade, inscribed with texts and tilted at a
slight angle, so that the hot air in rising caused it to revolve
gently. There were, besides, a few small tables with books, his
finely chased teacup, and an ancient painted scroll of some
deity under his "fearsome" aspect. A rug was laid for guests
to sit on; and a young monk, who was charged with the abbot's
personal service, kept up continual relays of cups of tea and
rusks of puffed rice.

There we conversed by the hour. The abbot's speech was
slow, but not devoid of a humorous turn. A wide range of subjects was touched on and it seemed to me that he was turning
over some plan in his mind that concerned me; but perhaps I
only imagined this.

One day he suddenly asked: "Why did you go up to the
Zemu and try to climb snow mountains? I would know your

true purpose." A difficult question to deal with on the spur of
the moment: to such a man the usual humbug about finding
it good for one's health or character, or that one was pursuing
some pseudo-scientific object, would have been an insult to his
intelligence. His piercing glance was like Ithuriel's spear, com-
pelling truthfulness. So I made a lame answer: "We love to go
to wild places for their solitude, to avoid the bustle of town
life." "You will never find it thus," he replied. "You have no
idea how to seek it. It cannot be won by such methods. It will
not be obtained nor acquired nor gained nor procured nor en-
compassed." (I have tried to give an impressionistic rendering
of his words in Tibetan.) "The solitude to seek is the concentration of your own heart; if you have once found it, it will not
matter where you are." Perhaps he was thinking of his own
spiritual ancestor who said: "For him who hath realized Reality
it is the same whether he dwell on an isolated hilltop in solitude or wanders hither and thither." Then placing a tiny image
of the Buddha on the table, he said: "Learn to fix your thoughts
on this, and then you may know solitude, but not otherwise."
"But surely, my lord abbot, the great saint Mila Repa himself
has sung the praises of mountain and wilderness, and recom-
mended them to those who wish to master the art of solitude.
He who aspired to Buddhahood within the span of a single
life found that the undistracted atmosphere of mountains offered the best setting in which to woo the solitary spirit. Does
he not introduce many of his poems with the couplet:

Obeisance at the feet of Marpa the Translator
May he grant me strength to persevere in my mountain re-
    treat?

I myself am weak and cannot easily learn even the elements of
this art in the middle of crowds. If Mila Repa found it helpful,
can we be blamed for wishing to escape from the turmoil
sometimes?"

I felt I had just kept my end up — not that I am presuming
to compare the love of solitude as the mountaineer knows it
with the retreats of a Mila Repa, or of the abbot himself either.
Such a comparison would be blasphemy or pure romancing.
Yet in the mountaineer's conviction that there is a fullness of
life to be found in the lonely places that is lost in the hurry and
noise of the world, he can claim to have more in common with
the contemplative ideal than with the uneasy ambitions of the
man about town.

It was now my turn to question. "Tell me truly, can anything be learned about solitude without a teacher?" "It cannot." "So it seems that a study of the sacred books by oneself won't reveal the way to it?" "It will not reveal it." "Is that, then, your final word? The first thing of all, for him who would enter on the Path, is to find a teacher?" "A teacher is essential; without him you will get nowhere, for you will not learn to fix your mind." He then quoted a popular proverb, in metre, the gist of which is:

> Without milk you won't make butter,
> Without barley you won't brew beer.

And so on, till it ends: —

> Without meditation you won't attain Buddhahood.

I then asked him: "Could we possibly stay on here now and study with you?" He replied: "Yes, if I were remaining here myself; but this year I have arranged to go to Tibet. This happens about once in six years. In a few days' time I start for Ṭashilhunpo." "And where do you advise us to go and seek our teacher?" He pondered a little and then spoke. "One of two places would suit you; either Ṭashilhunpo or else the monastery of the Great Accomplishment at Mindöling ('the place where Deliverance is ripened'): that's the place for you."

One day while we were in camp the young lama who, with a small kitten, was the sole attendant upon the hermit, arrived with a message. "Will Mr. Pallis please come at once to the hermitage? The Precious Master requests his presence." I hurried up the hill and found the hermit fingering a large book. "Be seated, please." To the novice: "Serve tea to the gentleman." Then again to me: "The other day you spoke of Mila Repa. Here is his Legend. I wish you to read it aloud to me." He pointed to a chapter and I began, regretting that I had left my reading glasses behind, though fortunately I was not helpless without them. After a few sentences the abbot interrupted me. "No, this is not what we want: it does not contain the important parts of Mila Repa. It is not the history, but the spiritual poems that you must read from." He turned up another volume and I began again. The language was classical and rather harder than the prose biography, and I was not proficient in the old tongue. I managed to extract a little sense as I went along, but must confess to have missed a lot. I read on and on. Whenever a stumble occurred, due to the worn printing of the wood-blocks, the hermit corrected me: he knew it all off by heart, no unusual accomplishment among Tibetans. Then he would recite or read a little himself and expound obscure words, turning them from the ancient into the modern idiom; sometimes he stopped to enlarge on the sense of a passage. It was a curious experience, alternating between moments of lucidity, half-understanding, and total obscurity.

The afternoon passed and still the reading continued. As the sun began to decline outside, the twilight in the room increased and the print was no longer clearly distinguishable. I began to demur slightly. Looking at the master, I perceived a strange look in his eyes, as if some change were about to come over him; but its nature was not, at the moment, plain. He remained silent for a minute or two and then said abruptly: "Now depart — go!" Closing the book of the poet, I rose and bowed. "And what of tomorrow? Shall I return in the morning?" "No, not until I send word. Perhaps the day after tomorrow." Next day, however, the novice came down to say that the hermit had entered into a trance out of which he would not emerge for several days. No one might seek speech with him or approach him. At that last interview his spirit must have been hovering on the brink, about to take flight to undreamed-of realms. I thought of the passage in St. Paul: "I knew a man in Christ above fourteen years ago (whether in the body, I cannot tell; or whether out of the body, I cannot tell: God knoweth); such an one caught up to the third heaven. How that he was caught up into paradise, and heard unspeakable words, which it is not lawful for a man to utter."

So ended my strange visit to the abbot. As he was about to leave for Tibet, we decided that there was no point in lingering in T'hangu in bad weather; otherwise we would have asked nothing better than to spend several months under his regular tuition. Leaving a letter to be delivered to him on his emergence from meditation, we packed up and walked down to Lachhen, overtaking Samḍub and another monk on the road. They were returning to the village for the services of the Sacred Month (May-June) in which the entry of the Buddha into Nirvana is celebrated, the climax of the Tibetan year that corresponds with the Christian Easter.

Chapter XIII

Of Missionaries and Moths

AT LACHHEN at that time there were living two lady missionaries who ran a school and an industry for the making of blankets. I wished to find out what was the attitude of the lamas
towards the representatives of an actively competing creed, so
I tried to sound Samdub by putting the innocent question:
"What do those missionaries do in the village?" "They teach in
a school, and weave rugs," he replied. Repeated inquiries entirely failed to elicit any resentful answer; the propaganda motive behind their work he seemed to ignore. I have had several
subsequent opportunities of discussing the question of missions
with other lamas, especially in Ladak, where the Moravians run
an old-established proselytizing agency; but on no single occasion have I heard a spiteful word. Once, when I was moved to
comment on this fact, I was told that "we are taught that it is a
sin to speak disrespectfully of other religions or to treat their
ministers in unfriendly fashion."

This precept, which goes back to the times of the Buddha,
has been faithfully observed by His followers, with few exceptions, and makes Buddhist history pleasanter reading than the
grim records of the more militant religions; and this open-
minded spirit is shared by all other Traditions of Indian origin.
The idea of the same truth presenting a different appearance
when looked at from several viewpoints, and of various paths
converging upon one centre, is familiar in Eastern thought.
Furthermore, with so impersonal a conception of Divinity as
the Orient tends to hold, it is almost impossible for anyone to
fall into the state of thinking that he stands in a privileged
position in regard to God. An anthropomorphic habit in referring to the Godhead makes it easy to ascribe to it partisan sentiments of the most blasphemous kind. The believer with God
on his side does not take long to identify his own rivals with
God's enemies. When he finds himself worsted he comforts
himself with thoughts of martyrdom.

The Buddha and other Indian teachers, being aware of the
human tendency to faction, showed foresight in formally condemning the sin of irreverence towards other religions and thus
cut the ground from under the feet of potential bigots. An edict
of the great Emperor Asoka, pattern for all humane rulers,
who reigned in the third century B.C., says: "Do not decry
other sects, do not run them down, but, on the contrary, pay
honour to all that in them is worthy of honour." One sometimes
wishes that the official teachings of Christianity had been
equally explicit in respect of this practical application of
Christ's law of Love. One has only to reflect on what would
happen if a band of "Evangelical" missionaries were suddenly
to arrive, as they do in the East, in an Irish parish and start
vilifying the Catholic Church, or vice versa, in order to admit
that in these matters we are behindhand. In such a case, even
if no heads were broken, or if the attacked party turned the
other cheek to the extent of abstaining from violent invective,
it is doubtful whether a question such as I put to Samdub would
have been answered without some derogatory comment or
other, possibly taking the form of ridicule. The early apostles
of Buddhism managed to bear their good tidings to distant
lands without stooping to heap abuse on existing Traditions.
They addressed themselves first and foremost to those who
were capable of forming a considered judgment, the intellectually and spiritually gifted élite. Thence, the Doctrine percolated
downward into the mass of the people, which it leavened more
or less.

The professional missionary stands at a disadvantage, for the
standpoint he takes up as a supposed dispenser of light to the
benighted heathen entails for him a perpetual temptation to indulge in self-righteousness. Moreover, it is unavoidable that he
should be much concerned with the counting of heads of converts, for these are required for the statistics of the societies
who collect subscriptions. The less scrupulous agents make use
of disguised bribery, such as the distribution of medicines or
the offering of free tuition. Ostensibly charitable deeds, operations in hospitals, gifts to the poor, and the care of orphans, can
become, for the doers, so many deceitful expedients with a view
to attracting converts.

Those who feel a Christian call to the service of the needy
can still do useful work; but then, in my opinion, they would
do better to leave the proselytizing to others. The man who

wishes to play the part of an apostle is ever well advised to come empty-handed.

Bringers of new doctrines have never been unpopular in the East. One has only to remember the treatment accorded to the Jesuit Desideri, who visited Lhasa in 1716. He was at once granted permission to preach, and when he wrote a book to refute the errors, as he considered them, of the lamas, far from resenting it, they all rushed to borrow it. Desideri himself says: "My house suddenly became the scene of incessant comings and goings, by all sorts of people, chiefly learned men and professors, who came from the monasteries and universities, especially those of Sera and Drepung, the principal ones, to apply for permission to read the book." This was happening only a few years after the Huguenots had been driven from France and when in most of Europe heretical books would have been publicly burned by the common hangman.

Though in our eyes uncharitableness and pride are among the worst temptations, I think I am right in saying that a Buddhist or Hindu would always consider them secondary to that of wilful Ignorance. He would reserve his strongest blame for the habit of attacking other people's beliefs without first, like Desideri's lamas, making a genuine attempt to understand those beliefs as professed by their ablest exponents, not only by the unlettered herd. A scientist who presumed to find fault with a rival's hypothesis without giving evidence of more than superficial acquaintance with its principles would make himself ridiculous in the academic world. In one who tries to make himself the mouthpiece of God this attitude, not at all uncommon, is not only intellectually censurable; it is a sin against the Holy Ghost.

Apart from doctrines, even in regard to actual statements of fact there is a temptation to try to paint a lurid rather than a balanced picture, underlining all possible moral and material abuses and suppressing whatever is favourable; otherwise the emotions of parishioners at home will not be raised to the pitch of inducing them to open their purses wide for the cause. In this respect there may be some honourable exceptions; but my meetings with a good many missionaries and the perusal of their literature have led me to the opinion that, on the whole, their activities in Asia are disruptive and their methods open to severe criticism.

When we returned to Lachhen we were informed that heavy

rains had washed away paths in the Tista Valley and that it would be advisable not to linger if we wished our baggage to reach Gangtok in safety. These rumours afterwards proved to have been exaggerated; but at the time, having no means of verifying them, we decided to stay no more than two days, just time enough to sort out the remaining stores and attend a service at the *Gompa* (monastery), to which we had been specially bidden by Samdub.

We were first, however, invited to tea by the headman, in his own house, where we were introduced to his wife and little son, as well as to his mother, who, as commonly happens in Tibet, ruled the home. There is no friction on that score, since family life is strong and governed by conventions that no one thinks of questioning. The interior of the house revealed an astonishing number of fine objects, considering the small size of the village. One has only to compare it with an Alpine village of similar character to see the difference in the level of taste. The living-rooms, as usual in Tibet, were on the first floor, the principal one being a combined chapel and entertaining room. On either side of the altar stood a tier of pigeon-holes, each harbouring a sacred tome; these books are probably seldom read; they are more often treated as mere objects of reverence. After taking our seats on rugs of very fair quality, we were served with tea in cups with finely chased silver mounts. There was chopped mutton with spinach for the meat-eaters, and rice in china bowls for all. The best thing in the house was a beautifully fashioned copper brazier used for keeping the tea-pot warm, with a pair of silver handles ending in dragons' heads and a delicate band of ornament running round the edge. The shape is classical all over Tibet; but this example was outstanding.

The important event, however, was the visit to the *Gompa*. The service was timed for noon. A little before that, we walked up the hill and were received with due ceremony by the lamas, who presented the usual white scarves. We were led into an upper chapel above the main temple — most Sikkim temples are built in two stories — where we were served with tea. When the monks had assembled in the temple, we were led down-stairs. In their anxiety to put us at our ease they unearthed their three European chairs and placed them in the porch facing the doorway, doubtless supposing that no sahib was capable of sitting on the floor. When the service began we occupied the chairs, but felt horribly self-conscious and out of the picture. I tried to compose my mind by repeating a few *Manis,* but it kept wandering, unable to focus on what was going on in the church. My chair seemed to be burning the seat of my trousers. I fidgeted and fidgeted till I was able to bear it no longer; at last I sprang up and slipped inside and squatted against a side wall.

The service was most impressive. Perfect order and attention reigned, but free from any suggestion of drilled precision. The clergy were arranged in two choirs facing inwards and seated cross-legged on low platforms covered with carpets. All had musical instruments: trumpets eight feet long, oboes with a strong reedy tone, various percussion instruments including drums of all sorts and sizes, and cymbals. Others held a handbell, with a very sweet note, in the left hand and a *dorjé* or thunderbolt sceptre in the right, the pair that symbolizes the marriage of Wisdom and Method, the inseparable precursors of Enlightenment. From time to time the orchestra played a refrain; then chants followed, accompanied by drums or bells. The participants seemed absorbed in what they were doing: there was no shuffling or gazing around such as we had seen in the slack monastery at Gangtok. One sensed the influence of the abbot's teaching, imbuing his pupils with real seriousness and devotion. Samdub happened to be sitting facing me. As he wielded his bell and *dorjé,* his hands described graceful ritual gestures. There is a whole language in these *mudras,* to give them their Sanskrit name, for one who knows how to read their message. A faint smile occasionally flitted across his seraphic countenance. Most of his companions knew the whole service off by heart; but he followed in a book placed on a stand in front of him, periodically turning the page over with a light flick of his finger. There was nothing to mar an atmosphere of perfect edification; the only thing that somewhat spoiled the picture was ourselves with our incongruously cut clothes, which seemed aggressively out of place. I felt as if I ought to be sent away like the man in the Gospel who attended the King's feast without a marriage garment. It is extraordinary how hopeless it is to try to reconcile importations from the anti-traditional world with any traditional scene. I longed more than ever to be allowed to take part in the life of these people under conditions that would relieve me of all constraint.

In the evening Samdub and a friend of his came down to supper at the bungalow. When the meal was served, we waited for our guests to help themselves; but they paused as if em-

barrassed. Thinking they might be shy, I dipped a spoon in
the curry, but had only just time to drop it unobserved as
they started to intone a long metrical grace. When it was over
they took some curry and conversation began. Samḍub told
us something of his life. He belonged to the village and was a
special pupil of the abbot, for whom he professed enthusiastic
admiration. They used to rise at five a.m. and usually retired
to bed about sunset. They apportioned the day between study,
occasional services, and meditation under the teacher's direction. They gave occasional instruction to the laymen of the
village, and the Precious Master preached a sermon from time
to time. They spent not less than three months of the year in
meditation; at a later stage even more time might be given to
it. During retirement they kept silence and each man attended
to his own needs. Samḍub was certainly a diligent pupil, with
a grace and refinement all his own. It was strange to think
that he came from one of the same peasant families as our
rather argumentative and uncouth porters. Probably, had he
not entered the Church, he would have been just like the
others. His refinement seemed to be largely the result of his
training, though with him the right material happened to be
present also.

The monsoon is the season for seeing the Sikkim forests in all
their glory. As we returned down the Tista Valley, which we
had only seen in the April drought, it was hard to believe that
so much growth could have happened in two short months.
Innumerable creepers, which on our earlier passage were only
just beginning their upward journey, had now overtaken the
trees and bushes, the new shoots of which were vainly striving
to escape their pursuing tendrils. A bewildering tangle of lesser
plants covered every inch of ground under the big trees — ferns,
selaginellas, heart-shaped leaves of a coppery red with variegated markings, strawberries with fruit equal in size to a medium garden variety but with a flavour that belongs only to the
wild. Round Tsungt'hang we came upon the giant white Sikkim
lily growing in the glades to a height of about eight feet. A
little way below the same village we found two species of white
orchid; their huge spikes described a prancing curve through
the air high above our heads. We recognized a woody creeper,
which wound its way luxuriantly round the boughs of smaller
trees, as a hydrangea; in all things except in its manner of
growth it resembled the homely potted variety in English
greenhouses.

We lingered to pick some green raspberries, as delicious as the strawberries, but we had to keep a careful watch for the small black leeches that swarmed in the undergrowth. We found that a well-adjusted puttee was a sufficient protection; but a few leeches managed to evade our vigilance and made their way to exposed parts higher up, whence, after gorging themselves with blood, they eventually dropped off unperceived. If detected, a leech can always be made to release its hold by a pinch of salt. It is useless to pull them off as they may leave their grappling hooks in the flesh, and in that climate the sore is apt to fester. The bites bleed rather a long time because of a liquid that the leeches inject in order to retard coagulation.

Towards Dikchhu, in the tropical belt, the splendour of the woods attained its climax. Among the trees broad-leaved varieties, reflecting much light from their leathery surfaces — a characteristic of warm damp regions throughout the world — contrasted with the feathery grace of acacias, tree ferns, and bamboos, and the twisted sheaves of sword-blade *Pandanus*. The air was laden with heavy scents from invisible flowers overhead. Sometimes the path itself was strewn with fallen blossoms, the confetti of some sylvan wedding. Passing through this ordered confusion of forms and tints, where every step brought us face to face with a new fantasy, proof against every effort at analysis, we felt we were in the grip of a vital power, in whose presence man and his ethical preoccupations were of supreme unimportance. It is her very indifference that makes men fly to Nature for comfort when they are in trouble, for she is a mother who listens, but volunteers no interested advice.

Endless diversity of green gives the character to these woods. Flowers only play a subsidiary part in the landscape. The task of supplying brighter colours is left to butterflies, which emerge in great numbers at the approach of the rains. Among the common varieties are many yellow or white butterflies, related to the orange-tips and clouded-yellows; also swallow-tails, mostly velvety black, with patches of white or red on their elaborately scalloped hind wings. The common Himalayan species, known to us from the Satlej, dusted over with gold and with a blue patch on the lower wing, is also abundant. Then there is the famous mimic, the Leaf butterfly, which, when its wings are closed, looks exactly like a leaf, complete with stalk and veinings, and the Map butterfly, white, with dark meridians and. parallels, and the brick-red *Charaxes* and *Apatura ambica*, shaped like an enormous Purple Emperor, but brown with a broad iridescent band of blue crossing both wings. When it is flying, the blue mirror flashes as it catches the light. This butterfly takes the place of the blue-winged *Morphos* of the South American jungle, from whose wings vandals have made ugly paper-weights and brooches. A fritillary, a near relative of our English Queen-of-Spain, lends a homely touch. In dry spots, especially on the path leading from Dikchhu up towards the Penlong Pass, various members of the *Danaine* family, relatives of the common Monarch of U.S.A., hover round the trees. They are all large butterflies, some reddish-white with black wing-tips, some dappled grey and others (of the genus *Euplœa*) dark-brown velvet suffused with sapphire, one of the loveliest of all Indian butterflies. In addition there are no less brilliant day-flying moths, and innumerable bees and wasps of monstrous size encased in metallic panoplies of green, blue, and purple. At night, moths, beetles, ant-lions, and praying mantises come out in immense variety; but we did not get much chance of observing them till we reached Gangtok itself, where the electric-light standards drew vast numbers every evening. Whether we were looking at a hawk-moth or the huge Atlas himself with his nine-inch wing-span or an almost microscopic plumelike species, we never ceased to marvel at the intricacies of the designs that had been bestowed on them. How hopelessly inadequate and artificial those theories seemed that attempted to account for such beauties simply on utilitarian grounds, and which till recently were supposed to have said the last word on the subject. The prevailing bright colour of an insect or flower can certainly be advantageous to its possessor as a means of calling a mate, or warning off a bird, or attracting the pollinating bee; but it is only an artist who can find a use for the minute lines and dots, the delicate scroll-work, the silvery hairs, the tiny points of colour that turn orchids and insects into so many miracles. Without the presence of some sort of inherent Will in all things, it would seem the maddest waste. For whose benefit must the controlling cells go to all this trouble?

At Singhik there occurred the first break in the monsoon. Till that time we had been almost continuously enveloped in mist, with heavy rain at times. We went to bed in Singhik bungalow without a hint of a change in the weather; but about midnight someone chanced to go on to the veranda and saw the mountains unveiled and silhouetted against a moonlit sky. At dawn we witnessed a great wonder. In front of us lay the garden, bounded by a fence of purple bougainvillæa and datura bushes covered with white trumpet-shaped flowers. Looking beyond, we could see up into the side valley of Talung, thickly wooded, which drains the snows of Simvu. Suddenly that mountain, scene of our defeat, and beyond it, the overwhelming mass of Kangchhendzönga, were aflame, not with the pink glow of the Alps, but with an orange so unearthly that a painter who faithfully reproduced it could hardly have escaped the accusation of fancifulness. Then the curtain was lowered once more over the peaks; but we walked down to Dikchhu in radiant and unwonted sunlight. The same evening, taking two stages in one, we reached Gangtok.

We were now forced to make fresh plans, if we wished to carry on with our studies; for Tibet for the present was out of the question. After toying with several proposals, each of which proved to contain insurmountable objections, we decided to go to Ladak, a small kingdom of Tibetan affinities, which an incongruous accident of history has united to the Indian state of Kashmir. Excepting western China, which would have involved too long and costly a journey, it was the only district outside the political frontier of Tibet where there were monasteries of sufficient size and importance for our purpose. It meant that we had to go down to Calcutta and take the train across to the western end of the Himalaya; but it was a case of Hobson's choice, so, after saying good-bye to our friends at Kalimpong, we set out for our new destination and were soon speeding across the great plain, which the monsoon had reclothed with the lively green of growing crops.

PART THREE

Ladak -- 1936

Chapter XIV

Kashmir and Purig

THE MOST PLEASANT WAY of approaching Kashmir is to detrain
at Lahore and then to continue by car across the foothills, by
the Banihal Pass, a journey that occupies two days. Jammu, the
old capital of the present ruling dynasty, is a possible half-way
house. It possesses a number of Hindu temples, with elegant
spires tipped with golden finials; but many people will be surprised to hear that one of its most interesting buildings is the
dak bungalow maintained for travellers. Its ceilings are exquisite examples of Kashmir painted and gilt wood, covered
with the most intricate geometrical and floral arabesques. Each
room has a different pattern; how many passers-by must have
seen them without paying the least heed! If some of my readers
happen to pass through Jammu, I hope they will not forget to
glance upward while they are having lunch in the dining-
room. Nails have been driven into the panels and electric fans
fixed: in time all will perish unless the archæological authorities can protect these lovely ceilings as they deserve.

Having emerged at last on the fabled plain of Kashmir, we
drove along straight roads enclosed between rows of white-
stemmed poplars to Srinágar, the capital. We occupied a house-
boat on the river Jhelam. Europeans were not permitted to own
freehold property, because the rulers of the state were apprehensive lest the excellence of the climate, which is like a dry
and sunny version of our English one, should tempt retired em-
ployees of Government or commerce to settle there in embar-
rassing numbers. As a result of this ordinance the foreign residents mostly inhabited house-boats. The waterfront fringed
with poplars, willows, and plane trees, with its long lines of
floating dwellings made fast to the bank, is reminiscent of the
Thames, though the river here is swifter. Kingfishers dart about
or perch fearlessly on the mooring-ropes while they gulp down
wriggling frogs. A beautiful species of paradise flycatcher is
also common: the male is white, the female red, and in shape

they are not unlike some birds-of-paradise, whence the name.

The European end of the city, where the General Post Office, the club, and the modern shops are situated, has become very trippery, and innumerable touts dog the footsteps of the tourist. The nuisance is less noticeable in the old quarters, where people are civil and where it is possible to wander unmolested.

Much of Srinágar looks like a blend of Holland and Venice, with a labyrinth of shady canals and bridges, through which the boats of hawkers of fruit and vegetables thread their way. There are little private landing-stages and spacious mansions dating from the seventeenth century, but now mostly falling into disrepair. The material is a fine mellow brick; the walls are broken here and there by windows or balconies closed with lattices of wood forming complex geometrical interlacings. On most of the roofs grass is growing, and the effects of impoverishment are evident on all sides. One wonders how long it will be before some municipal council affected with zeal for modernizing the city in the name of slum-clearance will condemn them to demolition. These noble and well-constructed houses, if people had any taste, would be reconditioned and become the most sought-after residential property.

They must have been magnificent in the heyday of Mughal power, when Kashmir became a regular summer resort for the court during the hot weather: the practice of moving the government of India up to the hills has, of course, continued to this day. Srinágar was a centre of art, renowned for metal-work, weaving, and painted wood. The Kashmiris, as a race, are exceptionally dextrous with their hands; but hardly any craft worth the name survives now, although a lot of hideous carving and papier-mâché is still turned out. One can purchase bureaux, prickly with the horns of dragons and the manes of lions in three-quarter relief, cigarette-boxes and trays covered all over with finicky flowers done in shiny paints, and white felt rugs imported from eastern Turkistan and embroidered locally in nightmare colour-schemes. Yet in most of these things, if trouble be taken to trace back the patterns through serial stages of degradation to their origins, these will be recognized as the lineal descendants of once harmonious designs. Only in the case of rough glazed pottery, used by the very poor, and despised by the better-to-do for its cheapness, have a few good traditional forms survived. We purchased a pleasing vase with a biscuit-coloured glaze for three annas (probably too high a price), which can hardly be bettered for showing off a branch of some flowering tree, or leaves turned to copper by the touch of autumn frost.

But what of shawls, the craft for which Kashmir is specially famous? Plain white shawls, as fine as a spider's web, are still woven and drawn through rings to impress the customer. But shawl-making as a developed art, with the flowered borders so popular in Victorian days, is now a thing of the past. During the nineteenth century, when no lady of quality thought her trousseau complete if it lacked its Kashmir wrap, and two hundred pounds was not an out-of-the-way price to pay for a good specimen, the weaving of shawls, under pressure from the dealers, was speeded up excessively, to the detriment of the workers' eyesight. In more modern times, to combat the abuse, the authorities are said to have discouraged the manufacture, though one would have thought that a rational control of hours and conditions of work would have answered the purpose. However, even had the shawl-making not been frowned upon, it is doubtful if it would have survived in the face of the universal tendency to falsify processes, which has ended by killing almost every art in the Orient within a couple of generations. As in carpets and other textiles, the first step would have been the introduction of chemical dyes because their violence was mistaken for brilliancy, or else on the flimsy plea of "saving time," though the proportion of time spent on the actual treatment in the vats bears no relation to the months needed for the weaving of a shawl. The colour-sense of the people, formerly unerring, once having been disturbed, deadly logic subconsciously working in the artist would have taught him next to alter the designs also, to save labour and thought. Patterns would have become bigger or more repetitive or more obviously striving after self-advertisement. The result would have been the same in the end — extinction. There seems to be no trifling with the artistic principles. To recover the sense of craftsmanship one must retrace one's steps right back to the point where the traditional and anti-traditional ways parted; but if, through a readiness to compromise on this or that, the true tradition be not restored in its integrity, imitation of earlier models still results in something alien. The neo-Gothic and neo-classical and neo-Indian and neo-palæolithic are examples of what follows in such cases.

In making preparations for a journey into the interior, the newcomer to Kashmir is faced with certain difficulties not met with in other parts of the Himalaya. Many of the agencies engaged in supplying the needs of tourists are far from reliable. The country is very cheap indeed, but the standard of honesty seems rather low and one cannot indulge in that carefreeness about prices and property that makes Garhwal and Sikkim so easy to travel in. We were fortunate in enjoying the advice of a leading resident of many years' standing, Mr. George Stavridi of the Oriental Carpet Company, and of his daughter, Miss Helen Stavridi, who had made several enterprising journeys in the interior and knew all that was worth knowing about local conditions.

A young Panjabi clerk was given the job of purchasing stores for the party; we were quite taken aback by the exiguous sums he expended. For this young man the bazaar was an arena, bargaining a sport, and price-cutting a subtle branch of psychology. For instance, one of the things he had to purchase was a small milk-can. He walked into a shop and asked: "How much is that?" "Eight annas." "What, do you take me for a millionaire?" He quitted the shop with an inimitable air of injured virtue and walked into the premises of the first shop-keeper's nearest competitor. "That fellow over there had the impudence to ask me eight annas for a milk-can. What will you give it for?" "Six." "You must be out of your senses; I've never in my life heard of such outrageous extortion." "But I will reduce it to — " Unheeding, he swept out of the second shop and entered a third. "I wish for a milk-can of this size: how much is it?" Before the man could quote a price, another shopkeeper who had been standing by, listening to the previous encounters, pushed his way up to our friend and, nudging him, whispered with a wink: "You come to my place: I'll let you have it for four"; but by that time a fourth man had rushed up and was offering it for three annas six pice and so on, till the whole street was afoot in fierce competition. The young imp was well aware of the lack of solidarity among petty retailers in India and their readiness to whittle their profit down to nothing in order to undercut their next-door neighbours. Finally, for the price of two and a half annas, he closed with the owner of the shop into which he had entered first of all, having in the interval circled right round the bazaar back to his starting-point. He bore off his trophy triumphantly, pursued by indignant cries of "Dirty Panjabi swine" and other still more colourful imprecations from the whole neighbourhood in chorus.

Guided by our friend's advice, we applied for our transport

animals to one Muhammad Ramzana, who keeps a shop on the
Bund or river front. He was a very straightforward man to deal
with and looked after us splendidly at most reasonable cost.
The ponies engaged to carry our modest baggage for the first
week, as far as Dras, were obtained from the village of Gander-
bal at the entrance to the Sind Valley: they were to meet us at
Wayl Bridge, eighteen miles from Srinágar; as far as that point
the road was fit for wheeled vehicles, so that everything we
needed could be carried in a small van. For our permits, and for
information about the Treaty road to Leh in general, we applied to the Residency office, where we met the secretary, a
Panjabi called Khan Muhammad Din, who had been sixteen
times to Ladak. From the first moment of being introduced to
him we perceived that we were dealing with a man of unusual
insight and kindness; this early esteem became cemented into
still closer friendship in the course of subsequent meetings in
Leh. I am glad to take this opportunity of expressing our thanks
to him once again.

We did not, of course, think of leaving Kashmir before paying a visit by boat across the marshes and lakes to the famous
Mughal pleasances of Nishat and Shalimar, the first built by
Shah Jahan and the second by his father, Jahangir. The craft
used was not the swift *shikára,* which is the easiest method of
communication on these waters, but a massive barge with a
hut woven of rushes in the centre, in which the boatman and
his family slept and cooked. These barges are punted in lei-
surely fashion through the reed-fringed channels that offer a
passage in the tangle of pond-weeds which choke a great part
of the lakes. Huge pink lotuses lift their heads high out of the
water; they are much overpicked by natives, who offer them
in bunches to tourists. In quiet backwaters the surface is starred
with a small yellow water-lily. Villages and cottages, surrounded by fertile market gardens, occupy the solid ground,
while floating islands formed of water-weeds bound together,
on which tomatoes and marrows are planted, allow the peasants
to push their productive holdings out on to the surface of the
lake itself.

Punting up one of the water-alleys cleared in the reeds, we
reached the steps of Nishat, below the principal pavilion of
the garden, which is a simple building with projecting balconies
closed with the usual lattices. Some officious hand has thought
fit to fix a notice with the name *Nishat* in large block letters
in the middle of the façade.

This dream-garden is planned on the classical Mughal model, with a row of water-channels and fountains passing down the centre and out through the main pavilion itself. The water comes from a source in the hills which provide a background to the garden, and flows down a series of terraced levels, leaping each wall by an ornamental shoot. Lawns, like the softest of carpets, are edged by beds of sweet-scented carnations, heliotropes, and every other sort of garden flower. It is probable that this part of the work has been enhanced by the efforts of recent gardeners, for the English can always be trusted to make the best of a garden. It is the one art that they will never allow to be filched from them. Most of the trees of the garden are gigantic plane trees, the famous *chenars*, introduced by the Mughals to console their homesick hearts with tender memories of the old domain of their family, away to the north of the Hindu Kush. The gardens must look very different now from the time, three hundred years ago, when they were planned and the young trees planted.

Another hour of punting brings one to the Shalimar, a name redolent of sentimental ballads. A short walk between rice-fields, some vivid green and some of a reddish brown, leads to the entrance. The plan is not unlike that of Nishat, but the slope is gentler and it is not possible to take in the whole at a glance; nevertheless it is just as lovely, and in the architecture of its two pavilions it surpasses its rival. One kiosk in particular, of black marble, is built in the characteristic square style of the time of Jahangir, with bracketed capitals and overhanging eaves that cast deep shadows, so that the sunlit garden outside has the magic of an enchanted realm. The ceilings are of the same decorated wood as in the dak bungalow at Jammu; but, curiously enough, the latter, though so recent and not built to house princes, is somewhat the better example.

The two gardens, rightly esteemed among the perfect achievements of human genius, must have been a rare solace to sovereigns weary of the cares of empire. One can picture Jahangir with his fascinating and masterful queen, Nur Jahan, picnicking at the Shalimar and being diverted by the recitation of Persian lyrics or witty epigrams, or else by the disputations of learned men, in which the royal pair took a special delight — surely a true sport of kings. Or perhaps they sat and turned over the leaves of albums illuminated by the incomparable skill of the Mughal miniaturists, that strange art in which the force of a common tradition made co-operation between artists possible to an unheard-of degree, so that three separate masters, each of outstanding genius, collaborated in the production of a single small page, one doing the drawing, a second putting on the colour, while the portraits fell to a third. Often the artists would exchange their respective functions, yet these miniatures show a unity that makes it hard to believe that they were not the creation of a single brain.

At Nishat one can picture the peaceful and compassionate Shah Jahan, under whom Hindustan enjoyed almost uninterrupted tranquillity and good government, sitting at sunset with the lady of the Taj, his adored consort Mumtaz-i-Mahal ("Crown of the Palace"). They are looking over the lake, which shimmers like molten gold, past the arch of a camel-back bridge, which marks the point where a raised road crosses the marsh towards the fort of Srinágar, showing up black against the orange transparency of the sky. It was then that the genial monarch lived his happiest moments in the enjoyment of perfect conjugal love, little dreaming of the bitter cup that he must drink in his old age, when his own son, the able but narrow-minded Aurangzib, was to depose him and reverse his tolerant policy, to the eventual ruin of the Empire. It is suggestive to note that the latter prince, with the typical prejudices of the puritan, was no friend of the arts; nor did he share his father's love of building — his mosque at Benares, the slender minarets of which can be seen from the railway, was put up rather in order to impress the Hindus than from any love of architecture. He removed his patronage from musicians and dancers, who had made gay the feasts of his predecessors, so they plotted a stratagem to soften the heart of their dour sovereign. One day sounds of mourning reached his ears as he sat near the window. When he inquired the cause, it was reported to him that a long and doleful funeral procession was passing in front of the palace. "Whom are they burying?" inquired the Emperor. "Sire, it is Music herself: the guild of musicians are holding the obsequies of her and of her instruments." "An excellent idea," cried Aurangzib; "tell them to dig the grave deep, that she may be in no danger of a resurrection!"

Among the minor campaigns undertaken by the generals of this harsh ruler was one into Ladak; the king of that country had invoked Mughal aid to repel a Mongol-Tibetan invasion. It was accorded, but only at the price of conversion to Islam. The Ladaki prince, however, reaped but a shortlived advantage from his nominal apostasy from the ancestral faith, for though the Mughals routed the host of the invaders in a great battle, as soon as they had withdrawn the enemy reappeared and dictated terms afresh. From this time the fortunes of the principality, which at the height of its power had extended over all western Tibet right into the valley of the Brahmaputra, fell into decline, though it preserved a precarious independence, with its boundaries curtailed to the present limits. But the Mughal Empire was also moving towards dissolution, largely as a consequence of Aurangzib's religious intolerance, which goaded the Hindus into revolt — by contempt and petty vexations, be it understood, for no case is on record where a single unbeliever suffered death or loss of property for his faith — and reduced most of India to anarchy, paving the way for the gradual subjugation of the peninsula by the British. During the period of disintegration, in the eighteenth and early nineteenth centuries, Kashmir, after a spell of cruel oppression at the hands of Afghan upstarts, which ruined its prosperity, fell, in 1815, under the new military power of the Sikhs. A general of one of their vassals, the Dogra Rajput prince of Jammu, pushed the invasion into Ladak and, though meeting with fairly determined resistance, overran it between 1835 and 1840. From that moment its story as a separate state was ended, and this once glorious kingdom, in violation of its ethnic affinities, remained henceforth an unnatural appanage of a state mostly inhabited by Muslims and ruled over by a Hindu; for when the Sikhs in their turn fell foul of the British, Kashmir, and with it Ladak, were handed over to the Dogra chieftain, who, from having been a petty tributary to the Panjab, now emerged as the ally of British India, the Maharaja of Jammu and Kashmir, and has remained in control ever since.

Srinágar to Leh is an easy journey of fifteen days, but the time can be shortened by doing double stages. Rest-houses have been built at intervals along the route and the villages are bound, as part of their taxes, to provide transport animals if required, rates of payment being laid down in a schedule obtainable at the Residency office. Supplies of fodder, firewood, and certain basic articles of food are also catered for, so that the traveller has not to forage far afield. In certain cases it is pleasanter to avoid the conventional halting-places and to split up distances in a different proportion, camping on ground of one's own choosing. Till one is clear of Kashmir proper, it is wise to be rather wary before turning pack-animals out to graze, as there exists a species of coarse grass that produces a severe and often fatal colic in any pony unlucky enough to swallow it. One of our ponies eluded the vigilance of its syce and grazed on this grass. Next day the animal showed signs of distress. Then with rest and care it seemed about to recover; but it died on the tenth day.

After crossing the Zoji Pass, one enters a country of stony mountains and high-lying valleys, its barrenness relieved only where irrigation by means of leats has been able to harness the torrent-waters. In such favoured situations there occur oases of an intense green, kept moist by regular flooding, which takes the place of rain in this region, where the annual fall dwindles to a bare ten inches or less. Set at convenient distances apart, *baghs* or gardens, grassy enclosures shaded by willows, have been planted, kept fresh by daily watering. They offer charming camping-grounds; but when occupying them, a watchful eye should be kept lest the caretakers charged with the duty of watering should open the irrigation channels without bothering to ascertain if any tents are standing in the grove. Otherwise the unsuspicious camper will suddenly notice a silvery edge of water stealing towards him across the turf. In a moment the peaceful camp is humming with activity; men snatch up blankets or stores from the path of the oncoming flood, others rush with stones to deflect it at a higher point, while yet others shout out to the villagers, not without uncomplimentary epithets, calling on them to run and block the main breach. The waters stop short in the nick of time, the hubbub subsides, and calm enfolds the camp once more.

The number of visitors proceeding into Ladak in any one year is wisely limited, so as to avoid throwing an excessive strain on the scanty resources of the province. But for this measure, the peasants, tempted by a prospect of ready cash, might improvidently barter away too large a share of their produce, leaving themselves short in the lean season. The whole administration of the Treaty road is simple, efficient, and to the advantage of all concerned.

At last the appointed day arrived (July 12) and we set out by car for Wayl Bridge; but before emerging from the warren of narrow alleys we passed under the walls of a vast building of remarkable appearance, forming a regular quadrangle, with a peculiar wooden tower, a cross between a pagoda and a belfry, surmounting the middle point of each of the four sides. Built from small, flat bricks of a lovely warm tint, on a foundation of stone, it was entirely without ornament; but the proportions of

every part and of the tunnel-like arch at the entrance were so
faultless that it did not seem conceivable that anyone could
wish to add to its perfections. Inquiry revealed that this was
the great mosque of Srinágar, erected during the reign of Jahangir in a style peculiar to Kashmir.

No one had the heart to hurry past, so we stopped the car
and, removing our shoes, entered the mosque. The interior is as
austere as the outside. Apart from a black marble niche showing the direction of Mecca, the building is plain and relies for
its effect entirely on the proportions of the surrounding arches
and the forest-like colonnades bearing the roof, each pillar being the smoothed trunk of a gigantic deodar tree.

In the centre of the court is a basin where the faithful can
make their ablutions, and also two old trees, which sound a tiny
note of tenderness in the presence of the overwhelming majesty of God under His aspect Unity, the doctrine that this
building seems to proclaim with a single voice. Nowhere has
the Islamic genius achieved a more crowning triumph; it is
strange that books on Indian architecture usually omit any reference to this mosque, though it must be admitted that it does
not lend itself to photography as easily as some more ornamental buildings. This mosque had a narrow escape from destruction on the annexation of Kashmir by the Sikhs. Ranjit Singh
closed it for a time and it fell into disrepair. It is fortunate that
no one laid covetous hands on its colossal timbers. Later on,
subscriptions were collected for its restoration, and the whole
population contributed handsomely.

At Wayl Bridge we crossed the Sind and followed its wide
and verdant valley, which yields crops of rice and maize. We
passed through prosperous-looking villages, shaded by huge
walnut trees. The containing hills were not steep and their
sides were clothed with conifers; we could have fancied ourselves in the Tyrol. Neither the valley itself nor the distant
peaks suggested anything on a Himalayan scale; but the narrow side valleys were wilder and more rugged. I followed a torrent some little way during a day's halt at Gund. The slopes
were extremely abrupt and savage-looking, with long drifts of
old avalanche snow lying about, through which sweet-smelling
bushes with white flowers, probably viburnum, poked their
branches. Delphiniums, almost as big as our garden varieties,
made brilliant splashes of blue on the steep sides of the cutting.
Chestnuts, with a few pines, formed the woods. The undergrowth was also chestnut, but of a different species, rather

lanky and profusely flowering with bunches of huge pink blossoms. This was true Himalayan country again.

The pass across the main range, the Zoji La, the lowest in all the two thousand-odd miles of the Himalaya, is reached from Baltal rest-house, on the Kashmir side, by a path that rises some 3,000 feet by easy gradients. Pines soon gave place to birches, the trees that usually are found nearest to the snows; then the path, rounding a rocky corner where, in shaly crannies, grew huge tufts of pearly-white columbine, unexpectedly took a level sweeping curve to the right. Here we saw the last of the birches, save for a few gaunt stragglers higher up the pass, gnarled and riven under the lash of the storms. A biting wind attacked us; through mist we caught a distant glimpse of white peaks. Before us extended an even snow-bed, in the centre of which lay the half-eaten carcass of a horse, with a solitary vulture perched on it. The great bird, so gorged that he could only rise a few inches off the ground, scuttled away, aiding its legs with the beating of its magnificently spreading wings. Shivering, we stopped to open rucksacks and take out warm sweaters and scarves, for the edge of the wind was keen; then on again over snow-beds for some little distance, till we suddenly became aware that the streams had begun to flow the other way. It was the top: we were astride the Himalaya, but we could not quite agree upon the exact point of the divide. Where the snow had melted, skeletons of animals had been uncovered, calling up images of some old slave-route in the Sahara. Though such a low pass (11,300 feet) and a simple walk under summer conditions, the Zoji is one of the most murderous, accounting for a number of animal lives, and human lives too, levying its deadly toll by means of sudden avalanches, or engulfing its victims in bottomless drifts.

In the winter months, though trade is quiet, a number of Turkoman *hadjis*, or pilgrims bound for Mecca, come from Yarkand to Leh by the Karakoram Pass on their way to India. They are a happy-go-lucky lot and frequently get stranded in bad weather, at the cost of frostbitten fingers or toes, which are in due course amputated by local practitioners or, if they are lucky, by an English lady doctor who works devotedly in one of the Indus villages. Then, disdaining prudent counsels of delay, the hadjis push towards the Zoji, their minds possessed by the sole thought of reaching the sacred goal and assured of a crown of glory if they should fall by the wayside. The inhabitants of the villages just north of the pass, though nominally

It should be noted that only the principal mountain chains have been indicated; most of the area shown, however, is mountainous.

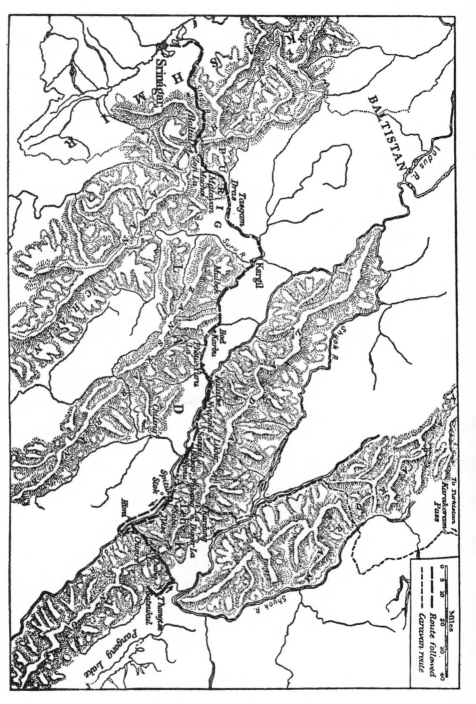

co-religionists, exploit the pilgrims unmercifully, withholding their help in crossing the pass until the travellers have consumed all their food, and then reprovisioning them at an exorbitant charge. Finally, having bled them white, they help them down to safety on the Kashmir side.

Four miles beyond the pass stands a rest-house called Machoi, and some way short of it there is a small cabin connected with the telegraph, in a flat alp where several glacier streams meet; it is a delightful place for a camp and would make an excellent centre for a climbing holiday. The grass cropped short by sheep is silver-grey with tiny edelweiss. It is said that the shepherds who frequent these pastures are given to pilfering, and it is unwise to leave a camp unguarded.

At Machoi we encountered a troop of Baltis with a slightly Mongolian cast of face, fine-looking men clad in serviceable homespuns, and of a cheery demeanour. We knew that their dialect belonged to the Tibetan group; but its harsh sound seemed far removed from the soft tones of the Lhasa dialect that we had heard farther east. Written Tibetan abounds in consonants; but the majority of these are now mute, only a single one, out of a group of two or three, being sounded. It suddenly occurred to us to address these Baltis in our ordinary Tibetan, but to sound all the mute consonants. In an instant they were beaming, and chattering to us in voluble Balti. Evidently in this remote land the language has retained very much the sound it had when the Tibetans first emerged into the light of history. At that time they were a rapacious tribe delighting in plunder and cruelty, dreaded over central Asia as the Vikings were once feared in Europe. Their tongue then matched their deeds, bristling with harsh combinations of sounds. Then came Buddhism with its genius for drawing the sting from the warlike lusts of peoples, and the Tibetan language seems to have softened in sympathy. Acting on this idea that the Balti language reproduced an early form, we not only pronounced the mutes, but racked our brains for all the obsolete words that we could remember. The plan seemed to answer, and we carried on quite an intelligent conversation and were credited with a mastery of their dialect — utterly undeserved! After some weeks among "Aryans" it was exciting to string the old monosyllables together in concise phrases and to see again flat noses and almond eyes.

Some way beyond Machoi, we came to the earthly paradise of Nimarg, again a meeting-place of several streams, where ev-

ery inch of ground was hidden beneath a carpet of irises, potentillas, delphiniums, gentians, verbena, onions — both metallic
purple and yellow — primulas, anemones, and other species too
numerous to mention. On certain slopes creamy *Eremurus,*
three feet high, stood up like lilliputian woods. A pink goose-
foot formed the foundation in most of the spaces left unoccupied by other flowers; but on the floor of the valley the prevailing colour was the blue of cynoglossum; pink lousewort and
edelweiss fringed the streams.

This alp owes its luxuriance to the fact that it receives the
residue of all the heavily charged rain-clouds that escape being
precipitated on the Kashmir side of the divide. Though Nimarg
is frequently drenched, the rainfall shrinks rapidly beyond this
point, being only 22 inches at Dras, a few miles on, while at
Leh it is no more than 3.26 inches.

A couple of miles from Nimarg, a group of mean hovels with
a sordid little rest-house marked the village of Matayan. Most
of the houses were too low to stand upright in, and the inhabitants seemed poor and suspicious of strangers. Though the
moisture had markedly lessened, there were still many flowers.
The marshy flats were rich with purple iris, and on one bank,
near the path, grew a specially lovely pale cream anemone. We
gathered seeds of this exquisite flower on the way back and
tried to induce them to germinate in a Cheshire garden, but unfortunately without any success. *Eremurus* was still found in
abundance just below Matayan; but each mile brought fewer
and fewer flowers. At Pandras, five miles farther on, the Alpines
had almost disappeared and plants characteristic of dry climes,
many of them aromatic, replaced them; thymes, camomiles,
huge umbels, and a few leguminous plants armed with thorns
were growing among rocks; great rose bushes made cascades
of pink blossom down the face of the cliffs. The banks of the
river were stony, and at times it raced furiously through narrow
gates of serpentine marble, like black slag. At Dras, which is a
fairly large village with a few general utility shops and a camping-ground in the usual willow grove, we felt that India was already far away. This was the highly coloured landscape, the
invigorating air, and the way of life of central Asia.

We had been told that we should pick up Ladakis at this
place, so we had only engaged our Kashmiris to accompany us
thus far. Actually the information was inaccurate and we were
compelled in consequence to take on Dras men as far as the

stage before the Ladak frontier. They were an unprepossessing crowd and none too trustworthy. We had to be watchful at night against theft: a blanket was actually stolen off a sleeping porter in the enclosed garden where we camped.

At most stages on the Treaty road, eggs are to be had from an official supplier appointed to attend to travellers; but if several parties happen to pass through the same village within a few days, there may be a shortage. Nevertheless, as a Kashmiri petty official assured us, it is the statutory duty of the *tehkidar* or caterer, as laid down by the regulations, to produce eggs on demand. "But what happens if the hens don't lay?" we asked. "They are bound to," he said pompously, "it is the Government rule." Acting on this assumption, we put in an indent with the caterer at Dras, a crafty-looking old fellow with a flowing beard; but he, after endless badgering, only managed to produce three eggs, one of which was cracked. We were beginning to entertain serious doubts whether the hens in Dras had really been sufficiently socialized to lay in obedience to Government behest, when our old friend Khan Muhammad Din rode up, having followed us from Srinágar on faster horses; for it was the time of his yearly inspection of the road to Leh. "Have you all you require?" he asked after greetings had been exchanged. "Everything, Khan Sahib, except eggs, which seem to be scarce." The Khan transfixed the caterer with a severe look. "What is this that I hear? Eggs must be found immediately." Then to us: "How many do you want? Oh! a dozen? All right, the caterer will supply a dozen eggs." The old peasant muttered something about tomorrow morning. "No, this minute. Bring a dozen here so that I may have a look at them," corrected the Khan sharply. The caterer went away and must have read the Riot Act to the fowls, for he was back in a few minutes with a dozen eggs, among which we even recognized the self-same cracked one of his earlier offer.

While at Dras we were invited by the local schoolmaster, a Hindu, to witness a drill display by his pupils in a field by the river. He was assisted by another Kashmiri dominie with a black beard and by a little Ladaki Moslem, dressed in the usual Tibetan garments, but crowned with a red fez, who acted as gym-instructor. It is curious how this profession seems to bring out the same characteristics all the world over. The little man was bubbling over with heartiness and energy and kept urging on the class in the same provokingly sharp voice that we re-

membered from gym practice at home. The orders were given
in three languages, mixed entirely haphazard, Hindustani, English, and Balti.

"*Ek, do, sum, bji* . . . left, right . . . one, two, *chik, nyis*
. . . wake up there, you . . . number three, wake up . . .
tin . . . *sum* . . ." (Here a sound thwack on number three's
shins.) ". . . double!"

The display ended with a tug-o'-war. The whole school took
part, and the two strongest boys were placed, not at the ends,
as with us, but in the centre. They used no rope, but the leaders
simply grasped each other's wrists, on which each took the pull
of some fifteen tough and excited young Baltis. The event was
fiercely contested, so it can be imagined what a strain their
muscles had to stand. One wonders why it should be necessary
to go in for a "Keep Fit" campaign with such people.

From Dras to Kargil is the hottest and least interesting part
of the journey. On leaving Dras, the path passes two ancient
stones carved with figures of Buddhist divinities and bearing
Tibetan inscriptions. There was evidently a time when this district, like Ladak, professed Buddhism, and its replacement by
the religion of Islam must have greatly altered the appearance
of the villages, which are bare in the extreme, as compared
with those to be found in the next province. There is one attractive halting-place some thirteen miles beyond Dras, where it is
worth stopping a night for the mere pleasure of camping there.
It is an oasis called Tasgam, set like a verdant island in the
midst of a sea of shimmering radiation, with multi-coloured
tangles of wild flowers along the edges of its cornfields, and a
bewitching willow wood to camp in. The inhabitants of this
and neighbouring hamlets vary greatly in the matter of physique: in Tasgam they looked healthy enough; but in villages
farther on they were afflicted with all sorts of nameless diseases.

The administrative headquarters of the whole district between the Zoji and Ladak, which is known as Purig, are at Kargil, a small township that has grown up round a bazaar of
Indian-owned shops, which draw their subsistence from the
Turkistan-India transit traffic. In addition it is the centre of a
considerable tract of fertile land, beautifully tilled and planted
with trees; its irrigated terraces reach far up the hillsides and
into the minor valleys all around. It is the seat of an official of
the Kashmir Government, who, among his other duties, is
charged with the examination of travellers' passes into Ladak.
The place is beautifully situated on a wide, fast-flowing river,

the Suru, and has an air of prosperity that makes an agreeable change after the miserable villages round Dras. The inhabitants are largely Baltis, clad in hard-wearing brown woollens, with flat round caps to match.

The greenness of Kargil is more than usually joyful because the last few miles before the village are tedious, with torrid stretches of sand, trying for both pedestrians and horses. After passing the head of an iron bridge, where the road to Skardu, capital of Baltistan, forks off, a bend brings one opposite a thin line of poplars, just over the river, which widens as one advances in the parallel direction, until the whole panorama is unfolded, with groves, bubbling rills of pure water, and waste ground covered with purple iris, different from the ones we found below the Zoji. These irises have been put to charming use by the peasants, who arrange them in tufted belts to mark the divisions of their fields.

As we entered the first grassy patch on our side of the river, we caught sight of a couple of tents, pitched close to a tempting spring of icy water which welled up from under a bank. Some small dogs and children were playing there, two or three women sat gossiping, and the menfolk lay stretched on the ground fast asleep. One woman caught our attention by her clothes, which were not of the style usual to either Baltis or Ladakis, but looked rather like those that we had last seen on Tibetan women at Kalimpong. A closer look left us in no doubt: this was indeed a true Tibetan, there was no mistaking her cast of features. Excitedly we greeted her and put a few questions. "Where have you come from?" "I come from Leh," she answered in the same dialect as we had used. "Are you a Tibetan? Where is your home?" "I belong to Tsang province; my village is close to Shigatze, but my husband is a Ladakpa." Then, in growing animation: "Wake up, you." (She shook her slumbering mate violently without making the slightest impression.) "Get up, quickly: do you hear? Here are some gentlemen speaking Tibetan!" She plied us with questions till she had satisfied her curiosity and then in her turn she told us her life-story. It was typical of that roving spirit which gains possession of so many Tibetans and sends them roaming from the frontiers of China to the edge of the Karakoram, quitting their homes without fear or care for the future. Our friend the T'hangu pilgrim was one of these wanderers; now here was another. Her father had died long since, but her mother was living when she quitted her home several years before. Though poor, she had made a pious resolve to go on pilgrimage to the Mountain of Precious Snow, better known by its Indian name of Kailas, close to the sources of both the Satlej and the Brahmaputra. All the way behind Nepal she trekked, now alone, now with others on a similar quest, till she reached the foot of her mountain. Then she took part in its solemn circumambulation, clockwise of course, for it, like a *Mani* wall, being sacred, must be passed on the left, with the right side turned towards it. The circuit concluded, instead of going back to her people, a desire was born in her to proceed still farther afield to other shrines and monasteries of the far west. So she found herself at last in Ladak. At Leh she had met her husband-to-be. Now they had a large family, and she was trying to eke out her scanty resources by breeding Lhasa terriers. She had some twenty dogs with her and was taking them down to Kashmir to sell to the English ladies.

This unexpected encounter seemed a good omen. We lingered for some time talking to her and then walked on towards our camp, at the far end of Kargil, where the Ladak road starts. We felt excited by the prospect of re-entering a Tibetan country the next day, where we would be free to take up those studies which so enticed us. We had been waiting for this moment to put into execution the long-cherished plan of adopting, as far as possible, the Tibetan way of living, in regard to both food, dress, and personal habits. We wanted to absorb the spirit of the Tradition by direct experience, subjecting ourselves to its laws to the greatest possible extent; for there comes a time when it is difficult to rest satisfied with the part of observer; one must participate, and if this spiritual association is to be thorough, the external trappings, which provide the framework, must also be made to agree.

But to accomplish such a purpose certain conditions must always be laid down; otherwise the plan may degenerate into a masquerade that will do no good to anyone. The conviction behind it must not only be sincere and strong, but also well informed. There is a price in knowledge that must be paid as an entrance-fee through the traditional wicket gate. Accurate observation of the people's habits and, still more, an appreciation of the motives underlying them is necessary, so as to preclude any danger of committing crude solecisms. Some slips are unavoidable at first; but the person who really knows what he is about and who has grasped the principles behind his new technique can usually arrest a slip so quickly and naturally that it passes unnoticed. After a time mistakes cease to occur, as right conduct becomes a matter of habit.

I regard this living of the Tibetan life as an extension of the study of language. There is speech in gesture, even in the way a cup is lifted to the lips, in a bow, in a thousand light touches that go to reinforce the spoken word and lend it additional point. Without them, language remains a foreign thing to the last. Externals, such as clothes, count for a great deal. The actor who wishes to live his part must first convince himself. He will find it much easier to transform his personality if he can banish as many incongruities as possible from his make-up. Kingliness is enhanced by the crown, a soldierly bearing by the sword, beggary by rags. Our intention was to be as thorough as possible. It was a way of saying to our hosts: "We wish to be as one of you. Please make no unusual arrangements on our behalf. We love your tradition, and hope it will not be rashly changed. We have found means of attuning ourselves to its ways."

I have studiously avoided turning any part of this book into an apologia; the recorded results must prove the soundness or folly of my methods. But I must make one slight exception, because I know that I have laid myself open to a charge of inconsistency. Someone is sure to offer the criticism, on the face of it a reasonable one, that here is a man who has all along gone out of his way to blame Indians and other Asiatics for copying Western dress and customs, yet he himself is doing just the same in regard to Tibet. I was never blind to this possible objection; nevertheless, I believe that I did not violate any of my principles; but I do not expect to convince everyone. I shall be satisfied if they admit that there was a *prima facie* case for my having adopted unusual methods.

My basic thesis is that between any traditional code of behaviour and the customs of an anti-traditional civilization like ours — the only one of its kind that history now remembers — there is no real equivalence. Modern Occidentalism is threatening to flatten out the whole world and mould it to a single, rather dull pattern, throwing away all that diversity whereby man has expressed himself through the centuries. Not only are all the Oriental civilizations in acute danger as a result of the Western encroachment, but also the West itself seems prepared to let go whatever was great or worth while in its own heritage. Our costume can no longer be associated with a civilized status; it has rather become the most general and characteristic symbol of this deplorable world-reducing movement. At home one

can but try to make the best of its rather narrow limitations;
but on stepping into a society that is still based on regular traditional principles, one cannot help feeling that in introducing
our manners and customs one may be helping to spread a taste
for things that will ultimately corrode the armour of Tradition,
thus paving the way for totalitarian materialism, which seems
to be the logical outcome of the non-traditional outlook. Furthermore, in the West no man can be said to follow the path of
Tradition without let or hindrance, even should he be so
minded, for conditions are against him, if not worse: one in
whose heart the traditional fire has somehow been rekindled
finds himself like a homeless exile and instinctively yearns to
taste the experience of a normal human life, free from profane
compromises. There was a day when all civilizations were
roughly equivalent and travellers from one to the other could
feel at home wherever they went. Now the scales are unequally
weighted, and world pressure is all from the anti-traditional
direction. Anomalous circumstances create their own problems,
which demand peculiar solutions.

In practice, I believe that I possess the requisite qualifications for making a free choice and that I could never have accomplished as much as I did had that choice been made differently. From the first moment I felt as if I had escaped from an
invisible barrier, within which, like a hen in the middle of a
chalked circle, I had been penned. I have felt at ease among
Tibetans of all ranks as I have not often done elsewhere. I
never felt that I was among strangers; rather was it a return to
a long-lost home. A lama with whom I was intimate explained
this quite simply by saying that it was no accident, but that I
showed unmistakable signs of having been a Tibetan myself in
a previous existence, whence I had inherited a natural sympathy with my former compatriots and a tendency to return to
them, like a homing pigeon. Whatever truth may underlie this
utterance, which should not be taken too literally, I can at least
say this about the next life: had I the choice, I should be well
content to be reborn as a Tibetan — always provided that Tibet
is still Tibet and has not been turned meanwhile into one of
many feeble copies of America. From my limited experience I
can endorse the words of that able French observer Professor
Jacques Bacot when he writes: "The Tibetans impress one at
once by the dignity of their persons. One sees them on horseback and nobly clad, scattered about the open spaces of their
deserts. . . . In all Tibet one would be hard put to it to dis-

KANGCHHENDZÖNGA AND SIMVU FROM SINGHIK   *See page* 113
From torrent to summit over 24,000 feet vertical

PAVILION IN THE SHALIMAR GARDENS   *See page 188*

Mughal Lattices and Inlays   *See page 184*

BETWEEN DRAS AND TASGAM   *See page* 198

SHEPHERD ON THE ZOJI LA   *See page* 191

OASIS NEAR KARGIL *See page 198*

KARGIL · *See pages 198–9*

MULBEK   *See page 205*

cover one fool. . . . The Tibetans are not barbarous or uncultivated; nor for that matter is their country. Under their rough hide they conceal refinements that we lack, much courtesy and philosophy, and the need for beautifying common things, whatever happens to be useful to them, be it a tent, a knife, or a stirrup. . . . Moreover they are gay, these Tibetans, and happy as is not the case elsewhere today, more so than our wretched workers in their wretched factories, armed with the whole arsenal of their rights. . . . The more densely the country is populated, the tamer is the wild game. The Tibetans are not much addicted to hunting. They have long since lost the taste for killing that we still retain. . . . I love their companionship during the long rides, for they are taciturn, or else they only speak with good sense, originality, and a taste for speculative things."

Chapter XV

Kargil to Yuru: Symbolism of the *Tantra*

FROM KARGIL ONWARD we had decided to take ponies instead
of continuing on foot; in a country where most people ride,
walking would have appeared eccentric; also there is no real
objection against traversing half-desert tracts fairly rapidly.
Small details count for little in such scenery, except within the
restricted belts of cultivation, whereas in a woodland like Sikkim a thousand subtle beauties of plant or insect life are to be
met with at every turn, past which it would be a pity to hurry.

Twenty-three hot miles separated Kargil from the next halting-place. At first the way crossed an arid plateau, its monotony relieved only by a momentary glimpse of an impressive
snow mountain lying to the south-west. The lifeless tableland
seemed as if it would extend for ever, when suddenly, without
warning, we found ourselves looking over the edge of a huge
sunken valley watered by a river from which numerous artificial rivulets conducted the life-giving water to smiling cornfields and shady groves. The place seemed so secluded and out
of keeping with the dead wastes immediately surrounding it
that it might well have been taken for a mirage. These unexpected encounters with life in the midst of desert are always
dramatic, and man never fails in his emotional response to the
first sight of green. It is one of the peculiar charms that belong
only to barren countries and cannot be shared by luxuriant
ones.

The track led down into the hollow and then hugged the
margin of the fields so as not to waste a foot of arable ground.
As at Kargil, here also the wild iris was planted to mark the
boundaries between properties. At the far end of the oasis the
road mounted sharply over a shoulder, missing the rocky gates
by which the river entered. We then rode on up-stream for several hours, past a few villages of rough construction such as
are found all over Purig. Wild rose bushes, armed with formidable prickles, were employed for hedging. Gradually the gorge

closed in: it was thirsty work riding through it in the heat of the early afternoon, especially as most of the ponies offered for hire along this road are rather slow.

As it was our first day on horseback and an especially hot one, we were beginning to feel rather sore and weary, when we emerged unexpectedly into a wider part of the valley with open views in several directions. There was a bridge to the right giving access to the small village of Shergol. From a gravel bank on the left several cold springs gushed out as if placed there specially for the convenience of thirsty travellers. But what immediately arrested our gaze and held it riveted was the sight of something like a stone bell terminating in a needle-like pinnacle — it was a *chhorten,* the symbol of Nirvana, found in all Buddhist lands. Presently, looking across the river, we discerned a cliff face some two miles away, against which nestled a white façade with a red frieze, evidently where some huge caverns provided natural chambers. Our first lamasery! We were in Ladak at last!

Yet a little farther on and Mulbek *Gompa* came into view, perched on the summit of a precipitous aiguille, its white and red walls outlined in the golden evening light. It looked like a small fortress, with its projecting balconies that hung airily over the gulf. Standards, like closed parasols, marked the angles of the roof.

Near the foot of the rock stood the village. Almost every house in it could lay claim to some artistic distinction. Even the meanest were of ample size, two-storied, with but few openings on the bottom story, for this was, as usual in Tibetan houses, taken up by granaries and stables. The classical plan consists of a central block with two wings. The rooms on the upper floor form three sides of a square, leaving a central space open to the sky, like a court with an arcade round it. The woodwork of doorways and window-frames was of simple but elegant design, while the more important upper rooms had graceful covered balconies of wood. Over the whole fluttered a forest of prayer-flags. One of the dwellings, which belonged to the headman, was a mansion fit for a duke.

A grassy flat by the river, here easily fordable, was chosen for the camp. Across the water could be seen an isolated farm or two, again constructed on generous lines. Judging from photographs, the style differs little from that of farms in other provinces of Tibet. It is extraordinary over how extensive an area the same design persists with but little variation. Beyond the

farms rose a fantastic escarpment of red sandstone that would
not have looked out of place in the southern Sahara. The camping-ground was close to the Government rest-house, which, unlike those found in Sikkim, was built in the style of the country,
with ceilings of rough poplar logs and a little porch held up by
wooden posts terminating in the spreading bracketed capitals
of the Tibetan pillar. Throughout Ladak the native style has
been kept in the rest-houses and even at the Residency of Leh.
The official who initiated this policy had two great qualities —
imagination and a readiness to let well alone; would that his
example had been followed throughout India. Unfortunately
these Ladak rest-houses are not very clean: we found that
some of them were infested with lice.

As we approached, the little bungalow presented an animated scene. Our friend Khan Muhammad Din was seated in
the porch, receiving petty notables and making his annual settlement of local business. A gay crowd of villagers was gathered round; their cheerful faces made a pleasant change from
the dour looks of many of the Purig people. Nor were the
women any less assured than the men. The Ladaki wife is anything but a doormat; more often than not, she is the real ruler
in the home, and children, when asked about their parentage,
will often give their mother's name before their father's. The
Italian explorer De Filippi was not wrong in saying: "The
woman has considerable influence in family affairs — though
the situation is hardly a true matriarchy — with a dignity, a social position, and a freedom not surpassed in any country in the
world."

The male costume is not unlike that of Khunu, consisting of
a long *chuba* or gown of brown or grey or sometimes purple
homespun, secured with a sash, in which are stuck a brass
spoon and a flute. It is common to meet people playing merry
tunes as they walk along the road. The shoes are quite different
from the high Tibetan model and are often decorated with
swastikas. The cap is peculiar to Ladak, made of cloth or of a
velvety material, flattened on the crown, but with the edges
turned up, something like a "cap of liberty." Often solid brace-
lets adorn the wrists, and the ears are pierced for rings. The
men tend to be big and strong-looking; nor do their looks belie
them, for they are about the toughest people I know. Even the
Sherpas do not treat cold or bad weather with such complete
disdain. At night they hardly bother to shelter if it will involve
them in the smallest extra trouble. They wear their hair in flow-

ing locks, and many grow a beard; the race appears to contain
a high percentage of non-Tibetan blood, though it has adopted
the language and customs of its conquerors. We noticed a wide
range of types, from those who looked closer to Europeans
in cast to others in whom Mongolian features predominated.
Whatever else he may be doing, whether walking or sitting,
the Ladaki is always assiduously spinning coarse woollen
thread; his little spindle hangs from the end of the thread
and revolves merrily under dextrous twists periodically administered, while a thick skein of crude wool is hung over
his elbow. The finished thread is wound on a stick. In this way
a continual supply of yarn is spun for weaving into clothes during the winter months. The women's dress is dark, trimmed
with sheepskin and decked out with silver ornaments of beautiful chain-work, one of which dangles from the shoulder; the
chains terminate in a tiny manicure-set with silver tweezers
and knives. A basket, like that of the Swiss peasants, is carried
on the back; under the basket a goatskin with the hair turned
outwards prevents chafing. The head-dress is extraordinary. It
consists of a sort of bonnet, shading the face and curling snail-
like over the back of the neck. On to this are sewn uncut turquoises, few or many, big or small, according to a person's
means.

We had not meant to stay at Mulbek more than just the one
night, but the place so charmed us that we needed little persuasion to remain a day longer. It also suited us to stay on, since it
was the date we had chosen for making the change from European customs to those of the country, by assuming the outward
and visible signs of our pilgrimage. The day finished with a
polo match got up to entertain the Khan, in which several villagers took part, playing with much spirit if with little apparent plan. The gay costumes and trappings called up visions of
mediaeval jousting, for which the setting was exactly right,
with the *Gompa* on its crag replacing the feudal castle.

On the morrow the Khan and his train set out with the dawn,
leaving us in sole possession. The first experiment with Tibetan
clothes made us feel slightly self-conscious; but we were helped
over the awkward stage by the fact that no one ever showed
the least surprise. It occasionally happened that a person asked
us what price we had given for this or that or, after feeling the
cloth, passed some comment on its quality; but *why* we chose
to wear them they never inquired. One or two Lhasa Tibetans,
or Ladakis who had spent many years in Tibet proper, did go

so far as to express positive pleasure. Usually we were treated
as if our use of Tibetan clothes was the most natural thing in
the world. Twice I was asked if I had lived many years at
Lhasa. What I soon noticed, however, was that the discrimina-
tive treatment accorded to Europeans was dropped automatically; people no longer tried to offer us chairs to sit on, and we
were everywhere expected to produce our own tea-bowls out of
our *ambags* — that is to say, out of the pouches formed by the
fullness of our gowns. The *ambag* hangs over the sash and
serves the Tibetans as a pocket to contain everything from a
purse to a pet dog.

The valley next to Mulbek was called Bod Karbu; it was
reached by crossing a long pass between rolling red downs.
This second valley was a good one in which to observe the typical features of Ladak farming. In addition to the biggest village, there were several small hamlets set along the lower
slopes of the hills, while all the flat lands were given over to
corn, out of which rose islets of trees and the pinnacles of
chhortens. The edges of the fields were a matted tangle of common wild flowers: cranesbills, vetches, blue chicory, and various clovers, which give to the country its individual honeyed
scent. Walls were hidden under white clematis and purple catmint. In one or two places the curtain of red rocky hills was
pierced by a narrow gatelike rent through which plunged a
small torrent. Peeping inside was rather like viewing a theatrical scene: everything resembled the main valley, but seen in
miniature — the stream with its stony bed, a few fields, a flume
of running water, a long row of *Mani* walls leading up to a tiny
village of fine stone houses, the whole crowned by a diminutive
white and red *Gompa*.

The peasant houses were a never ending joy throughout
Ladak, with their combination of the qualities of ampleness, solidity, classical plan, and appropriate detail. A mean or cramped
or ill-constructed dwelling was never to be seen, while a fair
proportion of the bigger ones made one feel positively envious.
This was true of every village through which we passed. Nowhere else have I seen houses to compare, on an average, with
those of the Ladakis.

The lower story is usually allotted to animals and stores, and
the family spends the summer on the upper floor in half-open
chambers round the pillared court. When it is very warm, people often sleep out on the flat roof, usually naked, with clothes
or a blanket thrown over them. Household furniture is con-

fined to necessities. Besides cooking-pots and wooden bowls and cups for eating and drinking, with perhaps a china cup or two for special occasions, there is always a red glazed pottery charcoal stove for keeping tea warm, in form not unlike a Greek urn; and one or two brass or copper teapots, often decorated with good chasing, as well as with *appliqués* silver plates and dragon handles, earthenware pitchers for beer, small carpets for sitting on, and low tea-tables painted gaily with flowers. All these objects are hand-made and of real artistic value; richer peasants sometimes possess quite fine utensils, and the woodwork of the principal rooms in their houses may also be richly decorated. There is no collecting of useless junk to clutter up the home. Special attention must be drawn to the common red pottery, almost Grecian in style, which is left plain and depends entirely on perfection of shape.

In each farmhouse there is one room which claims pre-eminence in respect of furnishing and comfort; this is the family chapel, in which reside the images of the Tutelaries of the household, before whom lamas from time to time are summoned to hold services. Votive lamps are alight on the altar and painted scrolls line the walls. One family of peasants whom we knew, and who, though well-to-do, cannot have possessed much ready cash, told us that they were about to invest in a new *t'hanka* by the most celebrated living artist of Ladak, Rigzin. Could one imagine many of our farmers at home who, even if they could afford it, would dream of placing an order with a painter of recognised eminence? Yet it must not be thought that I am trying to make out the average Ladaki to be a highly intellectual or consciously æsthetic person. Quite the reverse; compared to the Tibetans, for instance, they appear rather simple-minded; but under the guidance of Tradition there is a diffusion of knowledge throughout the country that cannot be paralleled in modern societies, for all their compulsory schooling.

A pass, the P'hotu La (13,400 feet), separates Bod Karbu from Yuru, where the first of the great monasteries is situated. It is usually called Lamayuru on maps and in books, an Indian corruption of the real name, which should be Yuru *Gompa*. I was seized by a sudden longing to wander off alone while we were sitting at supper at the Bod Karbu rest-house, so I asked my friends to bring up the baggage ponies next day, and I set off for Yuru on foot. The mysterious peace of sunset possessed the landscape as I walked out into the sandy waste beyond the

last fields. The jagged rows of peaks that formed the sides of
Karbu Valley faded slowly from orange through dull red into
inky black. By an isolated *Mani* I saw in the half-light a figure
with clasped hands and heard the faint whisperings of his
prayers. Then night dropped its curtain and I was alone with
my thoughts. I walked on and on, forgetting time and distance.
Occasionally the dying gleam of a fire or the pawing of a horse's
hoofs indicated an encampment. After a time the track began
to rise and the shapes of mountains, huge and eerie, closed in
on either side. I was hoping to make the top of the P'hotu La
and then rest, waiting to descend on Yuru soon after dawn. A
dog began to bark far off to the left, another joined in, and then
a third; all at once a whole chorus broke out and began to surge
towards me in a menacing crescendo. I felt very much alarmed,
for it was evident that I had approached a shepherds' camp
guarded by some of those fierce mastiffs, rather like chows,
which are used as watchdogs all over Tibet. It would have been
most unpleasant to be attacked by several of them, for I was
not even carrying a stick. Picking up a couple of stones, I hurried along the path, hoping to get out of their range. I caught
a glimpse of a furious brute who refused to be shaken off till he
had seen the intruder well out of the way. It was a great relief
when the barking died away in the distance.*

I walked on, feeling rather nervous; then I heard another
dog just ahead. I wondered what was the best thing to do, for
it seemed unwise to proceed farther before daylight. I turned
up into the entrance of a ravine and decided to halt for the rest
of the night. I lay down on the stones by a stream and slept fitfully. At the first glimmer of dawn I got up and unpacked some
bits of wood that I had brought, to boil up a pot of tea. It was

---

* The instinct that drove me to pick up the stones would have been blamed
by several lamas of my acquaintance as a sign of weakness. Still more they
would have criticized the egotism, expressed as *fear of others*, root poison of
hatred, that prompted the act. They would probably have voiced their opinion
thus: "When you heard the dogs barking, no doubt your own fear aggravated
their ferocity. You underrate your own powers; for you might have proceeded
on your way calmly and resolutely, fending off the phantoms of this contingent
world with the buckler of profound Meditation on the all-embracing Compassion. Why put your trust in other defences?" I must record events as they
actually happened; but I admit that the criticism does not lack force. Viewed
from the standpoint of Enlightenment, my act of warlike preparation deserved
the epithet "ill-considered." I believe that it is no exaggeration to say that
persons capable of this degree of Non-Attachment even in the face of danger
are far from extinct in Tibet; for them the demons of fear and worry have
been exorcized, and they enjoy a serenity that even a savage mastiff might
respect.

the first time that I had tried to light a fire on a hearth of three stones, such as the natives use all over Asia. It is extraordinary how clumsy an inexperienced hand can be, even at an operation that one has watched hundreds of times. I wasted many matches and sticks before I got the draught properly regulated; but I derived a childish pleasure from my cup of tea, for this too was one more tiny step into the Tibetan world.

From the head of the pass the road descended a small stream-valley with gravel-strewn sides and sparse vegetation. It widened out near a point where a solitary *chhorten* had been set up, in the middle of the pebbly bed, as if to suggest that something important waited round the corner. The path turned abruptly left for a few yards up a small col with another *chhorten* standing on it. Then I stopped, in face of one of the world's wonders, overcome by the whirlpool of emotions that suddenly surged through me. A hollow, shut in between red hills, lay below, its floor filled by fields and a tiny willow copse; the brick-red background threw up the greenness of the leaves in unusually sharp relief. The road contoured round the left of the combe in a wide curve, to the foot of a huge sandstone cliff honeycombed with caves, which looked as if they had been specially designed to serve as cells for the meditations of hermits. On the crest of this cliff stood the magnificently proportioned pile of the *Gompa*, a tall central building, with a number of lower wings containing monks' quarters and on one side a warren of peasant houses.

A continuous line of huge *Mani* walls and white *chhortens* bordered the road, forming a sacred way and exerting on the eye an almost dynamic influence in guiding it in the direction it should go. Some of the larger *chhortens* had their bases moulded into bas-reliefs of dragons, horses, lions, and phœnixes. The monastery itself was white, with the usual red frieze under the roof. These bands are always made in the same way, by laying bundles of sticks, closely bound and painted red, so that the cut-off ends face outwards like a brush. The setting of Yuru *Gompa* is unsurpassed and the first view of it is an unforgettably stirring experience.

Unfortunately it seems to have suffered by its proximity to the main caravan route; being the first big monastery on this road, it is visited by every tourist who enters Ladak. Its monks give the impression of being venal, and they hold the record for the number of requests for bakshish that they address to the stranger. When I was going over the building, a group of nuns

from the village also assembled in the courtyard and unashamedly shouted "Bakshish" in chorus.

It is inconceivable that an edifice so rich architecturally
should not also have been correspondingly endowed with pictures, books, and other sacred furniture of the best periods; but
the movable objects must have been disposed of long since, for
most of what I saw in the temples was second-rate. It was plun-
dered by the Dogra armies in the forties; but that does not explain the matter entirely, for soldiers would tend to confine
their attention to objects made of the precious metals. Also the
decorative arts had not at that date shown any serious signs of
decline, and replacements of pictures and statues would still
have been possible without noticeable loss of quality. I suspect
that archæologists, curio-dealers, and travellers have played
their part in stripping Yuru of its treasures, abetted by the more
unworthy among its sacristans.

Though the movable furniture falls below standard, the same
cannot be said of the fixtures, such as painted woodwork and
paintings on walls. The former craft, which is lavished on all
rich houses or temples in Ladak, never ceases to delight by its
delicate drawing and brilliant colouring. The motifs employed
are much the same everywhere, consisting of sprigs of flowers
and pairs of dragons or birds, set out on capitals, brackets,
beams, and panels; but the variety achieved within the set convention is astonishing.

The temples of Yuru are in a poor state of repair. Cracks
have appeared in walls that have been painted only recently,
either because the plaster was too hastily laid on or, more
likely, because the outer wall itself is crumbling, but no one
bothers about it. Much of the work is extremely fine, being, I
think, by the same living painter, Rigzin, whose name was mentioned earlier and whose work is in great demand throughout
western Tibet. He is a native of the Indus Valley and started
life as a monk, but apparently reverted to the lay state.

In Ladak there are, besides Rigzin, two or three more painters of major rank and numerous lesser ones who execute designs
on furniture and woodwork. All these are kept continuously
busy serving the needs of less than forty thousand people.
From this an idea can be formed of the number of artists required by a community in which art products are deemed no
luxury, but something in which even common folk can share.
No great halo surrounds the artist; but if his work is above av-

erage, he enjoys the solid esteem that is to be earned among a people who still have the power to judge good workmanship.

The figures in the wall-paintings divide into two strongly contrasted types. On the one hand we have Buddhas and Celestial beings, their faces calm or lit up by faint smiles of rapture, seated on their lotus pedestals in attitudes of imperturbable serenity. On the other hand there are frightful apparitions, decked with crowns and necklaces of human skulls, dancing in convulsive frenzy on the prostrate forms of men or animals. It is not surprising that the casual traveller to Tibet takes these dreadful beings for demons more appalling than those who people the hells of Signorelli, Fra Angelico, or Dürer; but this view is far from the truth. Many of those diabolical-looking figures are in essence identical with those who look so gentle. The Tibetan divinities all have a variety of aspects according to the functions that they are called upon to fulfil, perhaps even more according to the state of mind of the beholder. There are benign or peaceful, fascinating, fierce, or terrifying aspects. Thus to the saint and to the evil-doer the same divinity will show himself in widely differing guise. To the virtuous soul the Divine is necessarily glorious and comforting, but to an evil conscience the same can be a cause of horror and anguish. Indeed, the lamas teach that the various states of existence that men and animals attain to, such as the abode of gods or the purgatories, are entirely subjective in character, forming part, as they do, of the general body of illusions from which the mind suffers so long as it has failed to attain Enlightenment. The illusory river that might appear to us in our human state as the Thames would seem to one of the gods like a stream of water of long life; but to one of the damned the same will be a spate of molten lava. The willow tree on the river bank is a Wishing-Tree, from which gifts can be obtained at will by the blessed spirits; but to him who is blinded by sin-nourishing Ignorance, the same tree is a mass of lacerating thorns. To the perfected saint, who has attained Knowledge, there is neither willow nor river, but only Emptiness; for he looks on the reality that these and all other phenomena mask. This is the theory behind the various forms of the Tibetan divinities.

A certain writer, noted for his research into the externals of what he called "Lamaism," has employed the words "fiends and fiendesses" to denote the "terrible forms" of the various divinities. This is an unhappy choice of terms, since in our language the word "fiend" is necessarily associated with a being unalterably evil by nature, in rebellion against God, whereas here it is but the stern aspect of a beneficent power that is indicated. I must therefore protest against the use of the word "fiend" in this connexion, as being likely to mislead the average English reader into thinking that the Tibetans practise "devil-worship." The real meaning underlying the "terrible forms" is not difficult to grasp, and it is of importance to do so if one wishes to appreciate the true implications of Tibetan metaphysic and art.

Another side of this doctrine of multiplicity of forms is equally important. Whoever tries to thread a way through the complications of the pantheon, not only of Tibet but equally so of India, will find that he starts by learning a bewildering number of names of apparently separate gods with their attributes. Later he will find out that each of these can be recognized under several forms, externally very different; and again, as he pursues his inquiry, he will find that these forms manifest themselves in yet other forms and that some of them merge into forms that have apparently been derived from other prototypes. This has been pithily expressed by Kipling in the line: "Kali — who is Párvati, who is Sitala, who is worshipped against the smallpox."

His humorous remark enshrines a profound truth. Reversing the succession of forms, the goddess whom the villager invokes to guard him from smallpox becomes, as one traces her upward by a sort of involutionary process, Párvati, the spouse of Shiva. The goddess can also be worshipped as Kali under both gentle and fearful aspects. Farther on we will see that Párvati is the Active Energy of Shiva Himself, wedded to Him in the same way as Wisdom is wedded to Method. Thus the mind, unable to find any single static form on which to rest, is led into recognition that all forms are really one, or to use still more accurate language, not-two, and that the whole complex is merely the total of Divine Manifestation in Form. The symbolism is here part of Method leading to a basic metaphysical concept, part of Wisdom. This, incidentally, disposes of the favourite accusation of polytheism which the wilfully ignorant love to level at the Hindus, Tibetans, and other "heathens." That the followers of these Traditions are clear in their own minds on this doctrine can be proved from innumerable quotations. I will give two of them: The *Brihadāranyaka Upanishad*, a Hindu scripture, says that "those who adore the Divinities, thinking that they are different from themselves, such men the Divinities make their beasts of burden." So also the *Varâha Purana,* another Hindu book, says: "What Durga (Kali) is, that is Vishnu and that also is Shiva. The wise know that they are not different from one another." In the Tibetan sacred writings whole books are devoted to a special form of spiritual training by which various "circles" or sets of divinities, with their attributes, are evoked as on a stage and then gradually made to merge one into another till all their distinctions are absorbed in the "Foundation of all, beyond Mind and Speech." Not only are divinities viewed kinetically, as a series of aspects of each other leading to recognition of the One, but even doctrines are repeatedly expressed in terms of each other, leading to their final coincidence in a single Truth.

In one of the chapels at Yuru stands a colossal image of the Bodhisat Chenrezig, the same one who is manifested through the Dalai Lama, under the form known as the All-Merciful Lord. He is portrayed as a tall figure with innumerable arms forming a circle that surrounds him like an aureole; he has not one head but eleven, disposed in a pyramid. This strange symbolism was explained to me by a lama, who was almost carried away by his own eloquence. "Chenrezig is filled with boundless compassion for all creatures," he said. "You simply cannot imagine how compassionate he is. When he saw their constant sufferings and struggles in the Round of Existence, from which they vainly sought a way of escape, so overcome with pity was he that his head burst and was shivered into fragments. Then his own Lama, the Buddha of Immeasurable Light, provided him with a fresh head, and this happened no less than ten times, making eleven in all." Chenrezig's typical representation, however, is not the eleven-faced form, but the likeness of a young and beautiful white prince, with four arms. That is why an imprint, indicating the rudiments of the extra pair of arms, is one of the signs sought for on the body of the baby that is chosen to act as the earthly sanctuary of the Bodhisat's influence.

Chenrezig is often likened to a shepherd in terms that cannot but recall the Good Shepherd of the Gospel. The Shepherd-like Lord, in the Tibetan version, is so called because his action is that of a shepherd who, having led his flock to the entrance of the fold, lets them enter in first and then, when all are safely inside, goes in himself last of all and closes the gate. Chenrezig, in his capacity as Bodhisat, is freed from sin and illusion and is able at any moment to assume Buddhahood; but moved by his compassion for suffering creatures, he "abstains" from final Deliverance while so many are left behind in their imperfections and sorrows. "What is it to be saved oneself if others are still lost and suffering?" He therefore elects to continue in the Current of Forms so that he may aid all beings to pass in together to Nirvana. Then, and only then, he also will take the final step across the threshold. Chenrezig and his fellow Bodhisats, who again are not to be regarded as objectively distinct personalities but rather as "stages in the Path" accessible to every one of us, represent the embodied aim of the Tibetan Buddhist doctrine, the Saviour, who, though sinless and all-knowing, offers himself for the Universe, in the supreme and eternal sacrifice of redemptive love.

In the Tibetan iconography there is another peculiarity that must be mentioned: namely, the fact that each figure is liable to be composed of two figures clasped in close embrace. This feature serves to illustrate a doctrine that has been the subject of much uninformed and derogatory comment under the name of "Tantrism," a word simply derived from the books in which it is expounded, called the *Tantras*. According to their peculiar symbolism, each divine Being is represented as a pair, composed of a male or non-acting and a female or creative principle. The latter is spoken of as the consort or wife of the former: in Sanskrit she is called *Shakti*, and an adept of this school is called a *Shakta*. The *Tantras* themselves are primarily of Hindu origin, being the latest set of sacred writings to be codified. Their inspiration is considered to be the work of Shiva Himself; but there are also a great many Buddhist *Tantras* of similar character, though the terminology is different. St. Padma, the earliest Apostle of Tibet, introduced the Doctrine under this Tantrik form. After him came the succession of the great Translators, one of whom was Marpa of Hlobrak, of whom I have spoken so often. In the Indo-Tibetan cosmogony, the process of manifestation of the Divine Power as Form is conceived as being subject to a rhythm comparable to breath, so that the expiration corresponds with the Manifesting Act and the intake of breath with the withdrawal of the Universe back into itself. Each of these cycles is termed a *Kalpa*, presided over by a supreme Buddha-teacher; the *Kalpa* contains fourteen *Manvantaras*, each made up of four *Yugas*, equivalent to the gold, silver, bronze, and iron ages of European tradition. Each sub-period has its appropriate scripture, a *Tantra* being suited to the needs of the last phase in the cycle, the black age of decay, when the average degree of spiritual perception is insufficient to allow of the truth being encountered face to face. It must then be viewed through a glass darkly, and communicated to the dwindling group of devotees chiefly by means of symbols.

"All these things are done in parables: that seeing they may see, and not perceive; and hearing they may hear, and not understand. . . . And with many such parables spake He the word unto them, as they were able to hear it. But without a parable spake He not unto them."

There are some who, by certain signs, think that the present time may be the death-throes of one such dark age, the blackest hour that precedes the dawn.

Almost every recent writer on Tibet who happens to have mentioned the word "Tantrik" has used it simply as a synonym for superstition. Certain professional research-mongers, whose publications are as voluminous as they are prejudiced, have peppered their writings freely with such words as "gibberish," "meaningless," "necromancy," and even "filthy" and "obscene." Less learned persons, such as explorers and climbers, have borrowed these fantastic slanders on the *Tantra* from the supposed authorities and retailed them to their public quite unsuspectingly. Thus in one book Himalayan porters were described as affected by "Tantrik superstition." From what I know of porters they are as innocent of any knowledge of what is in the *Tantra* as the man who used the unhappy phrase! Naturally, what the writer meant to convey was a sense of something sinister, savouring of black magic; all one can say is that people should abstain from the use of words they do not really understand.

The Tantrik books are chiefly concerned with methods for assisting the mind to emancipate itself from the tyranny of phenomena. We are indeed imprisoned within a world of form, whence we cannot escape by simply wishing to be free; the Tantrik teacher starts by accepting this fact, but contrives to use the very multiplicity of form as a means to freedom. He causes the thoughts of his disciple to dwell on forms, to juggle with them, to make of them puppet actors on his mental stage, where they play passions and moralities, till through the jungle of their multiplicity he begins to notice the narrow trail that leads out to the great underlying Unity. It is this kinetic idea that has been the womb of symbolical art in India and Tibet. At the cost of seeming to labour the fact, I repeat that, according to Tibetan ideas, each celestial figure is capable of a continuous succession of transformations, being himself or herself a form of a form and so on indefinitely. To regard the numerous figures seen in the temples as separate "gods" or "devils" whose "idols" are worshipped is an error that will rob the traveller of any chance of learning how to read the symbolical language that is unfolded for his edification.

But there is another and far more serious misunderstanding of the Tantrik symbols which demands to be refuted in the public interest. This error is spread by persons who have seen just a little more than the mere name and are vaguely aware of the worship accorded to the Divinity under the form of His own consort, the Female Energy. There is little doubt that many have persuaded themselves to suspect that under this representation there lurks some vile suggestion pandering to man's sensual appetites, and that the figures seen clasped in ecstatic union are really pornographical emblems.

I have read that in Peking there is a lama temple, resort of many a tourist, where the sacristans have tried to turn to profit the propensity of Europeans to cherish such notions by hanging a curtain in front of those twofold figures, ready to be drawn aside in return for a tip; by so doing, of course, they commit grave sacrilege themselves, for, in the Tibetan view, the Father-Mother pairs, as they are called, partake of a character of the austerest purity. In Sikkim also, in one chapel sometimes shown to English visitors, the custodian, this time in a well-meant attempt to save sacred things from being blasphemed, has curtained off the Father-Mother picture. Though the intention was good I take the view that the means were mistaken. Anything savouring of mystery will only seem to lend confirmation to the theory that there is something to hide. Rather should a point be made of displaying the picture and explaining its true purpose on every possible occasion. The trouble really arises from the rather prudish conventions prevalent in Europe itself, by which open reference is always avoided to whatever is connected with the act of procreation, while it is deemed utterly inconceivable that a visible portrayal thereof could have a reverent purpose. In the Orient the subject is treated without reserve: it need not be mentioned in whispers and its emblems seem the natural ones for associating with an actively creative power. As to those who so easily fly to conclusions about the "indecency" of the "Father-Mother" pictures, one is bound to say that such people reveal nothing but the nastiness of their own minds.

I have borrowed one final example out of a *Tantra* called *Demchhog*, or Highest Bliss, because the Divinity who passes under that name, and who personifies a theme propounded for contemplation, is described with great wealth of detail, while a plain explanation is given of what each of these details stands for. No better instance could be given of how the Tantrik symbolism works. I can only offer an abridged paraphrase of the passage, for to quote it all would take several pages.

The Chief Divinity, "Circle of Higher Bliss," has four faces, symbolizing fourfold sets of ideas — among them the Elements of earth, water, fire, and air, which, with ether, constitute the material Universe, and the Four Boundless Wishes, which are Compassion, Affection, Love, and Impartiality; but there are several other sets of a still more profound character. The body is blue, to symbolize that He never changes from "the Wisdom, which knows that the things that are coloured differently and the like are really not so, but they are all of a single nature and taste." Each face has three eyes, to show that the Three Worlds — the Sensual, the World of Form, but without sensual craving, and the Formless Spiritual World — are under His vision, and also that He knows the Three Times, past, present, and future. He has twelve arms, which represent His knowledge of the Twelve Interdependent Origins of the Round of Existence.

To prove that Perfected Intelligence is both the Void (that is, the Absolutely Real, which we can only indicate through a privative word, since for us the Real cannot but be void of determination, form, relativity, and all that we can possibly conceive of) and Compassion (the pure sacrificial Love that characterizes the Bodhisat, the highest goal of Buddhism), He holds in the upper hands a *dorjé* (thunderbolt sceptre) and a bell. To show that Method and Wisdom are ever in union, the first pair of hands clasps His Spouse or *Shakti*. The next two hands hold a raw elephant hide, which they are tearing asunder: this is the emblem of Ignorance. The third right hand holds a drum, proclaiming the most joyous tidings. The fourth hand brandishes a battle-axe, by which He cuts off births and deaths. The fifth holds a dagger to show that the six sins of pride, disbelief, want of serious devotion, distraction, inattention, and boredom are cut off. The sixth right hand grasps a trident, showing the destruction of the Root Poisons of Anger, Desire-Attachment, and Sloth (the inertia of Ignorance).

Now to turn to the left hands: the third holds a staff sur-
mounted by a *dorjé,* sign of supreme bliss, and the fourth
holds a blood-filled skull signifying that all ideas which regard things as either material or immaterial are done away
with. From the fifth hand dangles a noose, the Knowledge
that grasps the nature of sentient beings. In the sixth left
hand is the head of four-faced Brahmā, showing that all the
delusions of the Round have been finally shaken off.

Under His feet He tramples an emaciated figure of Time,
proving that out of His boundless Compassion He volun-
tarily remains in the world of sentient beings as Saviour. His
bent left leg spurns the form of a Black Destroyer, for Wisdom has got rid of every antithesis such as subject-object and
enjoyer-enjoyment. His hair is tied in a knot on the crown of
His head, because merit has been acquired in the fullest
measure. Each of His heads is adorned with a chaplet of five
skulls, standing for the five kinds of Wisdom. His face frowns
and His teeth are set, for by Him all heresies are overcome.
His ear-rings are Fortitude, His necklace Charity, His brace-
lets Chastity, His girdle Energy, the wheel of bone over His
head is Meditation.

Round His waist is draped a tiger-skin, not tightly fastened, because He is released from all belief in the real distinction of Body and Spirit. His limbs have symmetry and
grace, His visage is heroic, stern, and severe, He is full of
energy, He is awe-inspiring, and yet He is compassionate
and His features are of a peaceful cast. (This form belongs to
a type called semi-wrathful, not one of the "terrible" forms,
nor yet wholly "peaceful.")

We now come to His Consort-Energy, who clings to Him
in inextricable embrace. She is red in colour, because She is
devoted to the service of all beings. She has only one face,
because all things have but one taste — they are basically
one. She possesses two hands, for She comprehends both aspects of Truth, the apparent and the real. Her right hand
holds a curved knife, which is Wisdom-Consciousness, that
cuts away qualifying thoughts and all passions. This weapon
She thrusts in all directions. With Her left hand She clasps
Her partner. To show that She has untied the knot that holds
all things to be what they appear, Her hair is loose and flowing. She is naked, for She is free from the obscuring veil of
Passion. She, like Her male partner, is three-eyed and
crowned with the Five Wisdoms, shown by skulls. He should

be regarded as Appearance (that is, the Phenomenal Universe), as Method, and as Boundless Compassion; while She is the Void (the symbol of the Absolute, the Empty of all relativities), Wisdom, Tranquillity, and Bliss. The pair are inseparable, so they are shown interlocked in sexual union, touching at all possible points of contact. The marriage is consummated in the midst of a halo of flames, the fire of Supreme Wisdom, which burns up all obstacles.

A casual observer, uninitiated into the mysteries of these symbols, would almost certainly mistake this picture of Highest Bliss for a demoniac form. It only shows the danger of applying the artistic criteria of one land to another without sufficient information as to where there is concordance and where the symbolic languages part company. In the present example we have seen skulls, blood, weapons, and flames, which in Europe have usually been given infernal associations, made to represent such mild virtues as Chastity and Longsuffering! In the book that I have quoted, these descriptions are given for the benefit of meditating disciples, who evoke the images mentally; but they could equally well serve as models for the painter. It is obvious that in his choice of colours and many other details the artist is not allowed to give free rein to his imagination. For instance, "Highest Bliss" cannot but be made blue, and His Consort red; otherwise She would seem to have given up Her devotion to the service of beings, which red denotes. The artist can vary the shade of red for better or worse; and there are many other details in which he can indulge his fancy to the full. But the emblems that serve to express definite metaphysical concepts are unchangeably fixed.

Whoever wishes to delve deeper into the *Tantras* and their teachings will have to refer to the only comprehensive book published in English, compiled by a distinguished British judge of the High Court, who was also a Sanskrit scholar, the late Sir John Woodroffe. He applied the searching probe of the finest judicial mind to the investigation of this difficult subject. As a result of his work, long-unchallenged prejudices, circulated not only by European controversialists but also by some obsequious Indian writers, were dispelled. He never moved a step beyond his brief. Every statement was accompanied by the evidence on which it rested, for all to weigh up for themselves. The book is called *Shakti and Shakta* — that is, *The Female Energy and Her Devotee.* In addition Mr. Justice Woodroffe arranged for the editing or translation of several complete texts of *Tantras,* both Sanskrit and Tibetan. Some copies of one of his editions, bound in the two sacred colours, red and yellow, were taken by us as presents for the more scholarly lamas. One of the latter, on receiving the book, observed in matter-of-fact tones: "This is a great doctrine. I know the book and it will be very handy next time I retire for a few months' solitary meditation." By his manner of speaking, it might have been a dictionary or a railway timetable. But another lama warned us: "It is useless for anyone to try to apply these methods by himself, without the supervision of an adept. Attempts by the uninitiated to carry out these exercises may involve them in no little danger." To read something about these doctrines is open to all, but he who wishes to use and realize them as a help towards Enlightenment must not forget that a teacher, imbued with practical knowledge of the particular *Tantra* selected, cannot be dispensed with.

Chapter XVI

"If I Forget Thee, O Jerusalem"

BELOW YURU a rocky defile, straitly hemmed in by sheer cliffs, falls away in a succession of huge steps down towards the Indus. The sky, far overhead, shows as a narrow strip of blue. A rivulet, born of an insignificant trickle, is crossed and re-crossed. Gathering volume, it swells into a quite sizable river, which after an all too brief independent life goes to merge its identity, with breath-taking suddenness, in the coffee-like waters of the greater stream, which here races along between forbidding banks of scorching rocks and sand.

A mile or two eastwards from the confluence a suspension bridge leads over to the right bank, defended by a fort of sun-baked mud, built by the Dogra invaders of Ladak to command the passage. In this part of the Indus Valley the road goes through three villages, Kalatze, Nyungla, and Saspul, a few hours' ride apart. They are some of the most prosperous settlements in the land. Each of them has sprung up close to the entrance of a tributary valley, whence issues the torrent that, through its leats, allows wide terraces to be irrigated. Every large village thus owns its own hinterland, with a chain of lesser hamlets extending inland from the river. Usually in each of these districts there is one important monastery, which fills the part of feudal overlord for the valley and receives a contribution of novices from all the leading families around. Most of these youths, before being admitted to the rank of full choir-monks, must first visit Lhasa for a long term of study, so that the holy city continues to be a nerve-centre for all Buddhist central Asia. Young scholars from outlying provinces as far apart as Ladak and Mongolia gather there and meet their fellows from the Chinese border, Sikkim, as well as from every part of politically independent Tibet.

To the rider in the desert, the sight of long *Mani* walls dividing the road into two always heralds the approaches to a village. Some of these *mendongs* are colossal, especially those built beside the trails that converge on Leh. Huge *chhortens* are set up at intervals along the walls, which suggest a breakwater with lighthouses, except that here the ocean is of sand instead of water.

At the beginning of the fields the roadway passes under several *chhorten*-crowned gateways, which, though modelled to one pattern, yet somehow always contrive to reveal the play of individual fancy. So also the houses, though conforming roughly to the plan described in the preceding chapter, remain a never ending source of curiosity and delight. A long series of photographs of Ladaki houses would well repay the trouble involved; I regret that we were not able to allot more time to this. "Every man his own architect" is the motto in this country; it explains how it has been possible to reconcile such extraordinary variety and originality with adherence to one model.

The valley of the Indus, comparatively sheltered from the most biting winds, offers ideal conditions for the cultivation of the apricot. Fruit ripens almost as high as Leh, but there the climate is too rigorous. The city lies near enough to the orchards, however, for a daily supply to be brought in baskets during the months of July and August. A certain proportion of the crop is dried and stored for winter use. In this form apricots are an excellent food for travelling. They are delicious when stewed, and have a very sweet, slightly toffee-like flavour. They are also economical, for they require the addition of little or no sugar, quite different from the tart dried apricots slit into halves and stocked by grocers at home. The reason is doubtless that the last-named variety is picked unripe, while the Himalayan fruit is left on the tree long enough for the sun to complete its work. The low humidity of the climate allows of the apricots being dried without decay setting in.

The inhabitants of these villages must surely be some of the happiest on the face of the earth. One can only pray that no zealous enthusiast will feel impelled to "raise their standard of living" in the name of some sociological theory worked out under totally dissimilar circumstances. Certain writers have mentioned the poverty of the people, doubtless referring to their lack of ready money and their rather Spartan simplicity of life. There is no luxury, nor a big margin of surplus food, but if the enjoyment of a sufficient, if rather unvaried diet — composed of tasty, unadulterated materials — and the leading of a healthy, outdoor life in majestic surroundings, with work that has its leisured as well as its strenuous phases, the wearing of durable and comely homespun clothing, the dwelling in spacious, well-built homes, and the possession of a restricted number of well-designed objects — if all this be poverty, then let us deplore our wealth! To the above catalogue two more intangible amenities can be added: time to think without the sense of being driven, and the absence of organized persuasion and regimentation at the hands of the state or of a commerce that does not fall far short of it in power.

Some twelve miles above Saspul, in the upland valley of Likhir ("Circle of the Water-Serpent Spirits"), stands the great abbey of the same name, belonging to the Gelugpa or "Virtuous Custom" Order of monks, commonly known as "Yellow-Hats," in order to distinguish them from the red-hatted adherents of earlier conventual organizations; all, however, without exception wear red clothes. The Yellow-Hats were founded in the fourteenth century by St. Tsong Khapa, "the man from Onion land," born near the western marches of the Chinese province of Kansu: eventually they became the most powerful association in Tibet and Mongolia, including among their members the sovereign of the country, the Dalai Lama, as well as his spiritual compeer, the Panchhen Lama of Tashilhunpo. Some of their colleges number their students by the thousand, the biggest of all, Drepung ("mound of rice"), outside Lhasa, exceeding in membership both Oxford and Cambridge taken together. Tsong Khapa's new Order has been described as a "reform," and one ill-advised author even went to the length of naming him the "Tibetan Luther." No more misleading label could well have been chosen. It is a fact that he tightened up rules, in reaction against what he considered as excessive licence among the other monks of his day, but there was nothing the least bit revolutionary or anti-traditional in any of his ordinances. Comparable reforms have occurred at various times in the history of Christendom; the Yellow-Hat reform most resembles perhaps the Cistercian revival in the Benedictine Order, which amounted to nothing more than a variant on the original foundation, though one which, in its time, was fruitful in rekindling the fires of monastic zeal. In doctrinal matters Tsong Khapa went to some pains to make it plain that he was not an innovator, but was building his teaching on the foundations laid by the great Indian saint Atisha, whose re-evangelization of Tibet in the eleventh century was like a second spring for Buddhism in that country. So also in respect of the Tantrik doctrines, so unloved by foreign commentators (especially by those lacking first-hand knowledge), the founder of the Yellow-Hats expressly declared that his own doctrine is a synthesis of the *Sutras,* or ordinary public teaching of the Church, and the *Tantras,* a special intensive method handed down, under the safeguarding seal of initiation, for the use of those who hope to tread the "abbreviated way" towards Buddhahood.

The Gelugpa differ from earlier foundations mainly in allotting relatively more time to the daily offices, to the slight attenuating perhaps — or so their critics allege — of those exercises in pure meditation which the others continue to place before all else. The Yellow monk regulates his conduct by a statute of 253 clauses, which include abstinence from alcohol, meat, and marriage. The second rule is often disregarded in practice, by reason of the difficulty of obtaining enough vegetable food on the plateau of Tibet, and even more so in Mongolia, where the people remain exclusively pastoral, refusing to take to agriculture. But even so, no one presumes to defend the lapse into a carnivorous diet, and the minority who do remain faithful to the law against flesh-eating are generally honoured in the land. In contrast to the Gelugpa, several of the old Red-hatted schools — to speak of Red-Hats as one Order, balancing them as one whole against the Yellow-Hats, is a common inaccuracy in books — admit both fermented liquor and marriage.

Though the adherents of the various Orders (again I must protest against the misleading term "sects," which is so often applied to them) usually live in harmony, they would not be human if a little rivalry did not sometimes creep in; one has only to think of the petty bickerings of Franciscans and Dominicans in our own Middle Ages. The Yellow-Hats are given to reproaching the others with slackness, especially over the question of drink, and to congratulating themselves because of their zeal for book-learning; whereas the Red-Hats, who, though they have their books too, lay rather more preponderant emphasis on the oral transmission of doctrine, turn that very same fact into a counter-accusation. Referring to the frequent daily assemblies in the temple for the choral repetition of the office that the rule of the Yellow-Hats prescribes, one Red-hatted monk voiced his criticism to me by saying: "They go in for too much chatter." It is said that these rivalries occasionally have reached the point of acrimony where brawls with iron pen-cases (the students' weapon in Tibet) have broken out and have resulted even in the spilling of blood and the cracking of tonsured skulls.

In Ladak, though both Red and Yellow Orders are to be found, with a certain advantage of number in favour of the former, relations between them seem perfectly amicable. Likhir of the Gelugpa is one of the older and larger houses; it is so flourishing that a new wing containing monks' quarters has been planned. It enjoys a high reputation for strict observance, being surpassed in this only by the neighbouring convent of Rigzon, many lamas of which — so it was said — refuse to ride lest the horses should take it amiss.

On a day of July 1936 a band of pilgrims from a distant country arrived at Saspul bound for Likhir. By their apparel one would have taken them for Tibetans from the Central Provinces, or perhaps from Sikkim, where that fashion is copied. Instead of the Ladaki self-coloured woollen tunics, they wore kimono-like cloaks of a reddish black, girt at the waist with silk sashes, bright red, blue, or yellow; green is a colour usually reserved for the use of women. Their caps were of black felt, with a band of gold Chinese brocade and fur-edged earflaps, worn turned up. Their boots were of the usual high shape, bound with coloured garters; the soles were of rope, while the uppers were black felt, gaily decorated with bits of green, blue, and red cloth. There were three principal persons in the party, besides a few grooms, one of whom, a tall and striking-looking man called Norbu, acted as servant. Norbu had a large frame, but a heart of gold. He came from Timosgam, above Nyungla, which is the home of the best porters in Ladak. The baggage of the party was on a modest scale: one did not see the huge paraphernalia with which Europeans are wont to encumber themselves when travelling in the Himalaya.

The little cavalcade rode into Saspul in the afternoon and alighted at a caravanserai, where they made a meal of milk, eggs, big radishes resembling turnips, and ripe apricots of prime quality, thin-skinned and succulent: the newcomers must have been thirsty from having trudged through the torrid stretch that lies between Nyungla and Saspul, for each consumed a double portion of fruit and still was eager for more. After lunch they asked for a messenger to carry a note to Likhir, since it would have seemed discourteous to have arrived there without warning; in no land is the virtue of politeness cultivated more than in Tibet. A peasant boy volunteered for the job, and a letter, couched in suitably honorific terms and wrapped in the white silk scarf that betokens sincere respect, was entrusted to him. He set off at great speed, not by the usual tracks, but by a short cut across the hills, promising to be back with an answer soon after sundown.

While waiting for their envoy to execute his errand, the three strangers idled away their time strolling through the fields, where the tawny crops, ripe for the sickle, were being cut down and carried to the threshing-floors. When they felt tired they sat awhile in the dense shadow of the apricot trees; the deep, intense green of the foliage was gold-spangled with fruit, which kept dropping to the ground with every puff of the clover-honeyed breezes. The air had an aromatic tang that mingled with its sweetness, a fragrance as of incense that came from the catmint which covered the walls. The three friends sat and rested on the brink of one of the leats, screened from the sun by willow trees; the water at their feet ran icy cold, though only two yards away the stones were too hot to touch.

Returning to the fields, the newcomers stood watching some peasants winnowing, to the accompaniment of shrill women's voices raised in a tune that gave its rhythm to the teams engaged in treading out the grain. Apple-cheeked girls drove their yokes of four of five yak calves round and round in circles, while others, armed with long wooden forks, threw fresh sheaves upon the pile. The women took turns at keeping up the refrain continually; at that season the whole country resounds with song from daybreak till evening. Not only harvesting, but every kind of work has its appropriate tune. One of the most expressive is that of the log-carriers. Heavy poplar logs, to be split in half for roofing, are borne on men's shoulders. As they march along, a single voice sings a verse, which is then answered in chorus by the remainder of the gang. Similarly, when a big reservoir had to be dug at Leh, an oboe-player and drummer were engaged all day to give the rhythm to the labourers: surely the requisitioning of serious music for such a use betokens a high degree of civilization!

At nightfall the messenger returned from the monastery with a message bidding the pilgrims welcome. He also reported that the abbot of Likhir was absent in Lhasa, and that the prior had been left in charge and would do the honours.

Next morning the party rose at dawn and followed a sandy track that led away from the river into a small valley between gravel-strewn downs. Norbu acted as guide with great willingness, for that day's goal was his family *Gompa;* two of his brothers were at that time in residence, the one just ordained *Gelong* or full monk, the other a novice still in his early teens. After a few miles the path mounted more steeply till it emerged in the Vale of Likhir, one of the most attractive in all Ladak. It was a rich expanse of cornland, dotted about with charming homesteads, each standing in its clump of willows or poplars. Since every inch of irrigated ground was precious, here, as always, the road ran in the desert, though close to the margin of cultivation. It was marked by rows of *chhortens* and *mendongs,* on which pious hands had laid innumerable flat stones bearing the *Mani* formula: the long chain of *Mani* walls constituted the Sacred Way leading towards the Water-Serpent Spirits' abode.

Likhir *Gompa* stands on a bold eminence commanding a view of the whole valley; as one approaches it from the direction of the Indus, there is a break in the curtain of hills to the right, through which a shimmering panorama of snowy peaks appears, like an immense diamond tiara. These are the higher portions of the Ladak Range, mostly attaining about 19,000 or 20,000 feet.

The abbey forms a magnificent architectural pile, terrace upon terrace, which looks as if it is growing out of the very rock, an effect due to the fact that every wall, window, and door is given a slight inward slope. It is this habit that makes the Tibetan style fit ideally into a mountain landscape, so that the handiworks of man, far from detracting from Nature's perfections, seem merely to heighten and extend her rhythms.

About a mile and a half from the *Gompa* the party was greeted by a young and handsome lama who had been sent out to meet them. The distance to which a person walks to receive a guest is proportional to the latter's rank. For a prince they might ride out a whole week's journey. A ravine had to be crossed to reach the end of a spiral path that led round the hillock forming the emplacement of the abbey. As soon as the riders came within sight of the lowest bastions, the deep purr of a bass drum greeted them. Next, added to the rumbling of the drum, sounded forth the majestic voices of the twelve-foot trumpets that serve to hold a pedal in every Tibetan temple orchestra, the foundation-tone above which the higher-pitched instruments weave their symphonies. The players take turns in breathing so that the note may be maintained unbroken, heaving like the swell of some ocean of molten brass. The descant is rendered by oboes, not unlike bagpipe chanters, while complexities of rhythm are contributed by smaller drums, handbells, and cymbals. The clashing sonority produced is strangely thrilling when heard in the open, especially when the orchestra

plays accurately in tune. There is variability in this matter
among Tibetan as among European bands: that of Likhir was
beautifully exact; but in certain decadent monasteries, careless
ensemble and bad intonation reduced music to a mere cacoph-
ony; indeed, the standard of orchestral playing is often a very
fair index of the moral state of any *Gompa!* Raising their heads,
the wayfarers caught sight of the group of red-robed musicians
high up on the walls. Surely no crusading baron returning to
his castle from the Holy Land could have enjoyed a more romantic welcome.

As the riders rounded the last bend, a throng of lamas and
peasants ran out towards them. They dismounted from their
ponies and, casting the bridles into willing hands, advanced to
an alleyway where a tall and venerable figure stood a little
apart. He was the prior, before whom knees were bent and foreheads touched the ground. Signing to the party to follow, he
turned and led the way at a rapid pace, threading a labyrinth
of courts and stairs and passages to the topmost terrace of all,
marked at the angles by banners, rather like furled umbrellas.
Then he passed through the doorway of the abbot's private
apartment, which, as was customary, was situated at the top of
the building. They removed their shoes and stepped inside a
chamber of surpassing magnificence.

The roof was supported on wooden posts, the bracketed capitals of which, as well as all the beams, window-frames, and
other woodwork, were picked out in delicate patterns of flowers
and dragons of brilliant hue. The windows, which were flung
wide open, affording a grand view over the mountains, were of
Chinese design, with a kind of translucent paper to take the
place of glass. The walls of the room were hung with scroll
paintings representing saints or angelic beings, each picture being mounted on Chinese brocade of richest design. The ceiling
was like a tent, with an awning of peach-coloured Chinese embroidery of ancient date. Along one wall, facing the window,
stood the altar, behind which presided a row of gilt, lotus-
throned figures shaded by elaborate carved canopies. The floor
was spread with fine rugs of Turkistan and Tibet, on which the
guests were bidden to take their seats; a charming little carved
and painted table was placed before each man to hold his teacup and food-bowl. Each article was a work of art of real worth
and had been kept in spotless condition, though put to reasonable use. How differently works of art appear when they are
thus related to life, as intended by their makers, and not im-

prisoned, on the plea of safeguarding, within those vast concentration-camps called museums.

No sooner was everybody seated than tea — that inevitable preliminary to all business in Tibet — was served out of a fine teapot, which after use was kept warm on an earthenware stove. The tea was equal to everything else at Likhir, prepared from the best brand, with the usual butter and salt and a pinch of soda added. The Tibetans daily consume a prodigious quantity of this tea, which to our taste seems rather more like soup. At every sip the cup is promptly refilled to the brim, and this goes on until the guest, after repeatedly making a polite show of refusal, finally decides to make a stand and covers his bowl with his hand, turns it upside down, or hides it under the table.

After the guests had drunk a good many cups of tea, food was also served: apricots both fresh and dried, a hard crystalline candy, and a kind of rice pudding containing currants, lightly fried and dusted with sugar. During the meal the old prior and one or two senior monks sat on the floor and carried on an elegant conversation covering a varied range of topics, while the young novices crowded in the doorway to watch and listen.

The boys are carefully brought up and have excellent manners, each one being allotted to a tutor who instructs him in deportment as well as letters. They do not look repressed in any way, but are, on the contrary, extremely lively save on occasions when etiquette requires a grave demeanour. Up to the age of fourteen their duties do not amount to much more than pouring out tea at intervals during services, and playing instruments in the orchestra; but after that they are expected to leave the monastery and make the long journey to Lhasa for their university studies. Unless they choose to take a degree corresponding to our Doctor of Divinity, for which at least ten years' work is demanded, they go back to their monastery after a few years as fully fledged choir-monks, being allotted rooms of their own, more like those in an Oxford college than a friar's cell.

Our three pilgrims gained some prestige from the fact that their dialect, clothes, and customs derived from the Central Provinces. Their own home, however, was in New Babylon, on the farthest confines of the Lands of the Setting Sun, a region that was in process of being enslaved by three malignant demon kings named Progress, Hurry-Hasty, and Propaganda (like many felons, the last-named has several aliases, the commonest of which is simple Mr. Education); these tyrants forced their subjects to work at a rate so intense that they might well have envied the pyramid-builders. From time to time the three fiends would set their subjects to battle, inflaming one against another like fighting-cocks, so that they were roused to the pitch of blind and furious hatred. Possibly the motive behind all this strife originated from a desire to distract men from calm thinking, lest having leisure to view things, and themselves, as they really are, they might discover, in non-attachment to self, a way of escape out of the sufferings of the Round of Existence in which they were imprisoned.

The majority of the servants of the demons lived in want, but some of them had persuaded themselves that their lot was enviable and should be shared by other races that had so far managed to avoid adopting their customs. Numerous busybodies were recruited, under all sorts of specious pleas, and dispatched to remote corners of the globe in order to disseminate the demons' influence. The company offered up an earnest prayer that Ladak and Tibet might be spared as a preserving-ground for other ideas and that, by the power of the five kinds of Wisdom embodied in the Buddhas of the five directions, assisted by their active Consort-Energies under their sternest aspects, the malice of the demons might be exorcized, so that all mankind might return to peace.

After tea the guests were led into a small adjoining chamber, the bedroom of the abbot. In it there was a fine chest painted in delicate gold arabesques; otherwise the room was bare except for five large scroll pictures so wonderful that to describe them there are no words sufficient in language. Whether one sets more store on boldness of composition, clarity of drawing, wealth of detail free from all irrelevancy, brilliancy of colour, or the rapt devotion expressed in the faces, one would discover each of these qualities in the five masterpieces. The middle one of the set represented the red Buddha of the Western Quarter, "Immeasurable Light," seated under a canopy of fruits and garlands that might almost have come from Crivelli's brush, and worshipped by angelic servitors and every sort of animal, bird, and plant. The attention of the sacristan was drawn to a small crack that had appeared in the paint, due to the warping of a wooden roller from which the *t'hanka* hung, a frequent cause of damage in such scrolls. He undertook to change the roller and to engage a competent artist to repair the harm before it spread any farther.

Finally everyone repaired to the main temple or Hall of Assemblies for the afternoon service. It was a lofty church, di-

vided into three aisles by massive wooden piers, on which the
flat ceiling rested. The walls were brilliantly painted or hung
with *t'hankas,* so that every corner of the building offered to
the eye some new play of colour under the intense rays of
the central Asian sun, streaming in by open windows opposite
the high altar. There were two thrones, a higher one for the
abbot and one slightly lower, on which the prior seated himself. A double row of wooden platforms, raised a few inches
off the floor and covered with thick rugs, formed a choir on either side, facing in towards the central space. On these the
monks sat cross-legged, those of the inner row holding musical
instruments. Each man, before taking his seat, drew over his
shoulders a yellow cape.

All through the service a little black kitten, the pet of one of
the lamas, kept playing in and out under the platforms on
which the officiants were sitting. No one paid attention to it,
and it was allowed to gambol to its heart's content up to the
very feet of Him who did not try to distinguish between man
and beast, nor even between god and devil, in pointing out the
road of escape from suffering.

A brief meditation preceded the rite, the offering of the Universe to the Buddha. This idea runs through all the public worship like a central theme. St. Tsong Khapa, who fixed the order
of service for his own Yellow monks, tells them to start by im-
agining themselves each to be endowed with a hundred heads,
and each head with a thousand mouths, and each mouth with
unnumbered tongues, all eloquent in praise. In making votive
offerings, at first separate gifts must be presented, such as flowers, incense, and music. What cannot be given in kind may be
offered up in imagination, and gradually added to, until the
whole Universe is ready to be laid at the divine feet "as a gift
tendered by the mightiest of kings, its possessor."

The hands of the worshipper are joined in a gesture called
mandala (globe), which is the regular symbol of the Universe.
The hands are turned palms upwards, with the little fingers
crossed. The tip of the right thumb touches the left little finger,
the right index finger touches the left middle finger, and vice
versa. These four pairs make the four points of the compass, or
quarters. The fifth pair, the fourth fingers, sticks up in the middle and represents Mount Meru, the central axis, which is itself
the path of Exaltation, of ascent from the partial and limited to
the integral and infinite.

The passage from small tangible offerings to undefined imaginary ones is intended to evoke the idea of non-duality, of the basic unity of everything, which lies behind all the Tibetan metaphysic. An analogous idea can be read into the sacramental sentence taken from the Christian liturgy of St. John Chrysostom: "Thy own of Thine own to Thee we offer, in all and for all."

The office consisted of psalms, some sung to a marked chant, others merely droned in a low voice, diversified with symphonies rendered by the orchestra. The oboe-players, who held the main tune, blew their reeds before starting, with a familiar quack-quack that carried the mind back to the tuning-in of the London Philharmonic or any other of our orchestras. Some of the chants were metrical and supported by drum alone; with others handbells were rung. A precentor with a deep bass voice led the service, giving the signal with his cymbals to start or end each section. He had a peculiar way of indicating the final cadences, letting his voice sink in a long chromatic glissando into the depths of the bass, not unlike bagpipes from which the air is being emptied. Every ten minutes or so there was an interval, when everyone could relax and look about him; during actual prayers in the strictest Tibetan monasteries inattention is apt to be summarily dealt with by a censor, who surveys the congregation from a point of vantage, his leather scourge kept handy for administering instant correction. Woe to the man who stares about or shuffles his knees or makes a whispered remark and thinks he can elude the watchful eye. He is seized by the scruff of the neck and led out into the middle, where he can only bow down humbly and take his punishment like a man. When officiating, the monks are expected to sit motionless, though without stiffness; their hands only move in the ritual gestures. In the pauses for relaxation the novices get up and fill the wooden bowl set before each monk with tea out of a monster pot; they drink, and sometimes also add to the tea a little of the parched barley meal that takes the place of bread; this is kneaded into a lump and then eaten.

When the service was over, it was time to think, reluctantly, of departure. Many were the requests on the part of the good monks that the three friends would return later and make a stay of several days or even longer. The ponies were led round by a groom; before mounting, the visitors saluted the kind old prior, who, bending, imprinted on each of them a light tap with his forehead, bestowing a blessing. Then they turned and disappeared down the hill. How often since that time have they

LADAK PEASANT HOUSE   *See page 205*

LADAKI PEASANT *See pages 206–7*

THRESHING BARLEY *See page 205*

STORM CLOUDS OVER YURU   *See page 211*

PAINTING AT YURU   *See page 213*

Divinities with their Consort Energies under both peaceful and terrible aspects

LIKHIR   *See page 229*

LIKHIR   *See page 230*
Corner of a lama's room

THE PRECENTOR OF LIKHIR   *See page 234*

DESERT TRACK BEHIND SPITUK   *See page 236*

A Novice of the Gelugpa Order   *See page 225*

The Lama Dawa, Bursar of Spituk   *See page 237*

dreamed of Likhir and of the day when, like the foretaste of a beatific vision, they were admitted to the threefold joys of Nature, the Arts, and Human Intercourse combined in one single all-embracing synthesis! Now they are back in Babylon: how shall they sing the Lord's song in a strange land?

Chapter XVII

The Bursar of Spituk

THE RIDE from Saspul to Spituk, where the road enters the wider portion of the Indus Valley, is on the whole monotonous, with sandy stretches strewn with round pebbles — an unpleasant surface, whether for riding or walking. At first, abandoning the Indus, which is only rejoined close to Spituk, the Likhir path is followed for a couple of miles to a fork; there the Leh road turns off to the right up an extremely hot and sandy pass, and leads on to a wide plateau, which it crosses before descending into the next cultivated strip near the village of Basgo. This village is surrounded by apple orchards, and dominated by an ancient ruined castle built to command the entrance to a long side valley through which it is possible to approach the river Shyok. Possibly in olden times Turkoman raiders may have come down this way.

Another village, Nimu, lies on the route before the final long stretch to Spituk. It is a regular stage and possesses a resthouse; but it is worth pushing on farther, in order to put the dullest bit of the road behind one. The notable thing about Nimu is the headman's house, which is exceptional even in this land of fine houses.

After so many days in stony gorges the open scenery round Spituk came as a refreshing surprise. The banks of the river were marshy in many places, with reeds and low bushes, and strips of damp meadow where cattle were grazing. Spituk itself is dominated by a famous monastery of the Yellow-hatted Order; its silhouette stood out sharp in the evening light as we approached from the west. The main road to Leh passes, not on the river side, but between the hill on which the *Gompa* stands and a low line of fantastic limestone cliffs, where, so we were told, the lime is collected that is used for the foundation coating of the sacred paintings. On passing through the opening, one enters a great sandy amphitheatre, the meeting-place of several valleys. To the south the Indus, now broken into two or three shallower channels, is fringed on either side with a broad belt of cultivation, set here and there with clumps of poplars. At the entrance of each subsidiary valley there is a fan of irrigated land; the nearest of these to the north contains the city of Leh itself. Across the Indus, in the shadow of a snow mountain, stands Stok with its castle, half monastery, half palace, in which resides the descendant of the great line of Ladak kings, now a state pensioner, who still bears the courtesy title and owns the fief.

As we wished to visit Spituk monastery at leisure, we decided to stop the night in the rest-house and to postpone entering the capital for one more day. An abrupt staircase, up which we were taken at a breathless pace, led to the main buildings, which occupied different levels on the hillside. The main temple is a fine building containing mural paintings and festooned with scrolls. There we made our offering of five precious stones, which were taken over by a tall and lithe-looking lama with a very keen, vivacious face, who discharged the office of bursar. He asked if we preferred to have the stones set in a decorated *chhorten* at the end of the aisle or in the gilt diadem of Tsepagmed, whose beautiful image stood on the right of the Buddha, behind the altar. We chose the latter as the most suitable setting for the jewels.

From the first moment we felt powerfully drawn towards the personality of our new acquaintance, whose name was Dawa (Moon); he seemed to reciprocate the feeling, for he spoke to us as if he had all along been expecting our arrival and knew that our fates and his own, already connected by an unseen link, were predestined to move along parallel lines in the future. Looking back, I think that the bursar of Spituk is one of the most remarkable people I have ever met, though the abbot of Lachhen must be accorded the first place. The lama Dawa was a man who, both in theory and in practice, exemplified a dedicated life of high quality. Not only was he a well-informed exponent of the Doctrine, but he was the thing itself. It showed up in his smallest action and in his lightest word; above all, it revealed itself in the extreme detachment of his judgment. It had even affected his bodily movements, which had a peculiar flexibility that seemed more than just physical, a reflection of the suppleness of his mind. To this list of qualities there must be added a trenchant wit and a sweet and lovable disposition. He told us that he had three pupils, whom he

was coaching before they went off to Tibet for their final studies. He considered that a teacher could not adequately deal
with more than that number at one time; certainly they were
greatly to be envied in their master.

From the temple we were led to an upper chamber containing fine *t'hankas;* carpets were spread, and tea and rice pudding were served. The room belonged to the Incarnate Abbot
of Spituk, the Lord Bakula. We remembered the tributes paid
to the good taste, wisdom, and urbanity of that prelate in various writings of the eminent Italian anthropologist Professor
Giotto Dainelli. But his Bakula was no more to be found among
the living, and the monastery was being run by a prior, in expectation of the day when the newly chosen Bakula, now about
eighteen years old, should return and take his seat on the ab-
batial throne. He had been found by the process of divination
used for discovering the child on whom the influence of the
preceding line of abbots had again descended, and on reaching
the age of about sixteen he had been duly sent to Lhasa to the
vast College of Drepung, where the men of Spituk, as also
those of Likhir, usually take their course in divinity. The young
Bakula was due to return only after obtaining his degree of
Geshé or Doctor, which demanded many years of work.

Among some framed photographs hanging on the wall was
one of the old Bakula; the nobility of his countenance certainly
bore out the high character that Signor Dainelli had assigned
to him. There was also a photograph of the present Bakula
taken at the age of twelve, clad in the vesture and mitre of an
abbot. His was also a face of rare distinction and beauty; he
looked a born prince who, if appearances did not belie him,
would prove a worthy ruler over his community. There was a
good deal that needed attention at Spituk, for a certain musti-
ness, mental as well as tangible, seemed to have settled on the
place. The prior must have been rather slack and inclined to
let things slide, pending the return from Lhasa of the rightful
lord of the place. Among the lamas, the bursar Dawa's vigour
seemed rather the exception; and my impression of a service in
the temple was none too favourable, for there was a good deal
of inattention, always a sign of decay. This *Gompa* must be
rated only moderately good; it is much above the degenerate
houses like Yuru, but falls equally far below the happy state of
Likhir.

We invited the bursar to supper. Towards sunset he arrived,
but would touch nothing but a cup of tea, since he said that he

never took anything after the midday meal. He was very strict in abstaining from alcohol and meat, and pronounced severe censure against those who were self-indulgent in these respects. According to him, many of the monastic houses in Ladak had deteriorated markedly of recent years; even Rigzon, reputed to be of the purest observance, had somewhat lowered its standard, while certain of the other *Gompas* were falling into deplorable laxity and were simply vegetating, with hardly a thought to spare for the Doctrine. In Tibet he declared things to be, on the whole, much better, though even at his own University of Drepung he considered that devotion needed rekindling. "There are nine thousand monks and students there," he said, "but go any day into the temple and you will find it far from sufficiently attended." On the other hand the University of Sera, also near Lhasa, was still a model, he thought, while at Ganden, the third of the great trio of Yellow-Hat Houses at Lhasa, the standard was about average. There were scores of excellent teachers, however, to be found scattered over Tibet, but oftener in the smaller monasteries, both Yellow and Red, than in the ones with the biggest membership.

Our newly found friend then proceeded to inquire about our own doctrinal standpoint and this led to a discussion as to what constitutes a Buddhist and what test, if any, can be employed for his recognition. Any form of inquisition into a man's private views is considered impertinent. Buddhism, like Hinduism, has on the whole avoided the error of trying to stamp out doubt by organized pressure. Indeed, the duty of subjecting the doctrines one professes to the final test of realization is the advice given by every teacher, good and bad alike. There is no real knowledge other than the realization of truths already immanent and waiting to be unveiled as soon as the obscuring passions and self-delusions have been cleared away. Moreover, though reverence for the person of the teacher runs through the whole tradition like a central thread, it is not expected of the pupil that he shall blind himself to the fact of human deficiencies in his master's life. His private faults in no wise impair the authority of his teaching for the disciple, nor do they diminish the latter's obedience and devotion to the master. It is bad form, however, for the disciple ever to speak disparagingly of his master to others. Whatever he may notice, he must continue to treat him with the respect due to his function as mouthpiece of the doctrine. In this matter the wording of the books is emphatic and allows no loophole for evasion. The master-pupil relationship, in a regular Tradition, is something far transcending any actual individualities concerned. The chain is more important than any single link. If some of the links are made of baser metal, it matters little, provided that they hold. Moreover a man may have something extremely precious to communicate and yet suffer from weaknesses in a human sense. A professor of mathematics need not be reckoned less qualified for his job by the fact that he drinks or is unfaithful to his wife. An observed fault of character does not, in the Tibetan view, invalidate the truth of a man's doctrine, which, in spite of his personal failings, he may be correctly transmitting according to the tradition which he has himself received. Conversely, there may be flaws in the lessons imparted by men of the highest private virtue; care must at all times be exercised against letting the scales be weighed down by irrelevant personal and moral considerations.

The bursar's view on the touchstone for recognizing a Buddhist was summed up as follows: "Where the Refuge is present, there is Buddhism: if the Refuge is wanting, there is no Buddhism. The Refuge is a question of understanding and of action based thereon. This truth must be grasped and experienced and all actions must conform to its spirit. Except in the Refuge seek no other way of Deliverance."

The Refuge is a triple formula that has sometimes, inappropriately, been described as the "Creed" of Buddhism. It runs thus:

> I take Refuge in the Buddha
> I take Refuge in the Doctrine
> I take Refuge in the Congregation.

To these three Refuges there has been given the name of the Trinity of Most Precious Things. The line one must follow in order to realize them is suggested by the following passage, copied for me by my next teacher, the lama Gyaltsan of P'hiyang, whom I shall introduce in a succeeding chapter. It is taken from the works of Dagpo Hlardjé, surnamed Gampopa, who was a pupil of Rechhung, the disciple of Mila Repa:

> This is the lesson to be learned of how to go for refuge to the Three Most Precious Things. . . .
> In the integral lesson are contained six special lessons and five general ones. First of all, the special lessons contain three renunciations and three attainments.

To start with, behold the three things to be renounced:

1. Having gone to the Buddha for refuge, do not worship the gods who err in the Round.
2. Having gone to the Doctrine for refuge, do no injury to living creatures.
3. Having gone to the Congregation for refuge, do not form associations with heretics.

Here are the three things to be attained. For as much as you attain them in conformity with the word of Buddha, do so without forgetfulness and with reverence:

4. Respectfully raise on high even a mere fragment of a sacred effigy.
5. Having gone for refuge to the Doctrine, strive to hear, ponder, and meditate the imperative Doctrine. The writing that enshrines the Doctrine, even were it a tiny shred, raise reverently on high.
6. Having gone for refuge to the Congregation, to it — the Congregation — that is, to the followers of Buddha — also show reverence.
Associate with the friends of virtue; lastly also show respect to the yellow robe.

Here follow the five ordinary precepts:

1. Even at the sacrifice of your life, do not abandon the Three Precious Things.
2. Even for a very important reason, do not seek any other method.
3. Do not cut off periodic offerings.
4. Do not invent another Refuge.
5. In whatever direction you may be proceeding, worship its presiding Buddha.

A few comments on this passage may help to make it clearer. I have compared it with a corresponding passage in the *Lamrim* ("Stages in the Way") of Tsong Khapa, the most authoritative book of the Yellow Lamas, which therefore represents a separate, though parallel, strand of tradition. The wording is almost the same, which makes one suppose that both were based on the same original, probably an Indian text. The numbering of the various injunctions and their subdivisions is typical of Tibetan doctrinal books. They delight in numbered lists and it would be possible, could a sheet of paper large enough be found, to draw up a scheme of the whole development of a doctrine in all its ramifications, like a sort of family tree. The *Lamrim,* for instance, reads in parts more like a Government White Paper than an abstract treatise, with its broad classifications, and then its clauses, its riders, its listed grades of knowledge; and there is never a metaphor, hardly even a simile, to break the severe economy of its language. Tibetan sacred writings are often voluminous, but they are the reverse of discursive. Sometimes, indeed, they are contracted to such a point of pithy condensation that without the help of a teacher it would be difficult to extract any sense from their bare phraseology. *The Lantern of the Path,* by the great second Apostle of Tibet, the Bengali St. Atisha, occupies about ten small sheets of woodblock printing; yet it contains the kernel of St. Tsong Khapa's vast volume, the *Lamrim,* which was based on it: and the *Lamrim* itself, though so long, is far from diffuse; its every line is fraught with meaning, demanding unflagging concentration from the reader.

To revert to the Refuge, some of the phrases explain themselves and ask for no comment, but a few might give rise to doubt as to their exact significance:

The gods who err in the Round. They are one of the six classes of beings who share the Round of Existence (see Chapter xi, page 132). Though temporarily possessed of superior powers, they are our fellow creatures, subject to the same vicissitudes of birth and death as ourselves. To worship them is senseless and therefore idolatrous. Real worship can only be paid to what is permanent and truly divine — that is, to the Buddha, apart from whose essence nothing is, though we know it not, because of the illusion of individual existence and the dualistic notions to which it gives birth. Reality and permanence can only belong to That which contains within Itself Its own sufficient Cause, and That can only be One. To offer real worship to anything else is idolatry, though reverence of a qualified kind (what in Christian theological language was termed *dulia* as distinct from *latreia* or true worship due to God alone) is offered to saints and heavenly personalities of inferior grades, who play the part of teachers, protectors, and intercessors. This statement of doctrine is practically the same as that which has obtained in the Catholic Church since the Council of Constantinople, which settled the controversy over the revering of images and the invocation of saints. It is furthermore interesting to note that all these heavenly Lamas and Divinities, including the Bodhisats like Chenrezig, who fulfil the redemptive function on behalf of all suffering creatures, are comprised in the Third Most Precious Thing — the Congregation. They correspond in idea to the Church Triumphant, while the lamas on earth, members of the Order set up by the Buddha, the authorized transmitters of His Tradition, correspond to the Church Militant. The concordance with Christian doctrine here revealed is a striking illustration of the common thread that, under many external differences of form and expression, runs through all traditional teachings.

The Renunciations call for some further comment. The second one, which discourages us from inflicting harm on other sentient beings, is interpreted very strictly, and a man is considered to have fulfilled his duty in this matter in proportion as he finds it possible to avoid occasions for injuring even the lowliest creatures. Like many of the Jains in India today, the ancient Buddhist monks swept their path as they walked, lest they might tread inadvertently on an insect, and they carried a filter so that the water they drank might be cleared of animalcules that would otherwise have been swallowed. One of the first things that a Gelugpa, or Yellow monk, must do on getting up in the morning is to anoint the soles of his feet with spittle as a sign that he prays that any animals that he may trample on by mistake may be reborn in the happy sphere of the Western Paradise.

The third renunciation is open to slight misconstruction. The word that, for a lack of a better, I have translated as "heretics" is given in the original Tibetan as *Mutegpa,* which literally denotes a Brahmin devotee. It comes down from the early centuries when regular debates used to take place between rival sectaries in India. There are many tales of the discomfiture of the spokesmen of one or the other party — which party depended on the sympathies of the teller; but there is also little evidence that religious emulation ever led to bigotry: in this respect the historical record of all the Indian schools of thought is singularly blameless. I discussed the point about *Mutegpa* several times with a lama, and as far as I can tell, the passage means no more than that one should avoid associating constantly with people who are likely to try to distract one by their bad example; it must never be read in the sense of authorizing an unfriendly, standoffish attitude even towards aggressive opponents of the Doctrine.

Turning to the three things to be attained, one notices that the first proposition, the latter half of the second, and the third are all concerned with treating sacred objects with reverence — images, books, and persons who have the right to wear the sacred colour. The most positive of the Attainments is the first half of the second precept, which describes the process by which Knowledge is to be acquired. First one must listen to the Doctrine, then one must consider it in a theoretical sense, and finally it will be realized in Meditation. Then only can it be spoken of as Known.

"The writing that enshrines the Doctrine" — that is, books or portions of books — is reverenced almost more than anything else by the Tibetans. They will not pack up their belongings for a journey without making sure that the books have the place of honour on top and will not be crushed under everyday objects. If a Tibetan is handed a book, he will lay it on his head, murmuring a prayer that he may be helped to profit by its wisdom. People are almost morbid about a book or an image coming into contact with shoes. I remember one day, at the *Gompa* of P'hiyang, when we were sitting on the floor of our cell talking to our friend the lama Gyaltsan, that Dr. Roaf, who had just finished looking up some reference in a *Textbook of Pathology* by Professor Boyd, happened to put his feet lightly on that massive black tome. Suddenly Gyaltsan noticed it and, stopping in the middle of his discourse, said in shocked tones: "Excuse me, you may not know it; but you are treading on a book!" Dr. Roaf at once apologized and Professor Boyd's precious volume was duly picked up and laid in a place of safety. I think its learned author would have been surprised to hear of the honour done to his book by a lama in far-off Tibet, an honour that it has probably never received from one of his students in his own laboratory at home!

The five general injunctions call for little comment: the only one that is not quite clear is the one that refers to periodic offerings. I fancy that it means that those who devote themselves to the religious calling deserve the alms of the faithful for their support, but I am not quite sure if I have read this sentence aright.

One final remark must be added to this commentary on the Refuge. When a Tibetan is about to invoke the Three Precious Things, he usually precedes them with another Refuge phrase: "I go for Refuge to the Lama."

The Lama here referred to is not synonymous with the third Precious Thing, the Congregation: it denotes the disciple's private spiritual director — "his own Lama," or *Guru*, as a Hindu would call him — through whom the Doctrine is transmitted and in virtue of whose teaching the pupil is made an effective participant in the Tradition from the beginning of time. In the Lama is seen personified the Teacher function, the highest that can be conceived in the Universe. To him boundless reverence, obedience, and devotion are enjoined and no important step must be taken unless preceded by his formal authorization. He is the symbol of Tradition, through which the Three Precious Things are revealed.

These explanations about the Refuge are the fruits of several discussions. On that first occasion at Spituk we naturally could only begin to approach the subject. After talking for some time of the traits that denote the Buddhist, the lama Dawa, in his turn, addressed a few inquiries to us about the teachings of Christianity. "I have noticed that Christians, as a rule, seem indifferent to the sufferings of animals. Not only do they all eat meat freely, but they do not seem to mind killing animals on the slightest provocation. Tell me, have they the authority of their Founder for this? Did He really teach that sentient creatures can be exploited in the service of man and injured at his mere convenience? It is the one thing that appears to me evil in what I know of Christianity."

There is an instinct of loyalty in man that makes it repugnant to him to run down his own countrymen before a foreigner; one feels a strong impulse to present the least unfavourable case. I believe that Christianity has been one of the great traditional avenues for the revelation of true Doctrine, and I also think that the general idea of Charity as taught in the Gospel is utterly incompatible with the heartless exploitation of animals for supplying man's material wants. I deny that it is reasonable or indeed possible to practise Charity towards one's fellow men and callousness towards one's fellow creatures of the animal world, acting tenderly towards the former and cruelly towards the latter; though it must be confessed that some otherwise virtuous people have attempted to justify such a policy. The theory that creatures endowed with any degree of sensibility were created to be used at the unrestricted will and pleasure of one species, singled out of the whole of creation, seems to make of the Creator not a God, but a fiend of unexampled malignancy. That day at Spituk I would gladly have given the lama Dawa a simple statement that Christ's teaching on animals was as precise as he expected it to be, and that the deplorable practice of Christians in this matter was simply a falling away from their professed ideal.

But to a man of the highest intellectual honesty like Dawa one felt it impossible to give any answer that suffered from bias; he and his fellow lamas showed such a freedom from all tendencies towards special pleading when discussing the condition of their own Church that anything short of an equal frankness towards them would have been rank dishonesty. I have been surprised how rare false loyalty is among Tibetans; I have said rare, but I must confess that I cannot at this moment recall a single instance of facts being doctored, or evidence unfairly selected, for the purpose of showing up their institutions in a more favourable light. This does not seem to be one of their temptations, for the basis of their whole philosophy lies in the undoing of illusion. Whatever ostensible success is built on a groundwork of misrepresentation is for them *ipso facto* poisoned at the root and correspondingly shortlived; its fruits therefore, however sweet their temporary flavour, must in the long run prove to be bitter. There are liars for personal gain to be found in Tibet as elsewhere, but, in their heart of hearts, they do not so often cherish the lurking belief that out of a deception of themselves or others ultimately happy consequences can somehow be made to flow. This error is precluded even by a partial understanding of the doctrine of *Karman*, which is inexorable in declaring that as the sowing, so shall be the eventual reaping. That is why the nature of the religious label affixed to a person counts for rather less among them than among ourselves: nominal conversion to Buddhism, based on insufficient reasons, is worthless and can only turn out disadvantageously for the person concerned, as well as for his fellows in the tradition.

The answer that I gave to the lama's question was roughly as follows: "In the recorded life of the Founder of Christianity, contained in the four Gospels, it must be admitted that there are hardly any explicit allusions to animals. One can find two or three passages that could be read in a favourable sense; for example, the sparrows, not one of which can 'fall on the ground without your Father . . .' and 'the lilies of the field'; but there is nothing that could not be explained away as a figure of speech." It is therefore just to admit that in the Gospels the question of animals is practically not touched on and appears to be treated as a matter of no great urgency. It is my own personal opinion that the teaching of Christ in regard to the cultivation of a generally merciful and loving outlook is impossible to realize if it excludes animals. The Sermon on the Mount and many sayings of the Buddha are, in spirit, singularly concordant. I readily grant that the absence from the Gospel of any specific mention of our duty towards animals seems rather regrettable in the light of subsequent experience.

If one considers later Christian writers, again one is forced to admit that, for the majority, the question of animals hardly arose. More often it was taken for granted that animals were created primarily for the direct service of man, and that any kindness shown them was by the way. The frequent use of disparaging terms such as "brute" or "beast" suggests that animals possess no rights of their own. On the other hand, quite a number of saints, especially the early hermits and, of course, St. Francis — but there are also many others — seem to have felt as the lamas do, that to limit love is to denature it altogether. While believing that these men represent the true spirit of Christ, nevertheless I should be exaggerating if I pretended that theirs has been an average view. Christian history has, on the whole, shown a negative attitude on this matter, and the awakening of conscience that has taken place in recent times is largely traceable to influences that are not specifically Christian, such as the humanitarian movement that followed the French Revolution, which was in fact partly associated with religious doubt; though the salutary example of smaller Christian groups like the Society of Friends has doubtless made notable contributions to all humane causes, especially in England and the United States.

Much cruelty to animals still exists, and though few English or American people would now tolerate intentional cruelty, many still refuse to forgo activities that indirectly result in cruelty. If any extension of European influence in the Tibetan countries were to take place, it is to be feared that the thousands of wild animals that now live unmolested in the neighbourhood of the monasteries would become an immediate target for the fur-hunter, the collector, and the so-called sportsman. More disastrous still, their example would arouse the acquisitive instincts of the local inhabitants. To give one example, the tragedy of the giant panda is a recent object-lesson. This adorable creature had been left in peace for centuries until the exhaustive search for it, organized by a few thoughtless travellers, suggested to the natives that there was money to be made in attacking the panda; with the result that in several localities it is already threatened with extinction, a disaster that the original collectors might well have thought of. A similar fate is likely to overtake all the wild animals of Tibet if that country were to open its gates to foreign influences. For though several explorers and climbers who have been privileged to enter Tibet have commented with delight on the number and tameness of the animals that they have seen there, I suspect that were it not for the prohibition against shooting enforced by the Tibetan Government, those same travellers would have found it difficult to resist the temptation to collect trophies and to shoot "for the pot," even at the cost of destroying for ever the idyllic conditions that they have praised, and indeed some recent travellers have admitted it openly.

One other question was touched upon that evening, the question of Peace. The fear of war has held such a large place in men's thoughts during recent years, and there has been such perplexity of mind as to the duty of both Christians and non-Christians in respect of bearing arms, that the chance of obtaining an opinion from a Buddhist teacher of the highest authority was one not to be missed. The trend of Buddhism has in practice been markedly more pacific than that of Christianity; but there have been schools of thought, notably that of Zen in Japan, in which a warlike attitude has been accepted under certain circumstances. Even among the lamas there are differences of opinion; we know that several of the monasteries of Kham played a big part in resisting the Chinese early in this century and that the Lhasa Government's forces were actually placed under the command of a churchman, the Kalon Lama. Nevertheless the views of the Spituk bursar are probably fairly representative of a large section of opinion. He expressed himself as an out and out supporter of non-violence. "Whoever wishes to act in conformity with the Refuge, the same is bound to abstain from every sort of injury towards sentient fellow creatures whether by thought, word, or deed. You cannot pretend to go to war without trying to inflict injury. If you take up arms, there is no Refuge; if there is no Refuge, you are not a true Buddhist."

Those who, with our lama, share these conclusions will recall the story of the Sakyas, the clan from which the Buddha Himself sprang, and who inhabited a territory in the foothills of the Himalaya. News was brought to them of an impending attack by a hostile tribe and it was debated anxiously whether resistance should be offered or not. Eventually they decided that, as followers of the Doctrine, they were debarred from offering armed resistance, but must welcome the invaders as friends, so they threw down their arms. Pacifists among us are sometimes apt to say that peace not only is right, but will pay automatically. The heart of the enemy will be changed and victory will rest with the non-resister. While not denying that in many cases the example of returning good for evil may produce incalculable results, such as a revulsion of feeling in the aggressor, one cannot encourage the belief that such would be the result as a matter of course, nor yet, as the lamas would add, allow a faint appeal to potential self-interest to fog the issue and taint the motive.

The Tibetans, however, not being sentimentalists, admit that the story of the Sakyas ends as it might very well end in any similar case — every convinced pacifist must face this possibility: the enemy arrived and the Sakyas were massacred to a man, the gutters of their streets ran with blood, and their race was blotted out from mankind. Some people may argue that the sacrifice of the Sakyas was in vain; but, viewed in relation to the law of Cause and Effect, the chain of consequences derived from their brave refusal to compromise, even if all memory of the deed should fail, would add itself to the general store of merit on the cosmic plane, the *Karman* of the Universe as a whole; and in the second place, as a recorded historical event, the slaughter of the Sakyas might, by force of example, affect many individual *Karmans*. To the Sakyas themselves there accrued no obvious profit; that is as it should be. Also we must ever remember that their own personalities were to be regarded as dissoluble; it was idle for them to trouble their heads with hopes of reward, or regrets. The fruit of the Sakyas' sacrifice was nothing less than the Enlightenment and ultimate Liberation of all creatures.

Before we quitted Spituk the lama Dawa made us promise to return to him. He was most anxious not to lose touch with us. "If you have a doctrinal difficulty, please put it in writing, so that I may have leisure to think it over. And do come back after you have been to Himi." (We had told him that we proposed to visit that celebrated monastery.) "And be sure to tell

me your impressions." So he spoke, before we rode off across
the last five sandy miles towards Leh.*

* An additional note on the subject of "the Refuge" may prove helpful, in
the light of experience gathered long after this book was first published. In
turning the formula into English I hesitated for some time over the choice of
terms, especially over the use of the word "Congregation" for the third Refuge,
because the picture it evokes in Western minds does not correspond exactly to
the Buddhist conception. The Indian word originally used, *sangha*, means
"assembly," which is also the primitive meaning of the Greek *ekklesia;*
"Church" was another possible choice. But this word suffers from a similar
objection in that it suggests the whole body of "church members" in our sense
of the word, whereas in the Buddhist sense it is restricted to the assembly of
dedicated persons, followers of the Order established by the Buddha, and not to
"Buddhists" all and sundry. It is the Order of lamas, heavenly and earthly,
that constitutes the third Refuge.

Similarly the second Refuge is not easy to translate, as the original Sanskrit
word *dharma* (Tibetan *chhö(s)*) has no real equivalent in our languages. I
have rendered it by "Doctrine," but this must be taken in the sense of the
Truth itself and not merely its formal expression. Another usual translation,
which has much to recommend it, is "the Norm," that is to say, the "manner
of being" proper to each existence in accordance with the inherent possibilities
that determine for it its proper "path" and "law." Each being or natural
grouping of beings therefore has its norm, which can be expressed by a doctrine that teaches the method of its effective realization; all apparently separate
norms being finally cancelled out in the Supreme Knowledge of the One,
Eternal, and Universal Norm.

Chapter XVIII

Leh

A BELT OF WILLOWS standing in rather dry ground marks the outskirts of the city. As we came to the houses, our baggage animals turned off the road abruptly. The ponies stepped over a wooden bar at the base of a gateway and we followed, thinking it must be some short cut, and found ourselves all at once in the main bazaar, a broad and stately street flanked by rows of immense pollarded poplars. The vista is closed by the prodigious castle of the Ladak kings, its lower stories of Egyptian severity, while the upper ones are pierced with larger windows leading out on to wooden balconies. The scale of the building is colossal, dwarfing the rest of the town; though most of it is unoccupied, it is in a fair state of preservation. It is built at the end of a rocky spur, at the foot of which nestles Leh.

Immediately below the castle is the mosque — for there is a large Musulman community — built in the usual Ladak style of architecture. Later on, it became one of our regular pleasures to walk down to it at night and wait for the muezzin's call. The first time that we happened to be there, standing in the darkness of the unlighted street, we heard from the balcony of a house a tenor voice of rare sweetness singing a melancholy rhapsody. The man now and then paused in his song and then began again. His mellow notes floated out into the surrounding stillness; he seemed to be expressing some deep joy that lay close to tears. In style his songs reminded me of those of Greece, so that I at first suspected Turkish influence, for many Turkish traders come down from the north to Leh; but on inquiry the house proved to belong to a Panjabi.

Eventually he ceased; spellbound, we lingered in the hope of hearing him sing again. A bell clanged somewhere above our heads, and then the *Azan*, or Call to Prayer, resounded in ringing tones through the night, making known that: "There is no God but God, and Muhammad is the Envoy of God!" It was the first time that we had listened to these words; we fell, for the moment, under the spell of the directness and simplicity of the Islamic faith, which proclaimed, in terms that clove like a sword, the unity of the Principle of all Being and the dependence of all created beings upon It, its Prime Cause.

But this is anticipating: on that first day, as we rode into the bazaar in the noon sunlight, we could overhear the comments of the people, who asked each other whether or not we had come from Lhasa. Passing through the crowd to the far side of the town, we sought out a secluded lodging in a garden to which we had been directed; it belonged to a native Muslim called Ghulam. We pitched the tents, while our host, who proved to be the kindest and most attentive imaginable, regaled us with bread, a long untasted luxury, and tea prepared in the Turkish way, with plenty of sugar forming a thick syrup, and scented with roses.

We had been in our garden only a few moments when Khan Muhammad Din came to call and invited us to a tea-party at his office, where we were to meet the principal merchants of the town. There were two of these: one was an old Muslim of seventy-five called Hadji Muhammad Siddiq, who traded with Lhasa and Gartok and knew the former city well, a humorous and hearty old man with a large family; the second one was also a Lhasa merchant, a Ladaki Buddhist, Nono Tŏnyod Sha, quiet and courtly; we used to see him almost every day and we owe much to his kindness. They both asked us to their houses at once, so the next day was occupied entirely with visits.

The interior of the better Ladaki house is usually extremely elegant, with spacious chambers bordering on a courtyard, windows with translucent paper in fretwork frames after the Chinese fashion, and attractive painted woodwork, on which floral and dragon motifs are applied with an almost endless power of invention. The ceilings are of unsquared poplar logs laid across the main beams. The furniture does not differ in principle from that used by the peasants, except in its greater richness and finer workmanship. There are carpets, Yarkandi, Tibetan, and, best of all, Chinese, divans round the walls, and painted chests and cupboards; in the old Hadji's house there were also Turkish pipes. He and his family wore the usual costume of Tibet except for the head-dress, which in their case was a turban or red fez. We have since heard news of the Hadji's death; it is difficult to imagine Leh without his merry presence.

Nono Tŏnyod, the other merchant, possessed a magnificent

house, but his taste appeared to have been affected by his journeys to Kashmir; in the midst of many beautiful things we saw much worthless junk. A cabinet contained, for instance, some lovely chased silver vessels from Lhasa, side by side with cheap earthenware adorned in the style favoured by third-rate landladies at the seaside. A painted tea-table, a perfect specimen, stood next to a packing-case aggressively stencilled with the name of a firm in Bombay. Appalling modernized Yarkand carpets swore loudly against the soft texture, the warm browns and blues, of the corresponding Tibetan products. It was a curious, untidy medley, an indication of the mental confusion that follows interference with the traditional sense. In fact Tŏnyod was a typical transition case. In theory he was still a faithful adherent of the old ways; whenever he pronounced judgment on something that fell within the scope of his knowledge, he was a faultless judge of quality. But in regard to novelties his standards were chaotic and he could tolerate things in his house that most of us would have been ashamed to possess.

He showed us his treasures, not forgetting to serve delicious Tibetan tea and trays of dried kernels and sugar-candy. He had a prodigious collection of teapots, magnificent examples of the silversmith's art, also teacup-stands, one of which, made at Lhasa, was a real marvel. Later on we asked him if he would part with it — it is quite in order to offer to buy things seen in a private house — but he said we could have it only if he first sent it back to Lhasa to be copied. He had also some fine jewellery of gold filigree set with choice turquoises. Strangely enough, the central jewel of a magnificent pendant was only a cheap piece of red glass that might have come out of a Christmas cracker; but though this was intrinsically unworthy of its setting, the effect was not inartistic.

The merchant had a manager called Ishé Gyaltsan, a young man of energetic appearance, much more like a Tibetan than his master, who was a typical Ladaki of mixed blood. The manager looked after the Tibetan part of their business, while Tŏnyod himself dealt with the Indian end. Ishé Gyaltsan usually wore yellow shirts, which matched his face, so that we called him the "Yellow Man." We were surprised that he should wear yellow, for he spent some months each year in Tibet and had, so he said, lived there without a break for fifteen years, and it is forbidden for any but members of the clerical Order to be clothed in that colour. "But I am of the clerical Order," he protested; "I was brought up as a novice at Tashilhunpo and I still

can stay there whenever I like, though I have taken to trading."
There are many similar cases in Tibet. He also wore his four-
eared cap in a queer way, with three of the flaps tucked in, out
of sight, and only the left ear sticking up asymmetrically. It
gave his face a peculiarly comic air. Again we asked the reason
for this and were told: "It is the privilege of anyone who has
served tea before either of the two great Lamas. As a boy I
served the Panchhen Lama and now I always wear it thus, for
if I did not, people in the road might say to themselves: 'What
sort of man is this?' — now they know."

He told a story with great animation, and his face and hands
helped to act the part, so that one could picture the whole
scene. His description of an unworthy treasurer making off with
the monastery plate to sell it on the quiet was a screaming farce
— one could see the teapots being stuffed under his robe and
the man slipping out to meet the foreign art-dealer to dispose
of his ill-gotten wares. Yet though he was so amusing, we never
saw even the flicker of a smile cross his face. He was a curious,
self-sufficient character, extremely concrete in outlook and of
untiring industry in his work, for which he had a passion that
had little to do with the mere making of money. He used to
spend a large part of his life in solitary expeditions with only
his own picked servants, all pure Tibetans, for company, going
first to Gartok to the great fair that takes place there every autumn, and then eastward to Shigatze, Gyantse, and Lhasa, a
three months' journey on horseback.

He was just then organizing a caravan of forty ponies with
Yarkandi merchandise such as carpets, green jade cups, and felt
rugs, also Indian cotton, to take to Lhasa, whence he would return with the precious brick tea, grown in western China, which
the Tibetans in the remotest places love to drink in preference
to more easily obtainable Indian-grown varieties. Ceaseless ty-
ing up of bales continued all day long on Tŏnyod's veranda,
while piles of saddles were lying ready in the porch. The Yellow Man himself had not had his taste upset like that of his employer. He was quite clear in his mind about the excellence of
his own country's products as compared with the shoddiness
of most Western importations. All his private possessions were
of the highest quality, from his sturdy horse, splendidly capari-
soned, with high peaked saddle and fine blue pile saddle-cloth,
to his boots, riding-whip, and other personal objects. He had a
critical eye for quality of material and workmanship. His own
servants were picked men from Shigatze, a more vigorous and

lively type than the heavy, mild Ladakis. They were employed under a similar indenture to the one described in connexion with the boy T'hargya at Lachhen; that is to say, they earned pocket money, not wages, but were kept, fed, clothed, and treated familiarly; if they married, their families were also adopted into the household. They appeared entirely contented and devoted to their semi-feudal employer.

The Yellow Man had another amusing characteristic. Whenever he felt excited, he would repeat the last word of a phrase many times at great speed, for emphasis. He might be asked: "Do you think this is an excessive price?" "No, it is quite reasonable, not excessive at all, at all, at all, at all, at all. . . ." Or he would say: "To sell the sacred books to foreign collectors is entirely unlawful, unlawful, unlawful, unlawful. . . ."

He and I became fast friends; he seemed to make the overtures soon after we met. One day he explained himself: "You know, I took to you from the first moment, because it is plain to me that you really love and understand our Tibetan customs and know how to do things just as if you were one of us."

Another friend in Leh, of whose generous help we cannot speak too gratefully, was a Christian called Joseph Gergan, who, in spite of his change of religion, had fortunately not attempted to become like a European, as is too often the case with converts. He was a man who truly deserved the name of Christian, for never have I come across anyone in whom the love of Christ and the imitation of His life were more manifest. There was no attempt to evade the more inconvenient portions of Christ's teaching; in him was seen the simplicity of a child, side by side with the wisdom of a cultivated, well-formed mind. We always spoke of him as "Gergan the Translator," borrowing the term from St. Marpa and the other eleventh-century importers of sacred books into Tibet, for Joseph too was a man who only tried to impart to others a doctrine that he had first practised himself. He had been occupied for years on the tremendous task of turning the Bible into colloquial Tibetan; eventually he completed the work, but died before its publication, which has still to take place.

In the summer, when caravans from India and Turkistan enter or leave Leh almost daily, the scene in the bazaar is most picturesque. Here can be seen tall, thin, hawk-nosed Kashmiris in their unbecoming Euro-Indian rags. Across the way saunter some stocky Baltis in thick grey-brown homespuns and close-fitting caps. Tall Turks, fair as Englishmen, but with narrow

slits of eyes and rather unintelligent faces, stalk about the market, clad in white shirts, sheepskin caps, and high Cossack
boots. Their women wear fine orange or rose embroidered
dresses and are closely veiled, in contrast to their Ladaki sisters, who move about freely. A few red-cloaked lamas are always to be seen and occasionally a true Tibetan, or an Afghan
youth of great beauty, with white skin and long eyelashes and
oval face, an amorous prince from the brush of Persian Bihzad
come back to life.*

Huge yaks ruminate contentedly in the courts of the Turkoman caravanserais, over which, like a shower of wool, floats the
clinging white down of the poplars. The average condition of
the animals is quite good, but many ponies or mules employed
on long-distance traffic show the usual sore-marks from the
hard pack-saddles, suffered during the protracted journey
across the Karakoram. I have heard that many animals fall
from fatigue and are abandoned on the passes there, where
they fall a prey to the wolves. The Turks are extremely callous
and frequently inflict cruelties out of sheer stupidity. I cannot
say that I have witnessed any bad treatment in Leh itself, even
from Turks, or heard an animal abused; so I am prepared to believe that insensitiveness, rather than an actively cruel instinct,
is responsible for the evil.

The Ladakis, on the whole, treat their animals well and in
their attitude do not differ from other Tibetans. The only form
of ill usage that is common among them is the chaining of
watchdogs. Most large houses, and even monasteries, have one
or more mastiffs chained up in kennels by the entrance and
never let loose, so that their friendliness becomes perverted to
the point of extreme ferocity. When a stranger approaches,
they bark savagely and strain with all their might at their chains
in a mad impulse to fling themselves at his throat. Although all
Tibetans are born dog-lovers, they have come to treat the presence of a chained dog as a piece of household furniture and are
no longer conscious of the cruelty involved. In a peaceful country like Ladak, this practice is absurd as well as unkind. In
parts of Tibet there might be some excuse on the score of defence against robbers, but even that explanation is inadequate
when one remembers that the dog, if well trained, could do its

---

* Since writing this description I have heard that the regular caravan
traffic from Turkistan has been suspended owing to political machinations in
the province of Sinkiang.

work just as well unchained. We tried several times to draw people's attention to this evil, but without much effect.

From Nono Tŏnyod we managed to collect a good deal of information about the local craftsmen. The principal metal-worker of Ladak, who was the maker of many of the best examples in our friend's possession, did not live close to the capital, but in a village a couple of days' journey away, in a subsidiary valley on the south side of the Indus. The place is called Chhiling, and one large family, probably including cousins and brothers as well as children of the master, supplies most of the high-class copper and silver work for all Ladak. The master used to make periodic visits to the capital for a few weeks to take orders and carry out repairs. He luckily happened to be at Leh at the same time as ourselves, and Tŏnyod took us round to a house on the outskirts of the town where he was at work. He had set up his furnace under a huge tree and was busy mending teapots, assisted by a pupil. Later he came over to Tŏnyod's house to discuss with us the price of a new brass teapot. Several examples from his own hand were shown to us, in every degree of elaboration, from one covered with silver *appliqué* to a plain copper one tinned inside, with a particularly fine dragon for a handle; according to custom, its spout was inserted into the mouth of a tusked marine monster. We decided on one of the latter pattern, as the proportions were excellent and the price very reasonable; this teapot reached me in 1938 and proved to be a masterpiece of the art of the hammer.

We also wished to purchase a couple of small tea-tables of carved and painted wood called *chogtse*. Tŏnyod made us a present of an old one carved in the Tibetan province of Purang near the source of the Satlej. For the other he indicated to us the best woodworker in Leh, whose house was situated on the edge of the city, looking out across the forest of *chhortens* that rises out of the surrounding sands. He was a large man of cheerful appearance, with very little of the Tartar in his features. He came to us in our garden, holding an adze in one hand and a balk of wood in the other, which he had hastily carved to show what he could do. The moment we caught sight of him we cried: "One of the Mastersingers of Nürnberg!" The price for a carved and pierced folding table, with dragons and birds, came to about three pounds. We impressed on him that there was no hurry and that he could take his time one of our friends would post it to us later. He also promised to see that no foreign paint

was used on it, but only the traditional materials. He said that
he would not carry out the actual painting himself, but would
get a specialist in the colouring of furniture to do it, who lived
at Sabu, a village some six miles away.

It is instructive to note the distribution of the leading artists
in Ladak. The chief woodcarver and also the best jeweller lived
in Leh itself. Gonbo, the silversmith with the greatest reputation, dwelt at Chhiling, but the potter whose wares were most
valued belonged to the Likhir Valley. Rigzin, the leading
painter, came from down the Indus, while at Kalatze, on the
same river four days short of Leh, lived the only man with any
reputation for weaving rugs. Besides these there were many as-
sistant craftsmen and painters, both lay and monastic.

We were given an introduction to another merchant, this
time a native of Lhasa, who was married to a Ladaki lady and
lived out of the town in a country house at Sabu. I rode out to
pay him a call across a stretch of desert that was free from
stones and loose sand, thus giving the opportunity for an en-
joyable canter. The house, which was on the usual plan, with
the family apartments on the first floor, was approached through
a courtyard in which three chained dogs, veritable hell-hounds
(but made so by man's folly), growled threateningly as I entered.

The squire — for such a title seemed to fit him better than
that of trader — received me hospitably and accepted my present of a ring together with a white scarf, offered in accordance
with etiquette. I had chosen for him a silver ring with a cornelian; it had been designed to slip over a finger of normal size,
but he had great difficulty in discovering one thin enough to
take it. He was huge and burly, and surely one of the ugliest of
men; he was dressed in a dirty old shirt and greasy gown, with
high velvet boots such as are affected by smart Lhasa society,
all smeared with mud. On his head he wore a pointed hat of
violet silk, also in the latest fashion. He was rough of speech
and hearty, and he certainly might, but for the clothes, have
figured as the typical squire in the days when John Bull was
John Bull. He had two sons, eighteen and twelve years old respectively, both of them exceedingly beautiful and well brought
up. They waited on me at table with the grace of mediæval
esquires, bringing a basin and pouring water over my fingers
from a ewer between the courses; and when it was time to leave,
they ran out to hold my stirrup. Our servant Norbu was given
food in the same room; he squatted in a corner and interrupted

the conversation when he thought he had a useful comment to offer. After a pleasant afternoon's small talk with the worthy squire, we returned to Leh, which we reached at sundown, just as a light breeze was getting up, following on the torrid heat of the afternoon. A soft tinkling, as of elfin bells, was wafted towards us; we found that it came from tiny peals attached to the pinnacles of the *chhortens*.

Next morning we had scarcely finished breakfast when who should appear but the squire himself! Had we been more versed at that time in Tibetan customs, we would have known that it is conventional to return a call at the earliest possible opportunity. Luckily we managed to behave as though we had been expecting him all the time. "Please sit down," we said, "the tea is nearly ready," meanwhile hastily whispering to Norbu to make the tea. While our guest drank tea we had a breathing-space in which to cook lunch. Actually someone had to be sent post-haste to the market to buy bread and eggs, so that omelets, always so handy in such emergencies, could be prepared. In a few minutes lunch, or rather brunch, was served, to which, after the polite show of refusal prescribed by custom, he did full justice. When he had eaten enough of a dish, he passed his plate to his own servant to polish off the leavings. At the end we gave him a stiff tot of the medicinal brandy, so we felt that, though nearly caught napping, we had not fallen too far short of Tibetan standards of hospitality.

Chapter XIX
"Where Rust Doth Corrupt"

THE MOST CELEBRATED as well as the largest of the Ladak monasteries is that of Himi, situated some thirty miles from Leh on the farther side of the Indus. It was founded by one Stag-tsang Raspa ("Tiger's Den Cotton-clad"), whose spiritual influence continues to remanifest itself in every head Lama of that line. The present buildings date from about three and a half centuries ago, having replaced an earlier foundation that was destroyed by a landslide.

Himi is rich, owning considerable estates in various parts of the country; its subordinate houses are numerous both in the vicinity and even as far afield as Mulbek, on the border. The names of five hundred monks are inscribed on its roll. It belongs to the Order called Drugpa which, besides possessing several lamaseries in central and western Tibet, can claim for its own almost the entire body of clergy in Bhutan.

This monastery is considered to be one of the sights that must not be missed and most visitors to the province make an excursion there. We had come provided with a letter of introduction to the abbot, since we imagined his home to be a seat of learning, where it might be worth while staying for some time in order to study. The letter, wrapped in a silk scarf of the best quality, was dispatched to him by messenger, together with our customary offering of five stones, among them an aquamarine. In a gift of this sort, coins, or whatever else is tendered, should add up to an odd number, as an even one is deemed unlucky.

The bearer of the missive completed the journey from Leh to Himi and back in an amazingly short time, having started homewards the very moment an answer was handed to him. This is typical of the Ladakis when they travel; they pause as little as possible till they have accomplished all their business and can relax properly. Their speed never fails to astonish foreigners. The abbot's reply, duly signed in English "Yours sincerely S. Raspa," conveyed an invitation to visit him as soon as possible, since he was on the point of leaving for a tour of the neighbouring province of Spiti.

The ride from Leh to the great *Gompa* is sometimes taken in two stages; a halt can be made at a half-way house, the Muslim village of Shushot. After crossing the Indus, which here splits into several channels, the road follows the edge of a riverside strip of farmland for several miles, before entering the desert. A long and scorching ride lies ahead, over a tedious stretch of sandy ground. The reflection of the sun's rays from the dazzling sand is so fierce that fair-complexioned people are well advised to use some kind of protective ointment just as if they were crossing a snowfield. If this precaution is neglected, their faces may be severely blistered.

The monastery itself lies concealed inside a narrow side valley running down to the river from the south-west. Approached from Leh, it is not visible at all; the only indications of its presence are two long *Mani* walls flanking the two chief roads, the Leh road and the one leading along the Indus from the south-east, which converge towards the entrance of the glen. On nearing the point where the two *mendongs* meet at an angle, fields and a few trees appear, framed between the rocky hillsides, with a stream rushing merrily down the centre of the trough. Along the road stand numbers of *chhortens* of exceptional elegance, some of which are pierced by gateways with ceilings that were formerly decorated in bright colours, but are now half perished; under these pylons the track passes. Soon the glen narrows still further, and the view is blocked by a grove of trees; no big buildings are visible anywhere, and it is hard to believe that so extensive a place can remain thus hidden. It undoubtedly merits its title of *Gompa,* which means literally "a solitary place."

At length, after going past the houses of the village, one arrives suddenly close under the monastery, which forms an impressive block of buildings nestling up against the side of the mountain. From its upper story projects a row of wooden galleries of charming design, and this gives it an unusual lightness in contrast to the fortress-like severity of other *Gompas,* which are almost always situated on rugged eminences where they seem to grow out of the very rock; this magnifies the apparent size of the buildings, whereas in the case of Himi its real proportions are overshadowed by the mountain towering above.

Just under the lowest terrace there is a small guest-house with a pillared portico facing into a garden enclosed between

high walls, with a strip of grass down the middle and a row of
poplars along each side. As soon as we arrived we were met
and conducted to this lodging by the *chyagdzôd* or bursar, a
rather villainous-looking old monk dressed in grimy garments.
To do him justice, however, he had arranged the little rest-
house cosily, with fine brown and blue Tibetan rugs on mattresses along the platform under the porch, and a separate tea-
table for each guest. He asked if we would eat meat and drink
barley beer or *chhang* — his eyes lighted up as he pronounced
the magic word. We replied that we would gladly drink one
cup each, and that we did not take meat. We then took our
seats upon the dais, while food was cooked and served by our
own men. The bursar came and sat down beside us, after di-
recting that a big brass *chhang*-pot, like a jug with a very long
lip and a lid, should be set before us. We drained our cups, and
then there ensued a contest between us and our host as he did
his best to refill them, while we resisted, covering the cups
with our hands.

From this it must not be supposed that the beer is very potent. The *chhang* that we tasted in Ladak seemed mild, rather
like a sourish cider; it is not an especially exciting drink, though
acceptable after a parching ride over the desert in the noonday
heat. The peasants keep it deliciously cool by storing it in red
porous jars. It is said that on occasions of prolonged festivity
people do get drunk on it; if so, a vast number of pints must be
consumed, unless a much stronger brew than the beer given to
us is produced for special occasions. It is made by boiling bar-
leycorns and then introducing a ferment, which is allowed to
stand from three to five days. The reason why we were so determined not to drink more than just the single cup was that
we judged that the old toper would never leave us in peace unless we impressed him from the first with our firmness. Though
he filled his own cup time and time again, it seemed to hurt
him cruelly to think of all the good liquor being wasted while
there were still more throats down which to pour it. It is the
sign of a confirmed drinker to derive inordinate satisfaction
from vicarious tippling. At length we were able to pacify him
with the offer of some blocks of chocolate, which was found to
rank next to beer in his affections, so he went off happily, inviting the party to call on the lord abbot in the morning.

That day a small incident occurred that helps to throw light
on a certain trait of the Ladaki character. We had ridden
ahead of our baggage, but did not expect it to reach its destina-

tion very long after us, since experience had shown that the pony-drivers on foot could keep up with the riders extraordinarily well, in spite of the latter trotting their horses on favourable ground. We were rather annoyed, therefore, when the transport did not turn up for several hours. So unusual did this seem that we even began to feel a little anxious; but eventually the men appeared, looking fresh and unhurried, so we asked them somewhat sharply to explain the delay. They frankly admitted that they had lain down to have a good sleep; though they knew they had done wrong and were liable to a scolding, and even to some loss of pay, they did not try to make excuses. This is very typical; these people hardly know how to lie. An official subsequently related to us that when any small offence is committed it is only necessary to question the suspects in order to elicit a truthful version with full details. There is no regularly organized constabulary in Ladak, though the Wazir, in addition to his other offices, holds police rank. Apparently it is thought that among such an honest and law-abiding population the police, having no crime to repress, could only pass their time in creating it!

Our first contact with Himi did not seem too promising, nor was a walk round the monastery reassuring. The whole area was polluted, and the air was charged with nauseating smells, which, owing to the place being so shut in, never drifted away. We had been warned in Leh that the water was liable to produce a form of diarrhœa like a minor dysentery; but it is just as likely that it is not so much the water itself as the filth-infected dust that causes the trouble. By walking to a point well above the monastic settlement, water can be drawn where there is no reason for doubting its purity; whereas it is hardly possible to avoid consuming a certain amount of foul dust with one's food. Naturally any water drawn from below the inhabited area must be regarded as the most dangerous of all.

After a night lying on fine pile carpets — surely the most restful of all couches — we made ready for the visit to the Lama himself. Passing through a vast and stately courtyard, where several ferocious dogs struggled, howling, at their chains, we mounted a staircase to the upper story, holding our noses to keep out the stench of a leaky drain, and were ushered into a lofty chamber, magnificently painted with floral designs, carried out with the utmost delicacy and taste. The staring white dial of a huge post-office clock disfigured the farther wall, while the floor was strewn with a litter of papers, boxes, small mechanical toys, and nameless junk, out of the midst of which, like a reef half-submerged by the oncoming tide, rose a platform on which the prelate was sitting, while a secretary and the old bursar stood by and assisted him with correspondence.

The man himself was a heavy, insensitive-looking person, from whose countenance any traces of learning or intelligence, if he ever possessed them, had long since faded. He signed to us to sit down before him and welcomed us with a string of in- ane banalities, which made us feel every moment more de- pressed and uncomfortable and filled us with regret at having sent that beautiful aquamarine!

We spent the rest of the morning in a tour of the temples, which are of great size and magnificence, or rather were; for the state of the interior is enough to break the heart of any art- lover. Massive brass-studded doors, with bosses cast in the form of wreathed dragons, gave admittance to the three main halls of worship, which opened on the central courtyard. They were crowded to the ceiling with works of art, in various stages of disintegration. Marvellous paintings, executed when the art was at its acme of creative power, had once lined the entire wall-space. Fairly large expanses still kept their rich colouring, though the colours were mellowed by time to a certain sombre- ness, which did not detract from their beauty. But elsewhere the plaster had cracked and flaked off badly, exposing the rub- ble masonry beneath. Here the face of a Bodhisat, his finely chiselled features still composed under the impenetrable calm of Knowledge, looked out on us, though his body had all but crumbled away. There we saw a torso, there a pair of hands still making the gesture that bespeaks mercy. In a corner we discovered piles of books, volumes upon volumes, wood-block prints and manuscripts, all jumbled together, their loose leaves drifting about in hopeless confusion: who could tell what wis- dom was on its way to oblivion? Passing along a side-aisle, we came upon a stack of t'hankas, some tied up and others half- unrolled, all cracked, torn, and thick with dust. The piety of generations had turned Himi into one vast treasure-house; on every side were to be found scrolls, Chinese embroideries and statues; there was also a throne covered with exquisite flowers that we took for Persian lacquer, but which may have been Kashmiri work, the gift of some former ruler.

In a small upper room, as if a sharp contrast were needed to point the sad lesson, we discovered a wonderful set of t'hankas, a riot of figures, birds, and rainbow-like halos, all still in perfect preservation; also a collection of books, equally well cared for. Some of the volumes were bound between thick boards, with scenes in relief: the under sides were of gold lacquer, on which line-patterns were traced with a delicacy worthy of the Japanese. How this one corner came to escape the general dirt and untidiness was a mystery.

We wondered if any of the treasures would survive; in that climate the process of decay is slow, and a little timely energy might result in cleaning up the place and restoring some, at least, of its ancient glory; but with such a governor in charge the outlook seemed almost hopeless. "Fish stinketh from the head," as they say in my own country of Greece. I was told that a certain sum was once sent by the Maharaja of Kashmir for repairs to Himi; but there were no signs of recent restoration to be seen. Unless there is a big change, I fear that Himi and its treasures will soon have to be written off on the debit side of history.

In the afternoon we received another summons to the presence of the lord Raspa; reluctantly we reascended to his apartment, where tea was served. At the Lama's right hand was placed another low platform, on which sat an aged and decrepit priest, with one wall-eye, which gave him a curious look of dotage, yet he was evidently a man of some rank, for a silver-mounted cup stood on the little table in front of him, which attendants refilled at intervals. No further notice was taken of him, however, but a number of European volumes were produced for our inspection, chiefly books of travel or albums of photographs. The abbot signed to us to approach and, rapidly turning over the pages, stopped at one that showed a photograph of himself seated under some trees, together with the late "Raja" of Ladak, father of the present holder of the courtesy title. He pointed to the picture of the former Raja, and then suddenly turned with a curious gloating look towards the miserable old man on his right. "That's the same man," he said. We felt a wave of pity sweep over us. Could that poor old thing really be the lineal descendant of the talented dynasty that had reigned in the far west of Tibet for so many centuries and had endowed the country with all those marvellous monuments? Truly, "all is vanity and a striving after wind. One generation goeth and another generation cometh; and — "

"Can you get me any stamps of this country?" broke in the voice of the abbot, while his finger pointed to the title "Czechoslovakia" at the top of a page in a small stamp album.

"This thing isn't working, can you mend it?" A broken bicycle bell was handed to us.

"Could you please translate this set of instructions into Tibetan and write them down?" This time it was the secretary, who handed me an old dry-cell battery, with explanations for recharging attached.

Borrowing Sir Charles Bell's dictionary, a copy of which they happened to have, I tried to make a paraphrase, ingeniously dodging unfamiliar technical terms. Finally an old catalogue of the Bombay branch of the Army and Navy Stores was brought out and we were all kept busy trying to find descriptions and prices for various small machines. The amassing of gadgets was evidently a ruling passion with the abbot of Himi; this characteristic of his was even remarked on by De Filippi years before. His room was full of knick-knacks, none of them in working order. As soon as we had dealt with one problem to the best of our ability, he produced another and it was apparent that this was to go on the whole afternoon. We felt that if we stayed much longer in this lunatic atmosphere we might ourselves go crazy, so after a hurried whisper of consultation, one of us deflected the next proffered gadget by a desperate parry and we all three rose and bowed our farewells as briefly as Tibetan etiquette would allow and filed into the outer air. But even that seemed to be pervaded with a miasma of mouldy decay. After leaving Himi a full day passed before the nightmare impression could be shaken off.

The visit to Himi made us feel very downcast and we grudged spending any further time in the neighbourhood. Nevertheless it was too late to continue our journey the same day, so we had to sleep there one more night before we could shake its dust from our feet. The old bursar, who, gross as he was, did his best to be hospitable, gave us a supply of rice, butter, and tea for the road. It was our intention not to return to Leh by the same track, but to penetrate beyond the Ladak Range by an 18,000-foot pass, the Chang La or North Pass.

Apart from the interest of seeing new country, we wished to call on another important Lama, the abbot of Sgang-Ngon *Gompa*, which is situated not very far from Leh, at P'hiyang. Later on we spent a very happy time there. This dignitary, who ruled over Yuru and a number of minor dependencies in addition to P'hiyang, was believed to be staying at the distant *Gompa* of Satsukul two days beyond the Chang La. He enjoyed a reputation for holiness that, after seeing Himi, we

LEH AND CASTLE OF THE KINGS OF LADAK   *See page* 251

YAKS FROM A TURKI CARAVAN *See page 251*

THE LATE HADJI MUHAMMAD SIDDIQ *See page 252*

"The Yellow Man" *See page 253*

The Art of Pouring Tea *See pages 252–3*
Seated, the merchant Nono Tönyod

HIMI GOMPA *See page 260*

BEYOND THE CHANG LA   *See page 267*

BRIDGE OVER THE INDUS *See page* 261

LADAK TEMPLE DECORATION *See page* 274

MEETING IN THE DESERT NEAR SPITUK   *See page 276*
The author, Dawa the bursar, and his pupil

might have doubted, but for the fact that Khan Muhammad Din himself had described him as a sincere, God-fearing man. There is none whose certificate of godliness could be more safely relied on than that of the Khan. If he used the term "God-fearing" it was because he himself knew what that meant.

There used to be a bridge over the Indus just below Himi, but it had broken down under a flood and we had to make a long detour south-east and then return along the other bank, before we could strike off towards the north-east into the cultivated valley of Chimre, dominated by the village and monastery of that name. Farther up the valley, at the foot of a branch valley leading to the pass, lay the pleasant village and camping-ground of Sakti, where we stayed the night; we were received in friendly fashion by a small landowner, a friend of our servant Norbu.

The morning appointed for the ascent of the Chang La dawned stormily; we had hardly passed the last of the crops when showers of rain, turning to sleet and snow higher up, made us dismount, shivering, in an effort to warm ourselves by walking. Fortunately the storm did not last as long as we feared; by the time we had advanced well up the torrent valley the sun began to break through fitfully. After some time we crossed an alp in which some especially magnificent black yaks were grazing, and then we saw the final slopes close ahead. It was gratifying to note that we might have been walking at sea level for all the effect the altitude made on us. It was evident that our acclimatization in Sikkim had been thorough.

Just short of the crest of the pass there were many flowers growing among the stones. It was a joy to see the Alpines again after so long: there were yellow Welsh poppies — rather a surprise — a pinkish mauve pyrethrum creeping close to the ground, and mauve delphiniums with heavy blooms, the same kind that we had found in 1933 on Riwo Pargyul. In addition there were nettles, of a kind new to us, which, as Norbu reminded us, had been the food of St. Mila Repa.

The story is a famous one. The saint had been spending several months in a favourite cave of his, called White Rock Horse's Tooth. His principal food consisted of nettles, which grew round the entrance to his retreat and which he boiled in an earthenware pot. One day, weakened by fasting during an unusually protracted meditation, he slipped and fell on the threshold and broke the handle of his pitcher, so that it went rolling down the hill. It was smashed to bits; but the accumu-

lated layers of residue from the nettles came out as a single
greenish pot-shaped block. This episode forms the theme of
one of Mila's best-known poems:

In the same moment I had a pot and have one no more.
This example shows the whole law of the impermanence of
    things.
Chiefly it shows what is the state of man.
If this is certain, I, the hermit Mila,
Shall strive to meditate without distraction.
The desirable pot that contained my wealth,
In the very hour when it is broken, becomes my teacher.
This lesson of the fateful impermanence of things is a great
    wonder.

The crest of the Chang La is marked by a cairn adorned with
horns of cattle and flags. It is customary in Tibet, on reaching
the top of a pass, to cast a stone on the cairn and call out: "So,
so, so, so, so! Hla gyalo, De t'hamche p'ham!" which means
"Ho! ho! ho! The Gods conquer, all the devils are defeated!"
Travellers in the Himalaya should learn the formula and say it
either when crossing a pass or a bridge. They will find it will
give great pleasure to their porters.

The locality abounds in marmots, which are very tame. On
the way back, when the weather was sunny, many of these attractive animals were to be seen lying stretched out on boulders, basking in the warmth. Some way beyond the pass was a
good but cold camping-ground near a lake, the resort of many
water-birds. Near by there was a hut where fuel and food were
stored by Government order for the use of caravans. The fuel
of the country is dried dung, as in most parts of Tibet. It smoulders like peat and does not smell unpleasantly. A pair of bellows is a help when tending the fire, otherwise one must rely
on one's own lungs.

The sparsely cultivated valleys on the farther side of the
Chang La, which lie between the Ladak and Pangong ranges,
are watered by streams which flow into the Shyok. Riding
about eight miles along the nearest valley, we reached a place
that was marked by a number of unusually large Mani inscriptions clearly chiselled on the rocks. There the ways branched,
one leading up a side valley towards our own objective, the village of Satsukul, while the other would have brought us out
near the huge Pangong lake, which, however, we had no
time to visit. The spot where the ways divide, called T'hangtse,

is famed for its cross and carved inscription in ancient Syriac, recording the journey of an old Nestorian Christian.

The tracing of connexions between different cultures is the special delight of archæologists and some of them have not been slow to discover Christian influences in the ritual and beliefs of the Lamas. Such points of likeness are usually brought to one's attention in a tone that suggests "Now we've caught them! They're not even original!" One hardly ever opens an English book on Tibet that does not make some allusion to this question of borrowing from other traditional forms, as if that were necessarily a weakness. The prejudice in favour of unalterable adherence to earlier practice, as against a policy of assimilation of whatever extraneous elements can be adapted to the service of the Doctrine, is closely bound up with the Protestant, as against the Catholic, view of history. The theory that the Reformation marked a repudiation of heathenish impositions and a return to primitive Christianity becomes a measure to be applied to all religious annals throughout the world, giving rise to all sorts of false analogies and fanciful conclusions. Naturally, each case must be examined on its merits; but the enunciation of a general principle based on the antithesis of "primitive purity" and "foreign accretion" is to be deprecated.

The Satsukul Valley, which lies at an altitude of 13,300 feet, consists largely of sandy desert with a few restricted tracts where barley can be grown as well as a species of pea, quite pleasant in flavour, with flowers resembling those of a diminutive broad-bean. Along the streams there are marshy patches, which in the month of August are spangled with little flowers of bright gold, having one larger liplike petal bearing a black mark. The peasants' houses are not the ample and artistic structures of the Indus Valley, being markedly poorer in every way: it would almost seem as if one is nearing the limit where it is profitable to try to maintain human life. The people eke out a living under severe climatic difficulties; and they show the effects of hard conditions in their less good physique, for bodily and mental deformities seem not uncommon.

The *Gompa* itself stands out in the open, not on the customary eminence. It accommodates about thirty monks; but it must be fairly prosperous since we saw an extra wing actually in course of erection. At the moment of our arrival the whole village was gathered in the courtyard; loaded ponies and riding-horses stood by the gate, while there was a constant coming and going such as foreshadowed a move of some sort. On in-

quiry we learned that the abbot whom we had ridden so far to
visit was on the point of eluding us by departing to an even
more distant spot, to which there would not be time to follow
him. Before we could collect our wits we found ourselves hus-
tled into his presence, in a room crowded with chattering peasants. The Lama, an elderly man with a kindly smile, was standing up, ready to set out. Though we attempted to explain the
purpose of our journey from Leh, we really only had time for a
mere exchange of formalities. A few moments later he passed
from the room and, after donning a helmet-like mitre, mounted
and disappeared down the valley, followed by his train, to the
sound of the drum.

We were left a trifle bewildered by the abruptness of the
good Lama's disappearance and not a little damped at having
ridden so far in vain. It would indeed have been more in accord with the habits of the country for him to have postponed
his journey. Such an alteration of plan counts for nothing in a
land where time is no object and where people travel for days
and days on horseback. For him to have waited a little would
really have been quite a natural action. However, later on we
learned that the abbot, who was also reputed to be rather im-
pulsive, did not entertain a very high opinion of Europeans,
owing to an unfortunate encounter while he was in residence
at his other convent of Yuru, on the main road from Srinágar
to Leh.

The story told us was as follows; for its accuracy I cannot
vouch:

A traveller came along one day who was seeking archæological treasures and who had, up to then, been very successful in
inducing unscrupulous custodians to part with monastic property. There were some antiques at Yuru that he also coveted,
so he made an offer. On being refused by the abbot, the man
became more pressing. After repeated efforts at convincing the
would-be purchaser that the sacred property was not for sale,
the simple-minded old abbot thought that he might make his
peace by offering the gift of some delicious tea. It seems that
the collector was so chagrined at his failure to obtain his curios
that he threw the tea away in a rage.

We were tired after our fruitless journey, so we spent the
next day resting, except for a visit to the monastery. It proved
to be devoid of artistic interest. The *chyagdzŏd*, who exercised
his financial office in all the monastic houses under that abbot,
was a well-fed-looking person with small, piglike eyes and an

insolent expression. We had set aside a few rupees as a contribution for the new extension and in a weak moment we handed them over to him. He hardly even made a pretence of saying, "Thank you," nor did he go in for any of the polite attentions usual on meeting strangers, and, acme of impoliteness, he failed to offer us a cup of tea! This is reckoned great negligence among the Tibetans, an unpardonable offence against the code; and it was aggravated by the fact that he was aware that we had ridden hard and far in order to visit his own superior. His bad manners were the more noticeable in that this was the only occasion, during all our intercourse with Tibetans or Ladakis, when we were not treated with hospitality and politeness.

It was in the course of the return journey that we almost charged into the middle of a herd of *bharal*. We were traversing a mountainside and had just crossed a rib into a dip when we found ourselves among them. The wind must have been peculiarly favourable to have thus concealed our scent. The whole herd, which included a number of magnificent males, and also some charming young ones, charged away at a great pace over the slopes and in a very few minutes were no more than tiny moving dots in the distance. I hope that anyone who may be tempted to shoot in the district may, both out of pity for the animals themselves and in consideration for the scruples of the inhabitants, substitute the camera for the gun. That should tax the skill and endurance of the keenest hunter!

While we were camping at Satsukul, we were soaked by tempests of drenching rain, which seemed incongruous in such an utterly dry country; but the storm cleared the air, so that we were able to enjoy a glorious panorama of the snowy Zanskar peaks as we passed back over the Chang La. After camping once again on the old site at Sakti, we did a forced march in order to reach Leh in one day. We followed the bank of the Indus over a terribly hot and dreary stretch and eventually entered one of the longest and richest belts of farming in all Ladak, the chief centre of which was the fine monastery of Tiksé, which, however, we had only time to admire from the outside. The water was conducted all over the area through innumerable rills shaded by huge willows. The farmhouses were more than usually spacious and prosperous-looking. In the swampy flats the ground was thickly covered with iris, but they were not in flower. It must be a most attractive district in springtime.

The last stage of the return journey crossed the sandy and

stony plain that leads from the river up to Leh; these last miles were very tedious at the end of a long day. Night had fallen before we entered Leh and gained the old camping-place in the garden, where our friend Ghulam gave us a splendid welcome. Turkish scented tea was brewed, and bread, sweets, and apples were hastily sent for, which kept us busy till the baggage arrived. Not many moments after the tents had been pitched, we were asleep, and the phantoms of Lamas and *chyagdzôds* had all dissolved into nothingness.

Chapter XX

The Painter of P'hiyang, and Spituk Debates

LEH FORMS a compact little world, where the various elements necessary for a complete society are blended in nicely judged proportions, resulting in stability and contentment; while the comings and goings of central Asian caravans have until now contributed sufficient movement for the community to escape the danger of stagnation. This little country town gives the impression of being every inch a capital, worthy to act as the nerve-centre of a country, which possessing, as it does, a total population less than that of Scarborough but somewhat exceeding that of Margate, has produced from its deserts so wonderful a culture as to put to shame all devotees of the cult of size, wealth, and number.

Apart from one or two officials, the leading citizens belong to the little group of important merchants, whose operations constitute the chief link with distant countries. Next come the shopkeepers, mostly Indian, whose influence nowadays is unfortunately tending to lower the standards of taste. In addition to these there are the skilled artisans, such as silversmiths or woodworkers, who furnish artistic requisites. Lastly come those, the majority, whose livelihood depends directly or indirectly on the caravan traffic. There are also, at all times, numbers of peasants from the surrounding district who come to the town to do their shopping or to sell fruit, vegetables, and fodder; the market-place is thronged with cheerful country women carrying huge loads of fresh hay in baskets on their backs: riding through the square one must watch one's horse lest it should take a sudden nip at one of these fragrant bundles.

Higher instruction is the care of the clergy, few of whom, however, dwell inside the city, though some of them are constantly to be found there. In the days of Ladak's independence there must also have existed a powerful secular aristocracy. Nowadays the centre of fashion, in the eyes of the Ladakis, is Lhasa: it, and not the Occidentalized Indian centres, in spite of their wealth and luxury, still holds first place in the imagination of the people. As to the delegates of the then paramount British power, opportunities for contact with them occurred so seldom that the respect felt for them was not untinged with a certain naïveté. When, at intervals of a few years, the Resident in Kashmir decided to pay a visit to Leh in person, he was received with almost regal honours, to the accompaniment of holiday-making and general excitement.

It so happened that the day after our return to the capital coincided with the arrival of the Resident, Colonel L. E. Lang, C.I.E. All the notables rode out as far as Spituk to welcome him, and there a procession was formed and the King of England's representative was escorted into Leh amid the acclamations of the populace. Schoolchildren, drawn up in the square by their teachers, greeted him with a somewhat original variant on *God Save the King*, to an obbligato rendered *sempre con tutta la forza* by a lama band playing in a different key. Finally, a durbar was held, at which prominent citizens were presented.

On the following morning we were due to leave Leh for the valley and monastery of P'hiyang, about three hours' ride away, where we had been invited to stay. The monastery itself stands on the usual bold eminence, in the midst of a tract of beautiful cornland, with fascinating views up and down the valley. Looking up, one is faced by a huge amphitheatre of bare hills, which take on a myriad colours in the magical light characteristic of that part of the country. In the opposite direction, beyond the Indus, darker mountains rise up steeply to their sparkling diadem of snowy ridges and small glaciers.

The project of making P'hiyang, the mother-house of Satsukul and the seat of the elusive abbot, into our headquarters came about in this way: A few days previous to the Himi excursion we rode out for the day to P'hiyang to look at the architecture. We were led into one of the two big temples, the walls of which were covered with brilliant paintings. On all sides serene countenances of Buddhas, of every size and colour, greeted us, attended by smiling Bodhisats and saints in ecstasy. Terrifying Protectors writhed in flames and leaped on the bodies of victims, who personified the evil passions to be subdued within the soul. The whole showed boldness in composition and remarkable precision in the drawing. These paintings struck us as being of no great age, so we inquired of an attractive-looking monk, who was showing us round, whether they were recent.

"Quite new," he answered, "it is not more than five years since they were finished." "The painter was a most talented artist," we said; "was he a Ladaki?" "I painted several myself," he replied, "but I worked in collaboration with our best painter, Rigzin, and several junior assistants. The work took several years."

Here was a thrilling discovery indeed! We were in the presence of a gifted craftsman, engaged in producing work of a high order, by the methods that had been handed down to him through the long dynasty of his spiritual ancestors. The man himself, though he obviously took his work most seriously, yet spoke of it with little more emotion than a plumber discussing the installation of a new pipe.

We plied him with questions; did he also paint *t'hankas?* He said he did and brought out a nearly finished picture of Buddha with two disciples, excellently done. Our admiration so amused him that he burst out laughing. We asked to buy the *t'hanka*, but he explained that it was being done to the order of a fellow monk; if we so wished, however, he would paint others for us and we could select the subjects. We were much excited by this, for it offered a chance of watching each step in the processes of Tibetan painting and of going into minute particulars of the technique.

Later in the day, at tea, we learned more about our friend. His name was Konchhog Gyaltsan, which means "Banner of the Most Precious Things," and he belonged to a peasant family of the P'hiyang valley. His colleagues also told us that he was a man of unusual learning, well versed in doctrine, and an admirable teacher. Our chance had come at last. If we could make a longer stay at P'hiyang we would be enabled not only to observe the painting, but also to clear up various doctrinal questions at the same time. Our satisfaction was heightened by the discovery that the Order of Lamas to which P'hiyang adhered was a branch of the Kargyudpa or White-Tradition Order, which traces its descent back to St. Marpa of Hlobrak and St. Mila Repa himself. The Kargyudpa include several sub-orders: P'hiyang belonged to one of these, the mother-house of which is at Dikhung in central Tibet, a hundred miles north-east of Lhasa. We therefore did not hesitate, but asked at once whether we might return later as his pupils, I to study the Doctrine, and the other two for painting lessons. He agreed enthusiastically, and it was arranged that we should occupy a cell next to his own as soon as we got back from Himi. We also made our choice of subjects for the three new *t'hankas*. Richard Nicholson ordered another Buddha like the one already seen, Dr. Roaf appropriately picked on the eight Medical Buddhas, while I asked for the three Bodhisats, Chenrezig the Compassionate, Djamyan the patron of Learning, and Chyagdor the "Wielder of the Sceptre," who personify respectively the mercy, the wisdom, and the power of a Buddha.

As to price, we had some little trouble in fixing one, since Gyaltsan was not used to asking a fee. He usually worked for his brother monks or for his family chapel or for his own cell. After some hesitation a settlement was reached at a modest figure, though for some time Gyaltsan refused to name a price, and our efforts to coax him into a decision only reduced him to boisterous mirth. It was stipulated that any gold powder used should be charged separately, just as would have been done in Renaissance Italy. We were also to supply dark-blue silk for the mount, the canvas, and a little red and yellow silk for the double stripe in the sacred colours which always frames the painting itself.

It may well be imagined that after the disillusionment at Himi and the fiasco at Satsukul we were looking forward with added zest to our return to P'hiyang; but that did not make us forget our other friend, the good lama Dawa, bursar of Spituk, who had been insistent in making us promise to return to him at the earliest opportunity. So we sent him word of our coming and started for P'hiyang, intending to call at Spituk on the way. We had just reached the edge of the Leh oasis when we heard a tinkling of bells and caught sight of Dawa himself, riding a white horse, and followed by one of his pupils, a grave monkling of about fourteen, on a chestnut pony. The pupil wore no shoes, but gripped the edges of the stirrups between his toes.

The lama had been on his way to the town, but learning of our intention, he turned at once and the united party ambled back towards Spituk. The horses were left in a stable at the foot of the hill, after which we were rushed up the endless steep stairs, worse than any mountain, and deposited panting in the temple, while the abbot's apartment on the top floor was made ready. During our earlier visit we had not realized the splendour of the main temple: a wealth of good *t'hankas* hung round the central choir, and a set of excellent wall-paintings lined an upper gallery, depicting yellow-hatted saints of the Gelugpa. In a quarter of an hour a man came to summon us to the abbot's room, where carpets were spread and tea prepared. Besides Dawa and ourselves, the *khenpo* or prior of the monastery and another lama were present.

Dawa opened the conversation: "So you have come from Himi? How did you find things there? Which profound doctrines did you discuss with the Lama?" We recounted our sad tale of corruption at the famous *Gompa,* but the bursar, seemingly unheeding, continued: "Surely the Lama talked with you about the significance of the Refuge?" "He mentioned nothing of the kind; we heard no doctrine at Himi." Dawa burst out laughing. "When you declared your intention of making a pilgrimage to Himi in the hope of hearing some wisdom, I said nothing; but I was shaking with suppressed laughter." He continued to tease us ironically. "But did you really not discuss the Refuge? Are they not Buddhists at Himi?" It seemed to amuse him beyond measure to picture us riding out there, full of anticipation of deep spiritual experiences to come, only to be disillusioned in that ridiculous fashion. "So there wasn't a word about the Refuge?" he chuckled. "It isn't doctrines you should have sought at Himi: beer and women are more in their line!"

Strange though it may seem to anyone not used to the Tibetan mentality, there was really no uncharitableness intended in the bursar's rather grim humour. His whole behaviour was characteristic. Though he knew all the time what would happen at Himi, he deliberately let us go and find it out for ourselves, even at the risk of discrediting his Church, rather than try to prejudice the case by a warning. No man deplored the decay more than he did, yet he was able to discuss it quite coolly, without needing to relieve his feelings with epithets and denunciations. Of course the real joke for him was not the sins of the clergy, but the castles in the air that we had been building. The reader may possibly doubt this explanation; but whoever knows the Tibetans, especially the lama teachers and their ways, will not fail to recognize Dawa's attitude as typical.

Such humour is born of a certain ethical outlook, which not only deters a man from trying to screen his disciple from contact with temptation, but rather makes him prone to expose him deliberately to dangerous experiences, both as a test and to cool down romantic enthusiasms. Instances can be multiplied when a Master has gone so far as to command his follower to commit an apparently sinful act if he judged that it would, in the long run, make for his spiritual development. The Lama Marpa and his treatment of Mila Repa is a case in point. Innumerable similar stories could be quoted where the means employed for testing the pupil have been carried to the verge of ruthlessness and beyond. Nor are such examples by any means confined to ancient history.

It is all a natural corollary of the attempt to strip off every illusion, however dearly treasured, which might stand in the way of the acquisition of "Awareness," the real aim of the Buddhist training. Charity itself, as they see it, is but ill-founded unless it has its roots properly planted in the soil of the knowledge of the true nature of things. St. Mila summed up this idea in two lines of one of his last poems, which I quoted before:

The notion of emptiness (absence of real self) engenders Compassion,
Compassion does away with the distinction between "self and other."

Loving impulses are less likely to be upset by a swing of the emotional pendulum when they are firmly linked to sound theory — firstly to the consciousness that we and all the other creatures of the Universe are together similarly afflicted, struggling to escape from the same Round of birth and death, from the same Ignorance and Desire, and secondly to a recognition of the falseness of a belief in the enduring character of the Ego such as St. Mila refers to, which is the real foundation of the whole edifice of selfish ambitions and of the craving to enjoy the fruits of action. Intellectual honesty is one of the traits most noticeable in the better Tibetan clergy, who shine like highlights against the duller surface of kindly mediocrity that characterizes the multitude of ordinary lamas. This sincerity is evinced in their fearless facing of facts and in a readiness to discuss their most cherished beliefs without quarrelling.

To show how little favour sentimental appeals enjoy — a preacher is not specially admired for his power of sweeping an audience off their feet by sheer eloquence; rather is praise bestowed on the man who, speaking in an even, unimpassioned tone, expounds the Doctrine without having recourse to aids that might conceivably sway his listeners for irrelevant reasons. An unsound motive is enough to vitiate the merit of embracing any truth; its value is strictly proportional to the clear understanding of the issues. A true proposition accepted for an improper reason is tantamount to a lie; the inquisitorial person finds himself at a loss under a Tradition where the value of a mere outward conformity is thus discounted.

It is perhaps needless to harp on the fact that popular piety in Tibet, as elsewhere, does not always reach these high levels. Men in their degree of spiritual discernment show a widely varying range of capability. Yet nothing has struck me so much, in my life among the Tibetans, as the way in which the Buddhist idea, much diluted no doubt, still permeates the outlook of the common people with its gentle and humanizing influence, and to some extent with its metaphysical conceptions, even though these may have been heard as the faintest of echoes. Yet this has been accomplished without quelling the natural high spirits of the race. Some writers have alleged that real Buddhism is almost unknown in Tibet and that superstition has entirely superseded it; I, on the contrary, was surprised to find how deeply the Doctrine had left its mark even on simple, inarticulate souls.

My criticism of the management at Himi led naturally to a general discussion on *Tulkus*, or Lamas functioning as manifestations of the influence of known personalities, whether heavenly beings or saintly predecessors. I had long sought an opportunity for eliciting the views of a really thoughtful lama concerning these much-revered figures, so numerous and popular in the Tibetan Church. I put the problem thus:

"If a *Tulku* is the manifestation of a saint and yet is notorious as an evil-doer, by whom is the sin committed?" The question was meant for Dawa, but the other lama, not the prior, was the first to enter the fray.

"It is not legitimate to say of a *Tulku* that he is a great sinner," he said, "for you must not judge only by appearances. Truly the Holy One who uses the *Tulku's* body commits no sin; nor may it be taken for granted that a sin has been committed at all, even if it seems so in your eyes. It may be planned to try your faith, or from some other motive judged in reference to standards far removed from yours or mine."

I was prepared for this explanation, having heard of it before as applied to the history of the sixth Dalai Lama, who caused much scandal by indulging in carnal delights. So I pressed my question, repeating it in much the same form as before. The simple-minded lama, delighted at the chance of holding forth before an audience, proceeded to cite a tale by way of illustration: "A man who was on his way to visit a certain saint learned that the latter had committed the crimes of murder and adultery. Horrified, he said to himself: 'This man is no saint, but a wicked criminal: I refuse to stay with him'; so he promptly departed. Just as he was leaving, the saint picked up some dust from the road and placed it in the man's pouch, telling him to take it home. On reaching his house he emptied out the pouch and instead of dust found pure gold. He repented of his rash criticism and gave praise to the name of the saint. A thing may not glitter and yet be gold: so also are the actions of Ṭulkus."

The worthy monk, by the time he had reached the end of his parable, was beaming with satisfaction at his own eloquence. As for Dawa, he let his friend have his say before contributing his own share to the debate. To him we put a concrete case that had come under our notice in 1933: "A certain Ṭulku formerly known to us secretly parted with some of the sacred vessels of the temple to a collector. He seemed to know it was a sin, for he always transacted his business under cloak of darkness." (Scandalized exclamations from the prior!) "We refuse to take this action at anything but its face value — that is, sacrilege and theft. The explanation just given by our friend here seems inadequate: find us a better." To this he replied: "If a sin is committed by a Ṭulku, or by anyone else, it is no use trying to get away from the fact. The holy being who is believed to have taken up his dwelling within the Ṭulku being illuminate, it cannot be his act: it is surely some fiend who has taken possession."

If I had to state the case anew now, I should put it rather differently and cite an example that did not depend on an ethical test, but rather employed a metaphysical symbolism; for, couched in this form, the problem would be easier to bring home to the Tibetan mind and would carry greater weight. I should mention the case of the late Dalai Lama and the Panchhen Lama, who also died a few years ago in China. They had a political quarrel, and the Panchhen Lama, who by all accounts was of a gentle and benevolent nature, was driven into exile by his masterful opponent, whence he never returned. Both these high Lamas were Ṭulkus. The Dalai Lama is a manifestation of the Bodhisat Chenrezig, while the Panchhen Lama is animated by the power of Ŏpagmed, the Buddha of Immeasurable Light, whose disciple Chenrezig is. No deadlier sin can be conceived than revolt of the pupil against the Master, against "his own Lama." How then could the Dalai Lama representing Chenrezig make violent war against the Panchhen Lama into whom the influence of Chenrezig's own Teacher emanates? The problem, put in this way, would exercise the mind of any earnest lama, and I hope some day to hear Dawa's solution of this particular difficulty.

Lest any Western reader be misled, I must explain that no special duties attach to the condition of *Tulku*. Such Lamas are most often, but by no means invariably, heads of monasteries; but that office confers on them administrative powers, not authority to teach doctrine. The Dalai Lama, most famous of them all, is the sovereign ruler of Tibet, but he is no pope and has no greater inherent right to define dogma than any of his clergy. It may happen, and often does, that a *Lama Tulku* is a learned person and a teacher; but this he owes to himself and to his initiation at the hands of his own Master, and not to his quality of *Tulku*. The service offered to mankind by *Tulkus* is held rather to proceed from their presence among us, which in some manner localizes the sacred influence for the benefit of mankind, than from the doing of any set work. It is as if the *Tulku* carried out all the purposes of a sacred image, except that it is formed of flesh and blood, not wrought in bronze. In that case he must be reckoned as a special example of a "support" for worship and meditation, like any other religious object. I am inclined to think that the doctrine of *Tulkus* is correctly interpreted by this theory of "supports" and that our raising of a moral issue was quite beside the point. Moreover it must be remembered that the exercise of any function of a supra-individual nature is independent of all individual contingencies, such as the private character of its ministers. It is only proper that they should turn themselves into temples worthy of the service to be offered and they can be blamed for failing to do so; nevertheless, the sacred influence itself, in principle, remains as unaffected by the individual imperfections of its supports as by their private merits.

Another question that was submitted to the judgment of the lama Dawa was whether Deliverance was attainable without first passing through the state of a human being. We were desirous to see to what lengths the belief that men and animals are, in essentials, alike would be carried. First we referred to the fact that St. Mila Repa took what is known as the "Direct Path," which enabled him to attain Buddhahood in the course of a single life. "If that is so," we said, "is it not reasonable to suppose that a member of some other class of being, whether he belonged to the animals or even resided in one of the purgatories, could, after experiencing perfect contrition, follow a Direct Path and actually reach Buddhahood without having to be reborn into the human family?" The lama pondered a little and answered: "Yes, I am inclined to think one must accept this.

Whosoever, whether he be beast or even the most malignant of demons, finds the strength to do what Mila Repa did, overcoming the distractions of his environment, the same can become Buddha in one life as he did; but it is still more difficult for those pitiable beings, since their life does not favour nonattachment to self. Continual suffering or the daily need to slay other animals for food is a great obstacle in the Path."

I kept one more question to the last — in many ways it was the most important of all: "The various divinities are commonly portrayed and spoken of under separate names, with distinctive attributes; and so they are taken to be by many men. The countless forms, fierce or calm, or the Bodhisats such as Chenrezig or Djamyan the Giver of Wisdom, are these all separate beings, or should they be regarded as begotten only within our minds?" His answer was as follows: "From one point of view all those divinities exist, from another they are not real" — he was here following St. Tsong Khapa, founder of the Yellow Gelugpa Order, to which Spituk belonged. "So long as you are confined within the present world of forms and distinctions, so long will you personify them separately. But once a man has entered the state of 'Subduer of Foes' (Perfected Saint, who is the subduer of passions and illusions), and stands on the threshold of Enlightenment, being freed from the Round, then for him these separate things simply *are not*; for such a one, nothing at all is, except Buddhahood."

I must here add a note to Dawa's explanation in the hope of bringing out his meaning still further; but it is my own interpretation and I must bear responsibility for any error. He who enters into the realization of the Absolute has no more part in conditioned or determined existence, which ceases to have any appearance of reality whatsoever. For such a person, it can be said that our Universe, and all forms, are illusion. But so long as we still have our being within the world of form, we are forced to clothe all our ideas accordingly. The stages in the path of Enlightenment become personalities, the more distinct in proportion as we are unenlightened, the more disembodied as we progress towards the goal. What concern have we with Djamyan Lord of Wisdom, when once we have known Wisdom herself? I used the feminine of set purpose, for She is the active energy of Method, who must also collaborate if we are to hope for the unveiling of the One Light by which alone we are able to know ourselves. And Method himself, who is Compassionate Love, the same is clothed in the form of Chenrezig, for those who can only so conceive him. And he who has trodden the path of the Bodhisats and *knows* this Compassion beyond all chance of forgetting, the same knows Chenrezig, for he *is* Chenrezig. Even the Bodhisats are "supports"; when once Buddhahood has been attained, when there is Knowledge, Reality — things that at present mean nothing to us and are *Void* of all that we can possibly conceive of — then all supports can be done away with; they "simply are not," as the lama said.

I cannot refrain from quoting at this point a passage that might easily have been taken from some book of the Tibetan Canon, but which is, in fact, from an English work of the fourteenth century, called *The Cloud of Unknowing;* also another passage from a commentary on it, written in the early seventeenth century, by Father Augustine Baker, a Benedictine. Nothing could better illustrate the solidarity of all traditional thought, irrespective of race and period, than these teachings of an unknown Yorkshireman born over five centuries ago. Both the substance of the passage and its phraseology would be more readily intelligible to the bursar of Spituk than to its author's own countrymen of today.

> The nought . . . is God, to whom the soul may be united when she is nowhere bodily, nor hath in her any image of creatures. And when she is nowhere bodily then she is everywhere spiritually; and being in such condition she is fit to be united with the said nothing, which also is in all places. . . . And this union I have elsewhere called a union of nothing with nothing. . . . What is he that calleth it nought? Surely it is our outer man and not our inner. Our inner man calleth it All; for by it he is well taught to understand all things bodily or ghostly, without any special beholding to any one thing by itself.

> And when she [the soul] being in such case of nothing — that is as no imaginable or intelligible thing, but as another thing which is above all images and species, and is expressible by no species . . . doth further apply and add her foresaid nothing to the said nothing of God, then remaineth there, neither in respect of the soul nor in respect of God, anything but a certain vacuity or nothing. In which nothing is acted and passeth a union between God and the soul. . . . And so in this case of union there is nothing and nothing and they make nothing. . . . This is the state of perfect union

which is termed by some a state of nothing, and by others, with as much reason, termed a state of totality.

These quotations are strikingly akin to the Buddhist doctrine of Nirvana, and they would surely be acclaimed by the bursar of Spituk as bearing the stamp of universal truth.

These enthralling talks we had with him were spread over two days and made us reluctant to leave. We got him to promise, however, to ride over to P'hiyang to see us before we left for England, which he agreed to do all the more readily as he was a personal friend of the painter Gyaltsan, whom he held in high regard.

On reaching P'hiyang we found all made ready for our lodging. A certain monk named Sherab (Wisdom) had vacated his set of rooms in our favour — we later paid him a small rent for their use — and had arranged to sleep on the roof for the duration of our stay; sleeping out is customary during the summer months.

Our cell, which had a balcony with a glorious view, was approached through a small lobby where dung for the fire was stored. From the lobby a ladder led out on to the flat roof, from which tall prayer-flags floated their messages. We arranged to have our meals up there, for a small kitchen was attached.

The cell was furnished with rugs and mattresses and low tables. At the end of the room stood the altar, of white wood still undecorated, on which two large books occupied places of honour. The walls were hung round with about a dozen t'hankas of varying age, some of them painted by our friend himself; they depicted the patrons of the Kargyudpa Order in both their mild and their terrible shapes.

In the evening dozens of unexpected people kept peeping through the doorway or even walked right in, squatting down on the floor to gaze at us. Sometimes it was a monk, sometimes a couple of peasants; now they were silent, now in conversational mood. The young novices, in particular, left us no peace. Eventually we got used to visitors entering at awkward moments. If they were of superior rank we had to be patient and behave as if we had been expecting them. With commoner folk we let them satisfy legitimate curiosity and then turned them out good-humouredly. But unless one is engaged in meditation, which no Tibetan will willingly disturb, one must learn not to demand the strict regard for privacy that people expect to enjoy at home in England.

Chapter XXI

Painting Lessons and Leave-takings

OUR STAY at P'hiyang *Gompa* was, in a way, the climax of the expedition, for in it a hope was fulfilled round which our plans had revolved from the outset. Time was unfortunately short: we could have done with some of those extra weeks that had been frittered away earlier on, in preparations for the abortive Hlobrak project. Nevertheless the results of P'hiyang cannot be measured in time; not only does it mark a definite stage in our education, but also during that brief spell so much experience was gained, so many doubts were cleared up, and such wide vistas were opened that I look back on it as a time of accomplishment and of abundant harvesting.

Life began in earnest the day after our arrival, when we went round to Gyaltsan's room, the place where we were to spend most of our waking hours during our visit to his monastery. It was not a particularly large room. A wooden post stood in the middle supporting the roof-beam, and at the foot of this the lama spread out the rug upon which he used to sit when working. In the morning the sun shone full upon that side of the building, and large shutters were put across the window to subdue the glare. In the afternoon they were taken down, after the sun had moved round to fall dazzlingly upon the rampart-like white walls that faced south towards the Indus Valley and the Zanskar peaks beyond. Then the room was cool, with a soft breeze occasionally blowing through it, and it was filled with an even light, ideal for painting.

The furniture was more than usually well cared for, and it included two large painted cabinets, which Gyaltsan had decorated with floral designs. The paraphernalia of an artist was to be seen in various corners: trays of brushes, saucers of paint, stretched canvases leaning against the wall, compasses, rulers, and set-squares; but all was arranged with remarkable neatness and taste. Three or four *t'hankas* hung on the walls, one having been recently finished by Gyaltsan himself, and in a corner next to the altar there was a particularly fine scroll of some age, which he treasured highly. Sometimes, as I sat upon my rug by the window and watched Gyaltsan either painting or making extracts from books in his lovely handwriting, it was the easiest thing in the world to fancy myself in the workshop of a Master Jerome or a Fra Angelico.

Gyaltsan's personal novice, a boy about twelve years old, derived much entertainment from our presence in the monastery. He was constantly running to and fro between our room and his master's, but his favourite place was on our roof helping Norbu to cook the meals. I fear our coming somewhat interfered with the even course of his education. Nevertheless, on one or two afternoons he was put through his paces and made to recite in a high piping voice, while Gyaltsan, though he might appear half engrossed in other things, would pull him up at the mistakes without ever a reference to the text. The boy also waited on the lama when he was at work, ran errands, kept the room tidy and the floor clean, and brought in the tea at frequent intervals. Gyaltsan seemed to have a very successful way with him, and the boy had all the high spirits and insatiable curiosity of his age.

The boy novices have their appointed place in community life and perform all sorts of odd jobs for which children are particularly suitable. The monasteries in Tibet are much more comparable to our universities than to their nominal counterparts in the West, at least as these survive today. Each lama owns or hires his own rooms, which are often like a little self-contained flat, and keeps them up out of the money remitted to him by his own family. The lamas feed separately, and except for certain prescribed gatherings for worship in the temple each man is free to use his time as he thinks fit. This general statement must be qualified somewhat in the case of the Yellow monks, whose rule is laid down in greater detail, so that their life approximates rather more nearly to that of a Christian monastic community; but even in their case the points of resemblance can easily be exaggerated. If a lama desires to wander off on the highroad or to withdraw into contemplation in some remote spot, the permission that he must first seek is not the formal authorization of the abbot, but the consent of his own personal tutor, *his* lama; this is for everyone the final authority, from which the death of one of the parties is the only dispensation. Though children are dedicated by their parents to the spiritual life at an early age, before there could be any possibility of personal inclination, they are not bound for life in the sense that they have no means of release if they should come to doubt their vocation. The vows are dissoluble at any age and a certain number of persons avail themselves of this right; they are very much in a minority, however, for the lama is looked up to socially, and a return "to the world," though not penalized in any way, naturally seems rather a come-down.

One day I asked Gyaltsan in the presence of the little novice if he had a diligent pupil. He answered: "Well, I wouldn't quite say that; but on the whole he's pretty fair." "And do you sometimes have to scold him? What do you do to him — beat him?" From the burst of merriment that greeted my words from both master and pupil I gathered that the latter was in no great danger. I had put the question of set purpose, in order to draw Gyaltsan, since I knew that there were a good many Tibetan supporters of the school that puts unbounded faith in corporal punishment. On the whole, Tibetan educators do not believe in sparing the rod; even eminent *Lama-Tulkus*, during their years of probation, are liable to vigorous beatings if slow at their lessons or slipshod in deportment. The preceptor in such a case, after dealing out correction with due conscientiousness, prostrates himself at the feet of his charge to show that there has been nothing of personal pique or disrespect in his action. Similarly the young lama must prostrate himself before his corrector and thank him for his well-timed severity.

Every monastery owns a number of "mountain retreats," where those who desire to spend periods of contemplation can retire from the distractions of social existence. These cells consist of four walls, with a raised platform at one end, where the recluse sits. Food is pushed into the cell at stated intervals; those who bring it must on no account address a word to the contemplative or interrupt him in any way. Among the Kargyudpa many are found who, true to the tradition of their great saint Mila Repa, withdraw into caves in the cold regions of glaciers, where a cotton cloth is their only garment (*Repa* literally means "cotton-clad"). Many retreats are not so rigorous, but are simply small cottages, furnished like any other house and differing only in the absence of companionship. I remember talking to one Yellow monk from Lhasa, who had been telling me that he intended to retire for several months to a "mountain retreat." "Where is this retreat," I said, "is it in a cave?" The monk, who was a man who loved his comfort, made a gesture of horror. "Oh! no," he cried, "not a cave! My mountain retreat will be provided with every convenience!" It must also be remembered that the Buddhist conception of asceticism is quite unlike that which is familiar from the history of the Christian Church. There is little idea of mortifying the flesh by painful austerities. The Buddha formally condemned the extremes of both luxury and self-torture; He was born Himself to wealth and tried to escape into violent self-repression before He discovered its uselessness. Nothing that is calculated to damage health is to be encouraged, for impaired health may create added obstacles in the pursuit of Knowledge. The austerity of a Mila has a very different motive, the renunciation of all that might distract, the cutting off of all "purposeless" activity, the lulling of the senses into quiescence, so as to permit, rather than compel, the real Knowledge-Consciousness to arise. Neither are all contemplatives ascetics in the present-day sense of the word. St. Marpa, though he laid on Mila Repa the injunction of taking "a terrible resolution of meditating for the duration of his life for the profit of creatures," himself continued to live and work in the world: he tilled his farm and was happily married.

While we were at P'hiyang, I one day suddenly ran into our old enemy the bursar of Satsukul, whose office extended to all the monastic houses of a certain group. If I was surprised, he was astounded in still greater measure — in fact, disgusted would be a better word, for it must have come as a shock to him to find the three people whom he had treated so ungraciously making themselves at home inside his own monastery. He did not say much, but I heard that after we left he tried to vent his annoyance by making himself disagreeable to Gyaltsan.

The monk Sherab, from whom we hired our bedroom, was also a rather unprepossessing specimen, uncouth and always on the make. He was one of the bursar's chief cronies. One day when we saw them come down arm-in-arm (not literally so, for it is not a Tibetan habit), I could not help exclaiming: "Look at Wisdom (Sherab) and Method collaborating for the salvation of creatures!" The joke raised a general laugh, for everyone saw the reference to the mystic union of the two inseparables, and the bursar's covetousness was known to be nothing if not methodical.

The office of *chyagdzŏd* or bursar is regulated by a peculiar system of tenure in many of the *Gompas*. It usually lasts for three years. On appointment, the *chyagdzŏd* receives a certain sum, out of which he is expected to provide for the upkeep of those amenities which are shared by all the residents in the *Gompa*. At the end he must pay back the sum intact, but in the meantime he can use it as he wishes, for trading or lending; any profits above the original sum, after he has disbursed all that is needed for the common expenses, are his own. It can well be imagined that this post offers considerable opportunities for graft, especially in a large monastery, and is much sought after by commercially ambitious monks. The position of *chyagdzŏd* in one of the vast establishments near Lhasa might be worth thousands. It must not be supposed, however, that all holders of this office are corrupt. Our friend the bursar of Spituk, who discharged his duties with zeal and integrity, told us that he longed for the day when he would lay down the seals, for he found it an uncongenial task and a distraction from things of greater importance. Nevertheless the system offers certain temptations; doubtless the presence of a strict abbot would make all the difference.

Most of our time was passed in study. Both the art-pupils and I found Gyaltsan an ideal teacher, clear in exposition, strict, patient, resourceful, and infectiously enthusiastic. His methods had been well worked out, but were far from stereotyped. With myself he either enlarged upon some doctrinal point by word alone or, more often, copied selected passages from the book of St. Gampopa, from which my quotations on the Refuge in Chapter xvii were taken, and passed them on to me to make what I could of them before turning to him for help.

After I had proceeded as far as I could, the lama expounded the passage. This method of working was slow, so that the ground covered at the time was not very extensive; but we had agreed beforehand that we should not allow ourselves to race ahead, leaving unsolved doubts to harass us afterwards. To the grounding that I received from Gyaltsan I owe the knowledge that enabled me to compile the chapter on the Doctrine in Part Two of this book, though I did not feel the full benefit of his teaching immediately; it was reserved for my other good master, the lama Wangyal, to make his predecessor's work bear fruit, when he came and visited me in my Liverpool home. In my discussions with Gyaltsan I found that when I wished to illustrate this or that knotty point, I often was able to make use of stories taken from the New Testament or from the lives of the Christian Fathers, especially St. Thomas Aquinas. The quotations were always very much appreciated; the parables of the Gospel, in particular, appealed to our lama, nor did it ever occur to him to treat them as less authoritative because they belonged to a foreign religion. He was only interested in their bearing upon the points under discussion and he seemed just as ready to find truth in the sayings of "a certain ancient Lama in our country" as in those of other Lamas whose names were familiar. The lama Wangyal went still further. Speaking of Christ, he said: "I see that He was a very Buddha!"

At sunset Gyaltsan and I usually made a tour of the walls, which were formed by a single huge *mendong* ringing the *Gompa* without a break. In hot countries this is always an enchanted hour, when the spirit seems peculiarly sensitized and ready to take wing. Gyaltsan let his mind lead him whither it would, like a rider who drops the reins loose on his horse's neck and trusts to it to take him in the right direction. I well remember how on one of these circuits the lama began to describe the next Golden Age, the expected reign of Chamba, "the Loving One," who will be the Buddha of the cycle succeeding to the present one. I cannot attempt to reproduce his mood of exaltation; he spoke like a predestined prophet, and had the heavens opened in that hour and the world stood still to make way for the Second Coming, I should have felt little surprise.

While attending to me, Gyaltsan carried on simultaneously with the drawing-class. "Well now, what shall we begin with?" he asked my friends the first day. "Shall we learn how to do the Teacher's hands?" He handed out to each man a sharply pointed wooden stylus and a small drawing-board provided with a handle and shaped like a butter-pat. Then, taking one of the boards himself, he dusted it over with fine chalk and proceeded to draw with the stylus the hands of the Buddha in their classical position, one hanging down to the ground and the other supporting the begging-bowl. He made them watch carefully how he made his strokes and then try to repeat the operation. He did one model in the corner of each pupil's board. They set to work, and as they both already possessed some skill with the pencil, they made rapid progress and soon began to turn out passable copies. Whenever they made a false stroke they dusted some more chalk over the place and began again. This was the first lesson, repeated a number of times with a view to greater accuracy.

The next lessons were taken up with the Teacher's feet,

which were more difficult; then came His head, and after that His body. When they had reached a fair degree of proficiency with the separate parts they tried to combine them and so produce a complete nude. This course of study was spread over several days, till finally they were considered good enough to attempt to clothe the body. Gyaltsan's criticisms confined themselves to the question of exactitude; æsthetic considerations were left alone for the time being: in fact, I doubt whether they are ever mentioned as an end in themselves. When the figure appeared to have approached the model, Gyaltsan tested it with a pair of dividers in order to make sure that the measurements of the different parts had been related in correct ratio; for the main proportions of the Buddha's figure are not left to the artists' discretion, being considered to have been fixed for all time by divine revelation. Gyaltsan related the story thus: "One of the disciples of the Victorious One was desirous of placing His portrait on record for posterity; but when he attempted to measure His holy body he found no rule long enough, nor any measure sufficient. After repeated failures, he perceived the hopelessness of his task, so he prayed to the Buddha of His grace to vouchsafe to mankind the knowledge of His earthly form. The Teacher consented and the disciple drew the first picture, which has served as a canon ever since. For a Buddha is not like other men: He has all sorts of peculiarities — a mark between the eyes, a protuberance on the head, teeth in an unusual number; and His ears are not at all the same as a man's. His eyes are shaped like a bow bent by a skilful archer — and there are many other points that must be observed if you are to portray a Buddha faithfully."

During the early stages the whole aim of the teaching is to train hand, eyes, and memory. When the pupils have proved that they are able to copy the model several times with a considerable degree of sureness, they are made to do it from memory. At the first attempt my friends found that they had remembered only a part of what they had practised; nevertheless, after referring to the model and making one or two attempts, they began to retain the proportions in their mind's eye and Gyaltsan expressed himself as satisfied with their progress. A still more advanced stage is marked by trying to draw the same figure in a material where correction by rubbing out is not possible, that is to say, in Indian ink upon paper. From time to time, for variety's sake, flowers, clouds, and animals can be introduced. Drawing from nature does not come in at all: it is a question of learning control and of memorizing the principal classical subjects.

While the pupil is busy improving his drawing he also helps the Master in such jobs as grinding the stones and earths that make the paints, pounding them in a polished stone mortar, preparing canvases, and washing brushes. Later he begins to learn how to apply the paint and is allowed to help in the more repetitive and mechanical tasks such as borders, grass, flowers, or skies. Eventually the day comes when he may try his hand at a whole composition.

There was naturally no time for us to tackle anything but elementary drawing, so, as we were anxious not to miss seeing all the processes that go to the making of a *t'hanka*, we asked Gyaltsan to let us watch him work on some that were awaiting completion. We thus saw enough for me to be able to describe the various stages without omitting any important detail.

The first task is the preparation of a canvas. The material used is ordinary white cotton cloth of Indian manufacture. An oblong is cut to the required size, and it is hemmed round barley stalks, to give the edge a slight stiffening. Then it is fixed in an embroidery frame of much larger size, with a woollen thread running in zigzags all round from the canvas to the frame, lacing the two together. If the canvas sags at any time, the lace is drawn tighter and the tension is gradually distributed all round the frame till the free end is reached, which is then reknotted. When this has been done, a dressing of lime, mixed with a little size made by boiling yak-skin, is applied, but very thinly, so as not to interfere with the flexibility of the canvas, which must be supple enough to be rolled up. The surface is wetted, polished repeatedly with a flint, and allowed to dry after each polishing. In the end the canvas does not differ essentially from a wall, and the method of painting is akin to fresco.

When the canvas is ready, the drawing is put on with charcoal pencils, but comparatively roughly, for the artist trusts to his brush to lend due precision to the finer lines and to obliterate all trace of what lies underneath. After that it is only a question of applying the colours; as only body colours are used, either opaque or only very slightly translucent, it is easy to blot out a mistake. The folds of draperies and the features on the faces are the last details to be put in, apart from various finer embellishments in gold. Gyaltsan's art was a typical example of pleasing but not highly inspired school-work. But for the tradition, he would have been completely at a loss; but given the help of its guiding hand, his great sincerity enabled him to go to the utmost limit of his talent.

When drawing on a *t'hanka*, the artist leans his frame against a wall; it is never laid flat on a table or on the floor. In painting, the left hand holds a transverse ruler, which follows the hand that holds the brush, providing it with a steady rest. The left hand also grasps a sea-shell, which serves as a palette. Brushes are prepared by the artist from selected hairs of goat, and even cat, which he fastens on to a stick. Size is used to mix with the paints, which are first ground in the mortar. White of egg is not known as a medium; that is why it is incorrect to speak of the Tibetan mural paintings as frescoes, though they resemble them so closely in appearance.

The day before we were due to leave, some ritual dances were performed in a cloistered theatre just below our own room, in honour of the visit to P'hiyang of Colonel Lang and his party. The proper time of the year for this display is January; at that time over a hundred monks take part in the service — for it is really a sacred mystery — wearing splendid Chinese costumes, and also grotesque masks decorated with yaks' horns, antlers, and tusks. The dancers wear red silk skirts, banded with yellow, which describe brilliant circles of colour as they whirl round. Summer is not really the best time for such violent exercise. Gyaltsan, who acted as trainer and master of the ballet, allowed his troupe of about a dozen to perform three figures that lasted half an hour, after which they retired, sweating profusely. At the proper season all Ladak gathers at P'hiyang to watch the Kargyudpa mystery, which lasts two whole days.

For ourselves that last afternoon brought a gathering of friends. Khan Muhammad Din was there, in attendance on the Residency party. The lama Dawa also came from Spituk and the Yellow Man from Leh. Joseph Gergan, the Christian translator, sent a messenger bearing a kind present of cakes specially baked for us by his wife. When the dancing was over, we forgathered for the last time in Konchhog Gyaltsan's room and conversed about our future plans. "My advice to you is to go to our mother-house of Dikhung in Tibet," said Gyaltsan. "The Dikhung Lama is a true saint, and if he should receive you as a pupil you will have the happiness of studying the Doctrine under one of the greatest teachers in the land. What do you think, Reverend Doctor?" — he turned to the bursar of Spituk inquiringly. I rather expected that the latter would prefer to recommend a member of his own Yellow-Hat Order, but to my surprise he concurred, saying: "Yes, I believe you could not do better. If you should go to Tibet, seek out the Dikhung Lama. I would gladly come with you myself, if by that time I were free of the bursar's office."

Bidding good-bye to our friends should have made us sad; but after living among Tibetans, one begins to catch a little of their philosophy, which does not favour long-drawn-out regrets. Absences of months and years are such a commonplace in this land that people settle down quickly after the departure of a friend, knowing as they do that there is little likelihood of news being received, until the day when the absentee himself turns up unexpectedly to announce his own return. Stoicism and resignation are in the blood, and a worrying disposition is quite the exception. The lama Dawa left first for Spituk; the Yellow Man lingered a little longer and then rode off, telling us that he too expected to be on the road within a week, for he was starting for Lhasa with a caravan and might be away a year or more. Two days later we parted from Gyaltsan, who had ridden with us as far as Kalatze, on the Indus.

We reserved for ourselves one final treat, a day to be spent in revisiting our beloved Likhir. This second occasion brought no disillusionment, but on the contrary a renewal of the rapture of our first visit. When it was at last time to go, the old prior drew me apart into his cell and said that he would feel happy to welcome us back at any time for an indefinite stay, with every facility for reading or doing whatever else we wished.

The homeward stages were all taken as speedily as possible — Yuru, Bod Karbu and lovely Mulbek. When we crossed the frontier we shed our Tibetan personalities with regret and became our ordinary selves once more. We hurried through Purig, where the fierceness of summer had given place to the more temperate glow of autumn. Everywhere people were stacking their last hay or walking up and down the stubble-fields with an air of busy aimlessness as if to say "The work of the year is over; now for a long hibernation." At the alp of Nimarg, which we had left a garden in full flower, many plants had died down or been cropped short, leaving no trace; but a few late-flowering species still bloomed — gentians, a monkshood, and a delphinium new to us; they were making all haste to get through their life-cycle before the first snows condemned them once more to the enforced rest of months. We spent a day gathering seeds; there is no sound more gratifying to the ear than their metallic tinkle as the ripe pods are bent over and emptied into the envelopes. Then at last came the Zoji, now quite cleared of snow; once across the pass, we were in India again. In the Sind Valley the maize harvest was ripe and also the walnuts. Buying roasted maize-cobs in the villages made us think of Soho and chestnuts.

At last Wayl Bridge appeared and "civilization," represented by a couple of cars, stood waiting for us. A Kashmiri peasant with a badly abscessed hand stopped us and asked for medicine, so we lighted our last wayside fire to boil up water for Dr. Roaf, who operated there and then. It was the final bow before the fall of the curtain. We stepped into our car and were whirled in clouds of choking dust towards Srinágar, conscious of a mounting nervousness that could not be kept in check in spite of our recent sojourn in the land of disillusion.

PART FOUR

Afterthoughts

Sunset over Marshy Tract near Spituk   *See page 236*

P'HIYANG GOMPA *See page 274*

Konchhog Gyaltsan Painting   *See page 275*

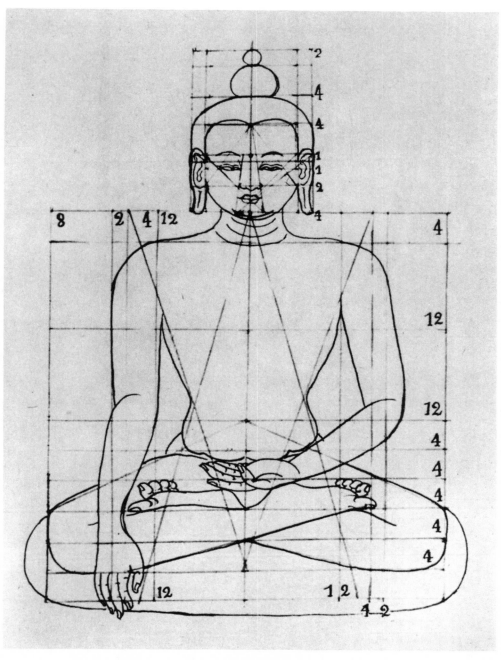

CANON OF PROPORTION FOR THE FIGURE OF BUDDHA   *See pages* 290–1

WAYSIDE CHHORTEN   *See page 61*

TRADING CARPETS *See page* 332

BEER JUG AND TEAPOT   *See page 332*

BRAZIER FOR WARMING TEA   *See page 332*

EAR-ORNAMENT FROM STATUE   *See page 333*
Silver-gilt filigree and precious stones

TEACUP WITH CHASED SILVER STAND AND LID   *See page 333*

Chapter XXII

The Presiding Idea

WHOEVER HAS HAD the patience to keep track, stage by stage, of the wanderings recorded in this book cannot fail to have gathered by now some kind of general impression of what life in one of the Tibetan countries consists of, both in respect of its outward conformation and even, to some extent, in respect of its essence. It goes without saying, however, that such a picture will remain incomplete in many ways; anything like a detailed analysis of the various strands that together go to weave the web of Tibetan life could only be undertaken after a prolonged stay in Tibet proper, where the civilization in question can be studied under its most typical as well as its most vigorous form.* Nevertheless, enough has been learned up to date to allow of a number of generalizations affecting the whole Tibetan world, since it is plainly evident that throughout its far-flung territories a certain type of human existence is recognizable, owing both its essential unity and its outward form to the influence of the selfsame tradition, having done so, moreover, for many centuries. One has but to compare the account contained in the biography of St. Mila Repa with what is to be seen today to become convinced of the extraordinary unity, as well as vitality, of Tibetan institutions. Apart from such changes as must come, almost imperceptibly, with the mere passage of time, the way in which people think, act, and speak and the standard by which they judge men and things do not appear to have altered in any very fundamental way since those early days, and the life of Mila Repa still provides the best-drawn picture of Tibetan life that exists, besides offering a most vivid commentary on that doctrine which, above all else, has given to that life both shape and direction.

The last remark calls for some additional comment, since it contains an allusion to a question of very wide import, one that

* Such a visit did in fact take place in 1947.

is of general applicability to all traditional civilizations and not
merely to Tibet — namely, the question of what is the principle of discrimination between one form of the Perennial Wisdom and another, causing them to be externally distinct as well
as consistent internally. For without the operation of some such
principle there would be no excuse for a formal discontinuity
as between the several traditions, serving as they all do as ways
and means of attaining to the realization of one and the same
universal Knowledge, from which every thought of distinction
is manifestly to be excluded, whether of form or otherwise.

The fact is that every civilization that can be called authentic is endowed with a principle of unity peculiar to itself, which
is reflected, in varying degrees, in all the institutions of the civilization in question. By a principle of unity is meant a pre-
dominant idea, corresponding to a given aspect of the truth,
which has been recipient of particular emphasis and for the expressing of which, if one may so put it, that civilization shows
a particular "genius." Emphasis on an aspect must, however,
have its price: that is to say, the highlight of attention cannot
be focused on one aspect of reality without producing its compensating shadows, affecting other aspects. Each separate formal embodiment of the traditional wisdom, therefore, corresponds, as it were, to a difference of intellectual perspective;
and the key to the understanding of whatever is explicit or implicit in any given form resides in a thorough assimilation of
the dominant idea running through that form — in other words,
of its principle of unity.

In seeking to determine which is the principle of unity ani-
mating the Tibetan civilization one must beware of being satisfied with an easy answer, such as saying that this principle is
no other than the Buddhist doctrine itself; for though this statement is correct as far as it goes, it lacks precision, failing as it
does to indicate which one, out of a whole body of ideas comprised within the one doctrinal plan, has been recipient of that
greater emphasis required for the moulding of an entire traditional structure according to a particular form, and, as it were,
in its image. Though one knows that Buddhism, by imposing
certain fundamental concepts, has become the rule of life over
very wide areas extending from Ceylon to Japan, and that this
has produced a certain community of outlook among all the
peoples that have come within the Buddhist orbit, one cannot
fail to recognize that in this general whole certain clearly dis-

tinguishable forms of civilization are to be found, the intellectual frontiers of which are in no wise determined by the Buddhist influence. The common presence of Buddhism does not, for instance, warrant one's placing the Chinese and Tibetan civilizations under one heading, even though they are next-door neighbours; and if Buddhism is admittedly a factor common to both, this fact has been insufficient to produce any very marked likeness in the two points of view, let alone identity.

The chief difference between them lies in the fact that whereas in Tibet the Buddhist tradition is everything, having completely replaced its *Bön-po* predecessor, in China Buddhism was something in the nature of a graft, admittedly a most timely and successful one, upon a civilization of which the pattern, in all essentials, had been already set before the arrival of the foreign influences. Since nothing in the existing Chinese form was found to be actually incompatible with the Buddhist point of view, the latest arrival from India found no difficulty in taking its place in the traditional life of the Far East on equal terms with its two other great constituents, namely Taoism, representative of an intellectuality so pure as to be adapted for the use of an exceptionally qualified "élite" only, and Confucianism, which is not, as is commonly supposed, a separate creation, still less a "religion," but which corresponds to that side of the Chinese tradition in which all without exception are able to participate, concerning itself as it does with social institutions and human relationships in general — the latter being given expression especially through its characteristic concepts of the race, the family, and the family ancestors. It might also be mentioned, in passing, that in the course of time Buddhism and Taoism engaged in many intellectual exchanges, some of which gave rise to that school, so rich in spiritual initiative, that is commonly known in the West under its Japanese name of *Zen*.

Similar considerations would have applied in India during the centuries when Hinduism and Buddhism coexisted there as separate currents of tradition: both continued to belong to the same civilization, the form of which had been laid down, under purely Hindu inspiration, at a time long anterior to the specific formulation of the Buddhist teachings. In any case, both in virtue of its origin and by the nature of its thought, Buddhism remains an Indian doctrine, having derived most of its basic conceptions, if not all, from the common root-stock of the Hindu metaphysic. It is not on that score that Buddhism can be called

original; nor, indeed, does it put forward any such claim, since
the Buddha Himself always was at pains to repudiate, as a monstrous heresy, any suggestion that He had come to teach something new in the matter of doctrine; it is only modern Western
writers, themselves imbued with individualistic prejudices,
who have been determined at all costs to discover in Buddhism
a radical innovation amounting to a revolt against the traditional spirit, and in the Buddha an early revolutionary working
on Reformation lines.

Where Buddhism was highly original, however, was in respect of its methods, affecting both the way of expounding the
principles and the form of the spiritual disciplines that went
with that knowledge. Indeed, but for a large measure of originality in the manner of restating the eternal truths the Buddhist apostles would have been unable to carry out their appointed task of adapting the Indian metaphysic so as to render
it eventually assimilable by non-Indian peoples, especially by
the yellow races, whose mentality was so very different from
that of the Indians. This task once accomplished, however, Indian Buddhism had little further cause to exist as a separate
form and gradually disappeared, gently subsiding back into
that Hinduism whence it had sprung and from which, despite
controversies on the surface, it had, at heart, never been entirely severed.

The Tibetan branch was one of the latest offshoots from the
main stem of Buddhism, having only come into being during
the seventh and eighth centuries after Christ, chiefly through
the work of Indian monks from Bengal and Kashmir. While
accepting all the basic ideas taught by the Buddha, which it
continued to share with all the other peoples of similar spiritual
allegiance, Tibet early developed certain clearly marked features of its own, to the point of giving rise to a distinct form of
civilization, comparable, on every count, with the other principal traditional forms of the world. This is possibly due in part
to the incorporation of such features of the previous *Bön-po*
tradition as could be usefully readapted; it was on the face of
it unlikely, however, that any element specific to a form actually in process of replacement by another would retain sufficient intrinsic vitality to provide a whole civilization with its
principle of unity, in the sense given to that term at the beginning of this chapter — that is to say, with an idea both distinct
and powerful enough to create and nourish its own forms, con-
ferring on them the means for perpetuating their own charac-

ter through long ages and of impressing it firmly and unmistakably upon the face of things and upon the thoughts of men.

In fact, the idea that enjoys pride of place in the Tibetan tradition is one that figures in the Buddhist doctrine as originally introduced from India. This presiding idea, colouring the outlook of sage and simple peasant alike (as we were repeatedly enabled to observe during our journeys), is the conception of Bodhisattvahood, the state of the fully awakened being who, though under no further constraint by that Law of Causality which he has transcended, yet freely continues to espouse the vicissitudes of the Round of Existence in virtue of his Self-identification with all the creatures still involved in egocentric delusion and consequent suffering. Such an attitude must not, however, be confused with a kind of sentimental "altruism" in the social sense; indeed, a moment's reflection will show that he who has finally been set free from the false notion of a permanent "I," to be individually experienced, is at the same time automatically rid of its correlative notion of "other." The Bodhisattva behaves as he does precisely because, for him, any kind of conceptual polarization is inoperative, because, to his singleness of eye, all contrasted pairs such as the Round and Nirvana, Bondage and Deliverance, Material Substance and Spirit, together with all the subsidiary oppositions born of such contrasts, are alike resolved in the unity — or, as the Tibetans would say, in the "two-lessness" — of That which he himself realizes as the All-Principle (Tibetan *Kun-ji*), the eternal Cause and ground of all phenomenal existence.*

The Bodhisattva's compassion, or what in human language is described as such, translates into individually intelligible terms the universal "non-altruity" of his point of view: even while in Nirvana he experiences the world, according to that measure of reality which belongs to it — and one must not forget that suffering, in the deepest sense of the word, is inseparable from the very fact of becoming, which cannot in any sense be experienced without it. Likewise, even when dwelling in the midst of a changeful world, he does not cease to know the changeless bliss of Nirvana, and if to us the two experiences seem distinct and mutually exclusive, they are not so to the possessor of true insight, because such a one never feels tempted to abstract one

---

* It is not difficult to see the likeness — nay, more, the identity — of this doctrine with that of the Hindus on the subject of *Ātman*, the universal Self; this in spite of various attempts made, by modern scholars and others, to oppose Buddhism and Hinduism on this score, by persistently misapplying the fundamental Buddhist teaching about the "non-selfhood" of all conditioned existence.

or other of them from the unity of their common and transcendent principle, so that, from his point of view, they are not
even conceivable apart. Thus the Bodhisattva, through a perfect realization of his own essential identity with all beings,
thereby suffers with them and for them, as the eternal victim
self-immolated upon the altar of their existence; but even in
that suffering itself he perceives the joy unspeakable — both
the light and its inseparable shadows alike yield up their clos-
est-guarded secret under the scrutiny of his incorruptible impartiality.*

The status of a Bodhisattva has been defined (though,
strictly speaking, the very word "definition," implying as it does
the idea of limitation, is here inapplicable) as that of one who
realizes Wisdom as Knowledge of the Void, and Method as
Universal Compassion; the first-named representing the purely
transcendent aspect of his realization, while the second implies
an unblurred recognition of the Face of Divinity even through
the veil of separativity, as constituted by the worlds — in other
words, a not merely theoretical but an effective awareness that
the transcendent aspect of Truth is not other than the immanent and vice versa. Thus, if the being is first called upon to
seek "deliverance" from form and its restrictions in order to become awake to that reality which dwells "beyond names and
forms," yet, in the deepest sense of all, it can be said, following
the *Lankavatara Sutra,* that there is really nothing to be acquired, nothing to be delivered from, no Way, no Goal, no
Round, no *Nirvana,* nor indeed anything needing to be done or
undone. However, lest this kind of paradoxical statement, so
common in the Mahāyānist writings, should be unconsciously
twisted into an excuse for taking up a "quietist" position, it is
well to remember that the knowledge in question itself implies
the most intensely "active" attitude conceivable, a concentration so impenetrable that it is a matter of indifference to its pos-

* A parallel, though one very different in its formal expression, can be
established by reference to Christian theology, in that it can be said that
the ultimate goal of the Christian life consists in giving complete effect to
the Doctrine of the Two Natures, central theme of the Christian tradition as
such, whereby Jesus, the Man of Sorrows, and the Glorified Christ eternally
seated at the right hand of Power are simultaneously realized as one and not
two; or, in other words, the Christ who suffered crucifixion temporally upon
the tree at Calvary and upon the cross of His own incarnation as a finite being,
and indeed cosmically upon the very fact of Creation itself, and that Word
of God by whom all things were made, though they respectively suggest
notions of blissfulness and suffering that to the eye of ignorance seem mutually
exclusive or, at best, successively realizable, are essentially inseparable conceptions neither of which can be fully realized in isolation from the other.

sessor whether he happens to find himself in the most secluded of mountain retreats or is engaged on exemplary and redemptive work among the crowded habitations of men, or else in one of the heavens — or the hells. His is not a solitude that depends on any special conditions of place or time, true solitude being indeed but another name for that Voidness which is also the Fullness, a first-fruit of that self-naughting which is also Self-knowing.

Three levels are broadly distinguishable in respect of the comprehension of Reality: First, things may be regarded from the point of view of Ignorance, which is that of the ordinary man, concerned as he is with appearances and with his own reactions to them. It is he, the "common man," held up to flattery in our day as if he were a very pattern of humanity, who is the pathetic dreamer, the incorrigible sentimentalist, the romantic, in contrast to the spiritual man, now at a discount, who is the only true realist, the "practical man" in the widest sense of the word. From an ignorant or "profane" point of view things are considered under the aspect of separativity only, and treated as if they were self-contained entities; that is to say, as if each of them were "carrying within itself its own sufficient cause." Under such circumstances the manifested world appears in the guise of an unresolvable multiplicity, in which the individualization and consequently the opposition of persons or things (through their mutual limitation and inescapable competition) is raised to the highest possible power, thus spelling insecurity and suffering for all concerned; such being, moreover, the inevitable fruit of dualism, of participation in the Tree of Knowledge of Good and Evil.

Secondly, one has the view that comes with an awakening perception of the fallacy underlying the world and its formal appearances. In that case the disillusioned being seeks deliverance in the formlessness of the Unmanifest, where all things subsist unchanged and unchangeable within the bosom of their parent cause, in a state that might be described as one of permanent actuality, whence their coming out to be manifested in one of the worlds can only partake of the nature of an illusion; that is to say, their existence pertains to a lesser order of reality that masks, by the various phenomena it gives rise to, its own lack of true selfhood.* This point of view corresponds with the

* One must remind the reader that current loose speaking has practically converted the word "illusion" into a synonym of "unreal"; and this in turn has given rise to frequent misunderstandings on the subject of the Buddhist

attainment of a Nirvana still able to be regarded as one of the
twin terms of an opposition, the other term being that state of
Ignorance mentioned previously, whereby beings remain imprisoned in the Round and subject to change and suffering.
Those who attain such a state of knowledge are usually referred
to, in the Mahāyānist books, under the name of *Pratyeka Bud-*
dhas (the Tibetan equivalent means *Self-Buddhas*), with whom
are also coupled those whom the Tibetans call "hearers" (in
Sanskrit known as *Sravakas*) and who are supposed, though
somewhat unfairly, to represent the devotees of the rival or
Hīnayānist school, that to which the southern Buddhists, those
of Ceylon and Burma, belong. These two types have provided
a favourite target for criticism on the part of all the Mahāyānist
writers, whose mention of them has come to constitute a kind
of refrain, a matter of "method," probably, rather than one to
be taken as referring to actual facts. Thus it is said that the
Sravakas and *Pratyeka Buddhas* rest content with deliverance
as far as they themselves are concerned (hence the name *Self-*
Buddhas), but fail to include in their point of view all their fellow beings still condemned to flounder in the whirlpool of the
Round; in other words, they succeed in breaking loose from
the world and its illusion, but they are unable to reintegrate it
positively, stopping short, as they do, at negation. For such as
them, therefore, Nirvana, though undoubtedly attained in one
sense, yet remains essentially as the *Non-Round;* just as the
Round itself continues to be similarly regarded as *Non-Nirvana,*
without any means being found of reducing the contrasted concepts to unity. Thus the withdrawal of attention from the
world as such, which marks a legitimate and indeed a necessary stage in the process of enlightenment, if it should ever be
taken for a final term, can land one in an intellectual blind al-
ley, bringing about a kind of lofty self-imprisonment, a withdrawal into a blissful supra-consciousness which yet implies
privation of the one essential thing, since it stops short of the
supreme non-duality.

Thirdly and lastly, there is the point of view (if one can still
describe as such what is really a total synthesis embracing all
possible points of view) of Bodhisattvahood, whereby the es-

---

teachings about the illusory nature of the world and its contents. Nothing
can ever be opposable to reality: something that is truly unreal cannot enjoy
any kind of existence, not even in imagination; whereas an illusion is something that makes game of the senses of an observer by seeming to possess a
character other than its own; typically, by appearing more self-sufficient than
it really is.

sential non-duality of the Round, symbolized by Form, and of Nirvana, symbolized by Voidness, is clearly perceived, compared with which Knowledge, as a typical Mahāyānist writer would probably have added, "all the virtues and achievements of countless millions of *Pratyeka Buddhas* and *Sravakas* during successive æons are nothing worth." This supreme realization, goal of the spiritual life, goes under the name of the *Prajna Paramitā* or Wisdom Transcendent (the Tibetans actually give it as "the transcending of Wisdom"); and a Bodhisattva is one who has succeeded in realizing this doctrine *effectively,* so that it can be said that possession of the *Prajna Paramitā* constitutes the characteristic *note* by which the Bodhisattva is to be known.* Once having realized it, and from the very fact of having done so, the Bodhisattva, though no longer involved in Existence under any law of necessity, freely decides — so the saying goes — "to remain in the Round as long as a single blade of grass shall remain undelivered from suffering," so that one and all may pass together through Nirvana's gates as the single, recollected Self that they already are in essence. Needless to say, however, the sentimentalism of the masses, even in Tibet, does not spare this doctrine altogether, for even there people will persist in reading into its symbolism some kind of moral lesson, according to which the Bodhisattva, in contrast to the selfish *Pratyeka Buddhas,* "refuses Nirvana," out of compassion for the beings (ourselves!) undergoing the painful experiences of the Round of Existence. Rightly interpreted, even such a coloured picture is not entirely devoid of meaning; its underlying implications are fairly clear, but naturally the tendency of simple minds is to take each detail separately and literally, thus sacrificing the unity of the idea in favour of some version more in accord with their own individualistic bias.

There is, however, one difficulty of interpretation which does actually arise from the fact that, according to the usual convention, Bodhisattvahood denotes the state penultimate to the attainment of Buddhahood and not the supreme realization itself. Thus it is said that the Bodhisattva "takes possession" of the fi-

* There is a famous formula that expresses this doctrine as concisely as possible; it is taken from a book bearing the same title of *Prajna Paramitā* and runs as follows:

> *"Form (it is) void:*
> *The Void Itself (is) form."*

By these words the Supreme Identity is given expression, hence this formula may be regarded as an epitome of all Knowledge. In translation, the unavoidable introduction of the word "is," wanting in the Tibetan version, destroys a great deal of the force of the original.

nal revelation that makes of him a Buddha, and similarly the
Buddha is spoken of as having been "still a Bodhisattva" at
such and such a time. In face of what has been said above it
may well be asked how a Bodhisattva can ever be regarded as
inferior in status to a Buddha, seeing that Bodhisattvahood, as
we have already seen, corresponds by definition to the state of
one who not only has realized the Void, in a transcendent sense,
but also has realized it in the World itself, in an immanent
sense, this double realization (as we are still forced to describe
it) being for him not twofold but one and only. It is evident
that the attainment of this, the supreme unitive Knowledge, is
in fact that which constitutes Nirvana or Buddhahood, so that
it is difficult to see how Bodhisattvahood can be referred to as
a penultimate state at all — yet the very existence of the two
separate terms must be intended to correspond to some reality
in spite of an apparent redundancy affecting their use, at least
in certain contexts.

The solution appears to lie in a twofold use of the name Bodhisattva itself. In the first place it can be used more loosely, in
order to denote the all-but-perfected saint, on the threshold of
Buddhahood, or even any unusually saintly person — I was
told, for instance, that "we will find you 'a Bodhisattva' to be
your teacher." In the second place it can be used in reference
to one who is identical with Buddha by right of Knowledge,
but who, in the exercise of his work of salvation for the benefit
of creatures, *recapitulates* some of the stages of the Way *for exemplary reasons*, as a "shower of the Way." * In that sense he
redescends into the Round rather than remains in it, though
the latter may be the impression produced on the minds of beings, ever prone to be deceived by external appearances. One
then has to do with an *Avatāra* (to use the well-known Sanskrit term); that is to say, with a specific descent of the Principle into Manifestation, a descent — to quote the words of
Ānanda Coomaraswamy — of the Light of Lights, as *a* light but
not as another Light. As I have just pointed out, such a descent
implies the assumption of a limit — in other words, of an individual form, or of something analogous if the descent were to
take place into a world other than our own, defined, as it would
then be, by another set of conditions; but such a self-limiting
need not shock us, since the realization of the *Prajna Paramitā*,
of the essential non-duality of the Void and Form, obviously
carries with it the power of assuming any and every form at

* This title is one that is habitually bestowed on the Buddha Himself.

will, as well as no form. Thus it is written of him who is established in the Knowledge of *Kun-ji*, the All-Principle, that "there will be no end of my *Avatāras*, who will appear in inconceivable millions of numbers and shapes, and who will adopt various methods suitable for the control of every kind of being."

At this point it may be advisable to guard against a possible misunderstanding as being one likely to arise in consequence of certain prevailing tendencies of present-day thought. That such might well be the case is evidenced by the following question that was recently put to me by a friend who asked whether, according to the precedent of the Bodhisattva's non-withdrawal from the Round of Existence, one was not justified in regarding as fundamentally sound the attitude of the man who says that he is prepared to make the best of the world as he finds it, enjoying life as far as he can, without troubling his head overmuch with thoughts of the beyond and the hereafter; was this not an indication of a more realistic outlook, it was asked, than the "other-worldliness" of the typically religious view of life?

At a first examination it might indeed appear that those who argue thus are not entirely at fault. Nevertheless, there is a fallacy lurking behind the question so put, even without taking into account the mixture of motives behind it, motives that are bound up with a hankering, on the part of the modern world, after a belief that the fruits of spirituality can be enjoyed without renouncing certain cherished habits and prejudices of an individualistic nature; while there sometimes also enters in a certain not entirely ununderstandable feeling of sympathy for the good-natured tolerance of the man who is prepared to live and let live, as contrasted with the narrow exclusiveness that so frequently mars the purity of a professedly religious outlook.

The real defect in the argument, however, is of quite a different order from these superficial matters of feeling, residing as it does in a false assimilation made on the strength of a purely specious similarity between the attitude of the amiable, easygoing, and common-sensical person already mentioned and that of the Bodhisattva, with his realization of universal non-duality. The two cases differ fundamentally for the simple reason that in the first instance the world is accepted *passively* — that is to say, is taken at its face value, under the aspect of separativity extending to everything within it, without any serious attempt being made to reduce things to unity through the knowledge of a principle superior to their multiplicity and distinction. The phenomenal reality of the world is thus treated as if it were valid in its own right; in other words, it is considered from the point of view of Ignorance, and this is as true in the case of a man who tries to make the best of things as of a confirmed pessimist. At most one has to do with a more amiable brand of profanity, as compared with what is obviously a more disagreeable one.

Such a view of things does in fact start off by ignoring what is a prime condition for any aspirant towards Bodhisattvahood; namely, an understanding of the essentially impermanent character of the world and its contents, not merely in a theoretical sense, as when one studies a doctrine through books, nor in an "ideal" sense, through developing a kind of vague sympathy for that same doctrine, but effectively, so that the knowledge in question may take root in one's very being, causing the apparent self-sufficiency of separate objects to lose all its fascination for the mind; for only when attention has been thus withdrawn from whatever is fragmentary and perishable will it be possible to become poised in "one-pointed" contemplation of That which alone possesses the true nature of Selfhood, "being unto Itself its own sufficient Cause."

The lama Gyaltshan at P'hiyang had repeatedly said to me that without an effective grasp of the Doctrine of Impermanence all further progress in the Way was an impossibility: in that negating of all that is in itself negative (because regarded in abstraction from its principle — note the use of the double negative resulting in an affirmation) is to be found the clue to the mystery. It can thus be readily understood that if the Bodhisattva is free to remain in the world for the sake of the creatures still subject to the delusion of separativity, he does so with his eyes open. Where they see "other" things all around them, things that seem to them only too solid and substantial, he only perceives their voidness, or in other words their lack of genuine Self-nature. Multiple forms that, to the creature, appear opaque and self-contained have become for him of such perfect transparency as to reveal, or to veil no longer (note the double use of a selfsame root) the supreme Thatness, *devoid* as it is of all particularization, restriction, relativity, distinction, and the like. Nay, more, to his singleness of eye, the negative voidness of worldly objects and the positive Voidness that translates a freedom from form and all other limiting conditions are but one Voidness unqualified, coinciding in that ultimate

Reality concerning which all one dares to say is "Not this, not this."

Whereas the profane man, the "ordinary person," is in the Round by compulsion of mediate causes, "under the law" as St. Paul would have said, the Bodhisattva is there but "playfully," that is to say freely, in virtue of his identification with *Kun-ji*, the Prime Cause of All, which being alone absolutely unlimited is also alone absolutely free. Where the former submits to the world and its ways, with or without a semblance of willingness, but in any case in passive mode, the latter may be said to reintegrate the world in active mode; while somewhere midway between these two positions can be placed the *Pratyeka Buddha* (with whom the common run of religious-minded persons might be associated, since their aim of a personal salvation is in many ways comparable with his, though on a somewhat lower plane), of whom it can be said that he has effectively rejected the bonds of worldly existence (in realizing its impermanence), but has stopped short of reintegrating it. In his case it is rather Nirvana that is accepted in passive mode, as against the Bodhisattva's realization, which is active through and through to the point of melting away every factor of opposition in the ultimate crucible of non-dual knowledge. Thus, for him, the realization of the impermanence of the world and the eventual reintegration of that world hang together; the first, leading to Knowledge of the universal voidness, corresponds to Wisdom, and the second, symbolised by the Bodhisattva's Compassion, corresponds to Method, this twofold realization being, as already mentioned, the "note" by which true Bodhisattvahood can be recognized — but by a Bodhisattva only, be it understood, since no one else is qualified for such an act of recognition, which can be arrived at by no inferential process, but only as the outcome of an infallible and direct perception — and any omission of the former realization will preclude all possibility of attaining the latter. This disposes of any claims made on behalf of the man who attempts to integrate either himself or the world without at the same time fathoming their impermanence in more than just the superficial sense of a theoretical admission that everything must some day have an end. It was important to clear up this point before returning to the consideration of the Bodhisattva as he appears from the standpoint of humanity — that is to say, under the inevitable fragmentation into aspects that goes with any view short of his own all-embracing comprehension. From the point of view of individual beings, that aspect of his realization which strikes them most vividly is his Compassion, the fundamental character of which has, so one hopes, been made somewhat clearer as a result of the foregoing rather long-drawn-out theoretical explanations.

It must be repeated that this "Cosmic Charity" (to borrow an expressive term belonging to the Islamic doctrine) is something essentially different from the ordinary human feelings of pity, hopelessly tangled, as they usually are, with self-pity; though it would also be true to say that whatever is genuine in human pity is a reflection, at the individual level, of the limitless compassion flowing out of the Bodhisattva's heart, for which reason even that feeling is able to be taken for an adequate symbol of its universal prototype. It is also good to remember that perfect charity is not a quality opposable to justice, to order or harmony in the widest sense, since its realization is an impossibility in default of an equally perfect impartiality or "non-attachment." Towards the suffering beings in the Round, severally drugged with the three poisons of Anger, Desire-Attachment, and Ignorance, the Bodhisattva, like the good physician that he is, will exercise his merciful office not with a view to the mere assuaging of symptoms that leave the more deep-seated causes of the disease untouched; but in the manner most conducive to his patient's real recovery he will be prepared to employ every kind of "skilful means," which may at times partake of the severest character, and he will show himself under every conceivable aspect, from the gentlest to the most appalling, nor will he stop short at any ministration however pleasant or however rigorous until, as the saying goes, "the last blade of grass shall have attained Deliverance."

This lesson is clearly brought out in the iconographical representation of the various Bodhisattvas, such as are displayed on the walls of every temple, for they are made to appear not merely under their benign or attractive forms but also in a guise no less fearsome to behold. Even the All-Merciful Chenrezig himself, the supreme protector of Tibet and explicit type of a Buddha's mercy, possesses his complementary form of *Nagpo-Chhenpo*, the Great Black One; similarly, the Bodhisattva of Wisdom, *Jamyang*, can also appear sometimes as *Dorje-Djigched*, the Ever-subsisting Maker of Fear, chosen to be the chief tutelary of the Yellow-Hatted Order, this aspect being depicted as a most terrible apparition, many-headed and provided with countless limbs, clasped in the arms of his equally bloodthirsty Consort-Energy and dancing ecstatically upon the prostrate bodies of men and animals, whose ignorance makes them his victims. Those who are able to penetrate into the symbolism of this redoubtable double of the All-Wise One will also know that his dance is no other than the Round of Existence itself and his kingdom the very process of becoming. If the presence of an individual form, with the restrictions that this implies, spells a proportionate measure of suffering for the being concerned, that suffering (which must of course be interpreted in the widest possible sense of the word) can itself be considered under either of the two complementary aspects of justice and mercy: under the first, because privation, such as is implied by the existence of a limit of any kind, produces suffering of its own accord, because, fundamentally, the suffering *is* the privation and not something added to it by way of retributive sanction or otherwise — though at a certain level of realization such a symbolism is both theoretically legitimate as well as useful practically when considered from the point of view of the being's own spiritual development; under the second, because suffering, in so far as it leads men into self-questioning, is able to become a pointer towards the spiritual path, being thus indeed counted as the first of the Four Truths that together constitute the Buddha's call to a radical change of heart, to that *metanoesis* which is so inadequately rendered by the word "repentance" with its implicitly sentimental notion of regret. Viewed under such an aspect, therefore, suffering must be regarded first and foremost as part of the mechanism of a merciful providence, but for which there would be small hope of deliverance for anyone. It is not a question of trying to explain away the facts of suffering "optimistically" by resorting to the use of a euphemistic phraseology, but of showing the place that it occupies in relation to the aspect of divine Clemency, as well as its more obvious connexion with the complementary aspect of Rigour.

The above considerations also have some bearing on a point that often has worried European students of Eastern doctrines, who fail to understand how desire, whether admitted to play the leading part in the Round of Existence ascribed to it by Buddhism or not, can ever come to be extinguished in a being, since it is evident that it cannot be restrained by sheer willpower such as can only stop short at dealing with the action prompted by this or that desire, either by way of impulsion or repression, whereas the desire itself will have arisen, in the

first place, out of the substratum of the being's unconsciousness where the will is inoperative; this quite apart from the
fact that the nature of Will itself is too closely related to that
of Desire pure and simple to provide an entirely adequate instrument for its control. For the average Western mind, with
its habit of concentrating all its attention on problems of moral
casuistry — that is to say, on questions concerning the right or
wrong use of will-power in respect of actions — the Buddha's
teaching on the subject of desire and its cessation is apt to
prove extremely puzzling.

Yet this side of the doctrine is not so abstruse as to defy at
least a theoretical grasp of the principles underlying it. What
is usually missed in the argument is the fact that, just as in the
case of suffering, unsatisfied desire, though in one sense an evil
in that it interposes a distraction between the being and its
realization of unity, is also just (therefore a good) in so far as it
genuinely registers a lack of something — the pertinent question is a lack of what? In fact all our separate desires are proportioned exactly to the measure of our privation of the One
Essential, and if we treat different things as successively desirable or the reverse, this habit arises from a failure to understand that nothing whatsoever can be called desirable excepting only *The* Desirable; whence it is easy to see that the
extinction of all desire and its fulfilment hang together, in exactly the same sense as death to self (the "self-denial" of the
Gospels) and birth to the Self spell one and the same thing.
Our alternate loves and hates, from the most trivial to the most
noble or ignoble, are, one and all, an unconscious tribute laid
by Ignorance at the feet of Knowledge, so that, in that sense,
they once again are as much an expression of the Divine Mercy
(because their attendant suffering is the factor that continually
impels a being to seek a way of liberation) as they are an expression of the Divine Rigour through the privation registered
by their very presence, which constitutes its own automatically
operative sanction.

Let us return, however, to the consideration of the symbolism behind the great variety of forms described in the Tantric
books or otherwise occurring in works of art of Tantric inspiration, a symbolism that, moreover, provides a most important
technical resource for the practice of the various spiritual disciplines attached to the Tantric doctrines, both Hindu and Buddhist. Thus one is led to see that the kindlier aspects can, when
necessary, be made to function as their own apparent opposites,

by which means both the complementarism and the interpenetration of the aspects of mercy and severity are vividly brought out, only to be succeeded by the coincidence of those same two aspects in a "two-less" identity that dissolves all the force of their opposition. Again and again the symbolical relationships are reversed in an unending play of antithesis and identification, as attractive forms give way to fierce ones, the most repellent features of which are, however, in their turn found to represent the characteristic attributes of the benign aspect and so on; until in the end, by dint of alternate manifestation, interchange and dissolution of forms,* Form itself loses its restrictive power over the mind of the devotee, leaving him henceforth free to contemplate through the eye of true Intelligence the non-duality of That which is to be known by those who find the way to carry their solitude ever with them, even in the world. So is one brought back once again to the Bodhisattva's knowledge, whereby the immanent is seen to be ultimately indistinguishable from the transcendent, the phenomenal from the real, the world of forms from the Void Itself. In all this there is never a question of any "monistic" or "pantheistic" confusion — one is bound to mention this point in view of repeated attempts to foist these purely Western notions, modern at that, upon Oriental thought, from a variety of motives — but of the realization of a unity which is called "two-less" from the very fact that in it all things are essentially "fused but not confused," to quote a phrase of Meister Eckhard.

This two-less Knowledge, possession of which constitutes the Sage, is as the warp to the entire weft of Tibetan tradition. One encounters it at every turn, now more explicit, now at once veiled and revealed by symbols, now faintly echoed in the thoughts and words of quite simple people, like a theme that unfolds itself in continual self-pursuit through an endless series of episodes and modulations, a fugue that will not modulate into its final close "so long as one insect or one blade of grass remains undelivered from the Round." The Bodhisattva provides the specific type of the spiritual life in Tibet, and it is in such terms that the idea of "sanctity" is always interpreted in all the lands where the lamaic tradition holds sway.

* The reader is again referred to the details given in the long quotation towards the end of Chapter xv. This text is typical of its kind, and is taken from a book primarily designed to serve as a practical manual for initiates working under direction of a qualified teacher or *guru;* the underlying aim of the discipline to which that theory serves as a key is a personal realization to be arrived at by means of the applied symbolism.

Space does not allow of anything like a comprehensive survey of the manifold applications to which the conception of Bodhisattvahood has given rise in all orders; nor would such an attempt work out profitably for the reader, since it could only result in leaving the essential idea snowed under a mass of indigestible, if separately interesting detail; the important thing to grasp, however, is that it is this doctrine that gives its form to the idea of spirituality as conceived in all the Tibetan world, especially under its two principial aspects of Compassion and Skilful Means. Sufficient has been said concerning what the former is or is not for little room to be left for misunderstanding as to the nature of this characteristic trait of the Bodhisattva; while in regard to the latter one can only point out the fact that the saint, in Tibet, is regarded first and foremost as one endowed with "skill," as it were an "artist in spirituality," and only secondarily under the aspect of individual goodness. Here one sees a certain difference of point of view, as between the Buddhist and the ordinary Christian picture of sainthood, bound up with the degrees of emphasis respectively given to ethical and intellectual values. Not that one wishes to suggest the existence of a fundamental incompatibility between the two conceptions; all that need be pointed out is that in the Buddhist tradition the practice of those portions of "the Eightfold Path" that relate to action and moral behaviour in general, though considered indispensable just as in the case of the sister tradition, are on the whole taken for granted when speaking of the saints, the chief attention in their case being drawn to the purely intellectual virtue of Perfect Contemplation, which forms the climax of the eightfold catalogue; whereas with Christianity, though its teaching on the supremacy of Contemplation over Action does not differ in principle from that of the Oriental traditions, there has been a certain tendency, much increased in modern times through the intrusion of "humanism" (itself an anti-Christian movement), to overstress individual and especially social considerations. Moreover, abuses apart, such a tendency always goes to a certain extent with the "religious" as compared with the purely metaphysical point of view, influencing not only popular conceptions but also many perfectly orthodox formulations of the doctrine itself.

Two examples will have to suffice as illustrations of the workings of the Bodhisattva idea in the spiritual life of the Tibetans. The one applies to the people at large, though admittedly at many different degrees of comprehension; the other to those who have proceeded a considerable way in the direction of realization, or at least whose aspirations and efforts are definitely set in that direction. The first example is taken from the widespread practice of invocation, usually on a rosary, of the *Mani* formula already mentioned in earlier chapters, which itself embodies a traditional communication the origin of which goes back to the Bodhisattva Chenrezig, the Patron of Tibet, for whose influence the person of the Dalai Lama himself serves as a focus.

When a person is about to begin saying his rosary he often preludes his reciting of the actual formula by a short dedicatory verse in honour of Chenrezig, its originator, addressed to him under his alternative name of the All-Compassionate. After this follows the repetition of the *Mani,* for a longer or shorter time, with more or less concentration as the case may be. When these devotions are finished, the invoking person (who incidentally will have been the recipient of a minor initiation qualifying him to use this particular ritual support) concludes with another short verse, the gist of which is as follows: "By the merit of this (invocation) to (my)self having accrued (i.e., by my having realized) the power of Chenrezig, may beings without a single exception be established in the land of the Norm (a periphasis for the supreme realization)." However attentively or carelessly these thoughts may be uttered, they contain an explicit as well as implicit reference to the "Bodhisattva's vow" not to enter Nirvana before all beings have been delivered from the Round and its suffering; the important thing to note is that this rite postulates a point of view that does not stop short at a personal deliverance, like that for which the *Pratyeka Buddhas* are constantly being reproached, since it goes as far as actually to envisage the redescent into the world with a view to its eventual reintegration in the Principle. That it should be possible for a conception of this order to be attached to a rite as popular as the *Mani* has become in Tibet is extremely significant.

Naturally too much must not be read into the above statement; the fact is that Tibetans, like other people, do often dream of spending more or less prolonged periods of care-free enjoyment in other and happier worlds, such as the Western Paradise presided over by Chenrezig and his teacher the Buddha Amitabha. The simple-minded likewise indulge in visions of a happy rebirth in a literal sense here on earth, forgetful as

they are of the oft-quoted phrase declaring "the individual(ity)
to be perishable, and devoid of true self(hood)": yet the fact
remains that even in the case of a rite so generally practised the
expressed intention goes far beyond the individual order — indeed, to the point of embracing the totality of beings and
worlds in a single universal synthesis in which individual distinctions find no place, so that one can justly claim that the
metaphysical horizon against which the rite is to be performed
is literally limitless by its own showing and that no concession
of principle has actually been made by way of encouraging self-
interest of the ordinary kind.

All that now remains is to speak of those who stand at the
other end of the intellectual scale from the many simple people who, in comparative unconsciousness, give utterance to the
Bodhisattva's awe-inspiring vow as they finish telling the beads
of their rosaries. I am thinking of those persons (and they are
by no means rare in Tibet) who have felt the call to self-dedi-
cation in the spiritual life so imperatively as to be unable to divide their energies any further, as between the pursuit of the
supreme knowledge and ordinary private interests of whatever
order. These people commonly go under the name of *naldjorpas,* meaning "obtainers of tranquillity," because they have cut
themselves free of the multi-directional pulls of a life lived
more or less profanely, leaving themselves in a state of "one-
pointed" contemplation that no distraction coming from outside is henceforward able to disturb. This wholehearted expression of the yearning for sainthood will provide us with our second example, which can, however, only be described in the
most general terms, since one who has not himself experienced,
at least in a high degree, the descent of the Bodhisattva into his
own heart is unfitted to offer any really profound comment on
the subject; and the same applies to his hearers, who unless
they are able, by resorting to the appropriate means, to approach a similar realization, will be equally incapable of understanding the deeper significance of the doctrine offered to
them. All that one can be concerned with here is not so much
the nature of the *naldjorpa's* experience in itself — about which
I am not qualified to pronounce — as the part which that experience, whatever may be its nature, plays in the Tibetan tradition as a whole and what kind of influence it represents in regard to giving its specific form to the idea of sainthood lived
according to the Bodhisattva pattern.

One reservation must be made, however; not everyone

loosely described as a *naldjorpa* is so effectively, and due allowance must be made for some who, though possibly qualified to embrace the life of spiritual abandonment, have for one reason or another strayed from the strait and narrow path, whether by yielding to the lure of unusual psychic and physical powers (such as often develop incidentally as a result of following certain disciplines) or from any other cause equally contingent.* These people, though they may continue to style themselves *naldjorpas* and be accepted as such, have really arrived at an intellectual dead end, or even worse in some cases. Nevertheless, the real thing not only exists, but it is that element which, above all, lends colour to the whole spiritual life in Tibet, constituting, as it were, the *axis* in relation to which all else must be situated and ultimately judged.

The genuine *naldjorpa*, in principle as in practice, stands outside the pale of society, so much so that if he has been a monk he usually casts off the monastic habit (and the rule it represents) as a sign that he has cut adrift from all that goes with organized existence, letting "the wind that bloweth where it listeth" carry him in whatever direction it will. Often he is to be met with among the hermits dwelling on the edge of the great glaciers, or else wandering along one of the many tracks that lead hither and thither across the plateau, and even sometimes, as at Lachhen for instance, staying quietly not far from human dwellings, in fairly close touch with social life though no longer involved in it; or if he be so minded, there is nothing to prevent him from seemingly participating in outward activities, of whatever nature, always provided that his solitude of spirit be such as to make it a matter of indifference to him where he is or what he is supposed to be doing or not doing.

Most, if not all, of these contemplatives are initiates of some particular spiritual line, of which a number exist, each having certain methods peculiar to it and requiring of its sons — one must not call them "members" — various special qualifications, apart from the general qualification that is implied in all initi-

---

* Professed spiritual seekers of European origin seem especially prone to develop an unhealthy interest in extraordinary phenomena of all kinds, and that despite the calculated warnings of so many of the great teachers of both East and West. An innate curiosity as well as an experimentalism that is constantly being stimulated by modern "scientific" training and propaganda is largely responsible for this tendency, which is only too apt to turn into an insatiable craving, as a result of which the person concerned, when he does not suffer serious psychological perversion, at least becomes fatally imprisoned in the world of appearances and in an egocentric enjoyment of marvels, real or supposed.

ability. Through an unbroken traditional succession from master to pupil, each such line may be said to constitute a separate current of spiritual influence, a channel that after issuing
from the same parent stream will by and by go to lose itself,
with all the others, in the uncharted ocean, large as the Bodhisattva's compassion, which is called Knowledge of the Voidness.

One misconception must be avoided, however, since it is
likely to arise with certain habits of mind and since it also
makes a peculiarly subtle appeal: the Bodhisattva's vow must
never be taken to imply that the saving of mankind, or even of
all creation, should become *an end in itself* for the apprentice
in spirituality. Nothing short of the naked Truth, shorn of all
contingencies and restrictions, merits to be called Desirable, its
pursuit alone can be called Activity unqualified; only one who
has been stripped of his attachments to everything except the
Truth without a rival or associate can hope to attain it. Having
attained it, he does, in fact, become qualified to save the world,
but should he at any stage yield to the supremely diabolical
temptation (the one offered by Satan to Christ upon the high
mountain) of making the world's salvation into his first aim,
then he must pay the price of his altruistic idolatry and remain
irremediably chained to the world and its otherness. A hair separates the two positions, and one can only recall in this connexion the remark quoted earlier to the effect that saving the world
is the Bodhisattva's play. The danger I have been speaking of
represents the ultimate temptation of the saint, being both the
hardest to detect and the most fatal if it is yielded to. This principle is, moreover, operative not only at the highest level but
even at inferior levels too; to causes of this order must be ascribed the non-success that, in so large a measure, attends the
well-meaning and often strenuous efforts of humanitarianly inclined people the world over, for it is their very obsession with
the cause of "others" that spells defeat from the start, in spite
of their own obvious sincerity.

Tibetans, on the other hand, even comparatively ignorant
ones, seem to have retained some grasp of the principle at
work; they look upon the *naldjorpas* as being first and foremost
the protectors of humanity, without whose "actionless" activity
the ship of mankind would irremediably founder. Unentangled,
as they are, in either duties or rights, whether of the family or
the state or of a professional kind, it is their very impartiality
towards worldly affairs that constitutes their power, in which

all those who are still, to a greater or lesser extent, "involved" by various ties of an individual and social order also participate, if indirectly. For this reason, it would appear not so much wicked as *suicidal* if society were, on any plea, to try to place restrictions in the way of those who wish to join the ranks of this spiritual élite, even while admitting that those ranks will contain a certain proportion of self-deceived persons and even some who are minded to make capital of the reverence in which they are held by the people at large.

Moreover, no one would even think of impertinently questioning the motives or methods of anyone so engaged. Every Tibetan understands that sainthood, at any degree of realization, will imply a different set of values from those that govern the judgment of the ordinary man: what the latter regards as important and obvious will often, to the spiritually minded, seem trivial and, in any case, highly contestable. Indeed, the last statement itself betrays an inaccuracy: for one who *knows* by the direct insight born of realization the kind of questions that trouble the ignorant do not even arise, nor do they enter into the realm of choice or discussion. True intelligence goes straight to the mark and requires no tortuous marshalling of pros and cons to bolster up its conclusions. Nothing would seem more illogical to the Tibetan mind than to expect the same kind of judgment from a Knower, even from one who is so to a partial extent only, and an ignoramus, which, in the deepest sense, is the state of the majority of mankind, including most of those whom the world looks on as learned or powerful or active, for it is they, and those who admire and follow them, who are the truly impractical visionaries, as compared with the *naldjorpa*, who is the unshakable realist because like Mary in the Gospel "he hath chosen that good part."

It must not be thought that this recognition of the freedom to be earned through following the spiritual path will imply any kind of antinomianism, though some may have been tempted to think so. A realization that places one in a state of complete harmony with the source of all law can dispense one from its manifold applications but cannot oppose one to it in principle; moreover it is knowledge that provides a valid sanction for all applications on the legal plane (I am referring to law in the very widest sense of the word), and not vice versa. At the very highest level, therefore, the realization that "His service is perfect freedom," from being merely theoretical becomes effective, and one who attains this state can rightly claim that he is no longer "under the law," but is, as the Hindus would say, henceforth "beyond caste."

The foregoing remark, however, gives rise to another, no less important in its way, since it affects those people — and they are not a few — who have come to yearn for a life of non-attachment, but who think that they will attain it by a premature and purely external casting-off of the bonds of form, whether religious or other. This state of mind on the part of the would-be "mystic" * is frequently evidenced by the habit of ceaselessly tilting at "orthodoxy," professedly in the name of "the spirit" as against "the letter," and by an instinctive fear and suspicion of whatever pertains to the formal order in general. Into this attitude of mind many different elements have entered in — individualism, sentimentalism, and other modernistic influences. What these people miss is the fact that there are two ways of being outside form, the one supra-formal, because form has been transcended, the other infra-formal, because its possibilities as a "support" of realization at a certain level have been neglected. The one gives access to the formless truth, seat of freedom and universality, the other represents the most abysmal kind of ignorance, compared with which the formal attachments affecting even the most narrow-minded person must be looked upon as a state of comparative liberty. Form, to be transcended, must first of all be realized and thus integrated; it is impossible to *skip* the experience of form, and the wish to do so, in the name of personal liberty, merely betrays a futile kind of self-conceit. This temptation is especially strong among Western advocates of a return to spiritual values at the present moment, by reason of the individualistic turn of their minds, fostered in the course of their education. On this whole subject of form a great confusion of thought has occurred, which has not spared even those who appear, in other respects, to be highly gifted. What so many people refuse to face is the fact

* Throughout this book any careless use of the term "mystic" and its derivatives has been carefully avoided. Whatever meaning this word may originally have borne, later and, more especially, recent usage has so confused the issue as to make it impossible of application outside the sphere where it belongs historically; namely, that of Christian theology coupled with certain modes of realization attached to the same. When, as now so often happens, the term is stretched to cover the Oriental traditions, its employment becomes not only loose but positively misleading, in that it suggests a close parallelism, if not an identity, as between things pertaining to very different orders, which, if they resemble one another at all, do so in respect of features that are largely external and superficial. To speak, as so many do, of a Tibetan or Indian or Islamic mysticism is therefore both inappropriate in point of fact and otherwise undesirable by reason of the false assimilations to which it can give rise.

that in a time of intellectual confusion form, "the letter," is almost the last life-line uniting fallen man with the sources of his spirituality, so that it would be about true to say that today it matters more to observe forms correctly than to be "good" — a hard saying, perhaps, and a paradox, but one worth pondering over.

In a country like Tibet — that is to say, anywhere in the wide world where the continuity of tradition still remains substantially unbroken — an intending *naldjorpa* will necessarily set out on his journey from a point situated somewhere in a traditional whole all the constituent forms of which will themselves already have been moulded or, as one might have said, *informed* under the influence of the selfsame idea that he is in process of realizing integrally and beyond every limitation of form: for this is in fact what tradition means — it is time people were reminded of it — namely, an effective communication of principles of more-than-human origin, whether indirectly and at several removes, through use of the forms that will have arisen by applying those principles to contingent needs, or else immediately, after an "exhausting" of whatever makes for formal restriction of any kind, including the human individuality itself.

Thus the true *naldjorpa* (after whom the aspirant is similarly named only in anticipation and, as it were, by courtesy) is both he who realizes fully and effectively what others at best learn only partially through the various theoretical formulations of the doctrine as well as through their own participation in the traditional institutions in general, and also he who, in having thus realized it, himself becomes at one with the eternal fountainhead of tradition; for him his approach to the goal is rather in the nature of a homecoming, a recollection, than a fresh acquisition in the spiritual field; while, on its side, the tradition, as revealed through the line of realized sages and their successors, is but a redescent, spontaneously undertaken, into that same world of men whence the *naldjorpa* had originally started on his way, in the days of his comparative ignorance. The intimate interconnexion between the two functions is not difficult to perceive.

Nor is it difficult to recognize the prototype of which this picture is a tracing: the twofold course of outgoing and return, which true insight knows as "not-two," the laborious ascent towards the highest eminences of awareness and the "compassionate" redescent into the valley, is not all this but another version of the oft-told tale of Bodhisattvahood presently renewed, whereby it is also made plain that Tradition is itself an aspect of that providential redescent into the Round, one of the "skilful means" wherewith the Bodhisattva "playfully" works for creatures? A traditionless existence, whether for a single individual or a whole group, is one in which the presence of the Bodhisattva passes unnoticed, in which the *naldjorpa* is without honour, in which mankind, refusing to listen to any talk of self-abandonment, is abandoned to its own devices, as the very name of "humanism" so obviously confesses. This is the first of the lessons to be learned by a sojourn in the places where Tradition still prevails, where it has not yet been entirely forgotten that without the guidance, both direct and indirect, of those who have themselves taken possession of the summit, thus qualifying themselves, if need be, for a retracing of the way for the benefit of all the creatures whom "otherhood" still holds under its spell, the supreme peak will remain for ever unclimbable.

One can but repeat it: a personal reintegration in an authentically traditional form, as well as a "normal" participation in its attendant institutions, is an indispensable prelude to any adventure into the path of non-formal knowledge; by this means the individuality is conditioned, "tamed" as the Tibetans would say, in preparation for the supreme task that lies ahead. To those aspirants after the spiritual life who, in a purely negative sense at least, have come to reject the modern world and its profanity, but who, as far as any positive action is concerned, waver on the threshold perplexed by doubts as to the next step to be taken, to such as these the only advice that can be offered is the traditional one: namely, that they should first put themselves to rights as regards the formal order (wherein they are situated in virtue of the fact of being individuals at all) by regular adherence to a tradition; after which they should make use to the fullest extent of the means provided within the framework of that tradition, all the while testing their own success or otherwise by reference to its theory — that is, to its canonical formulations. Lastly, if and when a call to the beyond becomes irresistible, they should place themselves under the guidance of a spiritual master, the *guru* or "Root Lama," who is destined to introduce them into the path followed through the ages by the blessed company of the "thus-gone" (*Tathagatas*) — call them Buddhas, Yogis, Sufis, or what you will.

But one must beware of unauthorized teachers and bogus initiations; for the modern world has produced a heavy crop of self-appointed free lances, mostly men who toy with the equivocal term "mysticism"; here again traditional "orthodoxy" is about the only available touchstone and safeguard, a case of form acting as a protective envelope for the formless, by lending it its body. But protection always will be purchased at the price of restriction — this rule holds good in all orders, including the social order — hence the danger of "idolatry," which precisely consists in ascribing to any form in itself the unqualified character that belongs alone to the integral and formless Truth. Anywhere short of the goal, the way of realization will imply a certain polar balance between these two conceptions, the provisional and "symbolical" validity of forms and the untrammelled freedom of voidness. The Way has been fittingly called "narrow" and compared to walking along a razor's edge: by describing His tradition as the Middle Way the Buddha was expressing a similar idea. Bodhisattvahood is the virtue of being freed from both horns of the eternal dilemma, Form *versus* Void, by realizing them alike in their common and essential twolessness. Likewise the Bodhisattva's compassionate mission for the sake of dwellers in the land of becoming is itself the free expression of that same non-dual Knowledge that is, for him, the source of his redemptive power as well as his own intrinsic qualification.

Chapter XXIII

The Present State of Tibetan Art

IN THE COURSE of the preceding pages there have been frequent allusions to the subject of art and artists, often to the accompaniment of considerable detail. These allusions have been linked up, however, with the casual incidents of travel. What is now proposed is that three chapters should be devoted to an ordered, though necessarily brief, survey, even at the cost of occasionally recapitulating points made earlier.

My purpose is to describe the state of the art at the present time, to show what needs it supplies in the life of the people, and to hazard some opinions about the tendencies that are at work within it. I profess no interest in antiquity as such, though the unity and continuity of the Tibetan Tradition permits old and modern examples to be used indiscriminately. Periods and origins, affinities and distinguishing marks dear to the specialist's heart are questions foreign to my purpose. Whoever wishes to pursue that side of the subject must delve among the notes and papers to be found in the journals of learned societies. He can also see for himself actual examples in museums; indeed, it is to be hoped that students will not be alone in so doing; this chapter will have been in part wasted if it fails to rouse the desire of ordinary readers to visit such collections as are available to the public, for in artistic matters, such people are often surer in their judgment than professional scientists obsessed with detail. In this connexion I cannot refrain from relating an anecdote about some lamas who were brought over to England a few years ago as a feature in an Everest lecture. A guide was appointed to show them round the sights of London: as they walked through one of the museums he said: "There, you see all these marvellous treasures from your own and every other country. They are the property of the entire people, so that any day, without having to pay a penny, anyone, from the highest in the land to the poorest, can come and enjoy them!" "Then why don't they come?" asked the lamas naïvely, gazing round the deserted halls.

It must be admitted, however, that the atmosphere of a museum is unfavourable to the appreciation of works of art. When, as in Tibetan countries, one has seen them in use, handled freely — even the most precious of them — in private houses or temples, one discovers how lifeless they are when withdrawn from ordinary use into institutions where irrelevant considerations, such as rarity or date, play a big part in their arrangement for display. Still, museums are perhaps better than nothing and should be made use of for what they are worth until the day when mankind will become enlightened to the point of allowing the bulk of the exhibits to be set free to re-enter the service of life; always provided that by that time modern "advances" in the methods of warfare shall not have proved effective in wiping out the whole artistic heritage of the past, so dangerously assembled in a few confined areas.

My present aim, then, is to give a picture of an art in being, with the tradition that is its life-blood still active. It is the last of the great traditions of which this can be said unreservedly, for in many countries where the artistic sense has not yet been strangled in the grip of mechanized materialism the lingering strands of tradition, by the eclipse of their unifying principle, are sadly tangled and torn. Not that Tibet has remained entirely immune to the influence of the same disintegrating forces that have destroyed art elsewhere, and with it all that pure intellectuality which makes itself recognizable in the sense of form: in recent years a downward trend has been evident, affecting both patrons and artists. The history of the last few decades in Asia reveals how quickly the virus can do its work. Three generations ago India, China, and Japan contained many fine craftsmen who still found a market for good work; now there is a race between these three supremely artistic peoples as to which can uproot its traditions the quickest in order to produce the most grotesque travesties both of its own now despised native style and of the European fashions that are taking its place. In these countries the wounds are severe if not mortal, and to recapture the traditional spirit a tremendous change of heart would be the first essential. But in the case of Tibet the injuries are as yet skin-deep and might perhaps not be beyond healing, if the ruling classes, on whose taste the existence of high art is almost wholly dependent, could be got to understand what is happening, warned by their neighbours' errors.

A singular consistency of style is observable throughout the vast territories where the Tibetan Buddhist Tradition holds sway, in spite of wide climatic and racial diversity. It calls for a trained eye to distinguish whether a certain painting was executed in Lhasa or Mongolia, and whether the photograph of a building refers to Ladak or to Kham, with over a thousand miles to divide them. A collection of hammered and chased teapots assembled from all the corners of the area is not easy to classify by local differences at a first glance. So also, going backwards in time, the dating of a picture or statue within anything nearer than a century calls for an expert. Change has taken place, as can be proved by comparing works separated by several centuries, but development has been by steps so gradual that they merge into one another imperceptibly.

Two great currents of influence have mingled in Tibetan art and have been assimilated and transformed by the creative genius of the race: the influences of India and China. The first has reigned in the sphere of sacred things — purely ritual objects such as pictures (there is no such thing as secular painting) or sculpture still clearly show their kinship with the types found in the old Indian Buddhist centres — while the second exerted itself more in the things pertaining to worldly life, because cultured society in Tibet modelled its manners on those of the court of Peking, which for centuries occupied the suzerain position. The interior fittings and furnishings of houses, window-frames, tables, carpets, and food vessels borrowed many of their forms and characteristic motifs from the Chinese. Certain domestic necessities, such as porcelain and silks, were never locally manufactured, but continue to be imported from China to this day.

Architecture is perhaps the branch in which native designs show least evidence of foreign influence, though the Chinese style has affected a good many of the minor details. The fact that in Chinese buildings wood always played a dominant part, whereas in most of Tibet stone and sun-dried brick were the only materials available in large supply, caused the borrowing of forms to confine itself to features where the use of timber was almost unavoidable, such as pillars and the high-pitched roofs of pavilions. But though I have drawn attention to the two influences in question, an impression must not be conveyed inadvertently that Tibetan art remains a hybrid, the offspring of two imperfectly mated parents. On the contrary, the Tibetans have shown a superb power of assimilation in everything that they have borrowed; so that though their character, to which such a concept as conscious originality is totally foreign, has made them copy some things with extreme faithfulness, yet they have never failed to imbue their own spirit into them, welding features derived from such different sources into a logical and harmonious whole.

Another important point to note is that in Tibet a comparatively small part is played by what is usually termed "peasant art." A rough-and-ready division is often made between the two categories of "folk art" and of "civilized art," by which is meant art that appears to have been practised in a more self-conscious frame of mind. This doubtful distinction is founded on the observation that the arts that have enjoyed priestly and noble patronage exhibit great variety between style and style, country and country, period and period; whereas in the art-products that serve the needs of the peasantry a surprising resemblance can be observed in the work of races widely separated in time and space and heredity. Typical patterns found in peasant art are those based on simple geometrical shapes such as checks, stripes, or diapers, as well as on highly stylized representations of men and animals. One has but to look at a few baskets and wooden bowls and embroideries, say from Rumania and Morocco, Sweden and Nigeria, Greece and Peru, to discover striking similarities of pattern and colouring. In music something of the same sort is noticeable; in "folk-songs" remarkable parallelisms have been pointed out between places as remote as Sicily and Ceylon, Scotland and China. Some have explained the phenomenon by saying that "primitive" conditions of life have everywhere produced similar results; others, judging more profoundly, attribute it to the survival of ancient metaphysical symbols that were once widely diffused throughout mankind.

The expression "folk art" can only apply, therefore, where there is a marked difference of style and content between the arts of high society and those practised by and for simpler folk; or else where a traditional synthesis is maintained on a lower plane, as among peoples leading a narrowly tribal existence. Both these cases can be called normal; but there is also the anomalous, not to say pathological, example of modern Occidental civilization, where those who would normally constitute the élite have proved false to their charge and have substituted an anti-traditional counterfeit for true culture. In the nations concerned, the surviving folklore is the last weak link with the eternal source of tradition. Its symbolical motives, though their deeper implications have been lost sight of, are still vehicles of real power to the peasantry, who delight in them, instruments of unconscious initiation. Once let these links be snapped, and the entire people suffers cultural death, sinking into the abyss of proletarian barbarism. The human dignity of the peasant is exchanged for the degradation and justifiable discontent of the wage-slave in the urban or the rural factory. It is no cause for surprise that some well-meaning persons, after comparing the simple sincerity of peasant work with the pretentious emptiness of modernist invention, should have been led into making a cult of folk art. If the sight of beribboned bourgeois trying to frolic round the maypole sometimes appears ludicrous, one must in fairness recognize that these antics reveal a pathetic confession of our general failure.

We have been discussing cases where folk art can be spoken of distinctively; in Tibet, as was pointed out before, this is hardly possible, because all the elements that have concurred to give its form to Tibetan civilization have been combined into a very completely digested synthesis, adapted to the needs of men of all ranks and capacities. Even ordinary farmers, for instance, possess many objects that do not differ in any essential respect from those of the aristocracy, though naturally they are rougher in execution and employ less precious materials. This is perhaps the most convincing evidence of how thoroughly the artistic tradition has permeated the whole of society. Many a rough fellow whom we met showed that he could look for just the right points in a rug or a teapot, with a sureness of judgment that few of our own educated folk could emulate.

The craftsmen whom we encountered on the Satlej, though sprung from peasant families, were no mere rustics in their outlook, and the style and technique of their work were not inferior to those of many Lhasa workers. From the small villages of Sugnam and Labrang the two leading masters were supplying the needs of a wide tract of country, and people came to them from a radius of many days' journey to place their orders. Again, when our friends at Poo wanted to commission a fine teapot, they sent specially to Hlari, a village of Spiti. The rich men of Leh gave their orders for plate to the silversmith of Chhiling, quite an insignificant place, while to Rigzin, native

PRIVATE CHAPEL   *See page 334*

In the house of the Raja and Rani Tobgay Sonam Dorjé at Kalimpong

BHUTANESE MUSICIAN   *See page 341*

KHAMBA DANCER   *See page 342*

TEAPOT   *See page 330*
Worked in 1937 by the Chhiling silversmith

BELL AND DORJÉ   *See page 351*
Emblems of Wisdom and Method

DOMESTIC ARTICLES OF EVERYDAY USE   *See page* 332
Tea-table, teacups, bowl for barley meal, teapot on brazier, pile rug,
t'hanka by Byaltsan of P'hiyang

WHICH STYLE LOOKS THE BETTER? *See page 380*

Schoolboys at Gangtok

"The Notion of Emptiness Engenders Compassion"   *See page 144*

"May All Sentient Beings, without Exception, Become Buddha"

See page 150

T'hanka BELONGING TO H. H. THE MAHARAJA OF SIKKIM   *See page 63*

CELESTIAL BEINGS   *See page 212*
From a temple at Yuru in Ladak

of the small village of Kalatze, people applied from all over western Tibet when they wanted the best paintings. This degree of specialization, and the general recognition by the public of grades in the skill of artists, as well as the wide diffusion, in rural areas no less than in the capital, of crafts of a high order, are sure signs of artistic health.

I must now attempt a review of the actual arts as they exist today. Instead of dividing them according to the nature of the technique employed, as painting, sculpture, textiles, and music — a method that always tends to run to technicalities — I will try to deal with them as a whole, in relation to the departments of life to which they minister. Starting with the homes of the common people, the peasants, I will then pass on to the houses of the richer merchants and nobles, and end with the monasteries, where the arts have received their highest and noblest exposition. To all these places we have already paid many visits in this book, so that it is now only a question of rounding off the knowledge gained.

It would be well to turn back to the illustration showing a big family farmhouse in Ladak, arranged on a plan that is followed, with small variations, over a great part of the country. In districts where wood is plentiful, that material replaces masonry to a greater or lesser degree and the style becomes less massive in consequence. As such districts are bound to be rainy, the roof will be sloped instead of flat and one finds a glorified chalet type of building, such as occurs in Sikkim and, to judge from photographs, attains its highest development in the superb domestic architecture of Bhutan. But the flat-roofed model, of generous proportions, with its solid walls, lightened in the upper or residential story by the wooden window-frames with their serrated arrangement of beam-ends, must be taken as normal in the dry climatic conditions that have chiefly helped to mould the racial character. Again the reader must be reminded that the house we are describing is an ordinary peasant residence, and that its spaciousness and good taste do not imply more than average wealth in the owners. Comparing it with the homes of people of corresponding rank elsewhere, it seems fair to claim that the Tibetan small proprietor enjoys the best housing in the world: in most other countries such a house could only belong to people occupying a much superior station.

Passing to the interior, one chiefly notices that there are no unnecessary possessions. The habit of using the floor for sitting and sleeping, instead of chairs or beds, protects the fine propor-

tions of the rooms from being spoiled by the presence of over-
bulky pieces of furniture: mattresses and rugs and low tables
provide all that is needed for comfort and rest. Many objects
of utility are made more pleasing by the addition of some decorative embellishments, but accumulations of pictures on the
walls, vases, and knick-knacks are happily absent. That evil
only arises with cheap, large-scale production, with its bewildering wealth of opportunities for gratifying passing whims.

The rugs are usually of small size, and knotted on a woollen
warp. The patterns are derived from Chinese prototypes and
usually consist of one or three circles on a central field, with a
key-pattern or other simple border. These rugs might almost be
classified as folk art. Complicated curves such as are formed by
the delicate stalks of Persian and Indian conventional plants
never occur in Tibetan work; some of their rugs are fine in texture, but this craft of carpet-weaving is not often carried beyond the elementary stages. A favourite colour-scheme in bet-
ter-class rugs is a combination of light blue, warm browns, and
white; again the Chinese taste reveals itself.

The little tea-tables called *chogtse,* when they are not plain,
are either painted gaily with bunches of flowers on flat panels
or, more rarely, carved with dragons and then painted; but
these more costly tables are not usually found in the houses of
peasants. Village headmen, however, often possess surprisingly
good things: we saw some superior rugs and silver cups in the
home of the headman of Lachhen; and our head porter Odsung's family at Poo on the Satlej, who were no more than petty
landowners, numbered among their heirlooms, so they told us,
some dresses of ancient silk damask that, judging by the period
in which they were made, must be of great magnificence.

The next class of objects are those for eating and drinking —
teapots, cups, bowls, braziers for keeping tea warm, pots and
jugs for beer. The poorer peasants usually drink from wooden
bowls, the bases of which are sometimes embellished with
chased hoops of silver. Almost everyone, when travelling, carries such a bowl in the folds of his dress and is expected, on
visiting a friend's house, to produce it to be filled with tea.
Their teapots and the little portable stoves that go with them
are usually of brown pottery, of distinctly "classical" appearance, but depending for their beauty on shape alone. Most families, however, have one or two better teapots of brass or copper, with chasing round the neck, on the lid, and at the base of

the spout. The more wealthy possess several such teapots; the best have bands of silver appliqué, often chased with great skill, and handles in the shape of dragons and spouts that issue from the jaws of tusked sea-monsters.

Silver stands and lids for china teacups are common in the Central Provinces, but are rarely possessed by peasants in the more westerly districts. The Lachhen headman had some very fine ones, chased all over with delicate floral devices and with the "eight auspicious signs," in higher relief: namely, the golden wheel of the Doctrine, the jar containing the elixir of immortality, the conch-shell with right-handed spiral, the standard of victory, the coiled lasso, the lotus, the goldfish, and the royal umbrella. These are among the favourite motifs occurring both on lids and teapots.

The fact that only a few personal possessions are needed for adequate comfort is one of the reasons why the average quality can be kept so high. People do not buy teapots every day and so can afford to get good ones, which they hand down to their heirs. As the materials of most of these things are not fragile, replacements are rare, and in the course of time, even at a slow rate of purchase, quite a store can be accumulated, which when displayed together makes an astonishing impression on foreigners. That is one of the great advantages of things not being too cheap; it encourages those possessed of modest means not to spend rashly, but to wait till they are in a position to acquire things that have an intrinsic value.

The clothes of the peasants, both men and women, are usually of plain but beautiful wool, spun and woven by themselves. A reddish black is the prevailing dye in central Tibet, but in the western provinces lighter self-coloured wool is worn, with a purple sash. Most Tibetans wear some pieces of jewellery, especially the women, who have a passion for it. In this craft, as might be expected, the mode varies greatly from place to place. It would be tedious to give long descriptions of the silver chains, star-shaped or square or cylindrical charm-boxes, necklaces of rough cornelian, agate and matrix turquoise, ear-rings, rings and beads of red coral, with which the people deck themselves on holidays. The decoration often takes the form of exceedingly fine filigree, and far the commonest stone is the turquoise, which is secured in its setting by a kind of sealing-wax in place of cement. The richest jewellery of all comes from Nepal, where the size of the pieces, the profusion of stones, and the frequent use of high relief as well as of filigree make one think that the Nepalis have borrowed some of their ideas from India.

The farmhouse always contains one room that is chosen out for special honour and where fine examples of craftsmanship are likely to be found — the family chapel. Here reside the household gods, and here priests are invited to celebrate rites, and guests of honour are often put up for the night. Sometimes it is an entirely separate chamber; sometimes the altar, flanked by tiers of pigeon-holes containing books, stands at the back of the chief living-room of the house. This is especially the case in smaller houses, with few rooms to spare; but in the large farms of Ladak the best room on the upper floor is almost invariably set apart as an oratory. In Khunu, private chapels are sometimes elaborate, being built on the roof and surrounded by richly carved wooden arcades, so that the outer walls, thus shielded from the weather, can also be painted.

The appointments are the best that the family purse can provide, consisting of rugs, metal altar-lamps and silvered bowls for offerings. Behind the altar are seated painted wooden images of all sizes; the walls of the room are hung with t'hankas mounted on brocade. These will often be crude, done by some itinerant lama, or just harmless school-work; but occasionally good examples are found in unexpected places. One need only recall the story of our servant Norbu, whose family were about to commission a t'hanka from Rigzin, the premier painter of Ladak; we contributed some gold wire ourselves to be ground into paint for it, since the gold is always charged for separately. At a rough estimate of half a million farming families in Tibet — which may be very wide of the mark in either direction — it can be calculated that there must be at least that number of altars to provide for, which at a modest reckoning would mean about three million each of statues and t'hankas, and a proportional quantity of minor appliances such as lamps. If to these there be added the vast quantities of higher-class objects made for the use of the wealthier laity, and the even vaster requirements of the hundreds of monasteries, where not only temples but every monk's cell has its own altar, it will be evident that the task of making good the natural wear and tear will occupy a great number of artists and craftsmen of every grade, spread all over the country, who work for a sure market in an encouraging atmosphere. As there is no outlet for spending money in the pursuit of ephemeral amusements — if one excepts gambling, to which many Tibetans are passionately addicted – a steady share of the surplus wealth finds its way to the artistic community, especially to the jewellers and the purveyors of sacred requisites. The sums paid, of course, are small according to our Western standards. Even in the best periods artists have never made fortunes, for the rate of work cannot be speeded up sufficiently for that. But there are other compensations, and so long as payment is regular and unaffected by the vagaries of fashion, the craftsman need ask little else of life.

All that I have seen of actual artists in these journeys has confirmed me in the belief that the traditional handicraftsman represents one of the most intelligent, independent, stable, and straightforward elements in a community, and that the value to it of his presence is beyond computation. The elimination of the craftsmen, including both the master minds who set and maintain the standards of taste and workmanship and the equally indispensable crowd of more modest artists who minister to the artistic needs of the people and transmit to them a steady standard of taste received from above, may represent, judged from a purely economic standpoint, no great material loss. The factories that drive them out of business can show a turnover beside which the total sum paid for their work in earlier times may seem trifling. But the intellectual wastage inherent in the extinction of a whole class of citizens noted for their sturdiness of character and for their varied gifts of mind and skill of hand cannot be measured in pounds, shillings, and pence.

The step from the richer peasant headman to the small trader or petty noble is almost imperceptible. Passing thence to the great merchants and officials and the heads of feudal clans, there is no fundamental difference in the character of the artistic objects in use. It exists only in respect of quantity and quality; but there the contrast is considerable. An opulent Tibetan's residence is often a veritable treasure-house, and his everyday possessions are further surpassed by those that are kept for use on state occasions. Such a man numbers his silver cup-stands and splendidly chased teapots by the dozen: when he entertains his friends he pours out tea for them into jade cups, and seats them on rugs of the finest quality.* On his walls hang scores of *t'hankas,* old and new, by good artists, mounted on rich brocades. His exquisite little tea-tables are of pierced

---

* Latterly the quality of the Tibetan rugs has fallen off sadly, thanks largely to the spread of chemical dyestuffs.

wood delicately gilded, while the jewellery of his wife and
daughters is worthy of the *Arabian Nights*, a profusion of filigree, turquoises, corals, and seed pearls. He may even employ
some whole-time craftsmen for the exclusive service of his
household. He clothes his servants, as well as himself, in silk
damask, and his library is well stocked with volumes, all sacred, printed from wood-blocks, or copied in manuscript of gold
and silver letters on a blue ground, each leaf being protected
by a slip of rare brocade and embellished with fine miniatures.
As he owns so much property, he naturally requires some big
furniture to contain it, in the shape of gilt and painted cupboards or chests. In his chapel, where a domestic chaplain is
constantly officiating, there will be hung the finest *t'hankas* of
all, and the images will be, not of wood, but superb examples
of brass casting, heavily gilded, an art at which the Newaris of
Nepal once excelled. The butter-lamps and other vessels standing on the altar are solid silver, and the chasing is carried out
with a sharpness that has rarely been equalled except in parts
of India. These fine examples of the goldsmith's craft are often
found, on inquiry, to have been made in Derge, on the eastern
frontier, which must be the very home of metal-work. And outside in the colonnade near the stables we find the master's sad-
dlery hanging up, the bridles studded with silver, and the sad-
dle-cloths consisting of small pile carpets, specially shaped, in
which blue and yellow predominate. We came across a little
gem of a saddle-cloth when returning down the Satlej in 1933.
We stopped the rider and looked at it; but in that case the
proud owner was no more than a prosperous farmer. Most of
these saddle-rugs are Tibetan-made, but in the far west one
comes across similar ones in the Turkish style from Khotan,
usually silvery-grey and crimson.

Lastly we come to the monasteries, those majestic structures
that seem to grow out of the very rock, and that have achieved
something of the solidity of the Egyptian style. Within their
walls the Tibetan Tradition is continually cherished and renewed, and art, as the visible signs of inward Grace, displays its
most perfect creations. I have said so much about them that
comment can be cut down to a few points.

Though the great era of building has naturally passed, since
the monastic population is fully accommodated in the buildings
that already exist, yet construction on a smaller scale has by no
means come to an end. Both at Likhir and Satsukul new wings
were being put up when we visited those places, and I have

been told that the exceptionally large monastery at Chiamdo, the seat of the Government of Kham, which was gutted in the Chinese wars, has been entirely renewed. Rich persons, otherwise disinclined to part with their money, frequently make considerable offerings for church work.

As for the internal equipment of the lamas' quarters, a monk's own room reflects in its furnishing the state of the home whence he came. His family is primarily responsible for his keep, and each child dedicated to the lamaic order has his wants supplied by his relations direct; thus the farmer's son will enjoy the best that the farmer can afford, the monk drawn from the feudal house will be provided with still choicer pictures and altar fittings, while the highest prelates, especially those who hold the rank of *Tulku* — these may be children of beggars or of lords — occupy chambers to which dignity has been lent by every means known to art. This must not imply that such Lamas pass their time in luxury — many of them lead a life that is extremely austere, making their beds on the hard floor or even sleeping in the seated position of the Buddha, while their food is meagre and of the simplest. There are also some whose conduct is not consonant with their professions; while others again belong to the class of urbane prelates, endowed with much book-learning, but affected by a somewhat worldly outlook, who feel more at home listening to the hair-splitting disputations of doctors, or exchanging courtly sallies with their friends while sipping their subtly flavoured tea from silver-mounted cups, than in practising the hard self-discipline of those who tread the "short road" towards Buddhahood.

The temple interior must be familiar to my readers by now; the stately pillared hall, the rows of low platforms covered with thick rugs for the choir-monks, the butter-lamps like huge night-lights in copper bowls raised on tall stems, gently glowing at the feet of rows and rows of lotus-throned figures, the well-known features of the Buddha, the Bodhisats like youthful Indian princes, the more human portraits of saints and defunct abbots, the skull-crowned visages of stern protectors who trample on the prostrate bodies of sins and passions or whirl in the cosmic dance clasping their female energies. All this shining assemblage doubtless is suggestive of a certain exuberance of treatment, but in practice the style keeps clear of all false pathos or self-assertiveness. Everything remains in due relation. Faces either are composed or show just a faint seraphic smile playing across their features, as when thoughts are turned inward in deep meditation. Even when meant to look terrifying, they are not made theatrical: bodies are never out of poise, ornaments, however rich and complex, always avoid fussiness or irrelevancy, minor details are executed with the same care and thoughtfulness as the principal figures.

The temple walls are almost invariably painted all over. Many capable mural decorators still exist in the country, though it must be admitted that their work usually falls short of the best ancient examples. It is not quite easy to lay one's finger on the discrepancy. It resides in a thousand subtleties rather than in any single cause: it is doubtless connected with the fact that in respect of the Doctrine itself, which alone gives its impulse and meaning to the art, there has in many places been a tendency to slothfulness. But even then, the old fire often is not really dead; it smoulders and only awaits rekindling. I have seen plenty of evidence of creative power, both potential and actual, reflected in the work of modern Tibetan mural decorators. As regards the actual style, the sombre colouring, sharp outlining, the manner of delineating drapery, the absence of cast shadows, and the generally flat treatment are in some ways reminiscent of the practice of the later Middle Ages in Europe, though the Tibetan style always remains more formalized at heart, even when it appears at its most animated.

The subtlest, most intimate creations of the Tibetan artist are to be seen on the innumerable t'hankas or banner scrolls that festoon every corner of the temples; often they are sewn at regular distances on to a band of red and yellow silk, which is hung along the transverse beams that rest on the main columns in a sort of frieze, with the banners falling like fringes. Brilliant colours, fine detail, and a slightly more individual expression on the faces characterize these smaller compositions. In the temple, though one seems to be surrounded by all the colours of the rainbow, the range of the palette is not very big. Half-tones, and the innumerable tints required when once shading has come to play a major part in a style, are absent. It is the extreme clearness of the colours and the skill displayed in their combination that is responsible for the variegated impression.

With regard to the system of tuition followed by Tibetan art-masters, whether painters or decorative craftsmen, the brief description of the lama Gyaltsan's teaching methods, given in Chapter xxi, is of fairly general application. The essential points to observe are: first, the small number of pupils working under any one master, who live with him, serve him, watch him constantly, and thus imbibe unconsciously a great part of what he has to teach them; and secondly, the preponderant part played by imitation of the teacher's own works. Copying them line for line forces the pupil to repeat, and therefore to master, every manipulation that has gone into the making of those works. Once the pupil has reached the point of being able to turn out finished copies, little remains for the master to teach him; it rests with the pupil himself henceforth to make what he can of his new-found skill. Thirdly must be mentioned the absence of any intentional fostering of originality. This quality is left to develop in the pupil, once he has become, in his turn, a master; but even then he probably never recognizes its existence as such, and continues to imagine that he is merely reproducing or adapting, with greater or less success, what he himself was taught by his master. I do not suppose that a single case could be found where a pupil has actually been asked by his teacher to try to invent something of his own. Among us genius tends to be looked on as a tender plant that is ready to wilt under every breath of discipline, especially in childhood; this is a notion that does not even occur to a Tibetan. The master's task is that of training his charges in precision — of hand and eye and mind — so that they may develop efficiency and control, and of teaching them the artistic canons representing the application of the Doctrine to the necessity of making things for common use. Finally one must keep in mind the power of the master-pupil relationship, which in respect of an art, as of everything else, is recognized as the highest human tie. The master's authority is semi-parental; from the pupil's side there is a rendering of the respect due to one to whom the pupil is related by spiritual filiation, and through whom he has been made a member of one great family, of the long line of masters and pupils that reaches back across the ages to the heavenly sources of Tradition.

Such ideals and methods have not, of course, been confined to Tibet, nor even to the Orient. With trifling variations, the same path has been followed by all the traditional schools of history, and is the one, if history is to be believed, that can best be relied on to lead to consistently successful results. A master can do justice to a very limited number of disciples at one time: they must be able to claim his undivided attention over lengthy periods. Of all branches of human knowledge, it would seem that art is the least fitted to survive under institutional conditions, or to be imparted rapidly in the form of a concentrate. The paradox is that those who have worried their heads least on the score of originality seem to have had that virtue granted to them in abundance and as if by superaddition; while those who, in their anxiety lest their precious personalities should suffer eclipse, have feared to subject themselves to discipline have been the first to fall into banality, whether unrepentantly or disguised under a veneer of pretentiousness.

The allied arts of music and dancing, which, besides ministering to the gaiety of life, play an important part in worship, can unfortunately be dealt with only rather sketchily, because during my journeys I did not have opportunities for studying them as frequently, or as closely, as painting and the domestic crafts.

The classical music of the temples has already been described, consisting of a solemn, though animated, style of chanting, and of orchestral interludes based on the pedal notes of the long copper trumpets, with the melody taken up by oboes, and the rhythm supplemented by a multitude of percussion instruments. The hymns, though always sung by heart, also exist in written form. The notation is in the nature of a graph of the rising and falling of the voice; large curves convey the basic tune, while smaller loops represent ornaments and other byplay. Though I had hoped for a chance of instruction in the reading of the signs, time proved all too short. The only way to learn would be to practise under a master till one could reproduce a few tunes exactly, and then try to relate them to the written notes; for it is likely to be found that in reading the notation much has to be taken for granted, having been treated as a matter of common knowledge and only vaguely indicated on the paper. Even in our own notation people are usually unaware of how much remains a matter of convention, without being indicated by precise signs; this is especially the case in the older music. In investigating such a new notation one should always approach the task the right way round: namely, after first learning the music in a practical way through the imitation of actual sounds. The way to write them down will follow in due course, after which the reading of any piece that has been noted in a book should be a simple matter. An over-hasty confidence in one's power of interpreting written symbols without previous experience in actual sounds is almost sure to result in a travesty; therefore for such a study much time would be required.

The singing itself is extremely moving. The words are articulated with perfect clarity and are given just the right stress, while the bodies of the monks sway gently to the rhythm of the music. Orchestral performances vary greatly as regards both ensemble and intonation. In communities that are conspicuous for zeal the orchestral tone is pure and balanced and well in tune, while in monasteries that are drifting into slack ways, the effects usual to under-rehearsal and inattention make themselves immediately discernible in performance, exactly as in other parts of the world. In these degenerate houses, the chanting also tends to become a gabble.

Outside the temples music seems to be of the "folk-tune" order. Simple songs, often on some humorous theme, lively and tuneful, but of no great depth, sung either solo or in chorus as an accompaniment to peasant dances, are heard everywhere. Tunes are also played on the flute, from sheer gaiety of spirit, while people are walking along or tending their flocks. In Ladak, and indeed throughout Tibet, one hears the shanties that workers use to mark the rhythm proper to almost any kind of work. One or two of these shanties are quite beautiful. In Ladak we also came across pairs of musicians called *mon*, one playing on a double-reed instrument like a musette, his companion on a drum. They seemed to be itinerant professionals who earned a few coppers playing at fairs and weddings, or accompanying work done out of doors, such as the digging of the new reservoir at Leh. Another instrument that we came across was the *damyen* or fiddle, used by dancers, played with a bow and yielding a thin, reedy tone. Once, at Chitkul on the Baspa, we heard a man softly plucking a lute-like instrument also called *damyen*; the piece he was playing was a sort of fantasia, of more complicated character than the usual folk music; it is the nearest thing to an abstract composition which we came across, and then only that once.

Both in music and in the sister art of the dance there is a certain distinction to be made between worldly and sacred. The former comprises all rustic styles, both the elementary ring dances in the village square and the far more complex and subtle figures of the troupes of professional dancers. Their performances are of an exceedingly high order. I do not know whether there exists any refined dancing among people of high society corresponding to the court dancing that was cultivated with such artistry in Europe in the sixteenth and seventeenth centuries. That remains a point for future investigation — I

have, however, never come across any allusion to it, and I
rather suspect that the aristocracy enjoy watching dances, but
do not often dance themselves.

It is in the sacred mystery plays, miscalled "devil-dances,"
that this art reaches heights almost undreamed of. They form
part of the regular ceremonial of the Church, given at certain
stated seasons of the year, but varying from district to district.
Every monastery has its dancing monks and costumes for these
mysteries. In the larger convents hundreds participate, and the
costumes are magnificent beyond words; the dresses are usually
of ancient Chinese silk brocade and embroidery, with an un-
derskirt banded in red and yellow, the two sacred colours. In
addition there are men dressed as skeletons and demons, and
effigies that are torn to pieces when the forces of evil are finally
overthrown by the heavenly hosts. Splendid ancient weapons,
ornaments of interlaced chain-work made of human bone,
heads and grotesque masks adorned with antlers or yaks' horns
complete the costumes. To an extraordinary agility are added
the qualities of a natural dramatic sense and an instinct for
effective spontaneous grouping, even in the case of large numbers of men engaged in violent action.

It must be borne in mind that the Tibetan sacred ballet is
primarily meant to tell a story. It is a church service, in the
fullest sense of the word, and not half-way to an entertainment.
For us, who have singled the dance out of the whole family of
the arts for banishment from the service of religion, except in
Seville cathedral, where alone it survives, it has become difficult to imagine that dignity and reverence can go hand-in-hand
with so exciting a performance. P'hiyang, where our friend the
painter monk acted as ballet-master, is annually the scene of a
two-day mystery depicting the symbolical history of the Kargyudpa Order; the ceremony draws a crowd from every part of
Ladak. A colonnaded theatre, with a high seat for the abbot,
galleries for distinguished spectators, and a covered platform
for the orchestra, has been built on the side of the hill below
the monastery. The people watch from above, looking over the
sides as into a well. But the P'hiyang play must pale before the
large-scale performances, involving thousands of dancers and
costumes of fabulous splendour, that take place at Lhasa and
in Bhutan. Photographs shown to us by one of the very few
foreigners — and long may their number remain thus restricted
— who have had the privilege of entering Bhutan gave the im-

pression of a performance that touched the heights, presented in a natural setting worthy of its perfections. One saw a great courtyard, either of a monastery or of one of the grand seignorial castles, round which a crowd of men and women of one of the most athletic of races were watching, either standing or seated on the ground, while the centre of the scene was filled by the lamas, arrayed in robes the least of which would have been worthy of a prince.

And now having passed through the whole gamut of the other arts, I must say a word or two about literature; but it can only be the briefest reference, for I have not read enough of the classical books to permit myself to offer criticisms. Judged quantitatively, Tibetan literature is staggering; the greater part of it consists of metaphysical treatises, some of which are actually in verse for the sake of those requiring to learn the texts by heart; there are also books on logic and medicine, and histories in which the tale of secular events is rapidly slurred over in order to enlarge on the far more important doings of saints and Lamas. To these must be added innumerable liturgical works, spiritual poems, an epic, and also a certain quantity of lyrical poetry, including the much-admired love lyrics composed by the sixth Dalai Lama, who was somewhat of a rake and came to a bad end.

There is one book, however, to which I have already made repeated allusions, and which is accessible to European readers in translation: namely, the autobiography of the ascetic poet Mila Repa, dictated to his pupil Rechhung. The story is most vividly told, with much human pathos; the dialogue is of the liveliest, as are also the descriptions of the country and its habits. An admirable translation of this masterpiece exists, by Professor Jacques Bacot of Paris. The text, which is introduced by an excellent short essay that helps to bring out salient points in the Tibetan metaphysic, has been turned into most beautiful French, yet keeps almost all the qualities of the original. I say "almost" not in order to reserve my praise, but only because there is one quality inherent in the Tibetan language that must needs be shed in translation: namely, that of an extreme, well-nigh laconic terseness. The power of stringing monosyllables together and the absence of true inflections cause one line of Tibetan to require two of any European language in translation. Besides the French translation just mentioned there is another, in English, by Dr. Evans Wentz. May I urge anyone really interested in Tibet to read Mila Repa's book if he has not done so already? If he will do this and also look at some paintings or other works of art in a museum, he will have made contact with Tibet and its spirit far better than through any words of mine, though this book may also have served its purpose by way of introduction.

Chapter XXIV

Tibetan Art (*continued*)—Its Connexions with the Doctrine

BEFORE EMBARKING on speculations concerning the metaphysical basis of Tibetan art a few words must be said about the care of works of art in Tibetan lands. Both monasteries and private owners vary greatly in their treatment of the treasures committed to their stewardship; a well-ordered, zealous community tends to keep its buildings and their contents in a fair state of repair, while a slack one, like Himi, suffers everything to go to rack and ruin. Nevertheless, compared with our own practice, works of art in Tibet are, on an average, treated with less meticulous care, except perhaps in a few aristocratic houses. At first sight this may strike one as strange on the part of people who have shown so much taste and who delight in all that is beautiful. Several reasons can be given to explain the paradox.

First there is the climate, which because of its dryness and the absence of insects is exceptionally favourable to the preservation of pictures, woodwork, and books. The ravages of time make their mark but slowly, so that the minds of the people are not trained to be particularly watchful.

Secondly, it has been noticed more than once in the course of history that the greatest solicitude in guarding antiques has been shown at those periods when art had sunk to a low ebb, and when consequently there was little hope of making losses good. The great days of collecting and safeguarding have been in Roman times and in the last two centuries in Europe; in the Orient, as the arts become extinct under the influence of the West, so will the examples that survive from the past, even mediocre ones, tend to find their way into glass cases and their names on to insurance policies. Among the artistic nations of olden times one exception must be noted; in China and Japan, even in their most productive periods, people appear to have

been conscious of the permanent value of masterpieces and to
have treated them more tenderly than has usually been the
case elsewhere. The normal attitude in any period when an uninterrupted supply of works of art can be taken for granted is
to be somewhat reckless, even with objects that are sincerely
valued and admired; the Tibetan temperament, moreover, contains a strong streak of slapdashness which also causes many
things to be handled more roughly than is necessary. This tendency frequently results in quite needless waste: I do not cite it
as an example to be followed, but as an illustration of a phenomenon that is often one of the accompaniments of artistic
health. In Tibet the deep-rooted reverence for the sages of old
and the repositories of their wisdom counteracts to a considerable extent the native carelessness over objects regarded as
works of art. By carelessness is meant an absence of anxiety
over their preservation, not carelessness in handling while they
are still in use. In this respect even rough people, such as our
coolies in the mountains, are often exemplary, and the continual breakages that ravage fragile possessions in an English
home are unknown even in camp.

Two opposing ideas war against each other in the Tibetan
philosophy, one of which tends somewhat to encourage neglect, while the other acts as a corrective in favour of due care.
The doctrine of the impermanence of things is so fundamental
and so deeply ingrained in the people's consciousness that
whenever a crack appears in a wall, or a bit of plaster flakes off
carrying with it the superimposed painting, this is apt to be accepted as one more example of the dissolution that awaits everything old or new, high or low, mountain or grain of dust.
Mila Repa says: "All worldly pursuits end in dispersion; buildings in destruction; meetings in separation; births in death." A
hankering after individual survival, even in the next world, is
reckoned the worst of illusions, so why go to any great trouble
to mend this or to underpin that? Rather let it crash, as a lesson and a warning to all men, and let something fresh be put
up in its place, to meet a like fate when its hour shall strike! In
India the same tendency has been evident — to rebuild rather
than to repair; it is in the West that people attach particular
importance to the idea of survival in a purely individual sense,
and by an extension of the habit of mind so induced treat things
as if they also could be made almost immortal. The virtue of
this attitude is that things are made to render service till the
last possible moment; its vice is revealed in an excessive attach-

ment to possessions, including life itself. On the other hand the Tibetan attitude, when carried to extremes, tends to obliterate treasures of art that could still be preserved for posterity; but it is perhaps the more realistic of the two views. In practice a middle path is preferable.

The compensating influence is the universally acknowledged duty of treating sacred objects with the utmost regard. The reader will recall the commentary on the Three Refuges and the injunction that if anyone should find the minutest fragment of a picture or book lying about he must pick it up reverently and lay it on the altar. Not to do so is a great sin. From this it is but a step to argue that failure to set right reparable damage, omission to bestow ordinary care, or an inaction calculated to bring about the dissolution of sacred objects into those very fragments that one is commanded to cherish, a day earlier than is necessary, is also a sin. Dissolution must needs come in the end, but the crack in the plaster may meanwhile be filled in, just as the sick man may be cured by medicine, because his hour has not yet struck. In addition, the ancient teachers say that worship should be carried out in clean and orderly surroundings, and that implies some degree of upkeep. Once or twice I have myself been instrumental in defending beautiful things from being thoughtlessly abandoned to their fate by quoting the above maxims, notably in an old temple at P'hiyang. I recommend this line of argument to other travellers similarly placed; and if they can lend a hand themselves with the work, so as to help the local people to overcome the inertia that sometimes holds them back from making a start, they will earn much merit. Sins of omission always weigh less heavily on simple minds than those of commission; but there is a fair chance that good counsel, offered in the manner suggested, will not fall on deaf ears except where corruption and apathy have brought things to a hopeless pass.

In the preceding chapter an attempt was made to survey the whole field covered by Tibetan art and to sort out the material on which generalizations might be based. Now is the moment to enter upon a more difficult stage in our inquiry by trying to deduce some of the principles that guide the Tibetan artist. What is the aim that inspires him? One can dismiss the obvious decorative purpose, which appeals to the sentiments of a people naturally fond of colour and ornament. This purpose will tend to be preponderant in those crafts that are chiefly bound up with domestic uses, though even here many ordinary emblems express some sacred symbolism. There is no phase of Tibetan life that is exempt from the all-leavening doctrinal influence, nor is it easy to pick out an object of which it could be said that its inspiration is purely secular.

In talking with artists or about them, the language currently used has a curiously utilitarian ring, which gives no inkling of the existence of any theory of æsthetics; it is doubtful whether such indeed can be said to exist, even in the background, so that the translation of many of those terms which are the stock-in-trade of criticism among us is no light task. For instance, the word "art" itself is not easy to translate; the nearest term that I can find is "science of construction," which can be made to cover all the applied arts, including architecture, but hardly takes in painting, since the latter is more usually considered by the Tibetans in conjunction with writing. Genius, originality, inventive power — though we know the Tibetans to possess all these unconsciously — are words foreign to them. They will speak of a beautiful woman or a fine horse, but will rarely apply such adjectives to inanimate objects. For a genius, one can only say "an exceedingly capable man," underlining the technical side of his skill rather than his gift of design. His work is either "well done" or "not well done" — again no mention is made of design, which is taken for granted. Where we tend to stress the individuality of the artist and to think of design first of all as an expression of individual genius, the Tibetan relies on finding a constant supply of artists who, when they do not feel capable of aspiring to great heights in their compositions, can always be relied upon to follow adequate, time-honoured models, to be varied according to taste. Genius, even when it is acclaimed, does not stand out in popular estimation like a mountain rising sheer out of a plain; rather is it comparable to a hill that happens somewhat to overtop neighbouring heights. According to the class of work that a person intends to carry out, so will he lavish or spare effort on the design. Their point of view, therefore, is seen to be the exact reverse of that current among us in modern times. We often noticed in our travels that when anybody gave an order for cheap work, comparatively little trouble was taken over the fine adjustments of design, and a decent and serviceable traditional model was followed, a safeguard against any great disaster; whereas when good work was demanded, the artists took no end of trouble over fine points of proportion, accuracy of detail, and quality of material. In Tibetan, when one wishes to make a specific reference to design, apart from execution, one can hardly avoid using a circumlocution such as "the shape is good and the pattern is well drawn."

The metaphor of "Creation" is one that they do not use, even in respect of the world itself; applied on the cosmic scale, they think of it as "manifestation in form," never in the sense of making something out of nothing. As to originality and invention, most artists, but especially painters and sculptors, might even feel rather hurt at being suspected, as they would think, of irreverent self-assertion. They always conceive of everything that they value, including ethics and art, under the guise of knowledge that is susceptible of being communicated through a chain of teachers and pupils. What the latter learn they adapt capably or incapably, that is all. The former are often the ones to whom we, viewing only the results, apply the term "original"; but, whether they really deserve the epithet or not, as many certainly do, they one and all maintain that they are simply carrying out, not inventing, designs prescribed by the traditional canons. Readers will recollect, in the chapter about the drawing lessons at P'hiyang *Gompa*, how Gyaltsan showed us the proportions of the Buddha's figure, which defied all attempts to measure them till, in answer to prayer, they were vouchsafed for the good of creatures to a saint by divine revelation: to presume to alter them would be nothing short of sinful. And if the painter were to find himself suddenly face to face with one of the Buddhas, or with Chenrezig, whose "portraits" — I nearly said "whose photographs" — he has been wont to delineate, he would feel awed, but hardly surprised.

How then could one try to convey to a Tibetan the meaning of our phrase "a work of genius," an apparently spontaneous creation by an artist, fit to become in its turn the starting-point of a new traditional chain of variations on the same theme? To try to translate the idea by bringing in the hated epithet "new" could only arouse prejudice and defeat one's purpose. The sentence that would best help to convey this idea, and would therefore be the most truthful, might run something like this: "That artist received the instructions for the picture directly from his Lama in heaven!"

When we were visiting Likhir for the second time, tea was served in the room of a monk who happened to be away; in it was hanging a particularly fine *t'hanka*, recently made at Lhasa, showing Gautama Buddha seated in the centre, with other Buddhas, Bodhisats, and awful Tutelaries of the Yellow Order as well as disciples, female angels and defenders of the faith severally disposed in tiers beneath Him, and a throng of Indian and Tibetan saints on either hand. The picture was brilliantly coloured, sparkling with burnished gold and azure. The subject is a classical one, found in all Gelugpa monasteries, and is named *Lamrim* or "Grades in the Way." We were told that the picture was private property, not owned by the monastery, and might be for sale; but as the owner was away for a few days, there was no chance to approach him. When we expressed disappointment at this, another monk came along with a book in his hand and said: "Here is another *Lamrim*, just the same as the picture; you can buy this if you like, instead." He spoke as if it were quite a matter of indifference whether one acquired a picture or a book, so long as the doctrine set forth were the same.

This little episode illustrates a point that has been mentioned before, but cannot be made too often; painting is looked on as equivalent to a language, which can be read in the same way as the written word by those who possess its key. The very term for "painter" in Tibetan bears this out: literally rendered it is "Writer of Gods." The colours, postures, and gestures laid down for the figures all express something perfectly definite: mercy, chastity, severity, or the sundering of Ignorance. Each detail is related to the special character that is considered to belong to a corresponding form of the Divinity. Similar gestures are also to be seen in real life, performed by living lamas during temple services, while the dancers in the mystery plays will reproduce the "fierce" deities on the temple wall. All the arts are in some measure interchangeable as aids to memory or supports of the same doctrine: they all are called upon to play their part according to circumstances. That is why, though purely decorative features may be varied to taste, the ritual elements are never altered. To change the emblematic colour would seem queer and eccentric as well as presumptuous; indeed, such an idea could hardly enter anybody's head.

But we have yet to come to grips with our original question; what, apart from obvious utilitarian purposes, does the Tibetan artist believe to be the end in view while exercising his profession? What, in his eyes, will be the test of success or failure, the criterion of good or bad art? The answer, in the absence of any authoritative pronouncement by a qualified person, must remain a matter of inference, an opinion pieced together out of chance comments gathered in the course of conversations with

Tibetans, especially with the painter Gyaltsan. I believe that my opinion is similar to the answer that might be given by any lama painter; but if I have gone wrong anywhere, I must bear the responsibility.

The aim of ritual — and ritual must be regarded as a synthesis of all the arts, acting as the handmaids of Doctrine and collaborating towards one end — is to prepare people for metaphysical realization, to spur them on to pierce the veil of the finite, and to seek Deliverance in Knowledge — that is, in identification with the Supreme and Infinite Reality. The latter is devoid of every determination whatsoever, even unity or goodness; that is why the least misleading title that the human mind is capable of inventing for It is the Void Itself. No symbol can stand for It save only vacuity. The Jewish Holy of Holies, containing nothing except an empty space, must be saluted as a triumph of art. Apart from this special instance, all art must occupy itself with forms; these are its principal concern. Once it has helped to pilot the mind up to the frontier between Form and the next stage, the world of Non-form, its task is over — he who penetrates to the beyond has no more use for art.

But within the formal Universe its value is enormous; indeed it can be called indispensable, as being one of the most potent and flexible means for expressing metaphysical truth in terms that are readily intelligible to the human mind. To attain to Wisdom, mere wishing is not sufficient, there must also be Method: that is why, under the emblems of the bell and the *Dorjé* or sacred sceptre, which every lama handles, these two, Method and Wisdom, are represented as an eternally inseparable pair and are said to be "married." So we, dwellers under the veil of Form, make use of ritual or art, a part of Method; since it is a most useful instrument for Form to use in the attempt to pierce a loophole and look out towards Non-form, the next veil curtaining us off from the Supreme Reality. This veil too must be penetrated in its turn; but that demands the use of quite other means.

Such is the theory underlying the sacred art of all the Traditions, intellectual rather than æsthetic. Ritual, contrary to the assertions of some Western writers, is not thought of as being efficacious in its own right — such a notion is included in the catalogue of obstacles to Enlightenment by the Buddha — but it remains strictly a means of exercising the mind and sharpening the perceptions, of providing for each of the senses its appropriate "supports," and as a help to canalizing attention to-

wards the point desired. In short, every possible artifice should
be called into play in order to facilitate and nourish the acquisition of the one essential faculty of direct, undistracted intellectual intuition of Truth, to which alone properly belongs the
name of Knowledge — with which discursive or rational knowledge must not be confounded, for that is merely one of several
earlier processes for clearing the ground in preparation for
Knowledge.

Whether painting is chosen, or the casting of images, or the
written word, or gesture, or the science of sound — called by
the Indians *Mantra* — or the public mystery plays, or the even
more extraordinary dramas performed by initiates into the
Tantra on the stage of their own minds, with themselves as the
sole audience, when actors and actresses, who are identical with
the divinities murally portrayed in the temple, are evoked,
amid scenic effects as unlimited as the power of imagination
— whether any of these methods be preferred separately or the
whole gamut of the arts be called into play at once, the end is
the same — namely, the attainment of metaphysical Knowledge.
To one man one method is profitable, to his neighbour a second, according to their respective mentalities. That which har-
monizes with metaphysical truth and leads naturally towards
it is good art, that which is rightly called inartistic betrays itself
by its lack of meaning and therefore by its defectiveness as a
means; the utilitarian purpose and the symbolical significance
of a work must go hand-in-hand, otherwise it will contain contradictory implications, which, if followed out to the end, will
logically lead to chaos.

The artist may therefore regard himself as an inventor of
glosses upon the Doctrine, a mediator between its pure spirit
and the intelligence of dwellers within the world of sense. He
is an alchemist who, after having been vouchsafed a vision of
the truth through direct intuition, transmutes it, insulating its
power in a symbolical envelope, so that eyes that cannot
yet face its naked intensity may gradually become fortified
through constant contemplation of the symbol, even to bearing
the sight of the thing symbolized.

Because I have gone into the doctrinal connexions of the
arts in such detail, it must not be imagined that beauty is not a
major concern of the Tibetan artist, as it has been elsewhere;
but he does not conceive it independently nor regard it as providing a self-sufficient motive for his work, whereas the mod-
erns have tended to separate beauty from meaning and pur-

pose, forgetting that *ars sine scientia nihil.* The idea that I am trying to bring out is the conscious attitude of the traditional artist to his own calling. Out of the various elements that go to make up a work of art, those which we usually choose to emphasize are just the ones that the Tibetans hardly think about; while we, on our side, are equally unconscious of those metaphysical implications which they delight in stressing. In the Middle Ages it would have been different, and the two points of view would have approached each other; but since the fifteenth century the Hellenistic influence upon our thought has asserted itself in an over-conscious emphasis laid on the pursuit of the beautiful. For us this has come to constitute an end in itself, an abstraction; the Tibetan still thinks of his art as one of several servants of Knowledge.

I have been criticizing the view of classical æstheticism; if we now turn to those who stand at the opposite pole, the iconoclasts and the puritans, who call in question the need for any art at all and who scoff at ritual aids in general, we will find that they display a singular inconsistency in the ways in which they give effect to their abhorrence. While they are inveighing against the "mummery," "idolatry," or "luxury" of this or that rite, they nearly always will be found to tolerate unconsciously practices that do not differ in principle from those which they have seen fit to condemn. A preacher, while denouncing the use of paintings or statues, will admit representations no less pictorial in principle when presented through the channel of literature. In the Bible or in his own oratory, he will overload God and the saints with epithets, including those very attributes which move him to indignation when they appear in pictures or images. The throne of God, the angels' wings, or the golden harps of the Blessed Souls are heathenish, so it seems, when looked upon with the physical eye; but if received through the ear and only viewed through the imagination's eye, they are edifying! The fury of the adversary tends to rage most hotly against visual supports, while music and words are accepted more easily. Others again denounce music, but allow themselves full licence to introduce the most anthropomorphic terms into their ranting oratory. Or they contrive strange compromises, like a revivalist whom I once met who enjoyed harmony in hymns when the parts moved note for note together, but disapproved of any attempt at movement in counterpoint!

Wherever the line is drawn, it is arbitrary, governed simply by the personal habits or preferences of the censor, who takes

it upon himself to deprive his neighbours of helpful rites and
symbols that he has not troubled to understand himself or that
call upon senses in which he himself is deficient; yet he toler-
ates the use of those aids which are his own personal favourites,
as when Luther, who happened to be fond of music, overruled
the objections of the more dour of the Protestant Reformers,
saying that he could not see why the Devil should be allowed
to keep all the good tunes. It is for this arbitrariness that Puritanism, which has afflicted most religious movements to some
extent, to the detriment of a full deploying of their intellectual
and artistic resources, merits the name of heresy in its etymological meaning of "choice" — that is, of capricious individual
choice that will not conform to any general principle.

To the claim: "*I* do not need eye or ear to help me in approaching the throne of God. What is the good of all this ritual
and art? Worship may not be, save in spirit and in truth," the
lama might make some such rejoinder: "Ritual is not an end in
itself, nor efficacious in its own power; but it is a means adapted
to the condition of men's minds: its diversity corresponds to
their diversity. Anything can become a symbol of your high aim:
things seen or heard or read or touched, your very breath. We
would enlist all kinds of activity into our service, turning everything into a mirror of the divine purpose, making the world
into one all-embracing Bible in which works of art, no less than
natural objects, have their part. In the practice of this doctrine
you will come to perceive the great liberating truth that distinctions are only an illusion, that there is neither This nor
That, neither I nor Other, neither Mine nor His. You will dispense with ritual aids on the day when you have achieved that
which is the end of all ritual. He who has reaped the harvest
need no longer water the field. He who enjoys the Beatific Vision needs no longer to view the Godhead through the trans-
forming symbols of art, nor is eloquence required for Its praise.
But to argue now as if you were in heaven already, and freed
from Form, is mere conceit. To advise others so to regard themselves is utter presumption. As to the idolatry of which you are
so afraid, first let us clear our minds upon what constitutes its
essential defect." The lama pauses and looks up. "Surely it is
rendering divine honours to a creature?" replies his friend. "You
have spoken well," answers the lama, "that is the test. No symbol, so long as it is recognized to be but a symbol, can ever of-
fend. That is how all images, and even the divinities whom they
represent, are meant to be understood among us, as well as

among the Hindus. Even the Buddhas of the five directions are manifestations in Form of the five kinds of Wisdom; but they themselves are phantoms from the viewpoint of that which lies beyond Form. The mass of men sees the symbol and perhaps looks a little farther; the spiritually more adventurous follow out these forms till they begin to merge into one another. Liberation is to pass the frontier of all distinctions, even those of unity and multiplicity. That, I repeat, is the end of ritual. You would, I am sure, be surprised to hear that we do not admit actual idolatry to be common in India and Tibet. Those who declare most of our rituals to be meaningless and our art to be merely picturesque do so only because they have not discovered the meaning — usually because they have not looked for one, having prejudged the case. Your people are ever prone to pay most attention to external appearances: one of your most quoted Orientalists has spent years of his life in cataloguing the details of ceremonies and deities and objects used for various cults, yet when it comes to main principles he is wildly libellous. One wonders why, if a thing be meaningless, it is worth devoting years and years to its study. Have you nothing better than research into human folly with which to occupy your leisure? It is also surely no compliment to human intelligence for a man to be so prone to assume that those things which have no meaning for himself are necessarily devoid of meaning for everybody else?

"To our way of thinking you should search for traces of idolatry nearer home," continues the lama, "for you sail perilously close to the wind in the language that you employ about the Infinite Principle of All, ascribing to It feelings and sympathies, even displeasure. Such attributes seem to belittle It; we, for our part, dare use no single adjective save 'Void' only. For every determination, even Unity or Goodness, is equivalent to a negation of Its Infinite character; therefore, Void of every determination, being the denial of a Negative, makes a Positive and is the most apt phrase — I ought to have said the least inept — that we can invent for referring to Its Uniqueness. It is our turn to question your wisdom in the employment of symbolism based on predominantly human attributes; but we will not do so, for we recognize that, like our own symbols, they too are intended to be used only as supports. Your greatest thinkers have tended to take a very similar view to our own. I need only remind you of a quotation from one of your Christian Fathers, St. John of Damascus: 'It is impossible to say what God

is in Himself, and it is more exact to speak of Him by exclud-
ing everything. Indeed He is nothing of that which is . . .
above Being itself.' Any lama would find himself on common
ground with the author of such a phrase.

"The prejudice in favour of 'equality,' which has become
your fetish in social matters and which you allow to invade
other spheres, makes you act as if you thought that all men are
equally able to grasp the essentials of the Doctrine; but this
seems to us to rest neither on observed fact nor on probability.
With us, it is recognized that the power of realizing a doctrine
is proportional to each being's stage of development; that
which is truth for one is far behind the truth for another, just
as all truth contained in this Universe is precisely nothing from
the viewpoint of Enlightenment. The truth must be given to
each man as he can bear it, to some in symbols and parables,
to a few less indirectly. We do of course admit equality of opportunity, inasmuch as all men — nay, the lowliest beast, even
the very mountains, as a Japanese has said — are potentially
Buddha." (How joyous a thought that we can claim some true
companionship not only with birds and trees, but even with
Scafell and the Matterhorn and cloud-piercing Everest!)

Then the lama adds his concluding remarks: "We are quite
ready to admit that some superstition — again I use it in its precise sense of something left over, a symbol that has continued
in use after its original meaning has been forgotten — is to be
found among us. The best cure for that is not misapplied invective against idolatry, but an exposition of the meaning of the
symbol, so that men may again use it intelligently. When that
meaning cannot be recovered, certainly let the outworn practice be discontinued. But may I also suggest that deification of
the nation, or even of mankind, now so prevalent in many Western countries, is a serious and destructive form of idolatry? To
read eternal qualities into things so utterly temporal is a symp-
tom of low intellectuality. Idols can be made of Work and
Service too, when they are taken out of their place in the hierarchy and given precedence over Knowledge. This results in a
restless and ultimately self-destroying world — cold comfort
for humanity. I can improve on your original test of idolatry:
I would define it as an upsetting of the natural hierarchy, to
the overvaluing of what is lower and the underrating of what
is higher. Whoever holds to this principle is in no danger of
misusing symbols, or of sacrificing to false gods, from the State
or his own ego downwards."

Whatever part iconoclastic tendencies may have played in certain phases of Buddhist history, they had been eliminated by the time the Tradition began to permeate Tibet, so that the unfolding of symbolical art in that country was unfettered even by the smallest of reservations. The ideal of the lama's life, at its most austere, excludes self-laceration not only on the physical but also on the moral plane. The passion for knowledge, the thirst for direct experience of the truth, produces a certain adventurousness, in contrast to the timidity of soul that comes of overstressing the dangers of falling into sin. This is perhaps the most striking trait that characterizes the best lamas. They hesitate to prohibit any practice that might conceivably prove helpful to seekers after Truth. They are more concerned with the potentialities of usefulness contained in such a practice than with the possibilities of its misuse. This boldness of outlook is a quality specially favourable to artistic achievement, because the artist is not hampered by restrictions invented by prudish and anxious minds.

If in the course of the preceding pages I have seemed to stray far afield at times, it has not been without a purpose. I have tried to demonstrate the close interdependence of every part of a normal Tradition, so that whatever starting-point may have been selected, the line of argument always leads back to the same Doctrine that gives coherence to the whole civilization, pervading its smallest part as well as constituting its centre of attraction. So long as the hierarchy of values be not overturned and intellectuality remains enthroned in the place of highest honour, both theoretically and as applied in the organization of society, health is maintained. The Tradition bears full fruit and has even the strength to assimilate to its own use elements drawn from outside, belonging to other traditional forms, if this should prove convenient, without any risk of endangering its own stability; it has also power to shed all that is found to be inconsistent with its principles. Metaphysic, ritual, law, government, art, social relations, even dress and the conventions of politeness, fit together like a jigsaw. I have been speaking primarily on the subject of art, but any other aspect of the Tradition would have served the purpose equally well and would have led us back to Doctrine just as surely. It is impossible to disentangle or pigeon-hole the components of a traditional civilization; a dualistic ruling of sharp boundaries between body and mind, material and spiritual, profane and sacred, is the first sign that the fabric is beginning to wear thin.

Out of distinctions strife is born, even to the eventual rending of the seamless garment of the Doctrine itself.

Once one begins tampering thoughtlessly with a corner of the fabric, one is soon committed to a policy tending towards its total disintegration. The very niceness of balance between the various constituents in the Tradition, which makes its strength while it yet remains harmonious, also makes it more vulnerable when a discordant element has crept in. Let a traditional society, from inexperience, be led into accepting some anti-traditional influences from outside — a danger non-existent when the whole world was parcelled out among different Traditions and when the anti-traditional spirit, if it ever arose, was feeble, but very critical of recent years, because of the temporary success of the modern humanistic movements — then it must reassert itself or go under. Herein lies the danger to Tibetan culture at the present moment, made more acute because there has been, as several lamas have testified, a certain drop in the intellectual level. Tibet is the last stronghold where Tradition rules intact, one might almost say the last authentic civilization governed by some sort of principle resulting in the observance of due precedence in the hierarchy of all its parts. Sheltered behind the rampart of the Himalaya, Tibet has looked on, almost unscathed, while some of the greatest traditions of the world have reeled under the attacks of the all-devouring monster of modernism. It is to its credit, too, that resistance has been, in part at least, conscious and intelligent; but the widespread Chinese defection from the traditional camp has exposed a flank, while at the same time the full force of world pressure has reached its maximum on all sides. Tibet and Bhutan are in the position of a healthy person who meets sudden and unaccustomed infection; he may succumb, when the rake and the weakling will survive. The only possible way to purchase immunity is by knowledge and by looking at things as they are, and not through rose-tinted spectacles — a habit that, of all forms of Ignorance, generates the deadliest poisons. It is with this disease, and the beginnings of its ravages, that my next chapter is concerned.

Chapter XXV

Tibetan Art—Dangers Ahead

IN THE PRECEDING two chapters I have dealt with the present state of art in Tibet under various aspects. We have seen what an important part it plays in the life of the country and how it is the expression of ideas that run through the whole social structure, binding it together and relating it to the universal values. Were I to end my survey at this point, I might seem to have given a rather idyllic picture. But such, alas, is not the case; for though Tibetan civilization is vigorous, balanced, and intellectually well anchored, it is being subjected to adverse influences that it will be hard put to it to resist, even with the best will in the world. Enthusiasm must not blind us to the fact that the last few decades have been marked by an unmistakable downward trend. The position is not yet desperate, because there is a genuine attachment among the Tibetans to their Tradition and because most of them are free from that conviction of their own inferiority to the West which has turned the so-called educated classes in most Oriental countries into their own culture's worst enemies. There seem to be a few, however, who are beginning to waver, having had their judgment upset and their cupidity aroused by the sight of our luxury, our speed, and our complicated amusements.

The arts are an excellent thermometer for judging the intellectual health of a nation. We will therefore begin by discussing the dangers which threaten in that field before we consider the future prospects of Tibetan civilization as a whole.

An impartial observer cannot but admit that the thermometer shows a steady, though still slow, dropping tendency, which appears to have set in some forty years ago at the most, hardly perceptible at first, but since then tending to increase. In painting, for instance, one notes that there is, on an average, far less expression in the faces than in older examples, a good deal of carelessness and hurry over detail, and often ill-blended, crude colouring, arising out of the use of cheap imported pigments.

In the better-executed pictures the deviation from the old standards is harder to define, for there is still much skill in drawing and a power of composition that calls for ungrudging admiration. Yet placed side by side with the works of half a century ago, there are few modern works that really excel. The difference is subtle; but one often gains the impression that fossilization is setting in and that a preponderant part of the merit is due to obedience to the well-tried, safety-conferring rules, and only a minor part to the devotional insight of the artists themselves. Yet there are still quite a number of excellent and conscientious men plying this calling, who keep their grip on sound principles and teach them to their pupils. My fear that symptoms of decay may herald a descent into the abyss and not into a temporary furrow rests not so much on the artists' work as on the deterioration in the critical powers of the other partner in the artistic directorate of a people, the educated class, on whose continued patronage the livelihood of the artists depends; because it is the people of education who are the arbiters of taste, whom the lesser purchasers are sure to imitate. I have several times been shocked by the poor judgment of persons who, by their social standing and by the artistic environment in which they have grown up, should have been able to discriminate.

The cause of this oncoming blindness is not far to seek. In most cases it can be directly connected with the importation of anti-traditional objects from abroad, glittering and vulgar products of mechanical or slave-man power, which, apart from their influence exerted directly through the eye, are calculated to affect taste even more severely through the glamour that they possess for the ignorant, because they come from the countries whose arms and commerce have subjugated the whole world.

Highly placed Tibetans who happen to travel down on business to Darjeeling, or even as far as Calcutta, come into contact with a section of European society that until recently had preserved the habits and outlook of prewar times. A socially privileged position, spacious living-conditions necessitated by a tropical climate, and remoteness from the storm-centres of world politics had together conspired to keep alive among Europeans in India the old nineteenth-century confidence and sense of undisturbed continuity, as well as the social customs that reflected those sentiments, and Tibetan visitors, having no standard of comparison, could not help basing their ideas of Europe on this apparently secure and comfortable picture. I was assured by one lama, for instance, that the inhabitants of Britain were one and all very clever and very rich! Latterly they have tended to transfer their dreamland to America.

This danger of misinterpretation is considerable; for were any large proportion of leaders in Tibet to convince themselves that we are, in spite of all our upheavals, fortunate people and worthy of their envy, nothing could save them from going the way of so many other Orientals. This point has not yet been reached, and many of the lay aristocracy, as well as most lamas, hold the contrary view. It is some of the younger men and women who are tempted, having been sent by well-meaning parents out of their country to schools run on modern lines. This problem of schooling is an acute one, and on its right or wrong solution the future largely depends. I propose to devote the next chapter to this question.

Some people have put forward the criticism that if the Tibetans — or, for that matter, the Indians or the Chinese or others who find themselves in a similar predicament — do not appreciate the good things that are their own, they deserve to lose them, for they show that they have mislaid the key to their understanding — indeed, everything is virtually lost already. This accusation is at best a half-truth. A man may have a genuine appreciation of his own things and yet may not possess the knowledge that will enable him to transfer his standards of criticism to the appraisement of entire novelties. Even the most highly trained and flexible mind has a circle within which it functions efficiently. The circle may be wide; but if its limits are overstepped, some degree of bewilderment is to be expected. Even in the Athens of the Periclean age, if all of a sudden one cinema, one chain store, and one radio station had been opened, I wonder whether the whole edifice of Hellenic civilization might not have come toppling about the ears of its creators, as surely as one machine-gun would have mown down the victorious hoplites of Marathon. Even a Phidias might have been momentarily taken in and a Zeuxis have exchanged his brush for a camera. One somehow suspects that Socrates would have seen through it all and stood firm; but he could always have been given his overdose of hemlock a few years earlier. A supreme power of discrimination can only go hand in hand with the highest Knowledge, and that is given to a few, not to the generality.

Whatever may be the correct explanation of the readiness with which people allow themselves to be caught on the hook of novelty, the fact remains that this failing is far from uncommon; therein lies the most acute danger for Tibetan art today. Any worthless machine-made trinket from abroad is apt to attract a man's fancy, so that he will set it up in a place of honour, next to the most supreme works of genius, without noticing the least incongruity. Madame David-Neel in one of her travel books relates how the learned abbot of a huge monastery of the province of Amdo, east of the Koko Nor, showed her his splendid apartments replete with the treasures of Chinese and Tibetan art. Enamel, jade, and the finest porcelain filled several cabinets; but in one of them she saw a collection of cheap European glass of the ugliest and most worthless description, displayed with a care which proved that these exhibits were no less admirable than the others in their august possessor's eyes. I myself, at Sangkar *Gompa* outside Leh, saw an empty ginger-beer bottle and a postcard of somewhere in Kent on the altar of the abbot's private chapel; in another temple in Khunu the sanctuary contained an empty tin marked "Flit." In the reception-room of the richest merchant in Ladak a whole set of sickly pink and green crockery of the most offensive type known among us reposed in a glass case side by side with precious examples of local craftsmanship.

A specially difficult practical problem has presented itself to the Tibetans since the Chinese republican revolution. For centuries China has been the country whence the bulk of imported art-products have been derived. Silk, porcelain, and the more expensive carpets, which have always come from China, still continue to do so, though their character has altered rapidly for the worse. Of these, the porcelain may still be comparatively harmless; but in the case of silk, required both for clothes and for the mounts of the painted *t'hankas*, the situation is more serious. Mechanical power has begun to be applied to its manufacture, though the better qualities of damask are often still copied from good patterns. The chief harm comes from the use of inferior dyestuffs. The materials intended for the surrounds of pictures, which have always tended to be brighter coloured than those meant for clothes, are daily changing in the direction of greater vividness and vulgarity. I have been told that the Lhasa people are not accepting this change without protest, but would give a lot to obtain fine silk as before.

Carpets are in the worst plight of all, for that trade has come entirely under the influence of the big importers into Europe and America, who demand of the makers both rapid delivery and frequent varying of designs, just for the sake of change. They often send out "Oriental" designs from Europe to the East, inventing glaringly conspicuous ones that will catch the eye easily. The patterns grow more sprawling every year and weird animals are preferred to geometrical or floral motifs. Vegetable dyes are abandoned for chemicals, largely because the latter will stand washing in caustic, to give a "silky sheen" — that is to say, a hideous celluloid-like surface. By these methods they have succeeded in destroying the art in China, as also in Turkey and central Asia, in a very few years. Tibet continues to buy in her old market, though a single one of these rugs is capable of upsetting the colour-scheme of any room into which it happens to be introduced.

In the modern Chinese rugs an objectionable feature is the general use of five-clawed dragons, once the privilege of the Imperial court. Now the four claws of the mandarin and the three claws of the common citizen are extinct, and everyone sports the Imperial badge. It is much as if in England the monarchy were to be abolished, and every vulgarian hastened to head his notepaper with the royal arms.

But the blame does not only rest with these degenerate Chinese articles. A new type of rug is creeping into the Tibetan market, probably of Indian or Japanese manufacture, which is nothing but a picture based on a photograph and stamped on the material. They are sold at a price within reach of the most humble purse. These textiles transcend the limits of ugliness; they deserve to be banned for moral poisons as surely as cocaine. I met a lama who possessed one of these rugs, on which was printed a group of camels, with their riders, in a neutral tint that could only be described as the colour of dirt. He was a friend of mine, who knew my views, so I offered him a little tapestry rug dyed with vegetable dyes in exchange, saying: "Let's set fire to the other and then all hold hands and dance round it." "Is that an English custom?" he asked gravely.

Among the imports, by far the most destructive are chemical dyestuffs, some of which are fugitive and almost all of which produce an ugly and heartlessly aggressive effect. The temptation to use them comes from the fact that packets can be purchased ready made up, whereas in the olden times the dyer had to exercise a little judgment when preparing his vats of indigo, bark, or lac. But then he was the master of his own colours; with the new dyes he must take what he finds. The difference in actual trouble is negligible, because weaving is a slow process, so that by comparison an extra day or two spent in dyeing hardly counts. It is curious how people who are models of patience in respect of spinning and weaving are ready to spoil their whole work by accepting the wrong colours; but the lure of the ready-made has everywhere been hard to withstand, especially for simple minds.

Examples can be multiplied almost indefinitely: here is one chosen at random from among many others equally possible. Certain notables of Gyantse, a town on the trade route to Lhasa, have lately begun to organize a local carpet industry for export to India. They use the usual Tibetan designs; but already they are beginning to corrupt them, as well as to apply inferior dyes. Each year brings some further step in the direction of crudeness and lack of artistic conscience. I do not suppose that the promoters of the scheme have ever given a thought to the ultimate effect of the changes in technique that they have been misled into sanctioning. I have reason to believe that they are persons who would repudiate any wish to interfere harmfully with tradition. A similar carpet enterprise is also carried on at Kampa Dzong, with the same result. Such mistakes are largely avoidable: a severe ban against the new dyes and an insistence that the traditional models should be faithfully followed would help to keep the craft in the straight path.

Chemical dyes are so harmful in the influence that they exert through the eye on the general colour-sense of both artists and their clients that they should be ruthlessly excluded, under pain of confiscation. Such a policy is not without precedent. John Claude White, the first British Resident in Sikkim, saw the danger long ago and actually caused the chemical dyes to be forbidden in the territory under his control. In this matter he showed remarkable foresight, when one remembers that he lived at a time when the evil was only just beginning, and when the world was fascinated by every new discovery of applied science, to which the meretricious glamour of Progress became immediately and uncritically attached. I should like to see White's policy enforced uncompromisingly not only in Sikkim, where at present it seems to be dead letter, but even more in Tibet and Bhutan. If it could be extended some day to the whole of India, so much the better.

To be logical one would also have to forbid the use of all cloth, silk, and yarn that was not dyed with vegetable colours; but this would mean interfering with a big trade in cottons and woollens. Before the war the importing of Polish or Italian broadcloth for gowns was seriously threatening the native-dyed and incomparably superior native cloth, and it would seem that here also restrictions are called for. But such action would affect important commercial interests and might be difficult to put into practice. Even if people have at first to be satisfied with a compromise, it is worth making a beginning and setting an example. So long as the people themselves are prevented from having access to chemical dyes, private dyeing with the good colours is bound to continue, and this art will not disappear for lack of practice.

One would like to see a policy on these lines applied to several other classes of imports. Much could be done if the nobles and richer merchants would show their disapproval by keeping such foreign goods out of their homes. It is their proper function to insist on the maintenance of artistic standards; where they lead, the rest of the nation will follow. If they abrogate their responsibility in this matter, the half-educated cannot be expected to show superior taste. Perhaps the simplest and most effective measure would be to legislate that no machine-made or chemical-dyed objects may be used for a ritual purpose, in temples or on altars. In a country where the prestige of sacred things stands as high as it does in Tibet, this would be a subtle way of discrediting the obnoxious articles, and it would probably react on their general use even for private purposes. The lesson would not be lost on the public mind.

The best measure that could be taken to protect and revive Tibetan art would be to start making locally many of those things which up to now have had to be brought from China, porcelain excepted, for which the materials are probably unobtainable in the country. But silk for clothes and *t'hankas*, as well as high-class carpets, could be woven in Tibet; it would chiefly be a question of importing a few good teachers. Willing and patient labour is there, and a general tradition of craftsmanship, which ought not to find it impossible to assimilate fresh techniques. Lhasa people have occasionally complained to me that they can no longer obtain fabrics of the old quality from China; there was also a kind of gold brocade that came from Russia in former days and that is much sought after for the little vests worn by high lamas. I was told that big prices could be demanded by anyone capable of turning out these things again. I have met at least one person who would be able to teach these crafts; and others could be trained. It is worth making the suggestion, in the hope that it may reach the proper quarter and be put into effect.

In the study of the present problem much can be gleaned from a comparison between districts where the arts are still to be found unimpaired, and others where decadence has already gone far. In our Himalayan journeyings, in every place where we had means of testing conditions, artistic excellence, both technical and in respect of design, was in strict inverse proportion to the amount of European social and commercial influence. Where this was great, the disaster had almost run its course; where it was small, there was some measure of bewilderment and inconsistency; but in places like the upper Satlej and parts of Ladak, where the people had been left to themselves, they seemed to find it impossible to produce anything meaningless or ugly. It is true that our friend the "Yellow Man" at Leh came into contact with European manufacturers in the course of his business, but this had not impaired his judgment, because he refused to be influenced by them. He represented the more vigorous and clear-sighted type of Tibetan, in whom should be placed the country's hopes: his attitude towards new things was quite matter-of-fact, not passionate: "They're shoddy and I don't like them. Anyone can see that they have not been properly made."

But we met others who were less discriminating, for whom the fact that things were from Europe or America outweighed questions of suitability and quality. Some of these people may have been brought to this pass by attending European schools; but by no means all of them would have felt happy had they perceived that they were likely to undermine the outer defences of the Doctrine of Buddha itself and were yielding up their own and their children's souls to the modern materialism. One can only say to such people that they are not really facing up to the facts, but are letting themselves be seduced from their allegiance, merely because they cannot resist the lure of a few mechanical novelties. Surely this is not the moment to plunge into rash changes, for the fate of the Occidental world itself is trembling in the balance and even its most fanatical admirers have been somewhat shaken in their optimism about its future.

It is, however, always possible that whatever the Tibetan peoples may elect to do, the decision will be taken out of their hands. Just as Japan, forced against her will to become Westernized, learned her lesson only too well and caught the nationalist infection as badly as anyone, so China, in her efforts to resist foreign encroachment, may also find that natural self-defence has turned her into a militarized national State, with the mentality that belongs to that condition. In case of a serious invasion from that quarter, Tibetan independence would be precarious; and resistance to an army fully equipped with modern weapons could only result in a repetition of the Abyssinian tragedy. But till it is clear which road China is going to tread, one worthy of her glorious and pacific past or one leading to yet another version of the modern barbarism, this issue must remain in the balance.

The tragedy of the Western penetration of Asia has lain in the fact that it has resulted in a breakdown of tradition, not in a mere reorientation, such as has mitigated, even if it has not justified, some of the other conquests of history. But someone might ask why the spread of Western influence need necessarily undermine every culture. Surely, it will be argued, history records cases, both of military conquest and of peaceful penetration, when the subjection of one civilization by another has eventually resulted in the creation of a new synthesis, legitimate heir to the excellences of both its parents. Unfortunately the European colonizing urge came at a time when in the West there had been a definite break with tradition as such. By the time that the impulse to expand had passed its maximum, the conquerors had lost grip even of the last lingering vestiges of the traditional sense; reversing the relative values in the hierarchy, they had become fanatical devotees of the practical, to the disparagement of the dignity of the spiritual order. The supreme aim of metaphysical realization became the concern of the outmoded few, while art was treated as one among the many minor luxuries reserved for the wealthy. To the average man, tastelessness and vulgarity were his allotted portion, justified by the typical argument of the demagogue: "Why shouldn't the public enjoy what it likes?" Yet there was a day in the European city of Florence when Cimabue's Madonna was borne in triumph through the streets. Now it would be the captain of a victorious football team who would receive this honour.

When appreciation of the fine things in our own inheritance is confined to an ever shrinking class at home, it is not to be expected that much of it will be carried overseas. It is humiliating to discover the things that pass for specimens of European taste in the estimation of the average Oriental. How often

have I been regaled with "English music" by the proud possessor of a wireless or a gramophone, even by persons of high station, without being asked on a single occasion to listen to anything better than the crudest examples of jazz or crooning,
blared out by strident brass bands or bleated by voices maudlin
with vibrato. These people's bad taste may be blameworthy,
but can one say that the models that have been set before them
have been characteristic of a highly civilized society? Are the
European communities in the East on the whole conspicuous
for the intellectual character of their homes or their pastimes?
As far as the arts are concerned, I have never come across a
case in the modern Orient when one good thing had been sup-
planted by another good thing; victory has always gone to
something utterly barbarous — which we as Westerners should
be ashamed to own — as if the operative law were a curious in-
version of natural selection.

It should also be remembered that the European conquerors
in the East differed in one marked feature from any of their
predecessors, in that they tried to organize themselves permanently on a temporary basis. The Saracens, the Mongols, or
the Turki invaders of India felt no great sympathy for the
ideas of their newly won subjects, but as they made the conquered provinces their home, time, familiarity, and intermar-
riage soon did their work in bringing about a fusion of ideas.
Alexander of Macedon went farther still, for he deliberately
set himself to hasten that fusion from the first hour of his success. Not only did he marry Roxana, the daughter of his rival
Darius, but he also assumed the dress and manners of the Persian court, as if to proclaim to his empire that he placed himself at the head of the existing tradition and was prepared to
fill the part allotted to the sovereign by its laws — a symbolical
act that abjured any breach of continuity. It is perhaps this
policy that, even more than his military exploits, has earned
him his title of "the Great." He became the national hero of
the countries that his armies overran; if he conquered men's
bodies, he also found the way to reign in their hearts. Even
now his name is one to conjure with all over the East, and
many an Afghan chief or Malay princeling is proud to trace
his ancestry to Iskandar, as the Orientals call the famous son
of Philip.

Whether or not one takes the view that, in the aggregate, European conquests resulted in greater or less harm, one cannot
but recognize that they did not partake of the same character

as previous invasions. Both settlers for purposes of commerce and the most conscientious of officials kept their thoughts fixed on the day when they would be allowed to retire to Europe with their families, there to enjoy their pension. Climatic reasons and the wish to avoid racial admixture both conspired to prevent them from striking their roots deep. But man is rarely willing to exert himself intellectually except in his natural surroundings. That is why Europeans in the East have largely kept to practical jobs, which they have often carried out with conspicuous ability if with little sympathy; but they have shown less inclination for the things of the intellect.

But the trouble is not confined to the expatriated communities. The same coarsening process that is robbing Asia of her arts has long been at work in the West itself, and the section of the population who can appreciate art and the things that make art possible, though it still survives, is restricted to small and dwindling numbers. If all works of beauty were to be blotted out tomorrow, including the monuments of the past, some tears, to be sure, would still be shed; but in the world at large, mourning would be far less widespread than over the loss of any popular sport, say tennis, though doubtless greater than if it were a question of the disappearance of ping-pong.

At present the Tibetans are resisting with increasing difficulty the sinister pressure of materialism, but there is also a chance that the modern idols may begin to lose their prestige as a result of their own self-destructive tendencies. If in the West itself materialistic values were to become discredited, there might be a hope of the whole world re-entering the Traditional Path. If this miracle should happen, it would be more than ever important for the few peoples who have so far kept themselves uncontaminated to be ready to lend the support of their example, whenever the day comes for building up a true *Western* Tradition again, complete in all its modes and degrees.

Chapter XXVI

Education in the Borderlands

I MUST NOW turn to the discussion of a practical problem, that of modern education, as it affects the peoples living on the borders of Tibet. We had ample opportunities for considering this question during our stay at Kalimpong and Gangtok, for, standing as they do on the frontiers of modernity and of the last traditional civilization left substantially intact in the world, they offer an ideal field for the investigator who wishes to observe the interreactions of these two forces. Independent Tibet is almost the only country where a considerable measure of consistent and conscious opposition continues to be offered in the face of the levelling tendencies of Pan-Occidentalism. In India, where there has also been some resistance, there is so much lost ground to make good that the final outcome is as yet impossible to forecast. There was a day when Japan hoped to remain like a second Tibet; but in her case, though the will was there, the menace of the guns of the squadron under Commodore Perry in 1854 forcibly opened her ports. In the light of events, how many people now living would have liked to undo that chapter of history and to see their dangerous commercial and political rivals safely back in the refined inoffensiveness of their feudal ages.

Tibet has been favoured by the remoteness of her geographical position and by the possession of a mountain barrier so impenetrable that she has found it possible to persevere in a policy impracticable for her larger and more powerful neighbours. Physical obstacles alone, however, would hardly have been sufficient to protect Tibet's isolation — nowadays engineers, given money and adequate time, might even force a way to the top of Everest — but Heaven, in its mercy, was pleased to make a great part of Tibet stony, sterile, and unattractive to lovers of comfort. A heart-straining altitude and the biting winds of the plateau have proved to be gifts more enviable than the fertility and kinder weather of temperate climes. It must also be admitted that Tibet's isolation has so far suited certain political interests.

This central area of Tibet has acted therefore as a preserving-ground for a society constituted on traditional lines, in the middle of a world which has thought that it could dispense with the traditional safeguards and which, when not actively hostile towards the ancient institutions, regards them with contemptuous indifference, dubbing them picturesque anachronisms. This epithet fits, if it is to be taken as merely meaning a minority carrying on in the old ways, when the majority of men, for reasons valid or unsound, have discarded them; but the word normally carries with it some additional notion of censure levelled at the discarded institutions, as well as an implication that such things as have been abandoned by the majority as useless have been rightly so abandoned and that the minority, in striving to row against the tide, is simply showing a retrograde tendency.

The late eighteenth and nineteenth centuries invested the word "progress" with sentimental attributes, picturing it as a continuous straight track along which humanity, with occasional unfortunate deviations, was fated to move steadily forward towards Utopia. The spectacular victory of the evolutionary hypothesis invested the new theory, in the eyes of the populace, with the same categorical authority that had previously been accorded to the old beliefs that it superseded. In its later developments, especially in the theory of natural selection, which Darwin had presented as no more than a blind force that was helping to mould the living world, the notion of evolution began to acquire moral, or rather moralistic, attributes. It was supposed that whatever was exterminated by something else showed, by its very weakness, that it was inferior to its destroyer and that its disappearance was required by the service of the new Juggernaut of Progress. It might just as well have been argued, when some epidemic carried off men in their prime, including the doctors and nurses engaged in fighting the plague, that the bacilli must enjoy a "higher" civilization than the scientists and the common folk who fell victims to their attack, and that the germs deserved their victory in a moral sense.

Lest my readers should think that this suggestion is too far-fetched, I quote a writer who in the year 1935 declared: "An attack by poisonous gas is another form of the effect of environment to secure the survival of the fittest and the elimination of decadent and unworthy persons and races." It is at least com-

forting to be assured that the gas will know how to select
its victims and will pass over the brave, the gifted, and the
healthy, even as the Angel of the Lord passed over the houses
of the Israelites in the land of Egypt — this is selection indeed! *

It can readily be seen how convenient such theories must
have proved, when they first came into vogue, in furnishing excuses for every brutal act of brigandage, political or commercial. They seemed to set the seal of Nature's approval on the
sordid tale of grab and exploitation. The victims were beaten;
therefore their defeat was a just defeat, their loss a public gain.
These dogmas — for theories soon harden into convictions —
form the darker side of liberalism; at the time of their general
acceptance they were acclaimed as the most epoch-making dis-
coveries, the scientific charter legalizing the subjection of the
weak and lowly to Nature's own strong men. Tender con-
sciences consoled themselves with the pious thought that the
Almighty had given them a commission to govern all "inferior"
or "native" peoples for their own good; they even went so far
as to dress up this duty in the garb of self-sacrifice, as expressed in the famous phrase "the White Man's burden," surely
the most smug and hypocritical that has ever passed human
lips. Humane evolutionists, such as Kropotkin, protested against
this travesty of biological theories, but to small purpose: the
new formula was far too convenient in providing the desired
theoretical basis for the working alliance between the two
dominant forces of puritanism and predatory commercialism.
The former contributed moral self-confidence and the latter
boundless material ambition and drive. In the firm of Messrs.
Mammon & God Unlimited, the lawless trader's vanity was
flattered by the fancy that in pushing his conquests he was acting under Providence as the agent of Progress, while the self-
appointed guardians of everyone else's welfare found the material rewards that accrued in the shape of social prestige and
all that went with it very much to their taste. Cecil Rhodes,
whose outlook, like Hitler's, was much affected by half-baked
Darwinism, put the idea very neatly when he said that a guiding principle of imperialist policy should be "philanthropy + 5
per cent."

* In fairness to the author of the above quotation it must be explained that
he was not condoning the use of poison gas: his aim was to goad slack citizens
into taking adequate defensive measures. My quarrel is with those who accept
the popularized view of natural selection and invest that hypothesis with a
moral purpose.

Brawny Gospellers and empire-building adventurers, as well as the new captains of industry, stood singularly close to one another in their outlook.

The same mixture of moralizing and cupidity enters into the actions of many comparatively respectable pioneers of the period of European expansion. In England this tendency has only begun to play itself out in our lifetime. I can remember the time when the old jingoism was still considered a respectable creed; but since then there have been some welcome changes in public and official opinion: imperialism is forced to look round for disguises. But the world is by no means rid of the old arrogance yet, only it has had to seek out new forms in which to disguise itself. "Democracy" may well prove to be one of them, on occasion.,

Nineteenth-century co-operation between religiosity of the "fundamentalist" type, always peculiarly untroubled by doubts, and the new commercial enterprise, flushed with the first-won victories of mechanization, brought about a concentration of forces acting in one direction such as had never been known in all previously recorded history. The Anglo-Saxon races led the vanguard of the movement and succeeded in cornering most of the places in the sun before other nations could follow suit, an initiative for which the world has paid in bitter jealousies. But most of the races of European blood, even those who did not participate directly in the colonial expansion, shared the extrovert mentality of the empire-builders. Drawn by this new focus of attention, all Western nations devoted their energies increasingly to large-scale exploitation and, in proportion as they did so, tended to approximate nearer and nearer to one model, and this in spite of the most violent national antagonisms. To the civilization that was thus produced I give the name of "Occidental," so as not to confound it with any genuine European culture, though nowadays some of its most frenzied exponents are of Oriental blood. This civilization seems totally unlike any of the others of which we possess records, whether in written form or inferred from archæological remains. One can almost go so far as to say that there is more in common between any two traditional civilizations picked at random — say Celtic and Inca — than between any one of them and that of modern times. Taking a bird's-eye view of history, would it be altogether far-fetched to speak of modern Occidental civilization as the one and only anachronism, the anachronism *par excellence*?

Among the ancients, nevertheless, there is one partial exception. The Romans seem to have tended, in some measure, towards a similar system. Among them we see the same preoccupation with purely practical ends, the same harping upon social applications to the disregard of the intellectual element, resulting, in logical consequence, in a deification of human society in the State. It is perhaps only the fact that post-Renaissance Europe was able, through the rapid development of the applied sciences, to harness material forces on an unprecedented scale that has caused us to leave the Romans so far behind; but their ideals, if one can give them such a name, were in many respects akin to ours, and it is doubtless no accident that the so-called Renaissance, the time of the final rupture with the regular Occidental Tradition, was characterized by an uncritical enthusiasm for everything Greco-Roman and by hatred and contempt for everything non-classical. The men who saw in Gothic cathedrals nothing but barbarous excrescences and who scoffed at the speculations of the Schoolmen were the spiritual ancestors of those who nowadays affect to despise everything Oriental.

Europe since the first World War has lost the comfortable sense of security of the nineteenth century; but it has not yet been able to shake off its habits; nor are there yet signs of any general abandonment of the notion of continuous progress. If anything, the trend is still all towards the elimination of lingering traces of tradition. Those who aspire to play the part of reformers usually look for their panacea, not in a rebirth of the genuine traditional spirit, but in a further development of the forces that liberalism brought into being, in more elaborate organization and in the organization of labour carried to greater and greater extremes. The ideal proclaimed is that of a world reduced to one vast insurance scheme; to this dream is attached the grandiloquent euphemism of "a pooling of the resources of humanity." But the pool has been carefully pre-engineered, so that the trickle that represents the united contribution of all the other civilizations cannot help being swamped by the drainage from the Euro-American quarter.

In Tibet and Bhutan, in so far as they still remain non-cooperators in this plan, the authority of Tradition remains unquestioned, and the more intellectually gifted persons usually profess the will to preserve it. "We feel that our institutions suit us best. Possibly your civilization suits you, though some of us think it has gone astray; but that is your affair" — this verdict sums up the attitude of many. But these countries are surrounded by a ring of small states and racially allied districts that, though they still look to Lhasa for their leadership, are living on the edge of two worlds and therefore cannot escape having to face a difficult problem of adaptation, one that does not so directly confront dwellers in the centre of Tibet. Residents on the border, whether they are engaged in business or in making social contacts with those, both Indian and European, who are partly or wholly imbued with Occidentalism, find themselves called upon to handle things that would not enter into their normal environment at home; to cite a few of them: cars, newspapers, radio, the persuasive technique of advertising, modern medicine, speed, bureaucratic organization, democracy and its catchwords; some things good, others evil, and others again more doubtful, able to make useful servants but bad masters.

To pick a way through this labyrinth, a certain knowledge is needed, mainly in the material field. Parents on becoming aware that their children, if they are to go on living on the borderland, must solve these problems or go under have also to decide how their minds are to be equipped for the ordeal. They find that their own education, however uplifting in a general way, requires supplementing in certain branches that lie outside its normal scope. Therefore the question of education is paramount, and on the method of its solution depends, to a large extent, the survival or the rapid disintegration of the culture of the frontier nations. If they also become Westernized, then the invading host, having pierced the outer ring of defences, will batter on the gates of the inner keep of Tibet proper with redoubled force. Even now, the Lhasa-Kalimpong trade-route, opened up by the treaty of 1904, offers one avenue by which a tentacle of the octopus can probe right into the heart of the land. Though foreigners are restricted from entering, their goods, less obviously suspect than their persons, do penetrate and serve to disseminate foreign tastes. Also, Tibetans and Bhutanese who come south to trade are liable to become infected with modernist influences. In studying this whole problem, the first step is to analyse the early reactions of all these people to Occidental contacts; nowhere can this research be carried out more conveniently than at Kalimpong and in Sikkim.

The Tibetans, like most of the yellow races, are imbued with an avid passion for learning and a natural predisposition in favour of education and schools and teachers, in contrast to that half-antagonism which the Englishman often shows and which, one must admit, has sometimes saved him from falling such an easy prey to regimentation as his more obedient Continental neighbours. Reverence for the teacher is a great asset provided the education offered be the right one; otherwise it is better to be a lazy and insubordinate pupil.

It cannot for a moment be maintained that the Tibetan race is devoid of education, and the culture of the country is everywhere vigorous and consistent. The clergy, natural custodians of learning, whose adequate leisure for study is effectively provided for by the social system in vogue, includes many lettered persons, whose marvellous memories enable them to repeat whole books by heart. Even among the poor I was surprised to find how many possessed a smattering of literacy and, still better, a power of judgment that is in no wise dependent on books. Higher education is preponderantly devotional: metaphysical treatises, chronicles of saints, legends, and sacred poetry form the bulk of the reading of the laity as well as of the lamas. Apart from these studies, writing a fine hand and the rudiments of reckoning complete the list. Officials, in addition, must acquire a mastery of the correct styles of address, which are often rather flowery; if to these be added the rules of grammar and logic, the result is an education comparable to that of the Scholastics in medieval Europe.

When foreign educators came and settled in places like Kalimpong and Darjeeling, it was rather natural that the well-to-do should hasten to place their children in the new schools, as being the best locally available, without stopping to peer with an over-critical eye into the drawbacks as well as the advantages of the tuition offered, and without feeling apprehensive of any possible evil results in the distant future. These institutions are of two sorts, either missionary schools of various denominations, or secular schools, endowed by Government, or, as in Sikkim, by the native State in imitation of the schools of greater India. Thus the children of parents who had themselves been brought up on strictly traditional lines, with sacred studies coming first, the art of courtesy holding second place, and secular knowledge counting third, came to be placed trustingly under the care of exponents of alien systems, actuated by motives that were either frankly hostile to the existing tradition, as in the missions, or simply indifferent to it, as in the lay schools. In both, the curriculum allots a preponderant share to information concerning material things, which is the chief pre-occupation of the West and which serves as the bait to entice pupils.

In mission schools there may or may not be a direct impart-ing of Christian teaching; but in either case the moral code and all sorts of undefined implications and tendencies derive from what is now commonly accepted in the West. The same teach-ing is there, whether the word "religion" be mentioned or not. A person who makes no secret of his hope for the eventual substitution of Christianity for Hindu or Buddhist belief can hardly be blamed if he shows at least indifference to the in-terests of the native civilization, inextricably interwoven as it is with the threads of metaphysical doctrine. In deciding what are the legitimate methods of implanting ideas into the minds of their young charges, some doubtless try to be nicely scrupulous, while others stretch a point here and there. In the case of a missionary teacher the more zealous he is, the farther he is likely to allow himself to go in the matter of deliberately un-dermining the foundation laid by the parents — or not laid, as is too often the case; for in a traditionally regulated society, where everything hangs together, the environment is suffi-ciently strong to relieve the private individual of some of his anxieties over these matters, so that the unwary may be lulled into a complacent mood that does not befit these times of crisis.

Whereas the missionary is, by his profession, inclined to re-gard the native beliefs as so much superstition, to the secular-minded modern teacher they appear rather in the light of primitive folklore, which education will force a person to out-grow. The man with the religious axe to grind will rush to implant his own official version of the Christian code; whereas the secular schoolmaster will probably expound a stoical sys-tem of ethics, possibly with a faint Christian tinge. He may also blend with it a sentimental belief in the magic benefits of "the public-school spirit," which regards competition as a virtue and sees in physical activity, as expressed in organized games, an automatic power to uplift; while gentleness is slightly suspect as a sign of weakness.

There are striking differences between the things that the pupil in the traditional scheme would have been taught and those that he is likely to acquire in an average Westernized school, even a good one. The sacredness of life, other than human, will certainly not be overstressed, even if it is men-tioned at all. The whole emphasis will be on Man and his

interests; everything else will be shown as ministering to these
— a very different story from the Hindu or Buddhist duty of
solicitude for all suffering creatures. A good many of the teachers in the more expensive secular schools, specially designed
for the rich and aristocratic, are keen on shooting. Therefore
it cannot be expected that they will go to any special trouble
in order to discredit that pastime in the eyes of their charges,
and the latter are likely to grow up to tolerate the idea. I
turned up a few Hindu, and even Buddhist, names at random
in the pages of *Who's Who,* and found that they nearly all had
put down "Shooting" under the heading "Recreation"! Most of
these poor people had been pupils at high-class schools in the
European style.

Secondly, the contemplative ideal placed before the true
Oriental as the highest possible calling for a man is dismissed
by modern Occidentals as equivalent to laziness. For them the
only ideal is "practical" work — that is to say, visible activity
confined to the material and social fields. The difference of
point of view is so fundamental that two educators, respective
adherents of these opposing philosophies, ought not to share
the same professional designation.

Thirdly, the aim of our education, even at its best, is the
development of individualism to its utmost, just as, at its worst,
by the cultivation of a blind *esprit de corps*, it encourages the
instincts of the herd, to the submerging of the sense of personal
responsibility. Both these aims are out of keeping with Buddhist doctrine, the first because it derives all its justification
from the belief in a real "Ego," which Buddhism denies, and
the second because it fosters an over-sensitiveness to public
opinion and makes easy a response to emotional stimulation
from outside which is incompatible with that deliberate, detached judgment which the true Buddhist must ever be at
pains to exercise.

Then there is the question of language. Since Macaulay in
his educational policy set out to turn the Indians into "coloured Englishmen," in the sincere belief that this was the
highest boon conferrable on any member of the human race,
irrespective of temperament, geography, or history, English has
been regarded as the chief vehicle of education throughout
Indian territory, and proficiency in English has come to be the
hall-mark of education above all others. In higher-class schools
a great part of the tuition is given in the English language and
so it comes about that a child of native parentage develops all

its early thought through the medium of a foreign idiom rather than through the tongue learned at its mother's knee.

A language is the faithful mirror of the thought and character of a people and becomes nicely adapted to the expression of its particular genius; no foreign tongue can be substituted without making it difficult for the thoughts themselves to take shape. If the means for voicing them are perfect, thoughts rise to the surface freely in a continuous flow; this state of affairs favours, through constant practice, the coming into being of fresh thoughts. But let the pumping-machinery be gritty and ill-adapted, then the flow will become irregular, and there will be a tendency for the well itself to dry up from disuse. As language is our principal vehicle for conveying our thoughts to our neighbours and as we act as a whetstone for one another's minds, faulty, slipshod, or inexact expression and the consequent interference with communication will also tend to bring about a drop in the general level of intelligence. Wherever any unnatural tongue has been adopted as the common vehicle of education, whether a foreign language has been chosen or even some insincere, pedantic version of the native language, the result has always been lamentable.

Travelling homeward, we happened to have as fellow passengers on the boat a number of Indian students on their way to join English universities. We noticed that a good many of them tried to talk English among themselves, especially in the public saloons. At first we thought that they must have come from provinces lying far apart, where different dialects were spoken; but we found out that in some cases they were neighbours and that this was simply an attempt to show off their education. And what an English they spoke! It would take a Kipling to reproduce its ungrammatical and pompous verbiage. Such a practice argues a serious degree of demoralization.

In an education based on English the pupil not only reads the literature of a remote country before that of his own, but is also brought up on history as viewed through foreign eyes. Similarly the excessive importance attached to games is such as to alter a boy's outlook permanently. There is also a danger of the children acquiring some of that gaucherie and shyness which we associate with the "awkward age." When travelling in the Himalaya, I noticed that all the children were free from this self-consciousness; it made one ask oneself whether its regular incidence among us was not due to some preventable maladjustment in the school system. It is not a fault to be ignored.

The only Tibetan pupils whom I ever found to be suffering
from this ailment were boarders in a European school, and
they had been badly affected.

And lastly I must again mention the question of dress. In
nearly all schools run by Europeans in the border districts I
saw a large proportion of the pupils wearing European clothes.
In certain mission schools of a high class this change had been
imposed under the specious plea of a school uniform. That
foreigners should come to a country and demand on any
grounds whatsoever that their pupils should abandon their
own dress in favour of that of their teachers is outrageous, for
it contains the plain implication that the native dress is the
badge of an inferior status. Were this not the case, it would be
just as simple to design a uniform modelled on the local costume. Could one imagine an alien headmaster founding a
school in England or America and requiring his scholars to
adopt any alien style of costume — let us say a German or
Russian school uniform? Would a single parent entrust his
children to such a person, however tempting the educational
facilities offered? In accepting such terms for their children,
many Orientals show a singular lack of self-respect.

The intangible influences must not be forgotten either, the
imperceptible effect of surroundings upon habits and taste.
Furniture will be different and will be used differently. The
floor will be replaced by the desk — a considerable physical
change for growing children and an even greater social one,
liable, later on, to make them feel uncomfortable among their
own people. As soon as an Oriental begins to require chairs
and tables, his domestic outlook has already undergone a tremendous revolution. There are also pictures on the walls, in
which the symbolical and decorative treatment of traditional
art will have given place to the conventions of photographic
naturalism, a dangerous experience for the innocent eye of a
child, which may well mean that the child's own art will eventually become a closed book to him. It would be easy to mul-
tiply these examples, but enough has been said to indicate the
main lines of criticism.

But surely there are the holidays, it will be argued; that is
an opportunity for parents to provide a counter-influence. First
it should be observed that under a fully traditional education
both parents and teachers are exerting their authority along
parallel lines. There is never a question of pulling different
ways. Once the two influences part company, the result is

bound to be a compromise if not worse, with the scales becoming weighted more and more against tradition and in favour of innovation as each generation passes. In most cases people just let things slide, in which case only one result can be expected. To counteract a dangerous influence deliberately needs foresight and discrimination, and one cannot yet expect that from the average man.

If the foreign educators, whether secular-minded or religious, were to use their schools openly for the proselytism of the pupils, parents might be roused to action at once, to the point of withdrawing their children. But there is no need to go as far as that; indeed, no one but a fool would thus invite trouble. The insidiousness of the poison lies in the fact that children, being at a plastic age, unsuspicious, naturally docile, and keen to learn, are only too ready to assimilate an unseen influence administered in small doses. The Jesuits are credited with having said: "Give me the child before it is eight; after that you can do as you like with it." They knew, from age-long experience, that early impressions count heavily in after-life and that if only a doubt can be sown early, or the embryo of an idea implanted, it may continue to work like a ferment capable of destroying the most ancient loyalties. In the case of the Jesuits, of course, the end in view was not to undermine, but to preserve a certain tradition against the temptations of unbelief.

Once the sense of reverence towards ancient customs and ideas has been weakened, the influence of the doctrine that permeates them will itself be on the wane. If the child who has been exposed to the new schooling does not lose its hold on the Doctrine in the first generation, the children of the next generation will be well on the way to deserting it; for they will start, not with a clean sheet, but from the point where their father and mother left off their own education. Whatever traditional ideas may survive to the third generation will be mere remnants — superstitions in the true etymological sense of the word. It is at this point that the chance of proselytizing to another religion is at its greatest; though in the modern world it is far more likely that atheism or agnosticism or mere nihilism will follow.

It is almost inconceivable that Oriental children who pass through a modern schooling of the ordinary type, whether well or badly run — the more efficient the school, especially if it is a boarding-school, the graver the danger — will retain a real sense of reverence. The feeling may survive for a time in an impaired form in good homes; in slack homes it will die or only show itself in a few lingering external customs. The children will become moral and intellectual half-castes and in the following generation all will be lost. The old people will eventually wake up to the puzzling fact that they, who tried, as they thought, to give their children " the best available chances of education," are now regarded by them as:

Credulous old fogies; back numbers;
Half-savages.

The children will also think that:

Their parents' doctrines are nothing but fairy-tales.
Their works of art are to be put in glass cases as antiques.
Their clothes are out of date and ridiculous.

Are the teachers then to be accused of having acted dishonestly? Doubtless there exist flagrant cases of unscrupulousness; but in general one cannot expect them to teach principles that they do not believe in themselves. If they are conscientious, they will do the best they can for the pupils according to their lights. If parents are willing to send their children to the foreign schools, the decision is their disaster, or rather the childrens' and that of the whole nation. For the parents it is a great temptation to make use of educational advantages that happen to lie so close at hand and that call for no effort on their own part. For the sake of the lesser, but immediate, advantage, they turn a blind eye to the cost — the loss of things that they should think most precious.

From the opposite point of view of the teacher, who feels that he is a bringer of inestimable benefits to a "backward" people, the methods followed all seem justifiable and even meritorious. To influence the children has proved to be the effective way, not only in Asia, but also in every part of Europe; that is why the new absolutist states have concentrated their biggest effort on the immature, rather than on the adult, mind, with the certainty of reaping the harvest in due course. In the case of religious schools, the type of man who feels the call to the mission field is not usually an impartial philosopher who wishes to see both sides — true philosophers do not take kindly to a life of propaganda, with its inevitable hurry and superficiality; the qualifications needed are a one-track mind and the sense of superiority that comes from the flattering conviction that one possesses and can dispense the message, the true message, and nothing but the message. The men who take up these tasks — but there are of course exceptions — are bound to hold the native culture to be worthless, or at least unimportant. It is difficult for them, even when they intend to act honestly, to judge the meaning of the word "scruple"; for in their eyes the prejudged result overshadows every other consideration. The attitude of the secular-minded school-teacher is less positive; but he also cannot be expected to go to the trouble of bolstering up a lot of "mediæval nonsense," to the prejudice of the "real, practical things" that he sets out to teach.

The fact is that in regard to the fundamental things of life impartiality is not easy in practice, even if the wish be present. Admittedly, there is such a thing as unscrupulous and dishonest abuse of the sacred calling to educate the young; but even apart from this, every person disseminates ideas by the mere fact of being himself. It is only one who himself participates in a living tradition who can be said not to be opposed to Tradition, at least unconsciously. It is not a question only of how many hours are to be spent in imparting set religious or moral teachings; it is the imponderable influences and the general atmosphere that surrounds the pupil that count even more than dogmatic instruction. The various totalitarian opponents of the Christian Church have been vehement in their determination to wrest the control of growing children out of the hands of the Church and, to a great extent, of parents. They are banking on the effects of early school environment becoming permanent. Let this be an object-lesson. To those Asiatic parents who have proved so unsuspicious in entrusting their own children to alien cares one would like to put the following questions: If, for example, the Communists were to found a school in England equipped with every modern appliance, would non-Communists be likely to send their children there? Or if a non-Catholic school, giving the most up-to-date education, superior to what is available locally, were to be opened in the west of Ireland, do you think that it would get many pupils?

It is not a question of approving narrow-mindedness, much less personal hostility, towards the purveyors of unacceptable creeds. Grown-up people ought to be able to look after themselves in these matters; but children are in no such position, and to expose them to outside pressure of that sort at a tender

age is not a sign of open-mindedness, but of sheer foolhardiness. It is astonishing the risks that many Oriental parents are
willing to take. In this we see the trustfulness and toleration
of the Oriental character pushed to a vice. A little of the
Occidental promptness to react might be borrowed with advantage. Some time ago the papers reported a speech by a
missionary leader in a Buddhist country who was speaking
optimistically of the prospects of his mission, consequent upon
the breakdown of the old traditions under the impact of modernity. He used the phrase: "The Wall of Buddha has been
smashed." This coarse expression, which should never have
crossed the lips of a professed Christian, can leave no doubt
as to the attitude to be expected of its author in educational
matters; yet in all probability in the schools under his control many children would still be found belonging to Buddhist families where the parents had been too inert to be aware
of the menace. Again it must be said that no one wishes the
Orientals to depart from their excellent habits of tolerance and
courtesy towards foreign religions; but if they withdrew their
children from the schools, it would be an act, not of fanaticism,
but of common prudence.

The time is certainly critical; to drift is to court disaster. If
there is a remedy, it lies in the parents' hands. The same applies to Tibetans, Indians, and all races similarly placed. But
though a man with his back against the wall should be ready,
in an extreme case, to abandon education altogether rather
than to agree to the cultural debauching of his children, he
need not give up hope of finding an alternative way till he has
exhausted every means at his disposal. There *does* exist an alternative, and that is to plan a system of education *consciously
founded on tradition,* but capable of including any supplementary information that local circumstances render necessary; ever remembering that, as between the various branches
of knowledge, the traditional hierarchy must be uncompromisingly maintained. Even so, many difficult decisions will have to
be taken; the best chance of deciding rightly will come to the
man who remains with his feet firmly planted on the rock of
his own traditional form and who takes the trouble to study its
principles even more diligently than ever before. Deliberate
choice is the sign of the free spirit; those who talk of political
or economic freedom without intellectual freedom are babblers.

If, through their earlier easy-going attitude towards the
pressing educational problem, the leaders of Oriental society

find themselves setting out late in the day to solve it, they must accept the fact and patiently start again from the beginning, without hoping to find a short cut. To have been caught unawares is no sin; but to persist in ostrich-like self-delusion will lead inevitably and deservedly to an utter breakdown.

To build up from the beginning in difficult circumstances needs vision, enthusiasm, and also a diligent attention to detail. The starting-point must be a firm adherence to Tradition, not mere pigheaded conservatism or patriotism, but reverence founded on the unbroken experience of the ages handed down through master and pupil in the intellectual élite or true spiritual aristocracy. In case of an inescapable choice between two courses of action one should always lean towards continuing the established usage; change should only be tolerated if, after due weighing up of the question, the existing practice is found to be hopelessly inconsistent with one's principles. In the same way the general trend should be against the importation of foreign usages; but that does not mean that there are not a few cases where these might be found to be definitely advantageous and could be accepted and digested into the traditional scheme, exactly like a foreign word that is assimilated into a language and takes on its character.

Let us now consider the possibility of creating new schools in the borderland of Tibet, as well as the practical details of their organization. They should be conducted in a manner consonant with Tradition, but they may also impart certain selected branches of knowledge borrowed, under careful control, from the West, to meet the special needs of those who are forced to dwell on the frontiers of two incompatible theories of life. It is assumed that, having experienced a revulsion of feeling against the present state of affairs, the minds of the leaders of the border peoples will have been cleared of all hankering after a compromise and that they will be firmly determined that, unless they can act in accordance with the spirit of traditional doctrine as applied in action, they will renounce school education altogether. A mere copy of the Occidental system, accepting its standards, plus the inclusion of, say, Buddhist or Hindu scriptural teaching in place of Christian, is no solution; a school run on these lines would be nothing but a disguised Occidental school. Ultimately it would be a sign that its founders valued the new material knowledge above the tradition, but wished to pay lip-service to the latter. Mere modified copies of existing schools will not do. A clean sweep must be made, but without impatience; whoever embarks on such a task must for a time rest content with small-scale beginnings. He must be prepared to make mistakes before he can work out his program to be both sound doctrinally and efficient practically. Quality must, as far as possible, take precedence over rapid results on a large scale.

What elements, in the traditional civilization, exist to provide the basis for such an enterprise? What is the fundamental principle of the existing education? We must not forget that it is fortunately not a question of starting education in an educationless society, but of applying the existing experience to certain immediate problems, almost entirely confined to the material field. The training of the person for the greatest and most essential of his functions — namely, the discovery of metaphysical reality — is an art so highly developed among the intellectual élite of India and Tibet that it would be an impertinence to offer any suggestions in that direction. The keystone of education can continue to be the selfsame agency that keeps Tradition itself perpetually functioning — namely, the reverence of the pupil for the teacher. The fact that in the Hindu and Buddhist Traditions it has been possible to combine such devotion to the teacher with a remarkable degree of freedom in respect of discussion and inquiry goes to prove that "orthodoxy" and narrow-mindedness do not necessarily go hand-in-hand, as some people would like to believe.

Accepting, therefore, that we shall build upon the teacher-pupil relationship from the start, it is important that all those external customs which help to nourish that relationship should be preserved exactly as they would be in Tibet itself. Outward ceremonies, courtesies, and other customs are a language that symbolizes the inner relationship. They are in the nature of sacramentals, acting as "supports" for the doctrine. For instance, a pupil in Tibet, desiring to learn the alphabet, presents himself before his master and, having done obeisance, asks for knowledge of the alphabet. Similarly his master, after having ceremonially repeated the alphabet and authorized the study, proceeds to the practical job of actually imparting the letters; thus this apparently simple and ordinary business of the alphabet becomes something more — it also affirms the master-pupil kinship, which carries the pupil through the entire chain of earthly teachers and heavenly Lamas back to the recognition of the principle of Knowledge itself.

As regards the curriculum, teaching should, in the main, be

carried out in the language of the pupils. If they need to learn English or Hindi or any other foreign tongue, they can do so, provided it is taught as a useful addition and is not turned into the main vehicle of education. Good literature, not only from the varied knowledge that it incidentally provides, but even more for its example of accurate speech and good style, must always take a high place; so should history by rights, if only it could be taught honestly and without nationalistic bias. "Modern" subjects must be fitted in circumspectly: they ought to be comparatively harmless if the foundation has been well laid in the first place, for then they can be linked on to principles far transcending their own limited scope. Doctrinal teaching should be carried out by the old methods, which can hardly be improved upon. This is too individual a matter to be taught through the medium of a class, and each pupil cannot do better than have recourse to "his own lama." If doctrine is allowed to take its place in a school on terms of mere equality with arithmetic or other such subjects, its pre-eminence in the hierarchy ceases to be apparent. The Monday morning scripture lesson must have done much to discredit Christianity in our own schools. As the Doctrine comprises and transcends all other knowledge, it seems unsuitable for treatment as an ordinary school subject; but that does not mean that its presence will not be felt all along. Far from it: in the general traditional atmosphere it will always be there, as the sufficient cause for all the rest.

Certain details are specially important: The traditional surroundings should be preserved in the school buildings and their interior fittings. Everyone should wear his own national dress, which he can be encouraged to make as pleasing as possible. The practice of doing lessons sitting on the floor should invariably be followed, unless there be a particular lesson that necessitates some other posture. Not only does this habit make for grace of pose and economize needless furniture, but it is a great safeguard against becoming Occidentalized. I believe that dress and the way of sitting are among the most decisive factors at the present moment.

There is no need to introduce a competitive system. The ideal of acquiring knowledge is the prize and privilege aimed at. To know which pupil has attained it the quickest is no help to anyone; and in so far as it strengthens the "Ego-forming" tendencies, it is anti-Buddhistic. A gentle bearing should be encouraged and the conventions of politeness as between pupils should not be relaxed in favour of a sloppy "free-and-easiness." A proper relationship with animals should be inculcated at all times, both by example and by the exposition of the correct doctrine. As regards games, national sports such as archery should, if anything, be preferred to imported ones; but there is no reason to restrict oneself very narrowly in this matter, provided games do not become exalted into a sort of religion; the ideal of games as a healthy recreation seems worth adopting.

If at any time it should be necessary to employ foreign teachers, as it might well be for special subjects, they should be carefully selected out of the ranks of those few who are willing, for the time being at any rate, to participate in the habits of the country. If possible, not less than five years of preparation should be demanded of the teacher, during which time he should try to master not only the words of the language, but also its spirit; he should spend enough time among the people for whom he is engaged to work to get used to their way of living and to cease to feel and act like a stranger. It is his duty and his privilege to make himself acquainted with their way of thinking and to let the spirit of their civilization sink into his heart. If he will adopt their clothes and manners, so much the better; for then the influence that he is bound to gain over his pupils will not be associated in their minds with something exotic.

At first there may be difficulty in obtaining the necessary teachers; if they cannot be found immediately they must be trained. Parents in educated families should be ready to lend a hand themselves if no one else is available. If they want to impart something that they do not know, let them first learn it themselves and then pass it on: in so doing they will acquire much merit. It is always through the leaders of society that corruption or improvement must come. If those who enjoy traditional rights become slothful about the duties that naturally devolve on them, they can act as destroyers of their country. Where the aristocrat goes, there the rest will follow. He cannot divest himself of his responsibility as national ruler or mis-ruler.

In dealing with the education of children, charity must always begin at home. If so-called traditional schools were to be organized for the children of the poor, while the aristocratic children still continued to be sent to the "modern" schools of Simla or Darjeeling, no one would be deceived, least of all the children themselves. The newly founded schools would then probably become nationalistic instead of national, anti-Christian instead of Buddhist. The full participation of the aristocratic element is demanded in any community governed on traditional lines. Besides, it is idle for a parent to profess devotion for his tradition unless he shows that he regards it as the highest good for his own children also. That is always the acid test, which shows what a man thinks in the secrecy of his innermost heart.

For the sake of anyone who may feel faint-hearted at the prospect of attempting to shut the sluice gates in the face of the flood, I should like to relate a true story about a poor woman who, with no private resources, was able to start an educational enterprise that is now both flourishing and widely recognized. Lest any misunderstanding should arise, it must be mentioned that her educational movement has no direct connexion with the question of tradition; the example is given simply to show what can be done by conviction, even against great physical and social odds.

She was born of slave parents in South Carolina, and her name was Emma J. Wilson. From an early age she showed a strong desire to be educated, but in those days only white children went to school. Eventually some ladies became interested in her and helped her to enter Scotia Seminary, where, after winning a scholarship, she completed a three years' course. She hoped to take up missionary work in Africa; but on her return to South Carolina she saw that her work lay elsewhere — to use her own words, she "found her Africa at her own door." She began a school in a disused shed; friends gave her a few books, and the children paid for their tuition in eggs, chickens, and vegetables, which her mother cooked and sold for the benefit of the work.

The school soon outgrew its shed, and the need for proper premises became urgent; but there was no money and the Negro community was too poor to raise funds. Undaunted, Emma Wilson decided to start for the North, where she hoped to find sympathizers. Her minister gave her the proceeds of the Sunday evening after-collection — just fifty cents! It seemed so little that she carried it home in tears; but her mother said: "Don't cry, child, God ain't dead yet." So she started off, begging her way or doing odd jobs of work till she reached Philadelphia. A Quaker, true to the wonderful charity of his society, was the first to listen to her story. After all sorts of rebuffs and trials she won through, and out of these small beginnings has grown the magnificently organized Mayesville Industrial Institute, with a hundred and twenty-two acres of farmland and five hundred pupils. It accepts people of many types — as Miss Wilson said: "It is the Lord's work and belongs to all."

Once, when her main building was gutted by fire, someone said to her: "You must not be discouraged, for you have done such wonders." She replied: "The Lord told me long ago He had no use for discouraged folks." That is the message that a great saint, Emma Wilson, sends across the sea to the borderlands of India and Tibet. If she, a simple coloured girl, daughter of slaves, and member of an abjectly poor community, could conceive and bring to success this wonderful educational enterprise, how much more ought it to be possible for wealthy nobles and merchants, heirs to an unbroken succession of rule, and members of one of the most vigorous and talented of races?

But someone may ask: "What is to be done at this actual moment by leaders of society in order to prepare their children, on whom the task of continuing their work will eventually devolve, for a certain amount of time is bound to elapse before anything new is organized? If the children are not to continue in their present schools, how is their education to be carried on?" In the case of those who enjoy a certain amount of wealth the problem is really not so difficult, for they have the resources to engage private tutors, who can impart to the children whatever knowledge may be desired. It is not even certain that for those fated to rule, this time-honoured system is not, on the whole, the best. One remembers the great tutors of fifteenth-century Europe and their accomplished pupils. Even if some of the tutors engaged were not found to be perfectly satisfactory at the start, one must not forget that they will be working under the eyes of the parents, who will thus be able to exercise a much stricter control over their doings. In the case of children of the great Lhasa families I believe that private tuition would expose them to far less danger than being sent to questionable schools. The selection of a private tutor is difficult; it is not sufficient for him to have won a good degree. The conditions that I suggested some paragraphs back in connexion with the appointment of foreign schoolteachers, should apply to private tutors with double force. A man who is willing or, better still, eager to conform to the traditional conventions, and who possesses the right personality, can mould himself into a tutor capable of discharging his high service. For purely native subjects, doctrinal and literary, the best lamas should be sought out, for their presence will set the tone to the whole educational environment. In that way too the supremacy of the spiritual Order will be publicly acknowledged.

If the present practice of supporting Occidental schools goes on unchecked, not only will the dangers already mentioned grow, but they will breed fresh ones and so accelerate the process of denaturing the children. Clever pupils will eventually be encouraged, as in India, to "complete their education" — that is to say, to attend foreign universities, whence they will return a prey to a chaos of undigested impressions. Later, some parents will be persuaded, instead of placing their children in schools in their own country, to give them a "pukka" modern education and send them to boarding-school in Europe or America. The results are likely to be equally lamentable. A child who has been brought up in a home still partially run on the old lines, if suddenly plunged into a whirl of complexities all new to his experience and asked to deal with them at the dangerous moment of adolescence, when all his ideas are still fluid, will be exposed to such pressure that even an exceptional character may well be swept away by the tide of materialism.

The suggestions contained in this chapter for dealing with the school problem have not been put forward with the idea that a solution on the lines indicated will necessarily save the day. Subversive forces are already very strong, and resistance may prove a forlorn hope. To expect to discover a panacea for deep-seated intellectual poisons in this change of system or in that measure of reorganization is a modern delusion that dies hard. If the common mentality, which tradition should normally inform, has been vitally affected, nothing can save the day. Nor can any multiplying or reorientating of activities replace Knowledge as the first and last remedy against Ignorance. All that can be said on the subject of improved schools is that in the absence of some such radical changes the end is a foregone conclusion, for the present easy-going policy is nothing short of suicidal.

Decisive action in this matter of education lies especially in the hands of the leaders of the nation, on both sides of the political frontier, for an increasing number of children of great families are also being sent even from Tibet to the schools of the borderland, and this is extremely dangerous. Were schools available, however, organized on a sound traditional basis, those pupils, officials of the future, would surely be diverted to them instead of being placed in the charge of those who care nothing for Tradition. The border peoples are stationed in the post of honour: may they not shrink feebly from the task confronting them. Every broad-minded European can wish them success, for we too continue to suffer from the degradation of our own traditional inheritance, due to the selfsame forces that have corrupted that of Asia. A turn in the tide, wherever it may occur, should be welcomed by men of goodwill everywhere, irrespective of their religion or race.

Epilogue

THERE IS a small book, of not more than five pages, written in verse, and called *The Powerful Good Wish*, which reveals the doctrine of One who is referred to as the "Buddha of the Beginning, the Altogether Good." He is the earliest Buddha known to mankind; but not the first in point of time, for the succession of Buddhas is eternal and cannot be assigned a temporal origin. The book opens with these words: "Listen! All apparent Being, whether of the Round or of Deliverance, is in Principle One with two paths and two fruits. This is the jugglery of Ignorance and Knowledge. By the good wish of the Altogether Good One, may all, entering the royal abode of the Divine Essence, manifestly and completely attain to Buddhahood."

These few sentences contain the pith of the Tibetan metaphysic, the central theme that echoes through the entire Tradition. The Principle is identical with what is styled the Void, lest by giving It any other name, one may be betrayed into limiting or qualifying It. In the Principle will be realized the ultimate Unity that belongs to all things alike, despite appearances to the contrary, a Unity so infinitely real that one dare not even give it the name of Unity, since this word too suggests an idea borrowed from worldly experience; one can only speak of Its non-duality, that which shall be known when all pairs of oppositions have been resolved in the Supreme Identity. Therefore it is said that under every form and seeming contradiction the illuminate eye will recognize Voidness alone.

But the multitude of undelivered beings cannot, by merely so wishing, rid themselves of their dualistic spectacles, nor of all the delusions associated with the conception of a permanently individual self, towards which the rest of the Universe still stands in the relationship of "other." A self-centred consciousness forces one to polarize every idea into two contrasted notions. Therefore, where there is essential unity, men will persist in seeing two paths, one might almost have said two realities. But the starting-point for any return into unity must still be sought somewhere in the existing dualism; thus so long as one stops short of the supreme realization it is quite legitimate to speak of two paths, that of Ignorance, which creatures are now following, and that of Knowledge, the path or current that they hope to enter. "Entering the current" is a usual Tibetan phrase referring to those whose course is fairly set for Illumination. The two paths as such are divergent; the one leads continually back into the Round of Existence, which is the product of Ignorance and of its associated Desires and Activities; the other path leads away from the Round into Deliverance, which is the product of Knowledge.

All this is compared to the byplay of a conjuror, a perplexing succession of mirages, now delightful, now terrifying, which will only fade away, leaving Reality unmasked, when all distinctions, even those of subject and object, Knower and Known, the Round and Liberation themselves, shall have faded into the Knowledge of the Foundation, the Void, which alone is causeless and uncompounded, finding within Itself Its own sufficiency.

The Good Wish is a prayer that all without distinction, having outgrown distinctions, may realize this Unity, the true Beatific Vision. Liberation, in order to be perfected, must be all-embracing — "What is it to be saved oneself, if 'others' are still lost and suffering?" Individual salvation, with its lingering strands of attachment to the idea of self, is of no interest to the follower of the Non-dual Doctrine. Therefore this doctrine, acclaimed by the Tibetans as the corner-stone of all Knowledge, is known as the GREAT WAY, in which the Bodhisats, those embodiments of impartial Love, are the guides, and all beings, down to the last and the least, are the pilgrims. The goal is Knowledge, and the Path is Method, which is non-attached and universal Compassion.

The story that has formed the subject of this book is a study in contrasts between two paths, the path of Tradition and the path of those who have cut themselves adrift from Tradition. Many aspects of the question have been considered, from the Doctrine on which all else depends, down to practical suggestions for applying traditional principles to special problems that have arisen in certain strictly delimited fields of action. The entire world is crying out for Reform; but that word must be understood, not in its most usual sense, but having regard to its derivation of Re-form — the remaking of the Tradition wherever there has been a deviation from its path, and the requickening of its influence in the hearts of lukewarm or bewildered followers.

Viewed in this sense, the present crisis does not connote the impotence of Tradition itself, but rather it affords an incentive to seek ways of applying traditional principles with renewed vigour. Any evil that cries out to be righted should be looked upon as a failure to apply Tradition's teachings with sufficient intelligence: in that case successful suppression of the evil should result in a reinforcement of traditional authority and in a change of heart in all who accept that authority.

This is the road of Reform; but there is the other path, the one that is already being followed by half the world, often semiconsciously and with hesitation, but which will be followed by all and to the bitter end, unless timely measures are taken; this second path is the path variously known as Progress and Revolution. To enter it always is a sign that the Tradition, in spite of all professions to the contrary, is no longer trusted; or it shows that people prefer to renounce their principles and to drift into a life of capricious opportunism. The revolutionary path, along which the West has proceeded with increasing velocity for some centuries, leads to the dispersal of thought in the whirlpool of multiple detail and action, and to the subjection of human effort to the low impulses of sentimentality, with consequent disregard of the truly intellectual element in man.

The derivation of the word "Reform" was suggestive; so is that of the word "Revolution." What picture does it evoke but of something that keeps doubling back on its own tracks? It is perhaps no accident that associates this idea with the Round of Existence, the circular eddy in which all beings flounder and find again and again their brief joys and recurrent miseries. Both Progress and Revolution imply an idealization of Change, which finally comes to be looked upon as something desirable in itself, in which case contentment logically becomes an evil and stability a reproach.

It is between these two paths that a choice has to be made. But choice itself implies intellectual detachment, a disinterested seeking after Knowledge. How can choice be exercised by populations weighed down by the fear of impending destruction and oppressed by the futility of any effort to avoid a fate that they see coming but cannot explain? The beings of the Round scurry hither and thither, listening to the glib per-

suasions of every quack and trying to charm away their anxieties by the narcotics of speed and mechanized amusements.
Yet if the right choice could be made, and if those who have
strayed and have perhaps learned the beginnings of wisdom in
the bitter school of disaster could be guided back into the traditional path, then there might be a hope that the pernicious
dualism expressed in the words "East is East, and West is West,
and never the twain shall meet" might disappear, together
with other similar oppositions, in Knowledge of the One Foundation. It is surely suggestive that the most violent hatred of
Europeans as men is to be found precisely among those Orientals who most admire European institutions and despise their
own Tradition: it is the anti-traditional mind, which has
learned its lesson well and longs to out-Westernize the West,
which stoops to the baser kinds of militant nationalism as well
as to irreverent vandalism directed against its own spiritual
heritage: the two things go together. This might serve as a
warning to the Westerners who first introduced the anti-traditional error, and even more to those Orientals, like the Tibetans, who still cling to the other path. The latter might then
realize how fortunate is their present lot and how precious
their intellectual independence. They would then guard their
inheritance more jealously than ever and redouble their cau-
tion when tempted by the meretricious triumphs of modern invention.

Tradition is the path along which pilgrims journey towards
the peaks of Wisdom; but without Method for a guide there is
ever a danger of straying from the route and being caught up
in the futility of the Round, through the allurements of blind
sentiment and attachment to self. The higher the doctrine, the
more abysmal will be the corruption if once the doctrine is
rejected. Lamas have compared the man who aspires to the
Light to a serpent struggling upward inside a hollow tube of
bamboo. There is little room to turn; one ill-judged movement
may cause a fall to the very bottom. This is Tibet's danger;
this has been the fate of those traditional civilizations which,
by force or consent, have been led into accepting the standards
of the modern West.

For myself, the writing of this book, and the two expeditions that led up to it, have been a single voyage of explora-
tion into a land of uncharted glaciers and unclimbed ranges,
the mountains of Tradition. From far up their slopes I glanced
back, and, in contrast with my surroundings, the prospect of

the lands whence I had come seemed dismal indeed. At the outset of my story I tried to climb peaks in a bodily sense; but in the end I discovered the Lama, who beckoned me onward towards immaterial heights.

A popular proverb says: "Without the Lama you cannot obtain Deliverance." Every good Tibetan — and all lovers of Tradition today might almost lay claim to the right of honorary citizenship of Tibet — before ever he seeks refuge in the Three Most Precious Things, the Buddha, the Doctrine, and the Congregation, first pronounces the words: "I go for refuge to the Lama." In a literal sense this refers to a man's own spiritual director, "his Lama," who is the visible "support" of Tradition and its audible mouthpiece: it is this quality of support that entitles the teacher to the disciple's unbounded reverence, irrespective of personal failings, just as a brass statue of the Buddha is worthy of worship, be the casting sound or flawed. But there is also an inner and more universal meaning inherent in "the Lama"; for behind every support there is the thing supported, which the symbol both veils and reveals. Here it indicates the divine guide whose hand sustains the climber as he strives to reach the summit of Enlightenment.

Taken in this sense, the Lama, the Universal Teacher, is TRADITION ITSELF.

Index

A NOTE ON THE TYPE IN WHICH THIS BOOK IS SET

The text of this book is set in Caledonia, a Linotype face which belongs to the family of printing types called "modern face" by printers — a term used to mark the change in style of type-letters that occurred about 1800. Caledonia borders on the general design of Scotch Modern, but is more freely drawn than that letter.

The book was composed, printed, and bound by The Plimpton Press, Norwood, Massachusetts. The illustrations were reproduced in sheet-fed gravure by Photogravure and Color Company, New York. The typography and binding design are by W. A. Dwiggins.

WAD